International Conferences on Interfaces and Human Computer Interaction (IHCI2025), Game and Entertainment Technologies (GET2025) and Computer Graphics, Visualization, Computer Vision and Image Processing (CGVCVIP2025)

Held at the Multi-Conference on Computer Science and Information Systems (MCCSIS 2025)

Lisbon, Portugal
23-25 July 2025

ISBN: 979-8-3313-2771-2

Printed from e-media with permission by:

Curran Associates, Inc.
57 Morehouse Lane
Red Hook, NY 12571

Some format issues inherent in the e-media version may also appear in this print version.

International Association for Development of the Information Society (IADIS)
Rua Sao Sebastiao Da Pedreira
No. 100, 30, 1050-209
Lisbon, Portugal

Phone: 351 21 3151373
Fax: 351 21 3151244

secretariat@iadis.org

Additional copies of this publication are available from:

Curran Associates, Inc.
57 Morehouse Lane
Red Hook, NY 12571 USA
Phone: 845-758-0400
Fax: 845-758-2633
Email: curran@proceedings.com
Web: www.proceedings.com

INTERNATIONAL CONFERENCES

ON

INTERFACES AND HUMAN COMPUTER INTERACTION 2025

GAME AND ENTERTAINMENT TECHNOLOGIES 2025

and

COMPUTER GRAPHICS, VISUALIZATION, COMPUTER VISION AND IMAGE PROCESSING 2025

part of the

MULTI CONFERENCE ON COMPUTER SCIENCE

AND INFORMATION SYSTEMS 2025

PROCEEDINGS
OF THE
INTERNATIONAL CONFERENCES
ON

INTERFACES AND HUMAN COMPUTER INTERACTION 2025

GAME AND ENTERTAINMENT TECHNOLOGIES 2025

and

COMPUTER GRAPHICS, VISUALIZATION, COMPUTER VISION AND IMAGE PROCESSING 2025

Lisbon, Portugal

JULY 23 - 25, 2025

Organised by

iadis

international association for development of the information society

As a member of Crossref (a non-profit membership organization for scholarly publishing working with the purpose to make content easy to find, link, cite and assess) each published paper in this book of proceedings will be allocated a DOI (Digital Object Identifier) number for its fast and easy citation and indexation.

Volume Editor:
Katherine Blashki and Yingcai Xiao

Computer Science and Information Systems Series Editors:
Piet Kommers and Pedro Isaías

Associate Editor: Luís Rodrigues

TABLE OF CONTENTS

COMPUTER GRAPHICS, VISUALIZATION, COMPUTER VISION AND IMAGE PROCESSING

SHORT PAPERS

INTERFACES AND HUMAN COMPUTER INTERACTION

POSTERS

FOREWORD

These proceedings contain the papers of the: 19th International Conference on Interfaces and Human Computer Interaction 2025 (IHCI 2025), the 18th International Conference on Game and Entertainment Technologies 2025 (GET 2025) and the 19th International Conference on Computer Graphics, Visualization, Computer Vision and Image Processing 2025 (CGVCVIP 2025), which were organised by the International Association for Development of the Information Society, from 23 - 25 July, 2025. These conferences are part of the 19th Multi Conference on Computer Science and Information Systems 2025, 23 - 25 July, which had a total of 608 submissions.

The Interfaces and Human Computer Interaction (IHCI) 2025 conference aims to address the main issues of concern within Interface Culture and Design with a particular emphasis on the affective aspects of design, development and implementation of interfaces and the generational implications for design of human and technology interaction. This conference aims to explore and discuss innovative studies of technology and its application in interfaces and welcomes research in progress, case studies, practical demonstrations and workshops in addition to the traditional submission categories.

This conference seeks to cover both technological as well as non-technological issues related to these developments.

Submissions were accepted under the following topics:

- Affective User-Centred Analysis, Design and Evaluation
- The Value of Affective Interfaces / Systems / Application / Interaction
- Generational differences and technology design
- Measurement of success of emotional technology / interfaces
- Supporting user populations from specific Generations
- Supporting user populations with Physical Disabilities
- Supporting user populations with Intellectual Disabilities
- Creativity Support Systems
- Emotional Design issues / methods / experiences for novel interfaces including tangible, Mobile and Ubiquitous computing, mixed reality interfaces and multi-modal interfaces
- Usability
- User studies and fieldwork
- Methodological implications of Emotional User Studies
- Participatory design and Cooperative design techniques
- Ethical issues in emotional design
- HCI and Design education
- Eliciting User Requirements

The Game and Entertainment Technologies (GET) 2025 conference aims to bring together research and practice from creative, social and business practitioners and researchers in this challenging field. The focus of this conference is on design, development and evaluation of games, entertainment technologies and the nature of play. Known to have been enjoyed since at least 30 BC, games and entertainment are a universal part of human experience and present in all cultures. Games and entertainment activities contribute to the social, emotional, psychological and physical well-being of human society. As game and entertainment technologies become increasingly more pervasive we are continually challenged in our work, learning and personal life by increased access to virtual spaces and communities that offer opportunities for everyday needs and aesthetic experiences. The 'Creative Industries' require design and development structures, techniques and methodologies that enrich, enhance and encourage new interaction modes, metaphors and in-depth co-creation.

Topics of interest include, but are not limited to the following areas:

- Development methodologies
- Design issues
- Controversial issues – we welcome debate and dissension, for example; games as art, entertainment as purely for monetary returns etc
- Special Effects
- Animation
- Mobile and ubiquitous games and entertainment
- Serious Games –applications, critiques
- Philosophical issues
- Prototypes
- Social and cultural uses of/for Play
- Tools and technologies
- Skills, strategy, rules and chance
- Genre
- Immersiveness and engagement
- Research methodologies in creative practice
- Usability and playability
- User/player centered design
- Psychological, social, and cultural differences in perception and participation
- Communities, networks, social interaction and social capital
- Cross-cultural and intercultural approaches
- Assessment of exploratory learning approaches
- Emerging practices

The Computer Graphics, Visualization, Computer Vision and Image Processing Conference (CGVCVIP 2025), intends to address the research issues in the closely related areas of Computer Graphics, Visualization, Computer Vision and Image Processing.

The conference encourages the interdisciplinary research and applications of these areas. Submissions were accepted under the following 5 main topics:

- Computer Graphics
- Visualization
- Computer Vision
- Image Processing
- Other Related Topics

These events received 122 submissions from more than 17 countries. Each submission has been anonymously reviewed by an average of five independent reviewers, to ensure that accepted submissions were of a high standard. Consequently, only 19 full papers were published. The overall acceptance rate corresponds to about 16%. A few more papers were accepted as short and reflection papers. An extended version of the best papers will be published in the IADIS International Journal on WWW/Internet (ISSN: 1645-7641), the IADIS International Journal on Computer Science and Information Systems (ISSN: 1646-3692), and also in other selected journals.

This volume has come together through the valuable contributions of many individuals. We extend our sincere thanks to all the authors who submitted papers, enriching these conference proceedings. Our appreciation also goes to the members of the organizing committee, as well as the delegates, invitees, and guests, whose dedication and participation were essential to the success of the conference. We are especially grateful to Professor Dr. Piet Kommers, UNESCO Professor of Educational Technology (The Netherlands), for serving as the keynote speaker at MCCSIS 2025.

Last but not the least, we hope that everybody enjoyed the presentations, and we invite all participants for the next years' edition of these conferences.

Katherine Blashki, Noroff University College, Norway
Interfaces and Human Computer Interaction 2025
& Game and Entertainment Technologies 2025 Program Chair

Yingcai Xiao, The University of Akron, USA
Computer Graphics, Visualization, Computer Vision and Image Processing 2025
Program Chair

Piet Kommers, UNESCO Professor of Educational Technology, The Netherlands
Pedro Isaias, Universidade Aberta (Portuguese Open University), Portugal
MCCSIS 2025 General Conference Co-Chairs

July 2025

PROGRAM COMMITTEE

INTERFACES AND HUMAN COMPUTER INTERACTION CONFERENCE 2025
& GAME AND ENTERTAINMENT TECHNOLOGIES CONFERENCE 2025
PROGRAM CHAIR
Katherine Blashki, Noroff University College, Norway

COMPUTER GRAPHICS, VISUALIZATION, COMPUTER VISION
AND IMAGE PROCESSING 2025
PROGRAM CHAIR
Yingcai Xiao, The University of Akron, USA

MCCSIS 2025 GENERAL CONFERENCE CO-CHAIRS
Piet Kommers, UNESCO Professor of Educational Technology, The Netherlands
Pedro Isaias, Universidade Aberta (Portuguese Open University), Portugal

INTERFACES AND HUMAN COMPUTER INTERACTION CONFERENCE 2025
COMMITTEE MEMBERS

Afra Pascual, Universat De Lleida, Spain
Alexander Kröner, Technische Hochschule Nürnberg Georg Simon Ohm, Germany
Andre Constantino da Silva, IFSP & NIED/UNICAMP, Brazil
Asterios Leonidis, ICS-FORTH, CSD UOC, Greece
Birgit Bachler, Fh Joanneum University of Applied Sciences, Austria
Bruna Carolina Rodrigues Cunha, Universidade de São Paulo, Brazil
Eduardo Tanaka, Eldorado Research Institute, Brazil
Elisa Boff, Universidade de Caxias do Sul (UCS), Brazil
Felix Albertos Marco, University of Castilla-la Mancha, Spain
Hilda Carvalho De Oliveira, Sao Paulo State University (UNESP), Brazil
Jesuk Ko, Universidad Mayor de San Andres (UMSA), Bolivia
José Antonio Macías Iglesias, Universidad Autónoma De Madrid, Spain
Juan Enrique Garrido Navarro, Universidad de Castilla-La Mancha, Spain
Kal Dhou, Texas A&M University Central Texas, USA
Larbi Esmahi, Athabasca University, Canada
Leonardo Tortoro Pereira, IGCE - UNESP, Brazil
Linghan Zhang, Eindhoven University of Technology, Netherlands
Maki K. Habib, The American University in Cairo, Egypt
Marcelo Romero Huertas, Universidad Autonoma del Estado de Mexico, Mexico
Michael Hohl, HS Anhalt/FB Design, Germany
Nadeem Faisal, National Textile University, Pakistan
Nadine Vigouroux, IRIT, CNRS, Paul Sabtier University, France
Otniel Portillo Rodriguez, Universidad Autonóma del Estado de México, Mexico
Paula Miranda, School of Technology, Setubal Polytechnic University, Portugal
Sandro José Rigo, Unisinos, Brazil
Silvio Cazella, UFCSPA, Brazil
Ulrich von Zadow, Technische Hochschule Nürnberg Georg Simon Ohm, Germany
Xiaokun Zhang, Athabasca University, Canada
Yacine Bellik, LISN Laboratory, Paris-Saclay University, France

GAME AND ENTERTAINMENT TECHNOLOGIES 2025
COMMITTEE MEMBERS

Alessandro Rizzi, Universita Degli Studi di Milano, Italy
Alf Inge Wang, Norwegian University of Science and Technology, Norway
Anna-sofia Alklind Taylor, University of Skovde, Sweden
Castulus Kolo, Macromedia University of Applied Sciences, Germany
Christos Bouras, University of Patras and Computer Technology Institute, Greece
Damon Daylamani Zad, Brunel University, United Kingdom
Daniel Cermak-Sassenrath, Uppsala University, Sweden
Daniele Aurelio, Università Degli Studi di Milano, Italy
Eva Hudlicka, Psychometrix Associates, USA
Gabriele D`Angelo, University of Bologna, Italy
Gerry Chan, Dalhousie University, Canada
H.Samar Qorbani, Macewan University, Canada
Harry Agius, Brunel University of London, United Kingdom
Ioana Andreea Stefan, Advanced Technology Systems, Romania
Josh Mccoy, University of California, Davis, USA
Ke Jing, Bytedance, United States
Kendra Cooper, Independent Scholar, Canada
Marcia Medeiros, UniFANOR (Devry Brasil), Brazil
Michael Katchabaw, University of Western Ontario, Canada
Michel Simatic, Telecom Sudparis, France
Mikael Collan, Lappeenranta University of Technology, Finland
Monika Gavriilidou, University of Thessaly, Computer Technology Institute, Greece
Nicolas Jouandeau, Universite Paris 8 - Liasd, France
Paolo Ciancarini, University of Bologna, Italy
Ralf Doerner, RheinMain University of Applied Sciences, Germany
Thrasyvoulos Tsiatsos, Aristotle University of Thessaloniki, Greece
Ulysses Bernardet, Aston University, United Kingdom
Xiong Shuo, Huazhong Univerisity of Science and Technology, China
Yoshihiro Okada, Kyushu University, Japan
Youquan Liu, Chang An University, China

COMPUTER GRAPHICS, VISUALIZATION, COMPUTER VISION
AND IMAGE PROCESSING 2025
COMMITTEE MEMBERS

Aiert Amundarain, Ceit, Spain
Angelica De Antonio, Universidad Politecnica de Madrid, Spain
Brian J. d Auriol, Gwangju Institute of Science and Technology, Republic of Korea
Bruce Campbell, Rhode Island School of Design, USA
Carlo Nati, Working Group for the development of technoscientific, Italy
Celmar Guimarães da Silva, Universidade Estadual de Campinas, Brazil
Cesar Alberto Collazos, Universidad del Cauca, Colombia
Creto Vidal, Federal University of Ceará, Brazil
Daniel Martin, Universidad de Zaragoza, Spain
Daniel Thalmann, EPFL, Switzerland
Daniel Wiegreffe, University of Leipzig, Germany

KEYNOTE LECTURE

A.I. FOR STUDENTS' METACOGNITIVE SKILLS AND CREATIVE THINKING

Prof. Dr. Piet Kommers
UNESCO Professor of Educational Technology,
The Netherlands

ABSTRACT

Similar to the advancements made in ICT three decades ago, the emergence of AI today signals to educators that the human learning process may be at risk. This keynote lecture will provide an additional perspective on this issue. It is crucial to recognize that the WWW supplies all the information that AI currently presents. The main difference lies in its rhetoric concerning establishing a specific viewpoint. In other words, AI now acts as a powerful catalyst for refining criteria for student assessments, concentrating on discovering unique creative solutions rather than merely elaborating on existing ones. The foundation of creative thinking is metacognition: the awareness of what one already knows, one's preferred thinking style, and an evolving intuition about how learning builds on prior knowledge. This lecture will outline a roadmap for innovative didactic, instructional, and curricular approaches in the future. Previous research into conceptual representations, ontologies, and metaphoric analogies has supported education in expanding the fields of knowledge elicitation and conceptual thinking. Once AI is integrated, we will witness a growing need among young people to navigate complexities, such as sources of information that do not rely on empirical and validated scientific evidence. This keynote will highlight new aspirations that have emerged and how to seamlessly incorporate them into 'standing education' at this very moment. Topics such as teacher education, student selection, and assessment will be discussed.

Full Papers

ESTIMATING INDIVIDUAL TASTE SENSITIVITY USING QUESTIONNAIRES ALONE

Emi Tamaki[1,2], Makoto Tomioka[1], Shinya Nakamura[1,2], Chihiro Okubo[1],
Homei Miyashita[3] and Hironori Ishikawa[4]
[1]*H2L Inc., Japan*
[2]*University of the Ryukyus, Japan*
[3]*Meiji University, Japan*
[4]*NTT DOCOMO Inc., Japan*

ABSTRACT

Individual differences in human taste sensitivity present a significant challenge in accurately conveying perceived taste experiences. Conventional approaches to assess taste sensitivity, such as taste sensitivity test kits, typically require more than three hours to administer, making them impractical for repeated use when taste preferences or lifestyle habits change. To address this issue, a novel method for estimating individual taste scores is introduced, leveraging questionnaire data related to taste preferences and lifestyle habits. From an initial pool of 98 questionnaire items, 25 items were identified based on their strong correlations with taste sensitivity scores obtained through conventional test kits. A machine learning model employing Support Vector Regression (SVR) was constructed based on these 25 items and the corresponding taste scores. The experimental results demonstrated that taste scores could be estimated with a high accuracy of 94.56% using only the 25 questionnaire items. This method offers potential applications in the preservation and reproduction of past taste experiences, as well as in the automatic adjustment of flavors tailored to individual sensitivities.

KEYWORDS

Taste Sensitivity Estimation, Remote Taste Transmission, Taste Transfer, Individual Differences in Sensation, Digitisation of the Sense

1. INTRODUCTION

Humans experience a wide variety of sensory events throughout their lives, many of which are tied to different meals and their associated flavors. Preserving and sharing these taste experiences with others or one's future self holds the potential to foster cross-cultural understanding, enable personalized food experiences, support the preservation and transmission of diverse food cultures, and create novel entertainment experiences. To this end, various food taste sensing devices have been researched and developed, and are actively employed ("Taste Sensor TS5000Z"). Especially, the digitalization method of tastes has been established using electrostimulation (Duggal, 2022, Kaji, 2022), ion electrophoresis in five gels (Miyashita, 2020), and chemical taste modulators (Ranasinghe, 2014, Brooks, 2023).

However, taste sensitivity significantly varies among individuals due to factors such as personal traits, dietary habits, preferences, routines, and age. For instance, it is well-documented that taste sensitivity tends to decline with age (Cooper, 1959, Schiffman, 1991). This phenomenon explains why foods that were difficult to eat during childhood, such as bitter vegetables like green peppers, can become palatable in adulthood, or why the taste of beer becomes enjoyable; a decline in sensitivity to bitterness could be a contributing factor.

Simply preserving the digital data of food flavors is insufficient to capture the uniqueness of individual taste experiences, share these experiences with others, or recreate identical taste experiences for one's future self. To address this, our aim is to estimate individual taste sensitivity scores and digitally preserve them alongside food flavor data, enabling the preservation of food experiences and their sharing with others or one's future self (Figure 1).

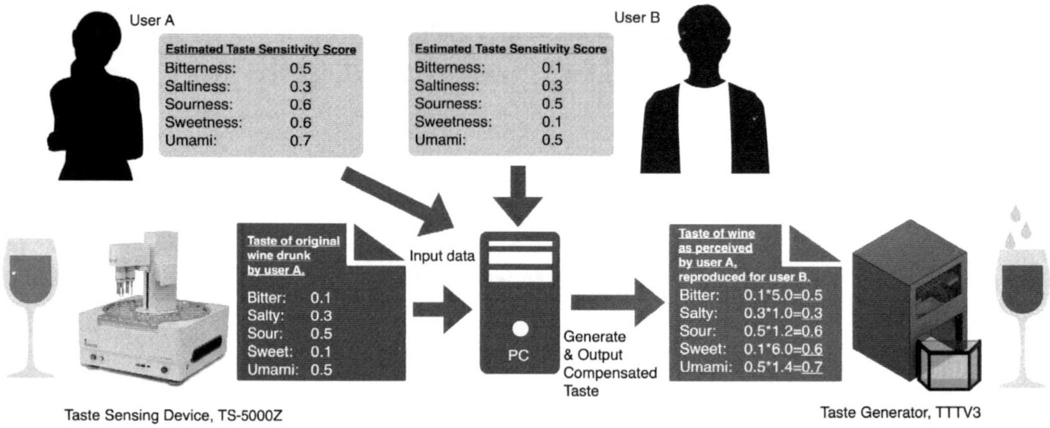

Figure 1. Our research goal. Preserving individual taste sensitivity scores and taste data to share food experiences and reproduce flavors for specific users (utilizing TS-5000Z ("Taste Sensor TS5000Z") and TTTV3 (Miyashita, 2024)

Figure 2. Method for calculating taste sensitivity scores using Taste Sensitivity Test Kits ("Taste Kit PRO Refrigeration Type")

Existing methods for calculating individual taste sensitivity scores include the use of electronic taste measurement devices ("Electric Taste Measurement Device TR-06A") and Taste Sensitivity Test Kits ("Taste Kit PRO Refrigeration Type"). Electronic taste measurement devices ("Electric Taste Measurement Device TR-06A") are designed to investigate the degree of taste sensitivity by stimulating the tongue with weak electrical currents. These devices were initially researched and developed to assess whether individuals suffer from taste disorders. Nevertheless, they fail to provide detailed information on multiple taste sensitivities, such as sweetness, saltiness, umami, sourness, and bitterness.

Taste Sensitivity Test Kits ("Taste Kit PRO Refrigeration Type") represent an alternative approach, wherein participants identify the type and intensity of tastes contained in several mystery bottles (Figure 2). Taste sensitivity scores are calculated based on the accuracy of their responses. These kits are primarily provided for food developers and are capable of assessing sensitivity to sweetness, saltiness, umami, sourness, and bitterness. While this method provides a highly reliable means of calculating taste sensitivity, it requires over three hours to collect data and calculate scores for a single participant. Additionally, the tastes in the mystery bottles are stored in frozen form, and once defrosted and used, they cannot be reused. Due to these limitations, the time and monetary costs associated with this method make it impractical for general users, as it is not feasible to incur these costs each time individual taste sensitivity changes as a result of personal traits, dietary habits, preferences, routines, or age.

The goal of this research is to suggest a method for estimating individual taste sensitivity scores using only questionnaires related to taste preferences and lifestyle habits, without significant time or monetary costs being incurred.

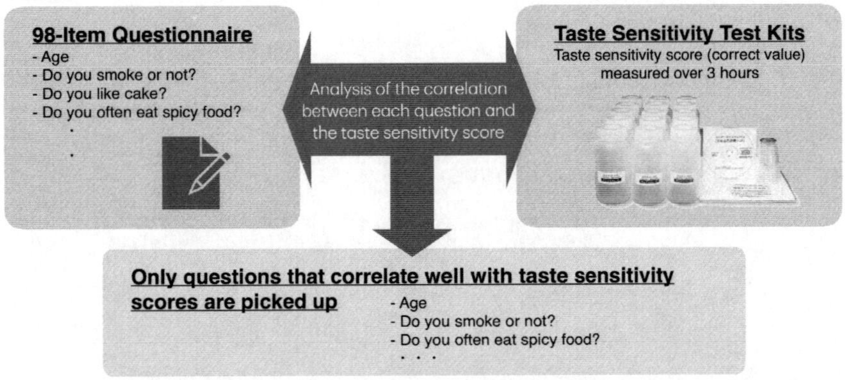

Figure 3. Overview of the method for extracting questionnaire items highly correlated with taste sensitivity

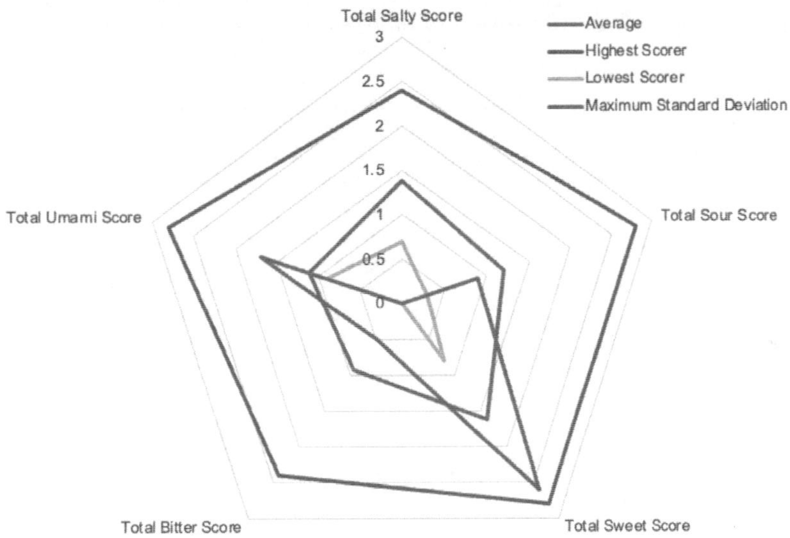

Figure 4. Averages, maximums, and minimums of taste sensitivity scores calculated from the Taste Sensitivity Test Kits

2. SUGGESTED METHOD

2.1 Extraction of Questionnaire Items Highly Correlated with Taste Sensitivity

The motivation of this study is to establish the method of using only questionnaires for estimation of individual taste scores, without taste-sensitivity test kits, which offers several advantages: it significantly reduces cost, enables large-scale studies, and better captures personal preferences and dietary habits. To estimate taste sensitivity scores based on questionnaire responses, the necessary questionnaire items were investigated (Figure 3). First, a dataset was created for each participant, consisting of their "taste sensitivity scores calculated from the Taste Sensitivity Test Kits" and their responses to "98 questionnaire items related to personal traits, dietary habits, preferences, routines, and age." A database comprising multiple participants was then constructed. From this database, only the questionnaire items that showed high correlation with the "taste sensitivity scores calculated from the Taste Sensitivity Test Kits" were extracted to create the final questionnaire.

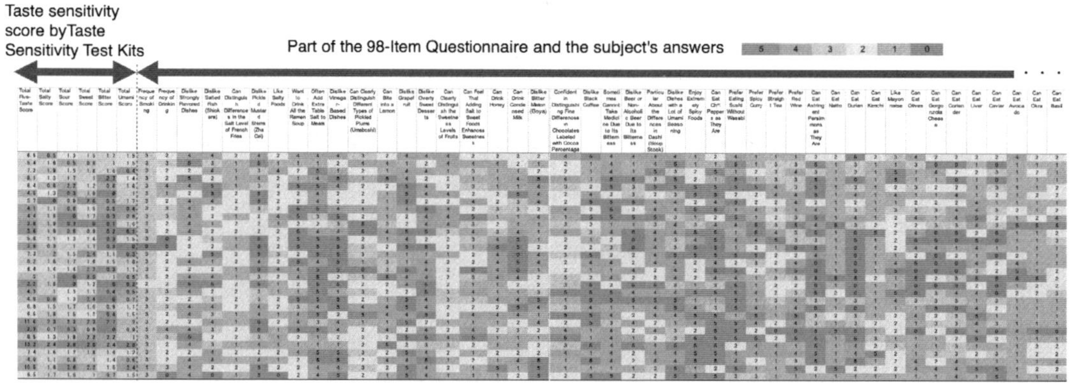

Figure 5. A portion of the database containing taste sensitivity scores and responses to 98 questionnaire items

Table 1. 25 Questionnaire items correlated with taste sensitivity scores

	Questionnaire
'Q1'	How frequently do you smoke? (0: Never, 5: Very frequently)
'Q3'	How much do you dislike dishes with strong seasoning? (0: Not at all, 5: Strongly dislike)
'Q6'	How much do you dislike zha cai (pickled mustard stem)? (0: Not at all, 5: Strongly dislike)
'Q11'	How well can you distinguish different types of umeboshi (pickled plums)? (0: Not at all, 5: Very well)
'Q12'	How easily can you bite into a lemon? (0: Not at all, 5: Very easily)
'Q14'	How much do you dislike overly sweet desserts? (0: Not at all, 5: Strongly dislike)
'Q17'	How easily can you drink honey? (0: Not at all, 5: Very easily)
'Q19'	How much do you dislike bitter melon (goya)? (0: Not at all, 5: Strongly dislike)
'Q21'	How much do you dislike black coffee? (0: Not at all, 5: Strongly dislike)
'Q23'	How bitter do you find beer and non-alcoholic beer? (0: Not at all, 5: Extremely bitter)
'Q26'	How much do you like extremely spicy dishes? (0: Not at all, 5: Strongly like)
'Q29'	How much do you prefer spicy curry? (0: Not at all, 5: Strongly prefer)
'Q31'	How much do you prefer red wine? (0: Not at all, 5: Strongly prefer)
'Q38'	How easily can you eat Gorgonzola cheese? (0: Not at all, 5: Very easily)
'Q39'	How easily can you eat coriander? (0: Not at all, 5: Very easily)
'Q41'	How easily can you eat caviar? (0: Not at all, 5: Very easily)
'Q53'	How easily can you drink olive oil? (0: Not at all, 5: Very easily)
'Q64'	How well can you distinguish between the spiciness of wasabi and chili peppers? (0: Not at all, 5: Very well)
'Q67'	How well does this statement describe you: "I dislike chili peppers but can eat wasabi"? (0: Not at all, 5: Very well)
'Q71'	How often do you eat citrus fruits with sugar added? (0: Never, 5: Very often)
'Q85'	How skilled are you at distinguishing sourness? (0: Not at all, 5: Very skilled)
'Q87'	How skilled are you at distinguishing sweetness? (0: Not at all, 5: Very skilled)
'Q89'	How skilled are you at distinguishing faint saltiness? (0: Not at all, 5: Very skilled)
'Q91'	How skilled are you at distinguishing faint bitterness? (0: Not at all, 5: Very skilled)
'Q96'	How skilled are you at distinguishing strong bitterness? (0: Not at all, 5: Very skilled)

In total, 30 participants (18 male, 12 female) were recruited, with an average age of 22.03 ± 4.95 years. The "taste sensitivity scores calculated from the Taste Sensitivity Test Kits" measured five types of taste sensitivity on a scale ranging from 0.0 to 3.0. The averages, maximums, and minimums of these scores are shown in Figure 4. As illustrated in Figure 4, taste sensitivity exhibits significant individual differences. Additionally, a portion of the database, which includes the taste sensitivity scores calculated from the Taste Sensitivity Test Kits and the responses to 98 questionnaire items related to personal traits, dietary habits, preferences, routines, and age, is presented in Figure 5. The 98 questionnaire was created based on terms related to all types of the sense of taste. Among the 98 questionnaire items, those with a correlation coefficient of at least 0.33 with the taste sensitivity scores were selected, resulting in a total of 25 items (Table 1).

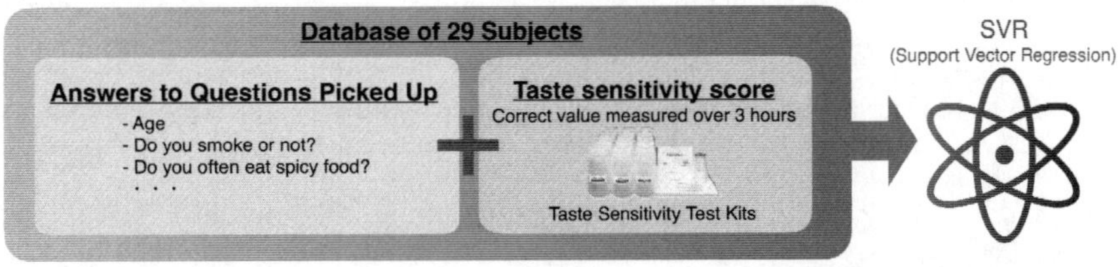

Figure 6. Dataset used to construct the machine learning model for estimating taste sensitivity scores

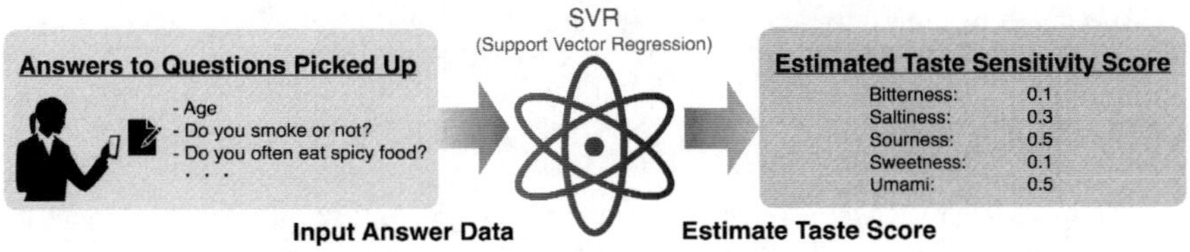

Figure 7. Estimation of taste sensitivity scores based solely on questionnaire responses

2.2 Suggested Method for Estimating Taste Sensitivity Scores from Questionnaire Response

A machine learning model was constructed using the dataset comprising the 25 questionnaire items selected in the previous section and the taste sensitivity scores obtained from the Taste Sensitivity Test Kits (Figure 6). This model was developed based on the dataset collected from 29 participants. To estimate taste sensitivity scores, it was essential to achieve quick result computation and provide detailed score estimations through regression analysis. Therefore, Support Vector Regression (SVR) was employed as the machine learning method. Using this machine learning model, taste sensitivity scores are estimated based on users' questionnaire responses (Figure 7). In the experiment described in the next section, a machine learning model was also constructed using the 98-item questionnaire to compare its estimation accuracy with that of the 25-item questionnaire.

3. EXPERIMENTS

3.1 Experimental Method

The estimation accuracy of the proposed method was evaluated by comparing the "taste sensitivity scores estimated using the proposed method" with the "taste sensitivity scores calculated from the Taste Sensitivity Test Kits."

Out of the dataset collected from 30 participants, a machine learning model was constructed using the data from 29 participants, and the taste sensitivity scores of the remaining one participant was estimated. This process was repeated for all 30 participants, ensuring that each participant's data was used as test data exactly once. Additionally, the estimation accuracy of the machine learning models constructed using the 25-item questionnaire and the 98-item questionnaire was also compared. The participants recruited at this stage were the same as those described in Section 2.1. In total, 30 participants (18 male, 12 female) were recruited, with an average age of 22.03 ± 4.95 years. The "taste sensitivity scores calculated from the Taste Sensitivity Test Kits" measured five types of taste sensitivity on a scale ranging from 0.0 to 3.0.

3.2 Experimental Results and Discussion

The results demonstrated that our proposed method could estimate taste sensitivity scores with an accuracy of 94.56% using responses from just the 25-item questionnaire (Figure 8). Additionally, using responses from the 98-item questionnaire, Our suggested method achieved an accuracy of 93.69% (Figure 9). These findings indicate that the 25-item questionnaire is sufficient for accurately estimating taste sensitivity scores, performing comparably to the much larger 98-item questionnaire.

Figures 8 and 9 also present the estimation accuracy of taste sensitivity scores for each participant. While the taste sensitivity scores of most participants were estimated with over 90% accuracy, Participant No. 25 exhibited an estimation accuracy of approximately 80%. Participant No. 25 is a specialist engaged in professional work related to taste, such as food development and sensory analysis. In contrast, the machine learning model was trained on a dataset consisting of non-specialists, including general workers and students, rather than specialists.

This discrepancy likely explains the lower estimation accuracy for Participant No. 25. Similar to methods that estimate body fat percentage based on bioelectrical impedance, which require separate models for athletes and non-athletes, it is inferred that separate machine learning models may be necessary for general users and specialists to estimate taste sensitivity scores accurately. Developing distinct models for general users and specialists remains a topic for future research.

4. A DEVICE FOR SHARING DINING EXPERIENCES

In this research, a system was developed for estimating individual taste sensitivity scores using the suggested method, preserving food taste data, and sharing dining experiences with others (Figure 10). The TS-5000Z ("Taste Sensor TS5000Z") was used for sensing food taste data. Additionally, the suggested method for estimating individual taste sensitivity scores and preserving food taste data was implemented using FEEL TECH, a human augmentation platform provided by NTT DOCOMO ("DOCOMO Announces World's First Technology that Utilizes Human-Augmentation Platform for Sharing Haptic Information Between People"). For taste synthesis and reproduction, the TTTV3 (Miyashita, 2024.) was employed. Participants required approximately three minutes to complete the questionnaire. Furthermore, the synthesis and reproduction of flavors, based on the stored taste data and the estimated individual taste sensitivity scores, were completed in about 20 seconds.

This system enables users to share diverse dining experiences easily. For instance, it allows adults to perceive the sourness of tomatoes as experienced by children or to recreate the taste of wine enjoyed by someone in a remote location.

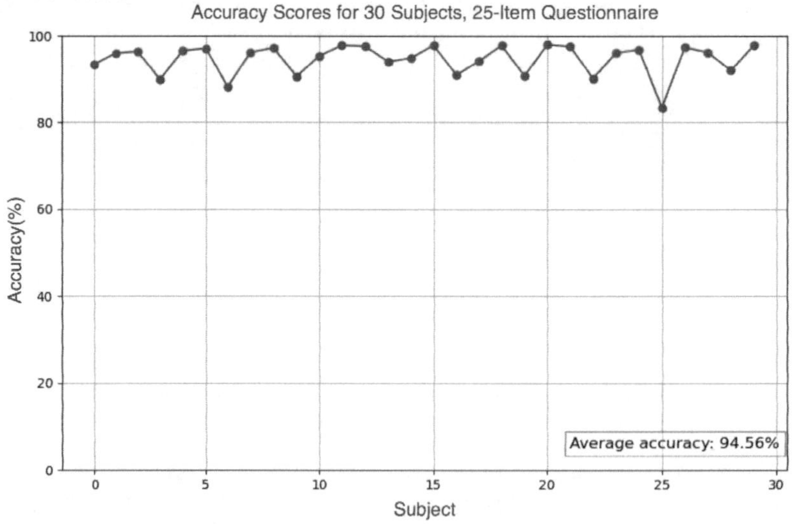

Figure 8. Estimation accuracy of taste sensitivity scores using the 25-item questionnaire and the suggested method (Number of participants: 30)

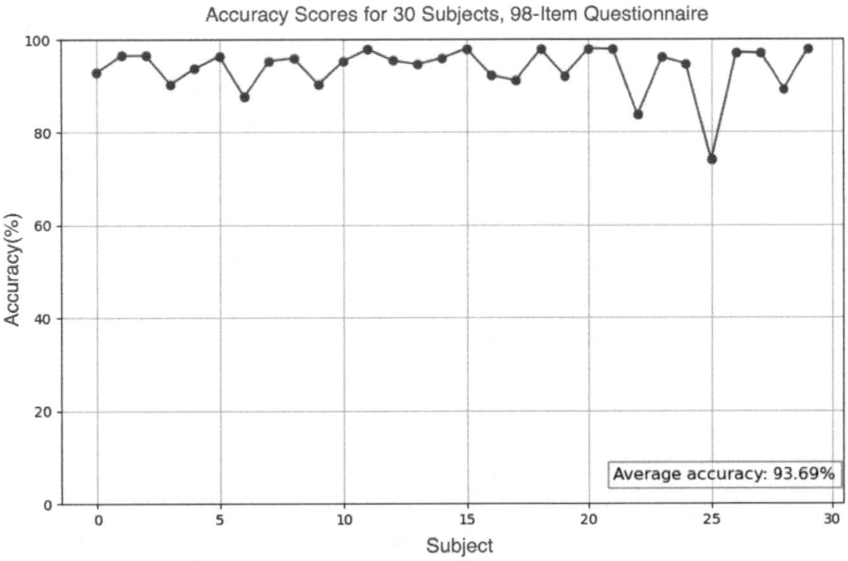

Figure 9. Estimation accuracy of taste sensitivity scores using the 98-item questionnaire and the suggested method (Number of participants: 30)

Figure 10. A device for sharing dining experiences using the suggested method for estimating individual taste sensitivity scores

5. CONCLUSION AND FUTURE WORK

To address the issue, a novel method for estimating individual taste scores is introduced, leveraging questionnaire data related to taste preferences and lifestyle habits. From an initial pool of 98 questionnaire items, 25 items were identified based on their strong correlations with taste sensitivity scores obtained through conventional test kits. A machine learning model employing Support Vector Regression (SVR) was constructed based on these 25 items and the corresponding taste scores.

The experimental results demonstrated that taste scores could be estimated with a high accuracy of 94.56% using only the 25 questionnaire items. However, it was found that the estimation accuracy of taste sensitivity scores decreased for taste specialists. It is inferred that separate machine learning models may need to be constructed for general individuals and specialists to accurately estimate taste sensitivity scores. This remains a topic for future research.

In this research, a system was developed that incorporates the suggested method for estimating individual taste sensitivity scores, the preservation of food taste data, and the sharing of dining experiences with others. This system demonstrated that the total time required for estimating taste sensitivity scores through questionnaire responses and reproducing flavors was approximately 3 minutes and 20 seconds.

Our suggested method and system is expected to be utilized for various applications, including the preservation and reproduction of previously experienced flavors, as well as the automatic adjustment of flavors tailored to individual preferences. Our method embedded within the system for sharing dining experiences is anticipated to be applied to an interactive system that provides past dining experiences, stored in a metaverse environment, as meals tailored to the preferences of individual users.

The use of a small sample for training the model might limit the generalizability of the findings, thus we would increase the sample number for further investigation in future work. In addition, it would be beneficial to explore the influence of age, gender, and other demographic variables, on taste sensitivity scores and how these variables could be accounted for in the model.

REFERENCES

Brooks, J., et al. (2023). Taste Retargeting via Chemical Taste Modulators. *Proceedings of the 36th Annual ACM Symposium on User Interface Software and Technology*, San Francisco CA USA, pp. 1-15.

Cooper R.M, et al. (1959). The effect of age on taste sensitivity, *J Gerontol.*, vol. 14, pp. 56-8.

DOCOMO Announces World's First Technology that Utilizes Human-Augmentation Platform for Sharing Haptic Information Between People [WWW document], NTT Docomo FEEL TECH, URL https://www.docomo.ne.jp/english/info/media_center/pr/2023/0125_00.html (accessed 1.10.25)

Duggal, A.S. et al. (2022). Digital taste in mulsemedia augmented reality: Perspective on developments and challenges. *Electronics*, vo1.1 pp. 1315.

Electric Taste Measurement Device TR-06[a] [WWW document], Rionet MedPort, URL https://medpo.rionet.jp/medport/product/detail/?tid=TR06A009 (accessed 1.23.25).

Kaji, Y., Sato, A., and Miyashita, H., (2022). Design of electrical stimulation waveform for enhancing saltiness and experiment on low-sodium dieters, *Frontiers in Virtual Reality*, vol. 3, pp. 879784.

Miyashita, H. (2024). Taste Media: Innovative Technology Transforms the Eating Experience, *In: Torra, V., Narukawa, Y., Kikuchi, H. (eds) Modeling Decisions for Artificial Intelligence(MDAI 2024) Lecture Notes in Computer Science*, Tokyo, Japan, pp. 8-16.

Miyashita, H., (2020). Norimaki synthesizer: Taste display using ion electrophoresis in five gels., *Extended Abstracts of the 2020 CHI Conference on Human Factors in Computing Systems*, online, pp. 1-6.

Ranasinghe, N., et al. (2014). Taste+ digitally enhancing taste sensations of food and beverages. *Proceedings of the 22nd ACM international conference on Multimedia*, New YorkNYUnited States, pp. 737-738.

Schiffman, S.S., Frey, A.E., et al., (1991). Taste of glutamate salts in young and elderly participants: Role of inosine 5′-monophosphate and ions, *Physiology & Behavio*r, vol. 49, issue 5, pp. 843-854.

Taste Kit PRO Refrigeration Type, Order No. 2-7423-11, AS ONE, Inc., URL https://axel-search.as-1.co.jp/asone/d/2-7423-11/ (accessed on 01.23.25).

Taste Sensor TS5000Z, Intelligent Sensor Technology, URI https://www.insent.co.jp/about/(accessed on 01.23.25).

EDUCATIONAL EFFECTS OF MATHEMATICS E-LEARNING WITH A STANDARDIZED MATH INPUT UI

Tetsuo Fukui
Mukogawa Women's University, 6-46, Ikebiraki-cho, Nishinomiya, 663-8558, Japan

ABSTRACT

Science, technology, engineering, and mathematics (STEM) education has become more important in recent years, and one of the challenges in digitizing mathematics teaching materials is inputting formulae. To address this issue, in 2015 we proposed an intelligent formula input user interface (UI) employing predictive conversion from ambiguous text. In mathematics education utilizing an e-learning environment, standardization of the UI is important for inputting mathematical formulae. In this study, we adopted the mathematics e-learning system Moodle+STACK to standardize the UI for inputting mathematical formulae. The effectiveness of this method in mathematics education was verified in a mathematics class for students at our university, and student reactions were investigated. Their responses were positive.

KEYWORDS

Mathematics e-Learning, Equation Input Interface, Learning Support Environment

1. INTRODUCTION

With science, technology, engineering, and mathematics (STEM) education becoming more important in recent years, the difficulty of inputting formulae has emerged as a challenge in digitizing mathematics teaching materials (Smith & Ferguson, 2005).

To address this issue, in 2015, we proposed a user interface (UI) that employs artificial intelligence (AI) for predictive conversion of ambiguous strings in inputting formulae. The developed UI system was named MathTOUCH. In 2017, we implemented MathTOUCH in answer format for teaching assessment using a computer algebra kernel, STACK (Sangwin, 2013), which is an online testing system that allows users to directly respond to mathematical expressions. In 2019, we proposed a mathematical graph maker that uses natural descriptions to draw graphs from functions entered using MathTOUCH, and in 2024, we proposed the MathTOUCH editor as a rich-text editor plugin for Moodle (Moodle, 2025), a learning management system (LMS) that includes mathematical formulae.

In this study, we adopted the mathematics e-learning system Moodle+STACK to standardize the UI for inputting mathematical formulae using MathTOUCH and verified its effectiveness in mathematics education. We used MathTOUCH in a mathematics class for second-year undergraduate students in our school and investigated the students' reactions. Their responses were positive.

2. PREVIOUS WORK

In this section, we explain the proposed mathematical input UI for STEM education and the various online support tools that apply it.

2.1 MathTOUCH: Challenge of Math Input Issues

In 2015, we (Fukui & Shirai, 2015) proposed MathTOUCH, an intelligent formula input interface that compensates for ambiguous human instructions to reduce the burden of inputting the formulae required to create mathematics teaching materials. MathTOUCH allows the user to enter the desired mathematical expressions using AI (Fukui & Shirai 2017) and predicts the candidates from ambiguous character strings. Our evaluation results show that math input is 1.2 - 1.7 times faster than conventional input methods, and user satisfaction was high.

Figure 1 shows a sample screenshot from MathTOUCH. A desired mathematical formula is constructed by first inputting a linear string of characters from the keyboard or touch pad, followed by selecting the desired candidate from a sequence of predicted candidates, and finally fixing by pressing on the Enter button. The linear string rule for mathematical expressions in MathTOUCH is to linearly set the key letters (or words) corresponding to the elements of a mathematical expression in the order of colloquial (or reading) style without considering two-dimensional placement and delimiters. For example, the case of "1 over a squared plus 3" is shown in the second line of Table 1. The third and fourth lines in Table 1 present comparative examples from the computer algebra system (CAS) command and LaTeX, respectively.

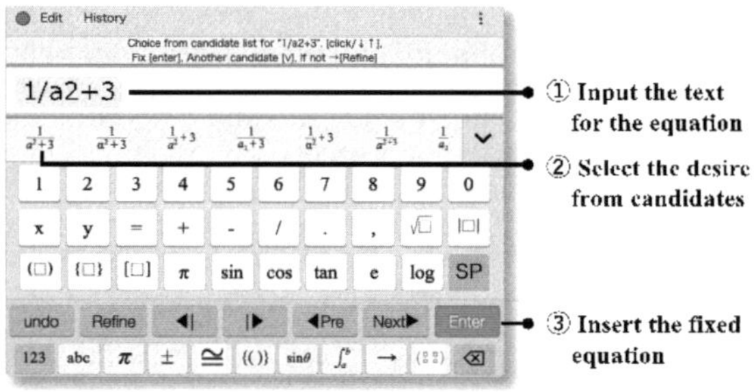

Figure 1. The screenshot of MathTOUCH and input operation steps

Table 1. An example of the linear string in the case of "1 over a squared plus 3"

Rules	Example in the case $\frac{1}{a^2+3}$
Linear string in MathTOUCH	**1/a2+3**
CAS command (Maxima)	**1/(a^2+3)**
LaTeX	**\frac{1}{a^2+3}**

2.2 Mathematics E-Assessment System Using MathTOUCH

In 2014 (Shirai & Fukui, 2014), we implemented MathTOUCH in an equation-answer format in STACK, which is an e-assessment system for mathematics. In our eight weeks of learning investigation (Shirai & Fukui, 2017), we observed that students were able to practice using MathTOUCH at the same learning rate as when using the current interface. Furthermore, the results of the questionnaire revealed a significantly higher level of satisfaction with memorability using MathTOUCH than with the current interface.

2.3 Rich-Text Editor for Math e-Learning Using MathTOUCH

The standard text editor on Moodle requires input in LaTeX text format, which is inconvenient for users unfamiliar with the LaTeX syntax. Therefore, we developed a rich-text editor using MathTOUCH implemented as a Moodle plug-in to reduce the burden of mathematical inputs (Shirai et al., 2018). Figure 2 shows a sample screenshot of the rich-text editor. The features of this rich-text editor are as follows:

- Mathematical expressions can be constructed using WYSIWYG.
- The proposed editor can seamlessly switch between the editor and MathTOUCH UI .
- The math input interface enables users to enter mathematical documents using a keyboard.
- The math input interface allows users to enter mathematical expressions with a low workload.
- This editor enables users to convert selected parts of mathematical documents into LaTeX format.

As a result of our evaluation, users were able to input mathematical documents approximately 1.5 times faster than the standard UI, with high subjective satisfaction (Shirai et al., 2023).

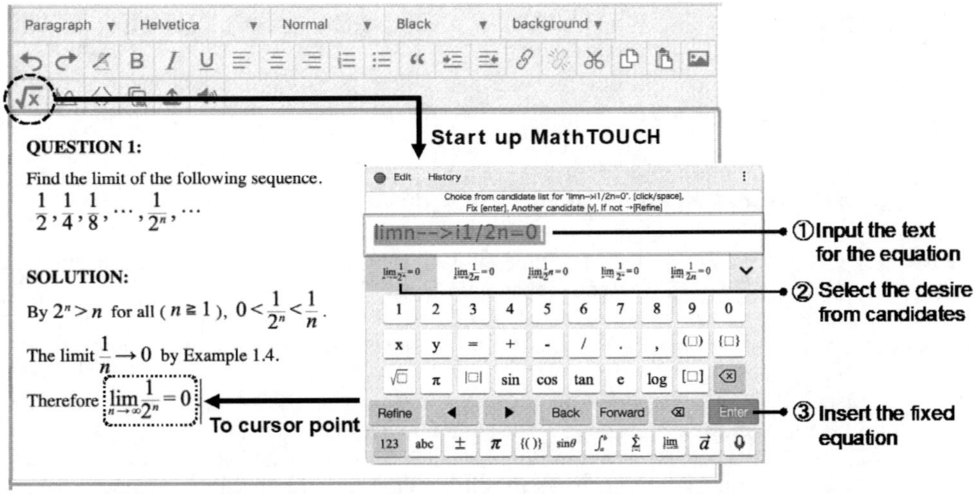

Figure 2. Screenshot of the rich-text editor using MathTOUCH

2.4 Graph Maker using MathTOUCH

In 2019, we (Fukui, 2019) applied MathTOUCH to propose a graph maker as a tool for online support in creating teaching materials for STEM education. Figure 3 shows a sample GraphMaker (MathTOUCH Graph) screenshot. The features of this graph maker are as follows:

- MathTOUCH facilitates the editing of graph equations.
- Equation labels can be clearly displayed on the canvas.
- Numerical values such as coordinates can also be expressed as formulae that include $\sqrt{\ }$, or π.
- Drawing command scripts for graph elements is easy to understand, as in mathematics textbooks.
- Graphs can be exported to various types of outputs.

The results of a user study with 62 students showed that the system usability scale (SUS) was 61.7%, and their subjective satisfaction with learning through the graph maker was greater than through classroom learning, with 82% of students reporting that it was easy to understand (Fukui, 2020).

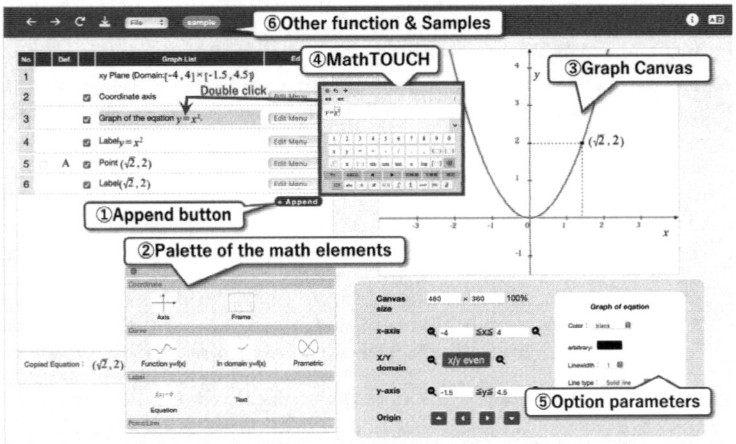

Figure 3. A screenshot of GraphMaker using MathTOUCH

3. MATHEMATICS E-LEARNING SYSTEM STANDARDIZED MATH UI

To integrate the results of our previous research and utilize them in an actual mathematics class, we constructed a learning support environment for mathematics e-learning with a standardized math UI, called MathTOUCH.

3.1 Learning Support Framework

The framework showing the flow of teaching material data is displayed in Figure 4. Specifically, we adopted Moodle as an LMS, implemented the above-mentioned mathematics e-assessment system STACK plug-in, and assigned the rich-text editor using MathTOUCH, as the standard editor for Moodle to create a mathematics e-learning environment linkable to the MathTOUCH Graph. This environment has the following important features:

- The MathTOUCH UI that allows inputting common quiz expressions, algebraic calculations, and function graphs, creating math notes, and submitting questions.
- Reusability such as copying and re-editing formulae from Mathematical quiz texts and notes.
- Math document accessibility with smooth collaboration between the editor and graph maker.
- Portability that enables loading and saving in LaTeX format. Therefore, numerous external mathematics materials are available in LaTeX.

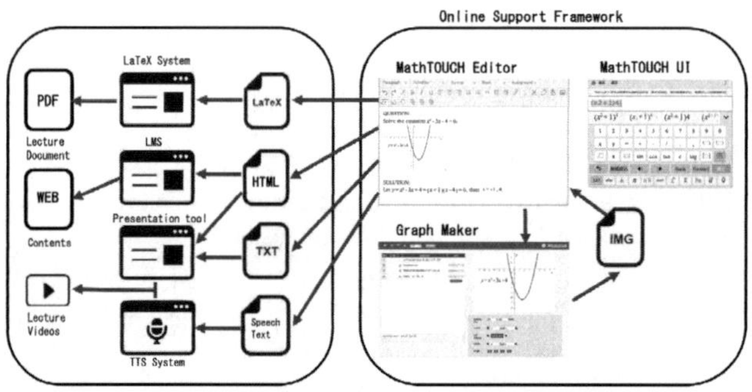

Figure 4. Online support framework for math learning

3.2 Activity and Resource

The activities and resources prepared for a Moodle course in a practical class (Figure 5), are explained in the next section. The four educational activities served four functions: 1. Mathematical chat (MathChat), 2. Forum, 3. Quiz, 4. Assignment. MathChat allows students to ask questions in class using MathTOUCH. The forum function allows students to contact each other and ask questions outside the class. The quiz function allows students to complete various practice quizzes online at any time. The assignment function allows students to answer mathematical problems through rich text and graphical submission. Resources in the course included the distribution of PDF files of course text, links to lecture videos on YouTube, URLs to websites containing MathTOUCH graphs, and sample programs related to the class.

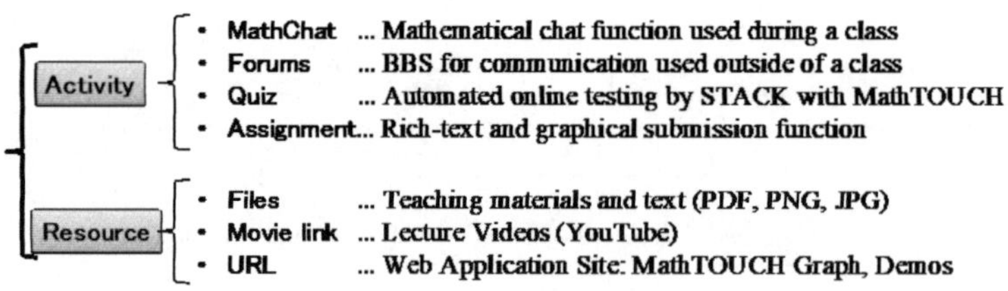

Figure 5. Activities and resources in the Moodle+STACK system using MathTOUCH

4. EVALUATION OF MATH CLASS EDUCATION

This mathematics e-learning system was introduced using standardized UI (MathTOUCH) to allow inputting mathematical formulae into my mathematics class, and its acceptance by students and effectiveness in mathematics education was further verified.

4.1 Course Content and Class Status

The proposed system was used in 90-minute lectures over a 15-week period on 37 second-year university students studying IT, AI, and data science. The students used their own laptops and took the course through LMS. None of the participants had any experience using Moodle or MathTOUCH before taking this course. In the first lecture, about 30 min was spent instructing students on how to use MathTOUCH, allowing them to practice taking online tests. From the second lecture onwards, they could operate the system on their own.

The course was an introduction to calculus and linear algebra, serving as a mathematical foundation for learning statistics and data science. Table 2 lists the primary learning items.

We investigated the subjects' prior knowledge in terms of their learning levels of "High School Mathematics I, II, and III" in the Japanese curriculum (MEXT, 2025). The results showed that 19% were at level I, 56% at level II, and 25% at level III. In particular, Level I students were learning calculus for the first time, and all students were new to matrix calculations.

Table 2. Content of the course using the proposed mathematics e-learning system

Chap	Learning title	Sec.	Main topics
1	**Basic mathematics notes for informatics**	1.1-1.2	Objectives and calculating formulae
2	**Functions and variations**	2.1-2.3	Exponential and logarithmic functions
3	**Differential calculus and its applications**	3.1-3.7	Derivatives, Newton method, indefinite integral
4	**Vector**	4.1-4.4	Components, inner product, and spatial shapes
5	**Differentiation of functions of multiple variables**	5.1-5.2	Partial differentiation and gradient vector
6	**Matrix**	6.1-6.3	Inverse matrix and linear transformation

4.2 Educational Activities

In the experimental lessons, the implemented teaching materials and educational activities using mathematics e-learning are as follows:

4.2.1 MathChat and Forums

Although the MathChat function was not used frequently, there were questions in some chat sessions about the meaning of mathematical expressions and definitions of vector symbols. Students received feedback on their mistakes through MathChat. The forum function was also used to communicate the weekly assignments and questions to students outside the class. Students also reported bugs in the MathTOUCH editor through the forum, to help improve the system.

4.2.2 Quiz

We prepared 195 STACK-type questions with mathematical solutions divided into 27 tests using the quiz function that the students could repeatedly study. Each test consisted of two to ten questions, and the answers were entered using MathTOUCH. The test was performed within a time limit of 10–30 minutes. The test results were automatically graded immediately after testing. Test takers could take the test multiple times within a one-week period, and the highest score was considered.

4.2.3 Assignment

The assignments in our course were mathematics problems designed to check the students' comprehension of textbook learning items, as shown in Table 2. Approximately one or two questions among the total of 24 questions were answered weekly. Students answered questions by submitting online reports that included mathematical expressions and graphs using the rich-text editor introduced in Section 2.3. In this case, manual grading was performed. MathTOUCH was used to input mathematical expressions and create graphs.

An example of an assignment question and actual student answer are shown in Figure 6. The questions were delivered in PDF format using LaTeX, and students submitted their answers online using the MathTOUCH editor.

An example of Assignments

[**Exercise 4.7**]

When $\boldsymbol{p} = \begin{pmatrix} 2 \\ -1 \\ -1 \end{pmatrix}$,

$\boldsymbol{q} = \begin{pmatrix} -4 \\ 2 \\ 0 \end{pmatrix}$,

$\boldsymbol{r} = \begin{pmatrix} r_1 \\ r_2 \\ r_3 \end{pmatrix}$,

find $\boldsymbol{r}$ such that $\boldsymbol{p} \perp \boldsymbol{r}, \boldsymbol{q} \perp \boldsymbol{r}, |\boldsymbol{r}| = 1$.

A student's answer of [Exercise 4.7]

Since $\boldsymbol{p} \perp \boldsymbol{r}$, $\boldsymbol{p} \cdot \boldsymbol{r} = 2r_1 - r_2 - r_3 = 0$. $\cdots$ (1)
Since $\boldsymbol{q} \perp \boldsymbol{r}$, $\boldsymbol{q} \cdot \boldsymbol{r} = -4r_1 + 2r_2 = 0$. $\cdots$ (2)
Since $|\boldsymbol{r}| = \sqrt{r_1{}^2 + r_2{}^2 + r_3{}^2} = 1$, $r_1{}^2 + r_2{}^2 + r_3{}^2 = 1$. $\cdots$ (3)
From equation (2), $r_2 = 2r_1$,
Hence, substtuting this into equation (1), $2r_1 - 2r_1 - r_3 = 0$,
then $r_3 = 0$.
Substituting these into equation (3), we get $r_1{}^2 + (2r_1)^2 = 5r_1{}^2 = 1$
which means $r_1{}^2 = \frac{1}{5}$.
Solving this, we get $r_1 = \pm\frac{1}{\sqrt{5}}$.
Therefore, the desired vector is

$\boldsymbol{r} = \begin{pmatrix} \pm\frac{1}{\sqrt{5}} \\ \pm\frac{2}{\sqrt{5}} \\ 0 \end{pmatrix}$ (where the compound order is the same).

Figure 6. Examples of assignment questions and student answers

4.3 Evaluation

To verify the educational effectiveness of the educational activities conducted in the mathematics e-learning environment described above, we analyzed the quiz and assignment scores and investigated subjective satisfaction with the class.

4.3.1 Result of Online Test (Quiz) and Assignment

Table 3 shows the status and average scores of the quizzes and assignments over 15 weeks.

Table 3. Results of quizzes and assignments over 15 weeks

Question type	**Automated online testing (Quiz)**	**Mathematics assignment report test**
Number of questions	27 tests (each scored 10 points)	24 questions (each scored 10 points)
Question format	Each test has 2 to 10 STACK type questions	Printed documents of mathematics problems
How to answer	Multiple instant online testing	Online submission of answers in rich text
Time limit	10-30 minutes per test	Within one week
Number of test takers	23-37 people	23-37 people
Average score (per 10 points)	8.37 (SD 0.6) points (min:7.18, max:9.50)	7.96 (SD 2.13) points (min:4.94, max:9.37)
Average number of attempts (per test)	2.52 (SD 0.73) attempts (min:1.6, max:4.4)	Only once

4.3.2 Analysis of Results

Figure 7 shows a scatter plot of the average scores between the quizzes and assignments (calculated from 100 points) for each of the 37 students. The average score for all students across all quizzes was 78.4 (SD 18.5) points, and the average number of times they attempted the same quiz was 2.52 (SD 0.73). The average score for all students on all assignments was 69.5 (SD 20.0) points.

There was a strong correlation (coefficient of determination $R^2 = 0.74$) between each student's quiz and assignment scores. These results suggest that students who practiced the quiz well also scored highly on the assignments, and the high average scores in the class suggest that the educational objectives were generally achieved.

4.3.3 Result of Subjective Satisfaction

Finally, students' subjective satisfaction with the class and proposed learning environment was investigated using a 12-question questionnaire (rated on a five-point scale ranging from negative to positive). Figure 8 shows a radar chart of the average results for each question between Q1-Q12 (Table 4). The overall evaluation showed that the class was in general conducted without any problems. In particular, the high evaluation of Q10 indicated that the students were very satisfied with the new knowledge and skills taught in class. In fact, according to comments from the students, the good thing about online tests was that the system allowed them to immediately check their answers and they could take the tests at any time. Approximately 70% of the students said that this learning environment was easier to understand than classroom learning.

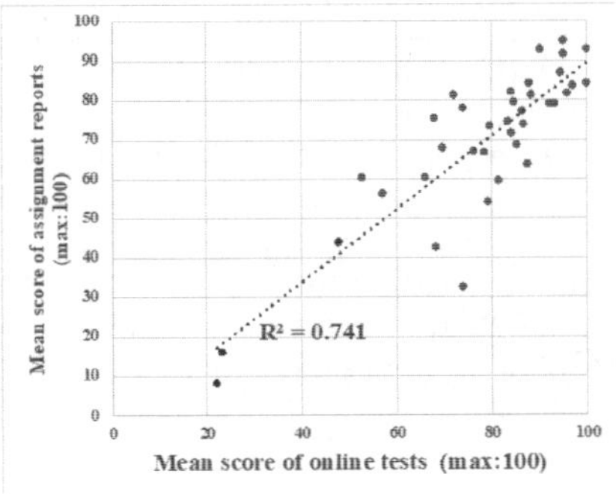

Figure 7. Scatter plot of quizzes and assignment scores

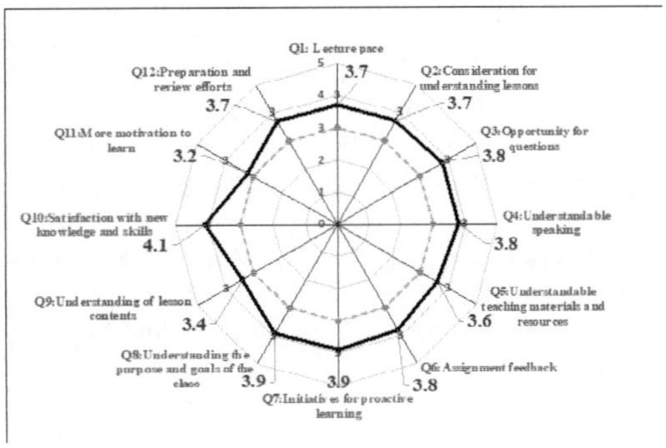

Figure 8. Radar chart of the results for each question

Table 4. Twelve-question questionnaire on mathematics classes

No.	Questions of questionnaire (1. Strongly disagree, 2. Disagree, 3. Neither, 4. Agree, 5. Strongly agree)
Q1	**Was the pace of the class good?**
Q2	**Was the content of the classes clear and organized?**
Q3	**Did the teacher give you enough opportunity to ask questions or exchange opinions?**
Q4	**Were the teacher's explanations and word choices clear?**
Q5	**Were the textbooks and class materials easy to understand and helpful for learning?**
Q6	**Did the teacher give you feedback on the assignments or the work submitted?**
Q7	**Did the teacher provide you with various ideas that helped you learn independently?**
Q8	**Did you learn and understand the objective and the goal of this class?**
Q9	**Did you clearly understand the contents of the class?**
Q10	**Did you learn new information and skills?**
Q11	**Would you want to learn more about the contents of this class?**
Q12	**How much time per week did you spend for class preparation and review, including out of class studying with friends?**

5. CONCLUSION

In mathematics education utilizing LMS, UI standardization is important for inputting mathematical formulae. This standardization is expected to reduce the burden of LMS operations, allowing teachers and students to focus on teaching and learning, respectively. In this study, we developed a mathematics e-learning system (Moodle+STACK) with a standardized equation-input UI, MathTOUCH. The effectiveness of such a learning support environment was investigated in a mathematics class. Primarily, we evaluated the (1) results of automatically graded online tests, (2) grading results of assignment reports submitted online, and (3) results of subjective satisfaction with classes through a questionnaire. In (1), the average score was 8.37 (SD 0.6) points (out of 10), which is very high, and the average number of times the students attempted the tests was 2.52 times, which shows that their efforts were effective. Although there were some inappropriate questions, such as setting a time limit, there were almost no complaints from the students regarding the testing operations in survey (3). Although online test exercises are useful for improving calculation skills such as formulae, they are insufficient for testing students' abilities to document and apply what they have learned. This should be evaluated using assignment tests. In (2), the average score was 7.96 (SD = 2.13) points (out of 10), which is a good result. However, there was variation in these tests, with only the outlier question on the indefinite integral of velocity scoring 4.94 points, which was outside the interquartile range. This was due to the fact that approximately half of the students did not understand how to solve the problem, suggesting that teachers should improve their teaching methods. Therefore, this outlier did not have much impact on the analysis of the students' responses.

In fact, as shown in Figure 7, in terms of the grade evaluation of individual students out of 100 points, the average score for the quiz was 78.4 points, and average score for the assignment report was 69.5 points. These are high and strongly correlated, suggesting that the proposed mathematics e-learning system can improve educational effectiveness. However, the number of subjects in this study (37) was insufficient. To verify the effectiveness of the method more precisely, the number of students should be greater.

Finally, in (3), the students were particularly satisfied with learning new knowledge and skills in response to Q10 and in general did not feel stressed operating the LMS. The free-form comments show that mathematics e-learning with a standardized UI is well received and accepted by students. Approximately 70% of the students said that this learning environment was easier to understand than classroom learning.

However, whether the educational effectiveness and high level of satisfaction shown by these results can be attributed to the standardization of UI formula input or the support of teachers is difficult to conclude without further evaluation experiments. In this study, we were unable to directly evaluate MathTOUCH as a human-computer interaction (HCI) nor could we evaluate its usability. In the future, we will conduct a usability test to evaluate these aspects and analyze the STACK answering process with detailed feedback design.

ACKNOWLEDGEMENT

This research was supported by JSPS KAKENHI (Grant No. 23K25724).

REFERENCES

Fukui, T. and Shirai, S. (2015). Predictive Algorithm from Linear String to Mathematical Formulae for Math Input Method. *Booklet of Abstracts of the 21st conference on Applications of Computer Algebra*, pp. 17-22.

Fukui, T. and Shirai, S. (2017). Predictive Algorithm for Converting Linear Strings to General Mathematical Formulae. *Human Interface and the Management of Information: Supporting Learning, Decision-Making and Collaboration, Lecture Notes in Computer Science, 10274*, pp. 15-28.

Fukui, T. (2019). Educational graph-creation tools based on the natural mathematical description. *Booklet of Abstracts of the 25th conference on Applications of Computer Algebra*, pp. 190-190.

Fukui, T. (2020). Evaluation of Educational Graph Creation Tool Based on Natural Mathematical Description. *Association for Computing Machinery, New York, NY, USA*, pp. 55-56.

MEXT: Ministry of Education, Culture, Sports, Science and Technology (online) available at (https://www.mext.go.jp/en/about/index.htm) (accessed 2025-4-28).

Moodle: Moodle (online), available at (https://moodle.org/) (accessed 2025-4-28).

Sangwin, C. (2013). *Computer-aided Assessment of Mathematics*. OUP Oxford, Publisher's location at (https://stack-assessment.org).

Shirai, S. and Fukui, T. (2017). MathTOUCH: Mathematical Input Interface for E-Assessment Systems. *MSOR Connections EAMS special issue,* Vol. 15, No. 2, pp. 70-75.

Shirai, S. et al. (2018). Intelligent Editor for Authoring Educational Materials in Mathematics e-Learning Systems. *International Congress on Mathematical Software 2018, Lecture Notes in Computer Science, 10931*, pp. 431-437.

Shirai, S. et al. (2023). MathTOUCH Editor: Rich-Text Editor for Math E-Learning using an Intelligent Math Input Interface. *Journal of Information Processing,* Vol. 31, pp. 775-785.

Shirai, S., and Fukui, T. (2014). Improvement in the Input of Mathematical Formulae into STACK using Interactive Methodology (in Japanese). *Computer & Education*, Vol. 37, pp. 85-90.

Smith, G. G. and Ferguson, D. (2005). Student attrition in mathematics e-learning. *Australasian Journal of Educational Technology*, Vol. 21, No. 3, pp. 323-334.

UNDERSTANDING OF VEHICLE INTENTION AND SAFETY PERCEPTION IN YOUNG AND OLDER PEDESTRIANS CROSSING IN FRONT OF TWO DRIVERLESS VEHICLES: IMPACT OF A BIMODAL EHMI

Aïsha Sahaï, Nicolas Souliman and Natacha Métayer
Institut VEDECOM
23 bis allée des Marronniers, 78000 Versailles, France

ABSTRACT

The foreseeable deployment of driverless vehicles in urban traffic raises concerns about pedestrian safety, as traditional communication cues used by human drivers to signal their intentions to other road users are set to disappear. Implementing external Human-Machine Interfaces (eHMIs) on driverless vehicles could restore communication with other road users, enhancing safety. The aim of this study was to investigate the impact of bimodal eHMI signals from two driverless vehicles on the crossing experience of young and older adult pedestrians. In a virtual reality setting, 44 participants (24 young adults and 20 older adults) were asked to cross a shared space while a car and a shuttle, both driverless, approached. The complexity of the crossing was manipulated so that the two driverless vehicles either had the same behavior (i.e., both yielding or both passing) or different behaviors (i.e., one yielding, the other passing). Additionally, the presence of a bimodal eHMI was manipulated so that the two vehicles could be both equipped with an eHMI indicating their respective intention (i.e., to yield or to pass) using visual and sound signals, or had none. After each crossing, the participants rated their understanding of the vehicles' intentions and their feeling of safety during the crossing, using questionnaires. Semi-structured interviews were conducted post-experiment to gather qualitative feedback on the participants' crossings and the bimodal eHMI. Results showed that the presence of the bimodal eHMI on the driverless vehicles improved the participants' understanding of the vehicles' intentions and their perceived safety compared to no eHMI. In addition, the older adults exhibited a better understanding of the vehicles' intentions than the young adults. Yet, different mechanisms appeared to underly the understanding of the car's and the shuttle's intentions. Moreover, a loss of perceived safety was observed in complex scenarios (i.e., when the two vehicles had different behaviors) during the participants' first interactions with the vehicles. Interview data revealed a clear preference for crossings involving eHMI-equipped driverless vehicles and provided design recommendations for bimodal eHMIs.

KEYWORDS

Bimodal eHMI, Pedestrian, Ageing, Crossing, Driverless Vehicle, Safety

1. INTRODUCTION

French authorities have supported active transportation and sustainable cities by creating shared spaces that are low-speed zones where vulnerable road users and vehicles move freely, guided by informal rules (Cerema, 2014). Yet, due to their potential benefits for road safety, traffic flow, and accessibility (Sharma & Zheng, 2021), driverless vehicles (e.g., robotaxis, self-driving shuttles) are expected to become increasingly prevalent in urban traffic. However, the non-verbal communication cues traditionally used by human drivers to indicate their driving intentions to the other road users (e.g., eye contact, hand gestures) (Rasouli et al., 2017), are set to disappear with this level of automation. Moreover, recent research has shown that even when a human is physically present in an automated vehicle, pedestrians may no longer rely on making eye contact with the passive human inside, highlighting a diminishing reliance on human non-verbal communication as vehicle automation advances (Sahaï et al., 2022). This poses strong risks for pedestrians in shared spaces with highly automated vehicles, given their vulnerability and the lack of formal traffic rules. Implementing external Human-Machine Interfaces (eHMIs) on driverless vehicles could bridge this gap by restoring communication with other road users (Bazilinskyy et al., 2019; De Clercq et al., 2019).

However, there is no consensus about the best eHMI signal to emit (Dey et al., 2020), highlighting the challenge of designing intuitive and universally understandable signals that suit diverse populations and contexts.

Indeed, most eHMI research has involved interactions with a single automated vehicle (e.g., De Clercq et al., 2019; Feng et al., 2023; Sahaï et al., 2024) which may fail to reflect the complexity of real-world scenarios involving multiple vehicles. Moreover, individuals aged over 60 are expected to represent 22% of the global population by 2050 (WHO, 2024). As cities evolve to accommodate both automation and an aging population, understanding how these two trends interact becomes critical to creating inclusive urban spaces. Therefore, including older adults in studies of interactions between pedestrians and driverless vehicles is essential to ensure their specific needs are met. This is especially important as older adult pedestrians already face mobility issues due to perceptual and motor deficits (Tournier et al., 2016). To date, only one study has investigated the crossing behavior of young and older adult pedestrians facing multiple driverless vehicles (Dommes et al., 2021). The study revealed that the older adult participants took longer to cross in front of two yielding driverless vehicles in a virtual reality (VR) scenario compared to the young adults, suggesting greater hesitation in the former case (Dommes et al., 2021). Moreover, the older adult participants anticipated this motor slow-down by initiating their crossing earlier than the young adults (Dommes et al., 2021). However, this strategy could be risky if driverless vehicles fail to yield. Notably, the driverless vehicles in Dommes et al.'s (2021) study were not equipped with eHMIs to signal their intentions to the pedestrians. This absence might have influenced the pedestrians' behavior by increasing uncertainty about the vehicles' intentions. To our knowledge, no study has investigated the crossing experience of young and older adult pedestrians in front of multiple driverless vehicles equipped with an eHMI.

In this context, we aimed to explore the impact of eHMI signals from two driverless vehicles on both the subjective and objective crossing experiences of young and older adult pedestrians in a shared space. To overcome the limited legibility of text- or pictogram-based eHMIs from afar, a colored LED-strip-based eHMI was implemented in the present study as visual communication for pedestrians. Moreover, recognizing that sensory limitations such as age-related vision or hearing loss could reduce the effectiveness of unimodal cues, the eHMI was designed to be bimodal by incorporating auditory signals alongside the visual cues.

2. METHOD

2.1 Participants

Forty-four participants took part in the experiment. They were divided into two age groups: young adults ($N = 24$) and older adults ($N = 20$). The young adult group consisted of 13 women (mean age = 26.08 years, $SD = 4.42$ years, range 21–34) and 11 men (mean age = 27.64 years, $SD = 4.70$ years, range 21–35). The older adult group consisted of 10 women (mean age = 72.60 years, $SD = 2.17$ years, range 70–76) and 10 men (mean age = 73.20 years, $SD = 5.03$ years, range 70–82). All participants had normal or corrected-to-normal vision, could walk 100 meters without difficulty, and met simulator-related requirements (height:1.60–1.90 m, weight < 110 kg). For safety reasons, pregnant women or those who had given birth within the past three months were not included. None of the participants required a walking aid to get around or had medical conditions affecting perception, decision-making, or mobility. All participants gave their consent before participating in the study. Participants received a financial reward of €50 at the end of the experiment. The present study was not submitted to an ethics committee, as it was not required under current institutional and national guidelines for non-invasive behavioral research.

2.2 Materials

2.2.1 Virtual Environment

The experiment was conducted on a treadmill (KatWalk Premium) with the participants wearing a VR headset (Vive Pro Eye) (see Cherni et al., 2021). Harnesses kept the participants secure and centered on the treadmill while rubber overshoes with pads enabled sliding onto the treadmill, sending walking signals to the simulation. The headset had a 2880×1600 pixel resolution, a 90 Hz refresh rate, and a 110° field of view. Moreover, the headset had an eye tracker with a frequency of 120 Hz.

The pedestrian crossings occurred in a shared space with a bus shelter located in front of the participants' starting point (see Figure 1). Buildings on both sides of the participants' starting point obstructed their visibility, causing vehicles approaching from either side to be perceived late. A road sign indicated the shared space with a speed limitation at 20 km/h. This virtual environment was developed using Unity 3D.

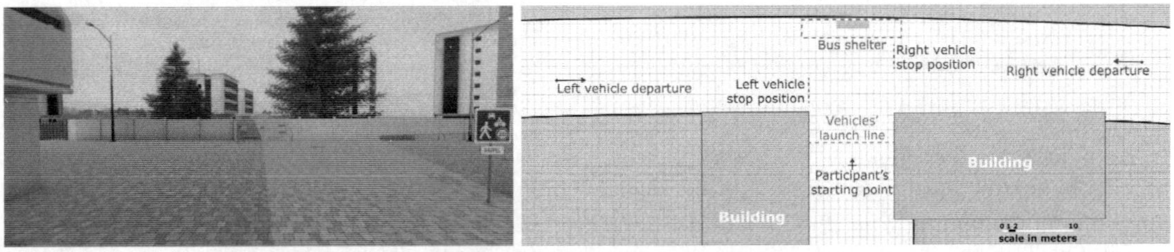

Figure 1. Front view (left) and schematic top view (right) of the shared space

Moreover, during the testing phase of the experiment, each participant systematically encountered two driverless electric vehicles: a car (Renault Zoé) and a shuttle (see Figure 2). Both were fitted with artificial sounds to mimic engine and tire noise, respectively proportional to acceleration and speed. The vehicles could be equipped with a bimodal eHMI (i.e., visual and audible) to indicate their intention to yield or to continue driving.

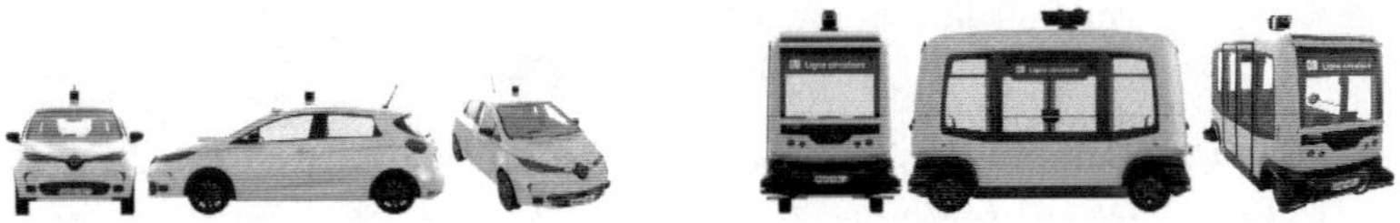

Figure 2. Front, lateral and three-quarter views of the car (left) and the shuttle (right)

When the driverless vehicles were equipped with the bimodal eHMI, LED strips located at the front of the vehicles emitted a cyan animated visual signal during the drive. If a vehicle intended to yield to the participant, the LED strips shifted from cyan to amber through three successive vertical sweeps during deceleration, coupled with a sound signal composed of three descending F notes (different octaves). Once the vehicle came to a complete stop and intended to wait, the LED strips displayed a looping amber horizontal sweep. This was paired with a sound signal composed of two quick D notes repeated five times with a 2-second interval, followed by four higher E notes, and ending with four repeated higher F notes to indicate the end of the stop period. When the vehicle intended to restart, the LED strips displayed a cyan vertical sweep followed by three cyan flashes. This was paired with a sound signal that gradually rose from F# to D, and upon reaching the pitch of A, continued with six successive beeps on that note. Once the vehicle resumed driving, the LED strips returned to a cyan animated visual signal.

Because green and red colors can lead to misinterpretation (Bazilinskyy et al., 2020), cyan and amber were chosen. Cyan was an emerging trend in automated vehicle communication (Dey et al., 2020), while amber was aligned with existing vehicle interfaces such as turn signals. Moreover, all the sound signals used were pre-tested against alternative sound signals with an independent sample of participants. The final sound signals were selected based on the participants' consistent and intuitive associations with the intended vehicle behaviors (decelerating, waiting, restarting), ensuring clear auditory communication. Braking and starting sound signals were designed to span more than one octave to be easily perceived in noisy environments.

2.2.2 Questionnaires

Four questionnaires were used during the experiment. The **socio-demographic and walking habits** *ad hoc* questionnaire was provided as a Word document to be completed. The first section required the participants to give socio-demographic information. The second section asked the participants about their walking habits.

The **technophilia** questionnaire (Agarwal & Prasad, 1998) was in the form of a Word document to be completed. It consisted of four items measuring attitudes towards new technologies to be rated on a six-point Likert scale ranging from 1 – "Strongly disagree" to 6 – "Strongly agree".

The **vehicles' intentions understanding** *ad hoc* questionnaire consisted of two items: "I have understood the intention of the car" and "I have understood the intention of the shuttle", while the **feeling of safety** *ad hoc* questionnaire consisted of a single item "I felt safe during my crossing". All these items were stated orally to the participants, who were then asked to rate each item on a six-point Likert scale ranging from 0 – "Not at all" to 5 – "Completely", by reporting their answer orally to the experimenter.

2.3 Procedure

Prior to the experiment, the participants completed the technophilia and the socio-demographic and walking habit questionnaires, along with reading the consent form to participate in the experiment.

On the experiment day, the participants signed the informed consent form. Then, they read an instruction sheet outlining the experiment's three phases: **familiarization**, **testing**, and **semi-structured interview**. The participants could ask questions at any time and the experimenter ensured all instructions were understood before starting. The participants were then invited to go to the VR treadmill.

After being introduced to the equipment, the participants received instructions on navigating on the treadmill and the eye calibration steps with the VR headset. They were then fitted with overshoes to facilitate walking on the treadmill. After this, the participants were safely installed on the treadmill, with the harnesses and the VR headset adjusted. The eye calibration was then completed, followed by the familiarization part.

The **familiarization** phase included two tasks. In the first task, the participants had to walk in a virtual environment depicting a tiled area to reach an orange-lit cylinder, twice. This task enabled the participants to become familiar with navigating in the simulator. In the second task, the participants were standing at a starting point and had to cross a shared space in order to reach a bus shelter while vehicles (automated or not) approached from both sides at 20 km/h. They were instructed to carefully look left and right before crossing. After completing their crossing, the participants received an instruction reminder, and the testing part began.

During the **testing** phase, the participants had to cross the same shared space as the second familiarization task, 32 times. However, only two vehicles were present: a car and a shuttle, both driverless, see Figure 2. These vehicles always traveled at 20 km/h on separate paths, ensuring one vehicle approached from the left and the other from the right, in a counterbalanced order. The participants had to initiate their crossings when they judged it safe. The vehicles' behavior congruency was manipulated, in a counterbalanced order: in congruent conditions, both vehicles either yielded or continued driving; in incongruent conditions, one vehicle yielded while the other continued driving. Each vehicle appeared equally from the left and right and those yielding stopped 6 meters from the scene center, approximately 13 seconds after the participants had passed the vehicles' launch line. Buildings on either side prevented participants' early vehicle detection, hindering the understanding of the vehicles' intentions from kinematics. During half of the crossings ($N = 16$) and in a counterbalanced order, both vehicles had a bimodal eHMI indicating their respective intention (i.e., to yield or to continue driving), consistent with their actual behavior. Importantly, the meaning of the eHMI signals sent by the driverless vehicles was not explained to the participants prior to the experiment. A break was set after the 16th crossing, creating two experimental blocks. In sum, there were 2 levels of vehicle arrival side × 2 levels of congruent vehicles' behaviors × 2 levels of incongruent vehicles' behaviors × 2 levels of eHMI presence × 2 repetitions, leading to 32 crossings. The vehicle arrival side was set for experimental control and was not included in further analysis. After each crossing, the participants completed the vehicles' intentions understanding and feeling of safety questionnaires. The items were read aloud to the participants, who responded verbally; their answers were then transcribed into a dedicated interface. The participants could also provide open feedback. Eye and walking behaviors were recorded throughout the testing phase, but these data were not included in this paper. Once the final crossing and questionnaires were completed, the participants exited the simulator and the equipment was removed.

Finally, an audio-recorded **semi-structured interview** collected the participants' impressions about their crossings and the bimodal eHMI. Then, the participants were thanked and the experiment ended.

3. RESULTS

One older adult discontinued early due to suspected cybersickness, and data from 3 participants were lost during the testing phase due to technical issues, resulting in a final sample of 23 young adults and 17 older adults. Statistical analyses were performed using R software. Main effects were analyzed using Wilcoxon tests (due to non-normal data distributions, all $ps < .10$), and interaction effects were examined using mixed ANOVAs with the participants' age group (young adult, older adult) as a between-participants factor, and the presence of the eHMI on the vehicles (yes, no), the vehicles' behavior congruency (congruent, incongruent) and the experimental block (1, 2) as within-participants factors. Pairwise comparisons were performed using Wilcoxon tests and applying the Bonferroni correction. The significance threshold was set at $\alpha = .05$.

3.1 Place of Residence and Walking Habits

Most young adults (67%) and older adults (53%) reported living in an urban city center. The remaining participants indicated residing in a suburban area. Moreover, 83% of young adults and 68% of older adults reported walking daily or nearly daily for trips lasting over 15 consecutive minutes.

3.2 Level of Technophilia

The Wilcoxon test revealed no significant main effect of the participants' age group on the participants' global technophilia scores ($W = 163$, $p = .10$, $r = -.07$, mean = 5.10, $SD = .54$). Thus, **no difference in technophilia levels was found between the young adults and the older adults prior to the experiment.**

3.3. Vehicle Intention Understanding

3.3.1 The car

The Wilcoxon test revealed a significant main effect of the participants' age group on the participants' understanding scores of the car's intention, indicating higher intention understanding scores among the older adults compared to young adults ($W = 107$, $p = .01$, $r = -.39$, $\text{mean}_{young} = 3.95$, $SD_{young} = .62$, $\text{mean}_{older} = 4.40$, $SD_{older} = .46$). Thus, **the older adults reported overall a better understanding of the car's intention compared to the young adults.**

Moreover, the Wilcoxon test revealed a significant main effect of the eHMI presence on the participants' understanding scores of the car's intention, indicating higher intention understanding scores when the eHMI was present compared to when it was absent ($W = 167.5$, $p = .002$, $r = -.35$, $\text{mean}_{eHMI} = 4.35$, $SD_{eHMI} = .58$, $\text{mean}_{no\ eHMI} = 3.93$, $SD_{no\ eHMI} = .81$). Thus, **the participants reported a better understanding of the car's intention when the vehicles were equipped with the bimodal eHMI indicating their respective intention compared to when the vehicles were not equipped with the device.**

No other significant main effects were found on the participants' understanding scores of the car's intention ($ps > .05$). However, the mixed ANOVA revealed a significant age group × vehicles' behavior congruency × experimental block interaction on the participants' understanding scores of the car's intention ($F_{1,38} = 9.46$, $p = .004$, $\eta p^2 = .20$, see Figure 3). Specifically, when the car and the shuttle had incongruent behaviors, the older adults reported higher intention understanding scores than the young adults during the second experimental block ($p = .04$), whereas no difference was observed during the first experimental block ($p = 1$). Yet, when the car and the shuttle had congruent behaviors, no significant differences were found on the participants' understanding scores between the young adults and the older adults both during the first ($p = .80$) and the second ($p = .08$) experimental blocks. Thus, **in complex crossings (i.e., when the car and the shuttle had different behaviors), the older adults reported better understanding of the car's intention than the young adults, but only during the second part of the experiment.**

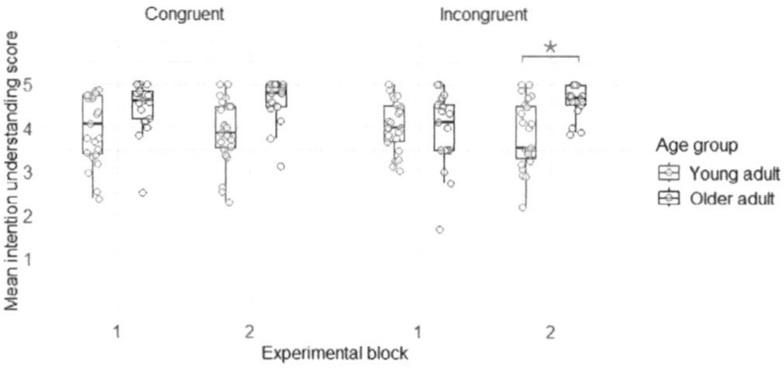

Figure 3. Three-way interaction on the participants' understanding scores of the car's intention, *: $p < .05$

3.3.2 The Shuttle

The Wilcoxon test revealed a significant main effect of the participants' age group on the participants' understanding scores of the shuttle's intention, indicating higher intention understanding scores among the older adults compared to the young adults ($W = 90$, $p = .004$, $r = -.45$, mean $_{young} = 3.89$, $SD_{young} = .64$, mean $_{older} = 4.48$, $SD_{older} = .32$). Thus, **the older adults reported overall a better understanding of the shuttle's intention compared to the young adults.**

Moreover, the Wilcoxon test revealed a significant main effect of the eHMI presence on the participants' understanding scores of the shuttle's intention, indicating higher intention understanding scores when the eHMI was present compared to when it was absent ($W = 127$, $p < .001$, $r = -.42$, mean $_{eHMI} = 4.36$, $SD_{eHMI} = .55$, mean $_{no\ eHMI} = 3.92$, $SD_{no\ eHMI} = .80$). Thus, **the participants reported a better understanding of the shuttle's intention when the vehicles were equipped with the bimodal eHMI indicating their respective intention compared to when the vehicles were not equipped with the device.**

No other significant main effects were found on the participants' shuttle's intention understanding scores ($ps > .05$). Moreover, the mixed ANOVA revealed no significant interaction effect on the participants' shuttle's intention understanding scores ($ps > .05$).

3.4 Feeling of Safety

The Wilcoxon test revealed a significant main effect of the presence of the eHMI on the participants' feeling of safety scores with higher feeling of safety scores when the eHMI was present on the vehicles compared to when it was absent ($W = 168.5$, $p = .002$, r = -.34, mean $_{eHMI} = 4.10$, $SD_{eHMI} = .62$, mean $_{no\ eHMI} = 3.76$, $SD_{no\ eHMI} = .85$). Thus, **the participants reported feeling safer during their crossings when the car and the shuttle were equipped with the bimodal eHMI indicating their respective intention compared to when the vehicles were not equipped with the device.**

Moreover, the Wilcoxon test revealed a significant main effect of the vehicles' behavior congruency on the participants' feeling of safety scores with higher feeling of safety scores for congruent vehicles' behavior compared to incongruent vehicles' behavior ($W = 102.5$, $p < .001$, $r = -.42$, mean $_{congruent} = 4.04$, $SD_{congruent} = .68$, mean $_{incongruent} = 3.82$, $SD_{incongruent} = .71$). Thus, **the participants reported feeling safer during their crossings when the car and the shuttle had the same behavior compared to different ones.**

No other significant main effects were found on the participants' feeling of safety scores ($ps > .05$). However, the mixed ANOVA revealed a significant vehicles' behavior congruency × experimental block interaction on the participants' feeling of safety scores ($F_{1,38} = 8.70$, $p = .01$, $\eta p^2 = .19$, see Figure 4). Specifically, during the first experimental block, the feeling of safety scores were higher when the vehicles exhibited congruent behaviors compared to incongruent behaviors ($p = .001$). In contrast, during the second experimental block, no significant difference in the feeling of safety scores was observed between congruent and incongruent vehicles' behaviors ($p = 1$). Thus, **during the first part of the experiment, the participants reported feeling less safe during their crossings when the car and shuttle had different behaviors compared to the same behavior. This difference in perceived safety was no longer present during the second part of the experiment.**

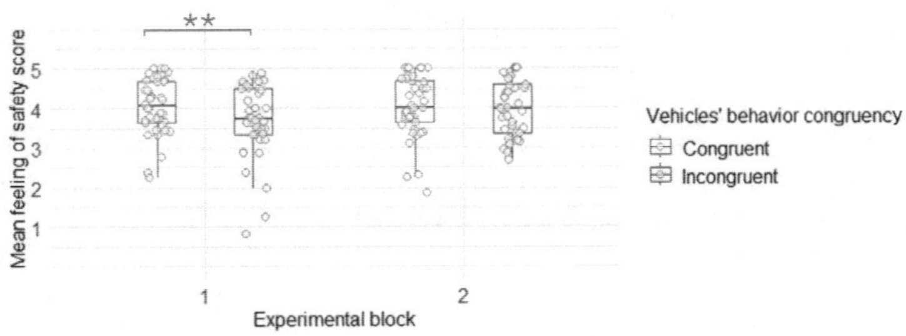

Figure 4. Two-way interaction on the participants' feeling of safety scores, **: $p < .01$

3.5 Feedback on the Bimodal eHMI

During the semi-structured interviews, 88% of young adults and 79% of older adults reported preferring to cross in front of driverless vehicles equipped with the bimodal eHMI, rather than without it. Participants explained that **the bimodal eHMI made them feel safer and more reassured, as it confirmed the vehicle's behavior and replaced human communication**.

However, 23% of participants claimed that it would have been **more suitable for vehicles to emit an amber light signal when it was not advisable for pedestrians to cross** (i.e., while driving) and a cyan light signal when yielding to them. For example, P30 (older adult) said *"As a driver, the orange traffic light is clearly an alert. It signals that I need to be ready to stop, not go. But here, it was the opposite."*

Moreover, 25% of young adults reported **difficulty identifying which vehicle was emitting the eHMI sound signal**. For example, P42 said *"If the car arrives first from the left and I start to cross, I am unsure if the other vehicle is stopping or not, creating a brief wait. The issue is that we can't really tell where the sound is coming from. I cannot tell if it is the car that has stopped that is emitting the sound, or if it is the shuttle that is making the sound and thus will stop."*

Additionally, 13% of young adults and 16% of older adults mentioned that **the acceleration of the sound signal during the vehicle's stop period was stressful and, for some, confusing**. For example, P34 (older adult) said *"Because the sound signal increases, it's stressful. It really increases. Well, you don't know if you should hurry, if the car is going to restart. And I think that since the light signal remains steady, we have time to cross. Otherwise, maybe it could cause some confusion."*

4. DISCUSSION

In the present study, age-related differences in the pedestrians' ability to understand driverless vehicles' intentions (e.g., to yield or to continue driving) were highlighted. Indeed, the older adults reported overall better understanding of the intentions of the car and the shuttle than the young adults. This might be attributed to the older adults' greater pedestrian experience, which could have helped them understand the vehicles' intentions more easily than the young adults. Another explanation could be that the older adults might have been influenced by social desirability bias, seeking to project competence and autonomy in their responses to the experimenter. Yet, when the car and shuttle exhibited different behaviors, the older adults showed improved understanding of the car's intention after repeated crossings, suggesting a learning effect for this age group in complex crossing scenarios. This learning effect was not observed for the understanding of the shuttle's intention, pointing out different mechanisms for interpreting the car's and the shuttle's behavioral intentions. These differences could be explained by bottom-up processes, whereby the participants' perception was influenced by low-level features such as the physical characteristics of the vehicles, notably size. Top-down processes may also have played a role, involving the participants' mental representations of each vehicle, with the shuttle being more readily associated with a driverless vehicle and the car with a human-driven vehicle. Further research is needed to clarify the relative influence of these processes.

Interestingly, we found that the presence of a bimodal eHMI on driverless vehicles improved both the participants' understanding of the vehicles' intentions and their feeling of safety during their crossings compared to scenarios without eHMI. These findings aligned with previous research showing that the pedestrian feeling of safety when deciding to cross in front of a single driverless vehicle was enhanced when the vehicle emitted eHMI signals to the pedestrian compared to when no eHMI signal was sent (De Clercq et al., 2019). However, our findings extended previous work (De Clercq et al., 2019), underscoring that the pedestrian feeling of safety benefits from an eHMI was not limited to the moment of the crossing decision making but persisted throughout the entire crossing, even when two driverless vehicles were present.

In addition, we observed that during their first crossings in the shared space, the pedestrians' feeling of safety was lowered when the car and the shuttle had different behaviors compared to the same one. This might reflect pedestrians' vulnerability due to uncertainty about appropriate behavior when vehicles act inconsistently. However, this decline in perceived safety in complex scenarios faded after repeated crossings, indicating an adaptive process. Indeed, over time, participants likely learned to manage complex crossings more effectively, which reduced their sense of vulnerability and, in turn, their perception of danger.

Furthermore, a preference for alternative eHMI color coding was suggested by 23% of participants, highlighting potential ambiguities in interpreting the visual signals of the bimodal eHMI, where the amber color, due to its potential association with warning, may be understood differently depending on whether pedestrians adopt an egocentric perspective (i.e., the signal is directed at them – they must not cross) or an allocentric perspective (i.e., the signal reflects the vehicle's behavior – they can cross). Nevertheless, ISO guidelines discourage providing explicit guidance to vulnerable road users (e.g., a crossing advice) to avoid legal and safety issues, and recommend instead communication of vehicle state, understanding of the environment and intentions (ISO/TR 23049:2018).

In addition, difficulties in perceiving the sound signals of the eHMI were reported, with 25% of young adults struggling to identify the source of the sound. Hence, considering the use of sound signals in bimodal eHMIs on driverless vehicles, it is crucial to select sound signals with acoustic properties that minimize the risk of confusion with ambient noise to avoid informational masking. This phenomenon occurs when an auditory stimulus becomes difficult to detect within an environment of similar acoustic properties (Kidd et al., 2008; Veyrié et al., 2023). The use of a bimodal eHMI is nevertheless recommended, as participants reported preferring to cross in front of driverless vehicles equipped with such a communication system. Moreover, the bimodal nature of these eHMIs may promote inclusivity by accommodating individuals with different sensory needs (e.g., individuals with blindness or deafness).

Despite these promising findings, several limitations of the present study must be acknowledged. Firstly, the relatively small sample sizes of participants analyzed (23 young adults and 17 older adults) may limit the generalizability of the results and reduce the statistical power to detect more subtle effects. Secondly, this study was conducted in a VR environment which, although offering controlled conditions, might not fully capture the complexity and emotional impact of real-world street crossings. In particular, risk perception might be reduced, as the participants were aware that, unlike in real life, they could not be physically hit by a vehicle. Moreover, pedestrians' crossing experience is closely dependent on individual factors such as social norms and culture (Rasouli & Tsotsos, 2019). Thus, the results obtained here with French participants may not be directly transferable to pedestrian populations in other countries.

5. CONCLUSION

In the present study, the implementation of a bimodal eHMI on driverless vehicles demonstrated a positive impact on pedestrians' perceived safety and their understanding of vehicles' intentions. Participants also expressed a preference for the presence of such a communication system, emphasizing its role in enhancing their crossing experience. However, further investigation is needed to consider improving the pedestrians' perceived safety and understanding of the vehicles' intentions from their very first encounter with driverless vehicles in complex crossing scenarios. Furthermore, to reduce confusion, LED signals should avoid colors like amber, which may be interpreted differently depending on the user's perspective. Moreover, when incorporating sound signals into a bimodal eHMI, designers should avoid overly intrusive sounds or closely spaced loops, as these may cause user confusion or rejection. Crucially, sound signals should be distinct and not easily confused with other ambient noises (e.g., bus horns) to ensure effective communication.

Taken together, these findings offer promising directions for the development of intuitive and inclusive communication systems between pedestrians and driverless vehicles, paving the way for safer interactions.

ACKNOWLEDGEMENT

This research was part of the SYDÉA project, jointly funded by the French National Research Agency under the France 2030 program, and by the partners of the project (RATP, RENAULT, VEDECOM).

REFERENCES

Agarwal, R., & Prasad, J. (1998). A conceptual and operational definition of personal innovativeness in the domain of information technology. *Information systems research*, *9*(2), 204-215.

Bazilinskyy, P., Dodou, D., & De Winter, J. (2019). Survey on eHMI concepts: The effect of text, color, and perspective. *Transportation research part F: traffic psychology and behaviour*, *67*, 175-194.

Bazilinskyy, P., Dodou, D., & De Winter, J. (2020, October). External Human-Machine Interfaces: Which of 729 colors is best for signaling 'Please (do not) cross'?. In *2020 IEEE International Conference on Systems, Man, and Cybernetics (SMC)* (pp. 3721-3728). IEEE.

Cerema (2014). *Les zones de rencontre en Ile-de-France.* https://www.cerema.fr/fr/actualites/zones-rencontre-ile-france

Cherni, H., Souliman, N., & Métayer, N. (2021). Using virtual reality treadmill as a locomotion technique in a navigation task: Impact on user experience–case of the KatWalk. *International Journal of Virtual Reality*, *21*(1), 1-14.

De Clercq, K., Dietrich, A., Núñez Velasco, J. P., De Winter, J., & Happee, R. (2019). External human-machine interfaces on automated vehicles: Effects on pedestrian crossing decisions. *Human factors*, *61*(8), 1353-1370.

Dey, D., Habibovic, A., Löcken, A., Wintersberger, P., Pfleging, B., Riener, A., ... & Terken, J. (2020). Taming the eHMI jungle: A classification taxonomy to guide, compare, and assess the design principles of automated vehicles' external human-machine interfaces. *Transportation Research Interdisciplinary Perspectives*, *7*, 100174.

Dommes, A., Merlhiot, G., Lobjois, R., Dang, N. T., Vienne, F., Boulo, J., ... & Cavallo, V. (2021). Young and older adult pedestrians' behavior when crossing a street in front of conventional and self-driving cars. *Accident Analysis & Prevention*, *159*, 106256.

Feng, Y., Farah, H., & van Arem, B. (2023, September). Effect of eHMI on pedestrian road crossing behavior in shared space with Automated Vehicles-A Virtual Reality study. *In 2023 IEEE 26th International Conference on Intelligent Transportation Systems (ITSC)* (pp. 2038-2043). IEEE.

International Organization for Standardization (2018). Road Vehicles — Ergonomic aspects of external visual communication from automated vehicles to other road users, ISO/TR 23049:2018

Kidd Jr, G., Mason, C. R., Richards, V. M., Gallun, F. J., & Durlach, N. I. (2008). Informational masking. *Auditory perception of sound sources*, 143-189.

Rasouli, A., Kotseruba, I., & Tsotsos, J. K. (2017, June). Agreeing to cross: How drivers and pedestrians communicate. *In 2017 IEEE Intelligent Vehicles Symposium (IV)* (pp. 264-269). IEEE.

Rasouli, A., & Tsotsos, J. K. (2019). Autonomous vehicles that interact with pedestrians: A survey of theory and practice. IEEE transactions on intelligent transportation systems, *21*(3), 900-918.

Sahaï, A., Labeye, E., Caroux, L., & Lemercier, C. (2022). Crossing the street in front of an autonomous vehicle: An investigation of eye contact between drivengers and vulnerable road users. *Frontiers in psychology*, *13*, 981666.

Sahaï, A., Puscasu, O., & Métayer, N. (2024). Age-Based Differences in Pedestrians' Feeling of Trust and Safety When Crossing in Front of a Real Communicating Self-Driving Car During Daytime or Nighttime. *Human Interaction and Emerging Technologies (IHIET 2024)*, *1*(1).

Sharma, A., & Zheng, Z. (2021). Connected and automated vehicles: Opportunities and challenges for transportation systems, smart cities, and societies. *Automating Cities: Design, Construction, Operation and Future Impact*, 273-296.Tournier, I., Dommes, A., & Cavallo, V. (2016). Review of safety and mobility issues among older pedestrians. *Accident Analysis & Prevention*, *91*, 24-35.

Veyrié, A., Noreña, A., Sarrazin, J. C., & Pezard, L. (2023). Investigating the influence of masker and target properties on the dynamics of perceptual awareness under informational masking. *Plos one*, *18*(3), e0282885.

World Health Organization (2024). *Ageing and health.* https://www.who.int/news-room/fact-sheets/detail/ageing-and-health

ACCESSIBLE EXPLANATIONS FOR ACCESSIBLE AI: EXPLAINABLE AI METHODS TO SUPPORT EASY-TO-READ TEXT GENERATION – A RAPID REVIEW

Susanne Dirks
TU Dortmund University
Emil-Figge-Str. 50, 44227 Dortmund, Germany

ABSTRACT

Explainable AI techniques offer significant potential for making AI-generated content more transparent and understandable for users with diverse explanation needs. The present study investigates the adaptation of explainable artificial intelligence (XAI) methods to support the understanding of AI-generated, easier-to-understand translations for users with disabilities. In a rapid review, the assessment of common XAI concepts such as LIME, SHAP and counterfactuals were investigated, and the main challenges and opportunities of these concepts were identified. Based on the results, recommendations on how to make AI explanations for accessible automatically generated easy-to-read texts were derived. The results of the study suggest that multimodal, personalized and simplified explanations hold considerable promise for enhancing understanding while maintaining the sensitive balance between appropriateness of explanation and cognitive accessibility.

KEYWORDS

Explainable AI (XAI), Artificail Intelligence (AI), Disabilities, Easy-to-Read (E2R), Accessibility, Human-Computer Interaction (HCI), Comprehension

1. INTRODUCTION

The complexity of contemporary machine learning models has increased exponentially, from relatively simple linear regression to sophisticated neural networks, CNNs and transformers. While these advances have improved predictive capabilities, they have also created 'black box' systems whose internal processes remain opaque to users (Hassija, Chamola and Mahapatra, 2024). This opacity poses a significant challenge for users with cognitive disabilities, who may require additional support to comprehend the process by which Artificial Intelligence (AI) systems transform information into accessible formats (Tielmann et al., 2024).

Explainable Artificial Intelligence (XAI) has emerged as a field dedicated to making AI decisions more transparent and understandable. Yet most XAI approaches are designed for technical experts or neurotypical users, potentially leaving behind individuals with cognitive disabilities who may benefit most from these technologies (Alnfiai, Alsudairy and Alharbi, 2025). Moreover, accessible interfaces and simplified text content can also benefit other people, e.g., older people, illiterate people and people with a different native language (Moreno, Petrie and Martínez, 2024). Developing accessible XAI approaches for text simplification systems addresses several important issues: promoting AI literacy among disadvantaged populations, fulfilling ethical obligations for inclusive technological development, and supporting the independence of disadvantaged people in an increasingly AI-immersed world. The present research investigates the potential of established XAI methods to support the understanding of AI-generated easy-to-read translations.

2. BACKGROUND

In this section, the theoretical background on the special requirements of AI users with disabilities and the current XAI concepts are briefly presented.

2.1 Accessible Information and Easy-to-Read

Recent studies have drawn attention to the difficulties faced by individuals with disabilities in accessing and using digital information. Despite increased awareness, a significant proportion of digital information and services remain inaccessible (Borina, Kalister and Orehovački., 2022). Nevertheless, digital technologies and AI-based technologies hold considerable potential to enhance the social participation and inclusion of disadvantaged user groups (Dirks et al., 2020). Research indicates that a simple user interface design, the use of easy-to-understand language, the provision of information in various formats, and the avoidance of distractions can improve overall digital accessibility (Borina, Kalister and Orehovački., 2022).

Easy-to-Read (E2R) is a linguistic concept that was developed to make information accessible to people with reading difficulties or cognitive disabilities (Bredel & Maaß, 2016). There are different sets of rules and standards for E2R in different countries, such as 'Leichte Sprache' in Germany, 'Easy-to-Read' in the English-speaking world or the 'Inclusion Europe' guidelines (Inclusion Europe). Automated generation of texts in E2R is a complex computational linguistic task that involves several levels of processing (Saggion & Hirst, 2017). Instead of rule-based simplifications, AI-based text simplification increasingly uses complex neural language models where the decision-making process is opaque. Reconstructing exactly how and why a model makes certain simplifications is difficult for users and developers alike (Stajner, 2021).

2.2 Explainable AI and Explanation Concepts

AI systems are increasingly involved in critical decision-making processes in areas such as healthcare or the justice system and influence the decisions that are made there. Consequently, it is of great importance that all users can understand how algorithmic decisions were made and what possible consequences they may have (Doshi-Velez & Kim, 2017). For this reason, increasing research efforts focus on XAI to reduce the opacity of complex machine learning models (Adadi & Berrada, 2018; Arrieta et al., 2020). The goal of XAI approaches is to provide explanations for the outcomes and decisions of AI-based processes that users can understand, control and ultimately trust (Gunning & Aha, 2019). Within XAI, the explanations necessary for understanding are broadly categorized into two basic types: local and global explanations (Molnar et al., 2020; Garouani et al., 2024). Users are generally categorized according to their expertise and their differing needs and goals into AI experts, agents, and non-experts (Bove et al., 2022). Research shows that non-experts are generally more interested in understanding the reasons for a particular outcome than in understanding how the general behavior of a system works (Bove et al., 2022). Since this paper is addressing the explanatory needs of non-expert users, the focus is on the use of common XAI methods for generating local explanations. The primary advantage of this approach is that it facilitates cognitive accessibility. Local explanations provide a rationale for the specific decision made by the AI system in a particular case. This phenomenon mirrors the way individuals seek explanations in their daily lives.

LIME (Local Interpretable Model-Agnostic Explanation) is a widely used XAI technique designed to explain especially individual predictions of any black-box machine learning model in a way that is understandable to humans (Ribeiro, Singh and Guestrin, 2018). It focuses on training a local surrogate model to approximate the prediction of the underlying black box model as closely as possible for a single instance. In contrast to the original model, the local surrogate models are transparent or explainable and are used to explain individual predictions of the black box model (Aechtner et al., 2022). This allows LIME to show which features were most important for the specific decision. LIME's power lies in its model-agnosticism – it can explain predictions from any black-box model without requiring knowledge of its internal decisions (Aechtner et al., 2022).

SHAP (SHapley Additive exPlanations) unifies several explanatory approaches through game theory principles. Developed by Lundberg and Lee (2017), SHAP assigns each feature an importance value representing its contribution to a specific prediction. The method is based on Shapley values from cooperative game theory and guarantees consistency (features with larger impacts on the model receive larger attribution values) and local accuracy (explanations precisely reflect the actual prediction) (Li et al., 2024). For each feature of a data point, SHAP calculates the contribution it makes to the prediction of the model. This is done by considering all possible combinations of features to determine the average influence of a feature. SHAP can provide both local and global explanations and can be used flexibly for different data types such as images, texts or tabular data.

Counterfactual explanations represent a fundamentally different approach to model interpretability. While LIME and SHAP focus on the importance of features for a given prediction, counterfactual explanations focus on the smallest changes necessary to achieve an alternative outcome. This approach was formalized by Wachter et al. (2017) and is conceptually based on the human tendency to think in counterfactual scenarios. Rather than explaining why a prediction was made, they show what modifications to the input would lead to a different prediction (Prosperi et al., 2020). Counterfactuals have become particularly important in the context of AI fairness and ethics (Kusner et al., 2017).

3. METHODOLOGY

Taking the state of research into account, it can be concluded that there are various XAI approaches that can be used to make AI-generated results more accessible to non-experts. The various XAI methods presented here have often been evaluated in areas such as image classification or structured data analysis. A brief analysis of the research field revealed that there is hardly any previous work on the use of XAI to generate E2R texts with explanations for people with cognitive disabilities. To answer the following research question '*Are common XAI approaches such as SHAP, LIME and counterfactuals suitable for providing comprehensible explanations for automatically generated, easy-to-read texts?*' a rapid review on XAI methods used to generate explanations for non-expert users was carried out.

The rapid review was conducted as single-reviewer-screening in accordance with the PRISMA 2020 guidelines (PRISMA)and the selection of literature was executed using Rayyan (Rayyan). Titles and abstracts were screened based on defined inclusion and exclusion criteria. Relevant hits were marked and annotated, and potential ambiguities were clarified in the full-text phase. The following inclusion criteria were defined: language English, period 2019-2025, articles from newspapers and proceedings, XAI for non-experts and users with diverse needs. Studies in other languages, older studies, gray literature and articles without user reference were excluded.

Search was conducted in the following databases: Scopus, IEEE Xplore, ACM Digital Library, and arXiv, using combinations of keywords such as 'XAI', 'explainable artificial intelligence', 'text generation', 'methods', 'SHAP', 'LIME', 'counterfactual*', 'user experience', 'non-expert*', 'cognitive disabilit*' and 'disabilit*'. After removing duplicates, the reviewer screened titles and abstracts for relevance. Full texts of included articles were assessed against the defined eligibility criteria. As the number of studies with direct user involvement was very low, studies that worked with user simulations were also included in the second analysis step. Of the 330 articles found in the first step, after removing the duplicates and applying the inclusion and exclusion criteria, 23 full papers were finally analyzed. An overview of the papers can be found in Table 1.

Table 1. Overview of the final analyzed full papers with author, year, doi and applied XAI methods

N	Author, Year, doi	XAI method
1	Jalali et al., 2023, https://doi.org/10.48550/arXiv.2309.11987	SHAP, LIME and counterfactual explanations
2	Förster et al., 2021. http://dx.doi.org/10.24251/HICSS.2021.155	Counterfactual explanations
3	Förster et al., 2022, http://dx.doi.org/10.1080/12460125.2022.2119707	Counterfactual explanations
4	Galhotra et al., 2021, https://doi.org/10.48550/arXiv.2103.11972	Probabilistic contrastive counterfactuals (compared to LIME and SHAP)
5	Zhong & Negre, 2022, http://dx.doi.org/10.1145/3477314.350702	SHAP
6	Fernandez et al., 2020, https://doi.org/10.48550/arXiv.2001.07417	Counterfactual reasoning framework (Comparison with SHAP)
7	Mothilal et al., 2020, https://doi.org/10.1145/3461702.3462597	Counterfactual explanations, LIME, SHAP
8	Vimbi et al., 2024, https://doi.org/10.1186/s40708-024-00222-1	LIME, SHAP
9	Chromik, 2021, https://doi.org/10.1007/978-3-030-85616-8_37	SHAPRap (SHAP)
10	Hase & Bansal, 2020, https://arxiv.org/pdf/2005.01831	LIME (and other methods)
11	Rao et al., 2022, https://doi.org/10.1109/IBSSC56953.2022.10037324	LIME, SHAP
12	Zhang et al., 2022, http://dx.doi.org/10.5220/0010900300003116	Global, local explanations, and counterfactuals
13	Salih et al., 2023, https://doi.org/10.1002/aisy.202400304	SHAP, LIME
14	Chromik et al., 2021, https://doi.org/10.1145/3397481.3450644	SHAP framework
15	Benk & Ferrario,2020, https://dx.doi.org/10.2139/ssrn.3748268	Counterfactual explanations and LIME

16	Aechtner et al., 2022, https://doi.org/10.1109/FUZZ-IEEE55066.2022.9882743	LIME, SHAP (and other methods)
17	Schulte et al., 2024, https://doi.org/10.1007/s10664-024-10469-1	LIME and SHAP
18	Dieber & Kirrane, 2020, https://doi.org/10.48550/arXiv.2012.000	LIME
10	Dutta et al., 2023, https://doi.org/10.1109/GLOBECOM54140.2023.10436967	LIME and SHAP
20	Warren et al., 2022, https://doi.org/10.48550/arXiv.2204.10152	Counterfactual explanations
21	Dost & Bendechache, 2024, https://doi.org/10.1016/j.csbj.2024.08.005	LIME, SHAP (and other methods)
22	Brughmans et al., 2024, https://doi.org/10.1007/s11750-024-0067 2	SHAP (and other methods)
23	Keane & Smyth, 2022, https://doi.org/10.1007/978-3-030-58342-2_11	Counterfactuals

4. RESULTS

Existing research on the three primary XAI methods, LIME, SHAP, and counterfactual explanations, reveals distinct strengths and limitations. Jalali (2023) found that LIME offers higher predictability compared to SHAP, though SHAP's comprehensibility is significantly reduced for samples close to model decision boundaries. However, Schulte et al. (2024) demonstrated that SHAP outperforms LIME due to lower ambiguity and higher contextuality when capturing sentence fragments, while both methods provide adequate explanations for error and non-error predictions. Counterfactual explanations emerge as particularly promising across multiple studies. Förster et al. (2021, 2022) found that counterfactual explanations are considered more coherent, realistic, typical, and feasible compared to other XAI methods. Similarly, Warren et al. (2022) showed that counterfactual explanations lead to higher accuracy, greater satisfaction, and confidence compared to causal explanations. Fernandez et al. (2022) developed a counterfactual reasoning framework that provides context-dependent explanations by identifying causal features relevant for system decisions, finding that importance weighting methods like SHAP are ineffective for explaining system decisions.

A critical finding across multiple studies is that no single XAI method provides complete explanatory power. Mothilal et al. (2020) demonstrated that feature assignment and counterfactual explanation methods complement each other, each providing unique insights into model predictions. However, their results indicate that the top features identified by LIME and SHAP are often neither necessary nor sufficient to explain model predictions, emphasizing the importance of considering multiple explanatory methods to fully understand model predictions. This complementary approach is further supported by Chromik (2022), who found that a combination of global, local, and textual explanations was reasonably effective in improving participants' understanding of predictive model behavior. Zhang et al. (2022) concluded that developing an accessible XAI system requires deep understanding of the AI system, application domain, and user groups.

Healthcare applications demonstrate a particular promise for XAI methods. Vimbi et al. (2024) identified several advantages of using LIME and SHAP in Alzheimer's disease detection, including improved confidence and interpretability for clinicians without technical experience. Rao et al. (2022) showed that XAI can help restore user confidence and make decision-making processes in autonomous disease prediction systems transparent. Dutta et al. (2023) successfully applied LIME and SHAP for generating real-time predictive explanations for technical non-experts in healthcare and showed that counterfactual explanations contribute to advances in health monitoring and personalized health support. Dost and Bendechache (2024) conducted a comprehensive review of XAI techniques in medical image analysis, concluding that both LIME and SHAP are well-suited to make results more comprehensible, with LIME being more suitable for individual decision comprehensibility and SHAP for representing model relationships. Zhong and Negre (2022) demonstrated SHAP's effectiveness in recommender systems, showing it can explain more than 95% of recommendations with high model fidelity.

User experience research reveals important insights about how non-experts interact with XAI systems. Chromik (2022) found that participants appreciated natural language explanations but missed more abstract or aggregated descriptions to understand the big picture. However, Chromik et al. (2021) revealed a concerning finding: participants overestimated their understanding of machine learning model behavior when using SHAP-based interfaces, highlighting the need for careful design considerations in XAI application.

Hase and Bansal (2020) showed that LIME improves the simulatability in tabular classification, though they emphasize the need for careful evaluation standards for explanatory methods, as current approaches often lack sufficient explanatory power. Galhotra et al. (2021) developed a system generating human-understandable explanations and compared it with LIME and SHAP, demonstrating the correctness and scalability of their explanation algorithm on synthetic data.

Several studies highlight significant limitations in current XAI methods. Salih et al. (2023) demonstrated that SHAP and LIME are highly influenced by the machine learning model used, with LIME particularly problematic as it assumes feature independence, which is unrealistic for collinear data and can lead to misinterpretations. Brughmans et al. (2024) found high inconsistency between different counterfactual explanations, raising concerns about reliability. Benk and Ferrario (2020) showed that LIME explanation comprehensibility depends on text instance structure and requires domain knowledge. Aechtner et al. (2022) demonstrated that other methods, such as Partial Dependence Plots (PDP), outperform LIME and SHAP in user evaluations, suggesting the field should consider broader methodological approaches.

The literature converges on several key recommendations. Keane and Smyth (2022) developed a case-based method and found that different methods serve different purposes: their developed method is particularly suitable for individual decisions, SHAP for model relationships, and counterfactuals for realistic, context-dependent explanations. The research emphasizes that a combination of different methods is often necessary to fully understand and explain AI systems. Dieber and Kirrane (2020) showed that LIME proves useful as an addition to conventional performance assessment methods in tabular models, while Zhang et al. (2022) stress that successful XAI implementation requires comprehensive understanding of the AI system, application domain, and target user groups. The collective evidence suggests that effective XAI systems should integrate multiple explanation types and need to be tailored to specific domains and user needs, while acknowledging current limitations and the potential for user overconfidence in their understanding of AI system behavior.

5. CONCLUSION

Based on these results, the following conclusions can be drawn. LIME proves to be a useful complement to conventional performance evaluation procedures (Dieber & Kirrane, 2020) and is particularly suitable for the comprehensibility of individual decisions (Hase & Bansal, 2020; Jalali, 2023; Anushree et al., 2024). SHAP, on the other hand, is particularly suitable for representing model relationships (Anushree et al., 2024), has high model fidelity (Zhong & Negre, 2022) and outperforms LIME due to lower ambiguity and higher contextuality (Schulte et al., 2024). Combined explanations from global, local and textual explanations effectively improve understanding (Chromik, 2022). Counterfactual explanations correspond best to familiar psychological patterns and are therefore perceived as coherent and more realistic, typical and feasible (Förster et al., 2021, 2022). They offer context-dependent explanations (Fernandez et al., 2022) and lead to higher accuracy and greater satisfaction compared to causal explanations (Warren et al., 2022).

Despite the proven potential, there are still many technical challenges and limitations. For example, the top features identified by LIME are often not necessary or sufficient for model explanations (Mothilal et al., 2020). In some cases, the methods lead to an overestimation of the understanding of the model behavior, e.g. SHAP (Chromik et al., 2021). Automatically generated counterfactual explanations can be very inconsistent, and their quality varies greatly depending on the method used (Brughmans et al., 2024).

5.1 Application of XAI Methods for the Automatic Generation of Accessible Easy-to-Read Texts

Text simplification systems represent complex decision-making processes where multiple linguistic features interact to determine transformation strategies. The opacity of these decisions limits user trust, system validation and iterative improvement capabilities. Local explanation methods like LIME, SHAP and counterfactual explanations address the interpretability gap in text simplification through distinct computational approaches. All three examined XAI methods are well suited for generating local explanations. This means that they can be used to explain individual simplification decisions in E2R systems, for example, why a certain word has been replaced by a simpler one or why a sentence has been split up. Table 2 shows an overview of the main strengths, possible applications and accessible implementation of the three approaches for generating E2R texts.

Table 2. Main strengths, possible applications and accessible implementation of LIM, SHAP and counterfactuals for generating E2R texts

Method	Main strengths for E2R	Applications	Accessible implementation
LIME	Greater predictability Explanation of individual decisions Improved simulatability	Explanation of why specific words have been replaced Assessment of text difficulty Transparency in sentence restructuring	Pictograms or icons instead of text features Color-coded scales with smileys or traffic light colors Reduction to 2-3 main features with simplified labels
SHAP	Display of model relationships High model fidelity Combined explanatory approaches	Explain global simplification strategies Representation of complex language model relationships Multi-level explanations (global/local/textual)	Layered icons or bars with explanatory emojis. Integration in scenarios or stories: Because you did [x], the decision was [y]'. Dynamic visualizations
Counterfactual Explanations	Realistic alternatives High coherence Good comprehensibility Context-dependent explanations	"What-if" scenarios Alternative simplification proposals Identification of causal relationships	"What-if" stories with comic illustrations Integration into dialog-based systems: If you had done a little more sport, the AI would have said YES'. Animation of decisions

As already shown in the results section, XAI research emphasises that single methods often lead to incomplete explanations. E2R systems should therefore use multiple methods to explain local system decisions: LIME for specific word or sentence split decisions, SHAP for understanding global simplification strategies, and counterfactuals for representing alternative simplification possibilities. Together, these methods can provide an accessible account of how and why a text has been simplified in a particular way, and what alternatives exist. A practical implementation of the three methods could look like this: 1. the translation system simplifies a complex text in an E2R format; 2. LIME identifies local decisions for individual sentence structures or words; 3. SHAP provides a global overview of the most important factors for simplification; and 4. counterfactual explanations show alternative ways of simplification. An integrated explanation system could then combine this information into a coherent, easy-to-understand explanation of local decisions. The research question: *Are common XAI approaches such as SHAP, LIME and counterfactuals suitable for providing comprehensible explanations for automatically generated, E2R texts?* can therefore be answered positively.

As stated before, the development of accessible XAI systems requires a deep understanding of the AI system, application domain and user groups. This is particularly relevant for E2R systems due to the special characteristics of the target group. In particular, the specific needs of different user groups (different cognitive abilities, educational backgrounds) and the application contexts (different explanation strategies for different text types) must be considered. In E2R systems XAI methods can be used to create transparency about simplification decisions, help users to understand the limitations of the system and thus help to build sustainable trust in automated simplifications.

Despite the fundamentally valuable results of this study, the existing limitations need also be noted. Although a single reviewer approach is efficient and scientifically sound, it represents a methodological limitation. Since this study was mainly conducted by one researcher, it may have affected the completeness and reproducibility of the results. The most important content-related limitation of the present study is the lack of studies that explicitly focus on users with disabilities. Instead, studies with 'non-experts' were used. The transfer of findings without empirical validation in the target group is methodologically critical. In addition, the analyzed papers focus on technical domains (medicine, banking, recommendation systems) and do not take cultural or linguistic diversity into account. Currently there are no studies on the application of XAI methods to E2R systems. Therefore, there is an urgent need for further research. Empirical studies with people with different levels of cognitive disabilities and longitudinal studies on the effectiveness of different explanatory approaches are needed. In the technical field, robust counterfactual methods, multimodal explanatory approaches (text, image, audio) and adaptive systems that adjust the type of explanation to the actual explanation needs of the user need to be developed. It is necessary to study the application of XAI methods to language models for text simplification and to analyse the explainability of different simplification strategies.

Inclusive XAI frameworks, such as the explanatory ontology model (Tielman et al., 2024) or proposals for reusable design patterns (Schoonderwoerd et al., 2021) should be combined with tangible technical developments. Future research should combine participatory approaches, methodological innovation and theoretical grounding to develop effective and accessible explanations for text simplification in E2R systems.

In summary, the current XAI research methods provide a solid, albeit incomplete, foundation for creating explainable and accessible E2R translation systems. LIME, SHAP, and counterfactual explanations can be used to enhance transparency in AI-driven text simplification by demystifying *how* and *why* complex inputs are transformed into accessible outputs. These methods bridge the gap between algorithmic decisions and human understanding, fostering trust in AI based decisions. While the methodological approaches are promising, the lack of target group-specific validation and the presence of methodological weaknesses require considerable further development. Although XAI methods have the potential to make AI systems more understandable, the explanatory methods themselves are not yet well understood or sufficiently validated for the target groups that need them most.

REFERENCES

Adadi, A. and Berrada, M. (2018). Peeking inside the black-box: A survey on explainable artificial intelligence (XAI). *IEEE Access*, 6, pp.52138–52160.

Aechtner, J., Cabrera, L., Katwal, D., Onghena, P., Valenzuela, D.P. and Wilbik, A. (2022). Comparing user perception of explanations developed with XAI methods. In: *2022 IEEE International Conference on Fuzzy Systems (FUZZ-IEEE)*. [online] IEEE, pp.1–7. Available at: https://ieeexplore.ieee.org/document/9882800 [Accessed 24 May 2025].

Alnfiai, M.M., Alsudairy, N.A., Alharbi, I. *et al.* (2025). Cognitive augmentation: AI-enhanced tools for supporting individuals with cognitive disabilities. *Cognitive Processing*. https://doi.org/10.1007/s10339-025-01258-9

Arrieta, A.B., Díaz-Rodríguez, N., Del Ser, J., Bennetot, A., Tabik, S., Barbado, A., Garcia, S., Gil-Lopez, S., Molina, D., Benjamins, R., Chatila, R. and Herrera, F. (2020). Explainable artificial intelligence (XAI): Concepts, taxonomies, opportunities and challenges toward responsible AI. *Information Fusion*, 58, pp.82–115.

Benk, M. and Ferrario, A. (2020). Explaining interpretable machine learning: Theory, methods and applications. *Methods and Applications*, [online] 11 December. Available at: https://papers.ssrn.com/sol3/papers.cfm?abstract_id=3721523 [Accessed 24 May 2025].

Borina, M., Kalister, E. and Orehovački, T. (2022). Web accessibility for people with cognitive disabilities: A systematic literature review from 2015 to 2021. In: V.G. Duffy, Q. Gao, J. Zhou, M. Antona and C. Stephanidis, eds. *HCI International 2022 – Late Breaking Papers: HCI for Health, Well-being, Universal Access and Healthy Aging*. Lecture Notes in Computer Science, vol. 13521. Cham: Springer, pp.240–257. https://doi.org/10.1007/978-3-031-17902-0_19

Brughmans, D., Melis, L. and Martens, D. (2024). Disagreement amongst counterfactual explanations: how transparency can be misleading. *Top*, pp.1–34.

Chromik, M., Eiband, M., Buchner, F., Krüger, A. and Butz, A. (2021). I think I get your point, AI! The illusion of explanatory depth in explainable AI. In: *Proceedings of the 26th International Conference on Intelligent User Interfaces*. New York: ACM, pp.307–317.

Chromik, M. (2021). Making SHAP Rap: Bridging local and global insights through interaction and narratives. In: *Human-Computer Interaction – INTERACT 2021: 18th IFIP TC 13 International Conference, Bari, Italy, August 30 – September 3, 2021, Proceedings, Part II*. Berlin, Heidelberg: Springer-Verlag, pp.641–651. https://doi.org/10.1007/978-3-030-85616-8_37

Bove, C., Aigrain, J., Lesot, M.J., Tijus, C. and Detyniecki, M. (2022). Contextualization and exploration of local feature importance explanations to improve understanding and satisfaction of non-expert users. In: *IUI '22: 27th International Conference on Intelligent User Interfaces*, Helsinki, Finland, pp.807–819. https://doi.org/10.1145/3490099.3511139

Bredel, U. and Maaß, C. (2016). *Leichte Sprache: Theoretische Grundlagen? Orientierung für die Praxis*. Berlin: Dudenverlag.

Chemnad, K. and Othman, A. (2024). Digital accessibility in the era of artificial intelligence—Bibliometric analysis and systematic review. *Frontiers in Artificial Intelligence*, 7, Article 1349668. https://doi.org/10.3389/frai.2024.1349668

Dieber, J. and Kirrane, S. (2020). Why model why? Assessing the strengths and limitations of LIME. *arXiv preprint* arXiv:2012.00093. Available at: https://arxiv.org/abs/2012.00093 [Accessed 24 May 2025].

Dirks, S., Bühler, C., Edler, C., Miesenberger, K. and Heumader, P. (2020). Cognitive disabilities and accessibility – Pushing the boundaries of inclusion using digital technologies and accessible eLearning environments. In: K. Miesenberger, R. Manduchi, M. Covarrubias Rodriguez and P. Peňáz, eds. *Computers Helping People with Special Needs. ICCHP 2020*. Lecture Notes in Computer Science, vol. 12377. Cham: Springer. https://doi.org/10.1007/978-3-030-58805-2_6

Doshi-Velez, F. and Kim, B. (2017). Towards a rigorous science of interpretable machine learning. *arXiv preprint* arXiv:1702.08608. Available at: https://arxiv.org/abs/1702.08608 [Accessed 24 May 2025].

Dutta, J., Puthal, D. and Yeun, C.Y. (2023). Next generation healthcare with explainable AI: IoMT-edge-cloud based advanced eHealth. In: *GLOBECOM 2023–2023 IEEE Global Communications Conference*. IEEE, pp.7327–7332.

Fernández-Loría, C., Provost, F. and Han, X. (2020). Explaining data-driven decisions made by AI systems: the counterfactual approach. *arXiv preprint* arXiv:2001.07417. Available at: https://arxiv.org/abs/2001.07417 [Accessed 24 May 2025].

Förster, M., Hühn, P., Klier, M. and Kluge, K. (2021). Capturing users' reality: A novel approach to generate coherent counterfactual explanations. *Manuscript submitted for publication*.

Förster, M., Hühn, P., Klier, M. and Kluge, K. (2023). User-centric explainable AI: Design and evaluation of an approach to generate coherent counterfactual explanations for structured data. *Journal of Decision Systems*, 32(4), pp.700–731. https://doi.org/10.1080/12460125.2023.2219325

Galhotra, S., Pradhan, R. and Salimi, B. (2021). Explaining black-box algorithms using probabilistic contrastive counterfactuals. In: *Proceedings of the 2021 International Conference on Management of Data*. New York: ACM, pp.577–590.

Garouani, J., Mothe, A., Barhrhouj, A. and Aligon, J. (2024). Investigating the duality of interpretability and explainability in machine learning. In: *2024 IEEE 36th International Conference on Tools with Artificial Intelligence (ICTAI)*, Herndon, VA, USA. IEEE, pp.861–867. https://doi.org/10.1109/ICTAI62512.2024.00125

Gunning, D. and Aha, D.W. (2019). DARPA's Explainable Artificial Intelligence Program. *AI Magazine*, 40(2), pp.44–58. https://doi.org/10.1609/aimag.v40i2.2850

Hase, P. and Bansal, M. (2020). Evaluating explainable AI: Which algorithmic explanations help users predict model behavior? *arXiv preprint* arXiv:2005.01831. Available at: https://arxiv.org/abs/2005.01831 [Accessed 24 May 2025].

Hassija, V., Chamola, V., Mahapatra, A. *et al.* (2024). Interpreting black-box models: A review on explainable artificial intelligence. *Cognitive Computation*, 16, pp.45–74. https://doi.org/10.1007/s12559-023-10179-8

Inclusion Europe, n.d. *Easy to read.* [online] Available at: https://www.inclusion-europe.eu/easy-to-read/ [Accessed 24 May 2025].

Jalali, A., Haslhofer, B., Kriglstein, S. and Rauber, A. (2023). Predictability and comprehensibility in post-hoc XAI methods: A user-centered analysis. In: *Science and Information Conference*. Cham: Springer Nature Switzerland, pp.712–733.

Keane, M.T. and Smyth, B. (2020). Good counterfactuals and where to find them: A case-based technique for generating counterfactuals for explainable AI (XAI). In: *Case-Based Reasoning Research and Development: 28th International Conference, ICCBR 2020, Salamanca, Spain, June 8–12, 2020, Proceedings 28*. Cham: Springer International Publishing, pp.163–178.

Kusner, M.J., Loftus, J., Russell, C. and Silva, R. (2017). Counterfactual fairness. *Advances in Neural Information Processing Systems*, 30.

Li, M., Sun, H., Huang, Y. and Chen, H. (2024). Shapley value: From cooperative game to explainable artificial intelligence. *Autonomous Intelligent Systems*, 4(1), p.2.

Lundberg, S.M. and Lee, S.I. (2017). A unified approach to interpreting model predictions. *Advances in Neural Information Processing Systems*, 30.

Molnar, C., König, G., Herbinger, J., Freiesleben, T., Dandl, S., Scholbeck, C.A. *et al.* (2020). General pitfalls of model-agnostic interpretation methods for machine learning models. In: *International Workshop on Extending Explainable AI Beyond Deep Models and Classifiers*. Cham: Springer International Publishing, pp.39–68.

Moreno, L., Petrie, H., Martínez, P. *et al.*, (2024). Designing user interfaces for content simplification aimed at people with cognitive impairments. *Universal Access in the Information Society*, 23, pp.99–117. https://doi.org/10.1007/s10209-023-00986-z

Kommiya Mothilal, R., Mahajan, D., Tan, C. and Sharma, A. (2021). Towards unifying feature attribution and counterfactual explanations: Different means to the same end. In: *Proceedings of the 2021 AAAI/ACM Conference on AI, Ethics, and Society*. New York: ACM, pp.652–663.

Pearl, J. (2009). *Causality*. Cambridge: Cambridge University Press.

Pichiliani, T.C.P.B. and Pizzolato, E.B. (2021). Cognitive disabilities and web accessibility: A survey into the Brazilian web development community. *Journal on Interactive Systems*, 12(1), pp.308–327. https://doi.org/10.5753/jis.2021.982

PRISMA, n.d. *Transparent reporting of systematic reviews and meta-analyses*. [online] Available at: https://www.prisma-statement.org/ [Accessed 24 May 2025].

Prosperi, M., Guo, Y., Sperrin, M., Koopman, J.S., Min, J.S., He, X., Rich, S., Wang, M., Buchan, I.E. and Bian, J. (2020). Causal inference and counterfactual prediction in machine learning for actionable healthcare. *Nature Machine Intelligence*, 2(7), pp.369–375.

Rayyan, n.d. *Rayyan – Systematic reviews made easy*. [online] Available at: https://rayyan.ai [Accessed 24 May 2025].

Ribeiro, M.T., Singh, S. & Guestrin, C. (2018). Anchors: high-precision model-agnostic explanations. In: *Proceedings of the 32nd AAAI Conference on Artificial Intelligence (AAAI 2018)*. AAAI Press.

Rao, S., Mehta, S., Kulkarni, S., Dalvi, H., Katre, N. & Narvekar, M. (2022). A study of LIME and SHAP model explainers for autonomous disease predictions. In: *2022 IEEE Bombay Section Signature Conference (IBSSC)*, pp. 1–6. IEEE.

Saggion, H. & Hirst, G. (2017). *Automatic Text Simplification*. Vol. 32. San Rafael: Morgan & Claypool.

Salih, A.M., Raisi-Estabragh, Z., Galazzo, I.B., Radeva, P., Petersen, S.E., Lekadir, K. & Menegaz, G. (2025). A perspective on explainable artificial intelligence methods: SHAP and LIME. *Advanced Intelligent Systems*, 7(1), p.2400304.

Stajner, S. (2021). Automatic Text Simplification for Social Good: Progress and Challenges. In: *Findings of the Association for Computational Linguistics: ACL-IJCNLP 2021*, pp. 2637–2652. Online: Association for Computational Linguistics.

Schoonderwoerd, T.A., Jorritsma, W., Neerincx, M.A. & Van Den Bosch, K. (2021). Human-centered XAI: Developing design patterns for explanations of clinical decision support systems. *International Journal of Human-Computer Studies*, 154, p.102684. https://doi.org/10.1016/j.ijhcs.2021.102684

Schulte, L., Ledel, B. & Herbold, S. (2024). Studying the explanations for the automated prediction of bug and non-bug issues using LIME and SHAP. *Empirical Software Engineering*, 29(4), p.93.

Seeman, L. & Lewis, C.H. (2019). Cognitive and Learning Disabilities. *Web Accessibility*. Available at: https://www.w3.org/WAI/people-use-web/cognitive [Accessed Day Month Year].

Tielman, M.L., Suárez-Figueroa, M.C., Jönsson, A., Neerincx, M.A. & Cavalcante Siebert, L. (2024). Explainable AI for all - A roadmap for inclusive XAI for people with cognitive disabilities. *Technology in Society*, 79(C).

Vimbi, V., Shaffi, N. & Mahmud, M. (2024). Interpreting artificial intelligence models: a systematic review on the application of LIME and SHAP in Alzheimer's disease detection. *Brain Informatics*, 11, p.10. https://doi.org/10.1186/s40708-024-00222-1

Wachter, S., Mittelstadt, B. & Russell, C. (2017). Counterfactual explanations without opening the black box: Automated decisions and the GDPR. *Harvard Journal of Law & Technology*, 31, pp.841–887.

Warren, G., Keane, M.T. & Byrne, R.M. (2022). Features of Explainability: How users understand counterfactual and causal explanations for categorical and continuous features in XAI. *arXiv preprint* arXiv:2204.10152.

World Health Organization (WHO). (2023). Disability and health. [online] Available at: https://www.who.int/news-room/fact-sheets/detail/disability-and-health [Accessed Day Month Year].

Zhang, Y., McAreavey, K. & Liu, W. (2022). Developing and experimenting on approaches to explainability in AI systems. In: *ICAART 2022: 14th International Conference on Agents and Artificial Intelligence*, pp. 518–527.

Zhong, J. & Negre, E. (2022). Shap-enhanced counterfactual explanations for recommendations. In: *Proceedings of the 37th ACM/SIGAPP Symposium on Applied Computing*, pp. 1365–1372.

PREDICTING THE VISUAL AESTHETIC DISTRIBUTION OF MOBILE GUIS USING DEEP LEARNING

Adriano Luiz de Souza Lima[1] and Christiane Gresse von Wangenheim[2]
[1]*Instituto Federal de Santa Catarina*
São José - SC, Brazil
[2]*Universidade Federal de Santa Catarina*
Florianópolis - SC, Brazil

ABSTRACT

Visual aesthetics is an essential and complex feature of GUIs and is typically expressed as a single score. However, this score may not reflect the different responses they evoke in users, even when they share the same background. One way to avoid this oversimplification is to present visual aesthetics as a distribution of ratings received from individual raters and compute its median as the degree of visual aesthetics, its average absolute deviation as the degree of disagreement among raters, and present it as a histogram for visual analysis. Here, we present a supervised learning approach to train models with different architectures and compare them when assessing GUIs created with App Inventor. As a result, we achieved a prediction with an MSE of .021 using a ResNet50 model. Although the correlation between the individual score prediction and the label was moderate, the medians showed a strong correlation (rho = .85). It also demonstrated excellent correlation with a model predicting single-valued visual aesthetics (rho = .97) and a Bland-Altman plot analysis revealed 95% agreement with their labels. These results indicate that it is possible to automate the prediction of the visual aesthetic degrees of mobile GUIs, not only as single labels but also as distributions of individual human rater responses.

KEYWORDS

Visual Aesthetics, Mobile Application, Score Distribution, Deep Learning, Automatic Assessment

1. INTRODUCTION

The importance of visual aesthetics for graphical user interfaces (GUIs) and its positive effects on users have gained increasing attention (Thielsch et al., 2019), making visual aesthetics a key construct in human-computer interaction. It has been shown to improve perceived usability (Tractinsky et al., 2006) and credibility (Oyibo et al., 2018). Moreover, since beautiful GUIs can attract and retain user attention (Takimoto et al., 2021), visual aesthetics should also be a design priority in mobile interfaces. Given its relevance, the visual aesthetics of mobile GUIs must be properly assessed (Moshagen & Thielsch, 2010). However, this is a challenging task, as it is highly subjective, and agreement regarding the aesthetic quality of an image is not always easy to achieve among a group of people, even when sharing the same background (Gresse von Wangenheim et al., 2018).

Several approaches for assessing GUI visual aesthetics have been proposed (Lima & Gresse von Wangenheim, 2021). Due to its subjectivity component, typical visual aesthetics assessments rely on target users' responses to understand their reactions when assessing GUIs. However, manually assessing individual GUIs is often inaccessible to small companies or self-employed professionals as it demands considerable resources (Miniukovich & De Angeli, 2015). Additionally, having a reasonably large group of people for every assessment makes it time-consuming and error-prone (Soui et al., 2020).

Alternatives aim to relate objective GUI features and subjective aesthetic judgments, enabling automated assessments of visual aesthetics to reduce effort and minimize errors. (Lima & Gresse von Wangenheim, 2021). These objective approaches range from simply counting and measuring visual elements on GUIs to extracting handcrafted features such as symmetry, complexity, or colorfulness (Altaboli & Lin, 2011). Nonetheless, the definition and design of these features require a broad knowledge of aesthetics and visual design (Bao et al., 2019). Additionally, while features like symmetry and color are clearly related to aesthetics, other visual properties may be less evident (Takimoto et al., 2021). More recently, deep learning techniques have achieved superior results when applied to assess photographs (Deng et al., 2017) and GUIs (Dou et al., 2019; Khani et al., 2016; Lima, Martins, et al., 2022; Xing et al., 2021). These results indicate that it is possible to automatically extract visual features related to visual aesthetics from images without manual feature engineering.

Assessment techniques express visual aesthetics in the form of a categorical label or a single numerical score representing the average perception of a group of users (Dou et al., 2019; Kang et al., 2019). It is used as a direct indicator of the visual aesthetics of GUIs that facilitates the comprehension of which ones are beautiful, and which are not (Bao et al., 2019). However, they may not represent the subjectivity of visual aesthetics because they do not truly represent the individual perceptions from which the assessment results derive (Murray & Gordo, 2017). For instance, two GUIs might receive identical average scores despite eliciting very different levels of agreement among raters (Kang et al., 2019). Therefore, it is inaccurate to assume they are of equal quality (Takimoto et al., 2021). When a group of people assesses a GUI as attractive, they seem to reach an intersubjective agreement about its aesthetics (Zen & Vanderdonckt, 2016). However, a score representing the mean or median value when all ratings differ cannot reflect agreement.

Before computing the final score that reflects the visual aesthetics of a GUI, these methods contain the distribution of the ratings received (Murray & Gordo, 2017). The mean and median scores, variance, and average deviation can be calculated based on this information (Bao et al., 2019). These scores, together with rating histograms, can help better understand the visual aesthetics of GUIs and how much the human raters agree about them, indicating the difficulty of the assessment (Jin et al., 2016). In addition, the variance or average deviation is a way of characterizing intersubjective agreement, which can be visually represented by a histogram. In conjunction with the visual aesthetics score, this representation may be a better indication of the aesthetic quality of the GUIs (Bao et al., 2019).

Here, we propose a deep learning model to predict the score distribution for mobile GUIs developed with App Inventor, as a step further from previous models that yield a single aesthetic score. From the score distribution, it is possible to compute the visual aesthetics degrees of mobile GUIs and the degree of disagreement between human raters. Automating this process contributes to improving the quality of mobile apps, addressing some usability issues early, and reducing development costs. With this research, we also expect to contribute to understanding how people agree about the visual aesthetics of mobile GUIs.

2. RELATED WORK

Previous research on applying deep learning techniques for visual aesthetics assessments of GUIs has focused on large screens (Dou et al., 2019; Khani et al., 2016; Xing et al., 2021), but also assessing mobile GUIs (Lima, Martins, et al., 2022). Khani et al. (2016) used a pre-trained convolutional neural network (CNN) with classical machine learning techniques. They trained a model that uses a support vector machine to classify web GUIs as having either "good" or "bad" visual aesthetic quality. After training with a dataset of 418 labeled website screenshots, they reported an error rate (root mean squared error) of 34.15%. Although Dou et al. (2019) also used a pre-trained CNN to train their model for assessing web GUIs, they adopted a regression approach instead. Using a dataset of 398 website screenshots labeled with the mean score of all ratings received on a 9-point scale, they reported an error rate of 20.41%. Xing et al. (2021) trained a Squeeze-and-Excitation VGG model with 38,423 GUI designs labeled with the number of "likes" they have received on a popular website and the number of user "collections" to which they belong as their visual aesthetics representations. They reported an error rate of 14.89% predicting "collections" and 25.38% predicting "likes," but it is not clear how they reflect visual aesthetics based on these predictions.

Despite the growing relevance of mobile GUIs, not much research has addressed their visual aesthetics assessment (Lima, Gresse von Wangenheim, et al., 2022). In addition to assessments based on handcrafted feature extraction (Alemerien & Magel, 2014; Miniukovich & De Angeli, 2015), one study used a pre-trained CNN to assess Android GUIs developed with App Inventor (Lima, Martins, et al., 2022). They trained a model based on the ResNet-50 architecture using 481 mobile GUIs labeled according to their visual aesthetics on a 5-point scale. Using transfer learning, an error rate of 14.85% was reported on the validation set. However, when evaluating the performance over a test set containing 20 new GUIs not used in the training, the error rate decreased to 12,88%. They justify the improvement of the model performance because the test set is composed of images with high agreement among the human raters, indicating that they present very characteristic features of each degree of visual aesthetics. To the best of our knowledge, a CNN model for predicting the visual aesthetic distribution of a GUI has not yet been presented. That illustrates the lack of research on machine learning to assess the visual aesthetics of mobile GUIs, particularly concerning the prediction of rating distributions that can represent the degree of agreement among users.

3. DEVELOPMENT

We applied the same methodology as in Lima et al. (2024), following the process proposed by Ashmore et al. (2021). Our goal was to train a deep learning model to assess the visual aesthetics of App Inventor app screenshots using a supervised approach. Specifically, we aimed to predict a distribution of five aesthetic scores in the range [0..1] for a given screenshot, based on a labeled dataset of 820 App Inventor screenshots with human-derived rating distributions. App Inventor is a block-based environment for Android app development, widely used in K-12 education and by non-programmers. Our model predicts rating distributions, where each bin represents the number of raters assigning a specific score. These distributions are ℓ1-normalized for comparison. Model performance is measured using the mean squared error (MSE) between the predicted and actual distributions.

Our dataset is an adaptation of a previous work that developed a model to directly assess mobile GUI visual aesthetics (Lima et al., 2024). It includes 820 App Inventor screenshots saved as PNG images with a resolution of 1080×1920 pixels. Instead of using scalar values to represent each GUI's visual aesthetics, we used score distributions indicating the frequency of individual ratings. Each GUIs is labeled with a 5-dimensional vector where the i-th element represents the number of ratings with score i. Ten human raters assessed each GUI on a 5-point semantic differential scale ranging from 1 ("very ugly") to 5 ("very beautiful"). For example, a GUI labeled as {1, 7, 2, 0, 0} received one rating of "1," seven ratings of "2," two ratings of "3," with no ratings of "4" or "5." These scores were then normalized to the interval [0..1], with "0" = "no ratings received" and "1" = "all ratings received."

For comparison, we used the same test set with 20 GUIs as in the previous work. The remaining 800 GUIs were randomly split into a training set of 640 (80%) and a validation set of 160 (20%). Screenshots were downsampled from 1080×1920 to 448×448 pixels. To avoid distorting image features relevant to visual aesthetic perception, we performed no further transformations, such as cropping. The dataset is publicly available at https://bit.ly/app-inventor-dataset-v2.

We used pre-trained models with ImageNet, one of the largest publicly available general-purpose datasets (Russakovsky et al., 2015). We employed fast.ai, a robust, adaptable, and research-focused CNN framework, to build our model (Howard & Gugger, 2020). We trained three network architectures to compare and select the one with the highest performance (VGG19, ResNet50, and EfficientNet B0). These architectures were chosen because they presented good performance in a previous study used for comparison.

The input layer was adapted to the image resolution of our dataset, which was represented by the screenshot vector and its label. The original output layers, which represented a categorical variable with 1,000 values for classifying ImageNet categories (comprising 1,000 neurons), were replaced with a layer containing five neurons. In this way, the model output is a 5-dimensional vector, where each element corresponds to a different score on the 5-point scale. The output scores range within [0..1] and are interpreted as the percentage of ratings received, with "0" = "no ratings received (0%)" and "1" = "all ratings received (100%)." We used the mean squared error (MSE) as the loss function.

The output layers of the networks were transfer-trained for 100 epochs, which, according to previous work, is sufficient for validation error convergence (Lima et al., 2024). Each architecture was trained using two strategies: standard training (fit) and automated hyperparameter optimization (fit1cycle) (Smith & Topin, 2019), resulting in six models for comparison, all using default parameters. After unfreezing intermediate layers, we trained each model for 20 additional epochs using the same strategy. Learning rates were defined using the method suggested by Smith and Topin (2019), yielding different ranges for each model.

All models improved after fine-tuning, and the best MSE was achieved by the ResNet50 architecture trained to predict score distributions using the fit strategy, reaching .02095 after fine-tuning. In comparison, the same architecture trained for direct regression yielded an MSE of .022049, while the VGG19 model with the fit1cycle strategy obtained .022129. The EfficientNet B0 model, also trained with the fit1cycle strategy, showed a slightly higher MSE of .022814. These results demonstrate that the ResNet50-based model for predicting visual aesthetic distributions performed best overall, surpassing even those models trained to directly estimate a single aesthetic score.

The medians of nearly half the predicted distributions (79 out of 160) matched those computed from the labeled data (Figure 1, left). For another 75 GUIs, the predicted and actual medians differed by only one point or less on the five-point scale. This suggests that, in most cases, the model can classify a "beautiful" GUI somewhere between "very beautiful" and "neutral" rather than "ugly." On the other hand, for six GUIs (3.8%), the median difference exceeded one and a half points (Figure 1, right). The worst case involved a GUI that received seven "1" ratings (i.e., "very ugly") from human raters but was predicted to have a median of "4" ("beautiful"). Nevertheless, such discrepancies in only a few cases are acceptable, given the high degree of subjectivity and variation in human judgments of visual aesthetics (Gresse von Wangenheim et al., 2018).

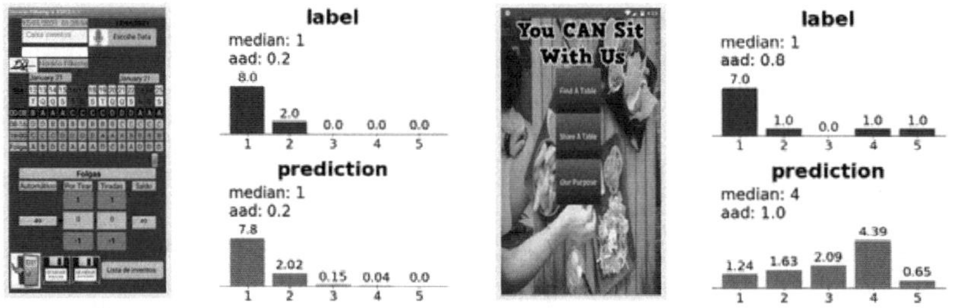

Figure 1. Validation set: best (left) and worst (right) predictions.

In general, the average absolute deviation (AAD) was higher for the predicted distributions than for the labels, indicating the model's tendency to assign scores higher than zero. However, the AAD was lower for some predicted distributions (24%) than for label distributions. For the worst predictions, the AAD was high, indicating difficulty in assessing the GUIs.

A similar performance was observed with the test set, with new screenshots without labels. The median of the predicted distribution of one GUI was two points lower than its label. All other medians differed by one point or less, with half of the predictions resulting in identical medians as the labels. The worst predictions in the test set also resulted in high AADs, suggesting a difficulty in assessing visual aesthetics.

4. MODEL EVALUATION

Studies using deep learning models typically evaluate their performances in predicting the sample labels in the validation set, using metrics that compute how close their predictions are to those labels. However, it is also essential to know how well the model performs on unseen images. To this end, we evaluated our model exclusively on a test set of 20 GUIs separated from the dataset before training. Although some studies for visual aesthetics assessments with deep learning adopt correlation analysis (Dou et al., 2019; Lima, Martins, et al., 2022; Xing et al., 2021), results can be misleading because they quantify only linear association, not actual agreement (Giavarina, 2015). Thus, to assess the degree of agreement between the model results and human ratings we also conducted a Bland-Altman plot analysis (B&A) (Bland & Altman, 1986).

We used Spearman's rank correlation coefficient (rho) to examine the linear association between the model predictions and human assessments because of the non-normality of the data (Bryman & Cramer, 1990). The correlation between individual predicted scores and label scores resulted in a moderate rho of .65. When analyzing the results, we observed that the model tended to distribute the scores along the scale. For example, in two cases where human raters reached consensus on the visual aesthetics of the GUIs, the model failed to assign any score close to 1. The highest predicted scores for these were only .74 and .71.

We also compared the medians of predictions with the medians of labels, which are less sensitive to outliers than the mean score. For that reason, the correlation was much stronger, with rho=.85. In this case, the median of the predictions was at most one point from the median of the labels. For example, the predictions were all correct for the GUIs with a visual aesthetic degree of 1 = "very ugly." On the other hand, the predictions were all wrong for the GUIs with visual aesthetics of 5 = "very beautiful," although the model was consistent here as it always predicted a median of 4. That indicates that the model presents a bias towards the lowest rates.

This result is very similar to the model predicting the visual aesthetics directly (Lima et al., 2024). When comparing the median from our results with the visual aesthetics degree directly predicted, the correlation was rho = .97.

Comparing the AADs of labels and predictions, a moderate correlation (rho = .67) was observed. Although this set contains GUIs with low AADs (.4 or lower), indicating high agreement among human raters, the predicted distributions had high AADs (> .27). As an example, one label had an AAD = .2 but a predicted distribution above 1. This shows the model's tendency to spread the distribution along the 5-point scale instead of concentrating it around one single rating.

We used Bland-Altman (B&A) plot analysis to assess agreement between two variables, as correlation analysis only reveals linear associations (Giavarina, 2015). The B&A plot shows the mean difference between two measurements and defines limits to characterize their agreement, identifying bias and calculating a 95% agreement interval (Bland & Altman, 1986). It does not determine whether automated models can replace human assessments, only quantifies bias and agreement range (Giavarina, 2015).

Analyzing the B&A plot for individual scores of the predicted distribution and those of the labels, we could observe that the mean difference between them is zero. This is an indication of bias absence in predicting the score distribution for the whole set. Nonetheless, the confidence interval (CI) is too large (-.46 to .46), meaning that 95% of the predictions can be between half of the labels up to two times greater. We could also observe that the predictions tended to be higher for the low scores and lower for the higher scores, suggesting a bias towards the middle of the scale. This may happen because more ratings received few or no votes than ratings that received all or almost all the votes.

The B&A plot analysis for the medians of the predicted distributions and the medians of the labels shows a different scenario. The plot also shows agreement between them because all their differences lie within the CI (-1,25 to 1,75) since the medians of the predicted distribution were never higher than one point different from the media of the labels. The analysis between the medians of the predicted distributions and the visual aesthetics degrees directly predicted displays even greater agreement. The mean difference between them was half a point on a 5-point scale, and the CI was (-.76 to .86). For only two GUIs, the median for the predicted distribution was one point higher than directly predicted.

The AAD is biased on the B&A plot. All differences are below zero, and the mean difference is -.49, confirming that the model outputs tend to have AADs higher than the labels.

5. DISCUSSION

Part of the challenge in assessing visual aesthetics lies in the subjective nature of this type of judgment. Because people are different, they tend to disagree about visual aesthetics, even when they share a similar background (Gresse von Wangenheim et al., 2018). Opposing judgments and varying degrees of assessments are common. A single score may obscure this disagreement, whereas a rating distribution allows both a central measure and a measure of disagreement, such as AAD, which can also be visualized in a histogram. This article presents the first model for assessing GUI aesthetics, generating rating distributions for mobile GUIs created with App Inventor. From these distributions, we compute the median for aesthetics and AAD for disagreement.

Our model obtained excellent performance, with an MSE = .0209, which exceeds other models for the direct assessment of visual aesthetics of web GUIs (MSE = .042) (Dou et al., 2019) or GUI designs (MSE = .0222) (Xing et al., 2021). It also resulted in a better performance than directly assessing mobile GUIs over the same dataset (MSE = .022), with the difference that we kept those samples with high AAD.

However, the correlation between the predicted distributions and the labels was only moderate (rho = 0.65). This may be attributed to the dataset's imbalance in rating distributions, with a greater concentration of low scores than high ones. Such an imbalance appears difficult to avoid when balancing for visual aesthetics degrees, defined here as the medians of the distributions. Extreme scores on the five-point scale (1 = "very ugly", 5 = "very beautiful") inherently require distributions heavily skewed to one side. Nonetheless, this moderate correlation between predicted and actual distributions does not significantly impact the model's performance in assigning visual aesthetics degrees. Although the correlation between predicted and actual medians was lower than that of the model trained for direct aesthetics prediction (Lima et al., 2024), both approaches showed near-perfect agreement over the same test set (rho = 0.97).

Despite the good performance, the model did not get the visual aesthetics scores right for any of the four "very beautiful" GUIs in the test set. That might happen because there are very few "very beautiful" GUIs in the dataset. Creating a more balanced dataset has been complicated because most apps available in the App Inventor Gallery have rather ugly interface designs, making it difficult to encounter beautiful designs in larger quantities. Moreover, as the final visual aesthetics score of these GUIs is the median of all individual ratings received, a GUI with a "1" or a "5" needs more than half of the human ratings assigning those scores. Regardless of this bias, the B&A plot analysis reveals that the difference is at most one point on the five-point scale for 95% of screenshots. That means that no GUI labeled as 4 ("beautiful") received a 2 ("ugly") from the model or vice versa. The only exception was a "very beautiful" GUI that received a visual aesthetics score of 3 ("not ugly nor beautiful").

Comparing the predicted distributions with the label distributions, we can observe that our model tends to inflate low scores and deflate high ones, leading to distributions with higher AADs than labels. One possible reason for that bias may be the unbalanced dataset concerning individual ratings and, therefore, concerning AADs. Although it was primarily built to be as balanced as possible in terms of visual aesthetics degree (distribution median), this is not reflected in the individual ratings as each median score may be the result of different distributions, and consequently different AADs. Maybe a larger dataset, with a balanced number of individual ratings, can contribute to mitigating the bias of the distribution and AAD prediction.

Threats to validity. One potential threat to this study lies in the dataset's inability to fully represent the spectrum of possible GUI aesthetic outcomes. To reduce this threat, we attempted to balance the dataset with respect to aesthetic ratings. However, full balance was not possible due to the limited availability of App Inventor apps with high-quality visual designs. Another threat concerns the rating process itself, especially when evaluators assess many GUIs in a single session. Fatigue may influence rating quality. To minimize this risk, we instructed raters to pause whenever they felt tired. For the evaluation, we adopted well-established methods from the literature to assess correlation and agreement. In addition, we selected well-tested CNN architectures that have been successfully used in related tasks. Regarding external validity, we used a reasonably large and diverse evaluation sample, including a variety of app types, which supports the generalizability of our results. Model performance was assessed using a test set of GUIs not used during training or validation. To facilitate comparison, we selected the same GUIs used in Lima et al. (2024), which were randomly drawn from the original dataset.

6. CONCLUSION

This article presents an original model for the automatic assessment of the distribution of visual aesthetics of mobile GUIs of Android applications developed with App Inventor. The model predicts a distribution of ratings on a 5-point scale. From this distribution, it is possible to compute statistical scores, such as the median as the visual aesthetics degree and the average absolute deviation as the degree of disagreement among individual raters. The model was trained with a dataset containing 800 GUIs labeled with 5-dimensional vectors representing the distribution of human ratings. We trained and compared three different CNN architectures. As a result, a ResNet50 model to predict the rating distribution achieved the best performance (MSE = .021), which was even better than a model to predict visual aesthetics directly. The evaluation results over a test set containing unseen GUIs indicate that it can support visual aesthetics assessments with high correlation and agreement with human perception, yet with a slight bias to lower visual aesthetics. The model can be used for effective and efficient visual aesthetics assessments during the design of GUIs of mobile applications, as well as to provide feedback to students in the context of computing education. In the future, we plan to improve the model's performance regarding the distribution of AADs so that it can better estimate the degree of disagreement among raters by expanding the dataset, as well as deploying the model in an online automatic assessment tool.

ACKNOWLEDGMENT

This study was financed in part by the Conselho Nacional de Desenvolvimento Científico e Tecnológico - Brasil (CNPq) - Grant No.: 302833/2022-6.

REFERENCES

Alemerien, K., & Magel, K. (2014). GUIEvaluator: A Metric-tool for Evaluating the Complexity of Graphical User Interfaces. *Proceedings of the Twenty-Sixth International Conference on Software Engineering & Knowledge Engineering*, 13–18.

Altaboli, A., & Lin, Y. (2011). Objective and Subjective Measures of Visual Aesthetics of Website Interface Design: The Two Sides of the Coin. In J. A. Jacko (Ed.), *Human-Computer Interaction. Design and Development Approaches* (pp. 35–44). Springer. https://doi.org/10.1007/978-3-642-21602-2_4

Ashmore, R., Calinescu, R., & Paterson, C. (2021). Assuring the Machine Learning Lifecycle: Desiderata, Methods, and Challenges. *ACM Computing Surveys*, *54*(5), 111:1-111:39. https://doi.org/10.1145/3453444

Bao, X., Shi, P., Pan, D., & You, J. (2019). Image Aesthetic Prediction Model Based on Deep Convolutional Neural Network. *2019 2nd International Conference on Information Systems and Computer Aided Education (ICISCAE)*, 122–125. https://doi.org/10.1109/ICISCAE48440.2019.221601

Bland, J. M., & Altman, D. G. (1986). Statistical Methods for Assessing Agreement Between Two Methods of Clinical Measurement. *The Lancet*, *327*(8476), 307–310. https://doi.org/10.1016/S0140-6736(86)90837-8

Bryman, A., & Cramer, D. (1990). *Quantitative Data Analysis for Social Scientists* (pp. xiv, 290). Taylor & Francis/Routledge.

Deng, Y., Loy, C. C., & Tang, X. (2017). Image Aesthetic Assessment: An experimental survey. *IEEE Signal Processing Magazine*, *34*(4), 80–106. IEEE Signal Processing Magazine. https://doi.org/10.1109/MSP.2017.2696576

Dou, Q., Zheng, X. S., Sun, T., & Heng, P.-A. (2019). Webthetics: Quantifying Webpage Aesthetics with Deep Learning. *International Journal of Human-Computer Studies*, *124*, 56–66. https://doi.org/10.1016/j.ijhcs.2018.11.006

Giavarina, D. (2015). Understanding Bland Altman Analysis. *Biochemia Medica*, *25*(2), 141–151. https://doi.org/10.11613/BM.2015.015

Gresse von Wangenheim, C., Porto, J. V. A., Hauck, J. C. R., & Borgatto, A. F. (2018). Do We Agree on User Interface Aesthetics of Android Apps? *arXiv*, 1–5.

Howard, J., & Gugger, S. (2020). Fastai: A Layered API for Deep Learning. *Information*, *11*(2), Article 2. https://doi.org/10.3390/info11020108

Jin, B., Segovia, M. V. O., & Süsstrunk, S. (2016). Image aesthetic predictors based on weighted CNNs. *2016 IEEE International Conference on Image Processing (ICIP)*, 2291–2295. https://doi.org/10.1109/ICIP.2016.7532767

Kang, C., Valenzise, G., & Dufaux, F. (2019). Predicting Subjectivity in Image Aesthetics Assessment. *2019 IEEE 21st International Workshop on Multimedia Signal Processing (MMSP)*, 1–6. https://doi.org/10.1109/MMSP.2019.8901716

Khani, M. G., Mazinani, M. R., Fayyaz, M., & Hoseini, M. (2016). A Novel Approach for Website Aesthetic Evaluation Based on Convolutional Neural Networks. *Proceedings of the 2016 Second International Conference on Web Research (ICWR)*, 48–53. https://doi.org/10.1109/ICWR.2016.7498445

Lima, A. L. de S., & Gresse von Wangenheim, C. (2021). Assessing the Visual Esthetics of User Interfaces: A Ten-Year Systematic Mapping. *International Journal of Human–Computer Interaction*, 1–21. https://doi.org/10.1080/10447318.2021.1926118

Lima, A. L. de S., Gresse von Wangenheim, C., & Borgatto, A. F. (2022). Assessment of Visual Aesthetics through Human Judgments: A Systematic Mapping. *Proceedings of the 21st Brazilian Symposium on Human Factors in Computing Systems*, 1–14. https://doi.org/10.1145/3554364.3560902

Lima, A. L. de S., Martins, O. P. H. R., Gresse von Wangenheim, C., von Wangenheim, A., Hauck, J. C. R., & Borgatto, A. F. (2022). Automated Assessment of Visual aesthetics of Android User Interfaces with Deep Learning. *Proceedings of the 21st Brazilian Symposium on Human Factors in Computing Systems*, 1–11. https://doi.org/10.1145/3554364.3559113

Lima, A. L. de S., Wangenheim, C. G. von, Martins, O. P. H. R., Wangenheim, A. von, Hauck, J. C. R., & Borgatto, A. F. (2024). A Deep Learning Model for the Assessment of the Visual Aesthetics of Mobile User Interfaces. *Journal of the Brazilian Computer Society*, *30*(1), Article 1. https://doi.org/10.5753/jbcs.2024.3255

Miniukovich, A., & De Angeli, A. (2015). Computation of Interface Aesthetics. In *Proceedings of the 33rd Annual ACM Conference on Human Factors in Computing Systems* (pp. 1163–1172). Association for Computing Machinery. https://doi.org/10.1145/2702123.2702575

Moshagen, M., & Thielsch, M. T. (2010). Facets of Visual Aesthetics. *International Journal of Human-Computer Studies*, *68*(10), 689–709. https://doi.org/10.1016/j.ijhcs.2010.05.006

Murray, N., & Gordo, A. (2017). *A deep architecture for unified aesthetic prediction* (No. arXiv:1708.04890). arXiv. https://doi.org/10.48550/arXiv.1708.04890

Oyibo, K., Adaji, I., Orji, R., & Vassileva, J. (2018). What Drives the Perceived Credibility of Mobile Websites: Classical or Expressive Aesthetics? In M. Kurosu (Ed.), *Human-Computer Interaction. Interaction in Context* (pp. 576–594). Springer International Publishing. https://doi.org/10.1007/978-3-319-91244-8_45

Russakovsky, O., Deng, J., Su, H., Krause, J., Satheesh, S., Ma, S., Huang, Z., Karpathy, A., Khosla, A., Bernstein, M., Berg, A. C., & Fei-Fei, L. (2015). ImageNet Large Scale Visual Recognition Challenge. *International Journal of Computer Vision*, *115*(3), 211–252. https://doi.org/10.1007/s11263-015-0816-y

Smith, L. N., & Topin, N. (2019). Super-convergence: Very Fast Training of Neural Networks Using Large Learning Rates. *Proceedings of the Artificial Intelligence and Machine Learning for Multi-Domain Operations Applications*, *11006*, 1100612. https://doi.org/10.1117/12.2520589

Soui, M., Chouchane, M., Mkaouer, M. W., Kessentini, M., & Ghedira, K. (2020). Assessing the Quality of Mobile Graphical User Interfaces Using Multi-objective Optimization. *Soft Computing*, *24*(10), 7685–7714. https://doi.org/10.1007/s00500-019-04391-8

Takimoto, H., Omori, F., & Kanagawa, A. (2021). Image Aesthetics Assessment Based on Multi-stream CNN Architecture and Saliency Features. *Applied Artificial Intelligence*, *35*(1), 25–40. https://doi.org/10.1080/08839514.2020.1839197

Thielsch, M. T., Scharfen, J., Masoudi, E., & Reuter, M. (2019). Visual Aesthetics and Performance: A First Meta-Analysis. *Proceedings of Mensch Und Computer 2019*, 199–210. https://doi.org/10.1145/3340764.3340794

Tractinsky, N., Cokhavi, A., Kirschenbaum, M., & Sharfi, T. (2006). Evaluating the Consistency of Immediate Aesthetic Perceptions of Web Pages. *International Journal of Human-Computer Studies*, *64*(11), 1071–1083. https://doi.org/10.1016/j.ijhcs.2006.06.009

Xing, B., Si, H., Chen, J., Ye, M., & Shi, L. (2021). Computational model for predicting user aesthetic preference for GUI using DCNNs. *CCF Transactions on Pervasive Computing and Interaction*, *3*(2), 147–169. https://doi.org/10.1007/s42486-021-00064-4

Zen, M., & Vanderdonckt, J. (2016, July). Assessing User Interface Aesthetics based on the Inter-subjectivity of Judgment. *Proceedings of the 30th International BCS Human Computer Interaction Conference*. 30th International BCS Human Computer Interaction Conference, Poole, UK. https://doi.org/10.14236/ewic/HCI2016.25

GENERATIVE ARTIFICIAL INTELLIGENCE IN 3D: EXPLORING AI CAPABILITIES IN 3D SCENE GENERATION

Ihor Romanovych[1], Sam Frish[1], Dmytro Kaliuzhnyi[2] and Mariia Bilova[3]
[1]*Softserve inc.*
Lviv, Sadova 2D, Ukraine
[2]*Individual contributor*
Wiltshire, Swindon, United Kingdom
[3]*National Technical University "Kharkiv Polytechnic Institute"*
Kharkiv, Kharkivs'ka oblast', Ukraine

ABSTRACT

The advent of generative artificial intelligence (Gen AI) has revolutionized creative processes across multiple domains, including 3D scene generation. This paper focuses on the transformative potential of Gen AI in supporting remote education and professional training, particularly in fields requiring practical, immersive experiences, such as architecture, design, education and employee on-boarding. By leveraging models like diffusion and transformer-based approaches, these systems enable the creation of photorealistic and customizable 3D environments with minimal human intervention, fostering accessible and scalable virtual learning spaces.

User interaction studies reveal that such technologies not only bridge geographical barriers but also provide hands-on experience in otherwise resource-intensive or hazardous environments (Bahroun et al., 2023). Moreover, the integration of Gen AI into educational and corporate workflows can streamline processes like on-boarding and skill development, offering adaptive, personalized training modules (Batista et al., 2024).

However, challenges persist, including usability limitations, computational demands, and ethical considerations such as biases and intellectual property concerns. This work proposes a useful tool to the growing discourse on the role of generative systems in shaping the future of virtual education and training, emphasizing their potential to democratize access to experiential learning and improve workforce readiness.

KEYWORDS

Generative AI 3D, Gen AI 3D, Interactive, Spatial Computing, AI-Driven 3D Scene Generation, Generative AI

1. INTRODUCTION

Gen AI is reshaping creative processes by enabling the rapid production of complex and photorealistic content. Applications such as gaming, virtual reality, architectural visualization, and film production have particularly benefited from these advancements. Traditional 3D content creation is often resource-intensive, requiring skilled professionals, substantial time, and significant costs. However, Gen AI offers a paradigm shift, speeding up many of these processes while maintaining creative flexibility and with scalability in mind.

At the core of this transformation are advanced machine learning models, such as diffusion models and transformer-based architectures, which can generate high-quality 3D objects and scenes with minimal input. These systems interpret user prompts, automate asset creation, and streamline workflows, enabling designers and developers to focus on higher-level creative decisions. Despite their promise, deploying Gen AI for 3D scene generation is not without challenges. Issues such as ensuring usability, providing adequate control to users, and addressing biases in generated outputs remain critical areas for improvement.

This paper investigates the capabilities of Gen AI in the realm of 3D scene generation, focusing on its ability to augment human creativity and optimize workflows. Through a detailed analysis of existing models and an evaluation of a novel AI-driven system, we explore how these tools can balance automation and user agency. Furthermore, this research examines ethical and technical concerns, including intellectual property issues, computational demands, and the inclusivity of generative models. By bridging the gap between AI capabilities and human-centric design, this study aims to contribute to the development of intuitive, collaborative, and efficient systems for 3D content creation.

The paper is structured as follows: a literature review outlines existing challenges in 3D content creation and explores AI-based solutions and their role in 3D; the methodology section details the proposed system and its operational workflow; the results section showcases results and provides a comparative analysis of cost and time efficiency. We conclude with an evaluation of the broader implications of AI-driven 3D scene generation across various industries. By addressing current limitations, this research aims to contribute to the development with a feasible future scalability, AI-driven solutions that will shape the digital worlds into a vibrant and accessible digital space.

2. BACKGROUND AND RELATED WORKS

The evolution of generative artificial intelligence has significantly impacted creative industries, particularly in the area of 3D scene generation. This section provides an overview of key contributions from recent research, focusing on the advancements, methodologies, and challenges associated with using AI for automated 3D content creation. Studies have explored various approaches, including diffusion models, Generative Adversarial Networks (GANs), and transformer-based architectures, which have demonstrated the ability to generate photorealistic and complex virtual environments. However, gaps remain in areas such as usability, scalability, and ethical considerations, necessitating further exploration of how these technologies can be optimized for real-world applications. By critically examining the state of the art, this review establishes the foundation for the proposed innovations in AI- driven 3D content generation.

2.1 Theoretical Background

Generative artificial intelligence (Gen AI) has rapidly emerged as a transformative tool in the creative domain, particularly in 3D content generation. This section reviews the theoretical foundations behind the AI models that drive such advancements, focusing on the underlying mechanisms of generative adversarial networks, diffusion models, and transformer-based architectures. These technologies, while distinct in their operation, share a common goal of automating and enhancing the creative process, offering significant potential for applications in virtual environments, gaming, architecture, and film production.

2.1.1 Generative Adversarial Networks (GANS)

Introduced by Goodfellow et al. in 2014, GANs consist of two neural networks—a generator and a discriminator—that work in opposition to create realistic data samples (Goodfellow, I. et al, 2014). The generator aims to produce new data that closely resembles real data, while the discriminator's job is to distinguish between generated and real data. The adversarial process encourages the generator to produce increasingly realistic outputs, making GANs particularly suitable for applications like 3D object generation and texture creation (Abdellatif, Elsheikh and Menke, 2024; Schnepf, Vasile and Tanielian, 2023; Sheremetieva et al., 2023). In recent years, GANs have been applied to the generation of photorealistic images and 3D models, demonstrating their potential for creative industries such as film and gaming (Karras et al., 2018; Schnepf, Vasile and Tanielian, 2023).

2.1.2 Diffusion Models

Diffusion models, another powerful approach in generative AI, simulate the process of transforming data into noise and then reversing that process to generate new data. Unlike GANs, which rely on adversarial training, diffusion models work by gradually denoising a random input to create meaningful outputs (Ho, Jain and Abbeel, 2020). In 3D content generation, diffusion models have shown remarkable capabilities in producing high-quality textures and complex scene structures, while often requiring less computational power compared to GANs (Wang, Li and Jiang, 2024). These models have recently gained popularity due to their efficiency in generating diverse, photorealistic results, especially in the creation of 3D environments for virtual and augmented reality (Kim et al., 2023).

2.1.3 Transformer-based Architectures

Transformers, initially designed for natural language processing tasks, have also found applications in generative 3D content creation. Transformer models, such as GPT (OpenAI, 2024), have proven to be effective in understanding and generating complex sequences, making them suitable for interpreting user prompts and generating corresponding 3D objects. When applied to 3D scene generation, transformer-based models can process large amounts of data, enhancing the automation of scene composition, object positioning, and texture assignment (Po and Wetzstein, 2023; Huang et al., 2023). These models are also highly adaptable, allowing for fine-tuning based on specific creative inputs, which is crucial for applications in industries like gaming and architecture.

2.1.4 Interplay of Models in 3D Content Creation

The integration of these advanced models (GANs, diffusion models, and transformers) enables the creation of high-quality 3D content with ability for human-design-abilities interactive augmentation (Kazi et al., 2017; Zhang et al., 2024). While each model has distinct strengths, combining their capabilities can lead to even more powerful systems that automate object generation, scene composition, and asset management, accelerating workflows in industries where 3D content is crucial. The synergy between these models is central to the ongoing evolution of AI-driven design tools, pushing the boundaries of what is possible in 3D content creation.

2.2 State-of-the-Art

2.2.1 Advancements in AI for 3D Content Generation

Recent advancements in generative artificial intelligence (Gen AI) have significantly transformed 3D content creation. A notable breakthrough has been the use of diffusion models and generative adversarial networks (GANs) for generating photorealistic 3D scenes and objects. Diffusion models, such as DALL-E 2 from OpenAI, have shown promise in generating highly detailed and diverse 3D objects from textual descriptions (Shi et al., 2023). These models enable users to specify the design of an environment or object in natural language, drastically reducing the time and effort required to manually craft these assets.

3D model generation has further been enhanced through innovative algorithms and frameworks. OpenAI's PointCloud Models are a prime example, allowing for high-fidelity 3D reconstruction from images and texts, improving the realism and accuracy of digital assets (Shi et al., 2023). These advancements are complemented by 3D CLIP search (Song et al., 2024), which leverages text-image matching to retrieve and generate relevant 3D objects from large datasets. The ability to retrieve 3D models based on semantic understanding of a scene has opened new possibilities for automatic scene generation, reducing the reliance on human-curated asset libraries.

Additionally, the application of Procedural Texturing and other texture generation methods has been revolutionized by AI. Procedural texturing algorithms allow for the creation of complex surface textures without the need for manual intervention, ensuring that textures scale dynamically with 3D models. Techniques like style transfer and neural network-based texture synthesis (Zhang et al., 2024) are now widely used to enhance the visual quality of 3D environments, enabling real-time applications in virtual worlds and simulations.

Furthermore, Structured Domain Randomization (SDR) has been applied to improve object placement and scene generation. SDR techniques randomize scene variables such as object placement, lighting, and background to train AI models in diverse scenarios, enhancing the robustness of 3D environments for applications like robotics and autonomous vehicles (Prakash et al., 2020).

2.2.2 Application Across Industries

The potential applications of AI in 3D content creation are vast, with industries like gaming, virtual reality (VR), architecture, and film production leading the way. In gaming, AI-driven 3D generation tools enable developers to automate world-building, creating expansive, interactive environments at a fraction of the traditional cost. Services such as Animate Anything (based on the CLIP model) have introduced AI-powered character and environment animation directly from text prompts, empowering creators to generate entire gaming worlds dynamically (Zhang et al., 2024; Po and Wetzstein, 2023).

In virtual reality, AI-based 3D content generation facilitates the creation of immersive worlds tailored to individual users. By combining procedural generation techniques with AI-driven texturing and asset generation, VR developers can quickly populate virtual spaces with realistic, interactive elements. This scalability is crucial as VR applications demand high-quality environments with constant updates.

Architecture and design also benefit significantly from AI-based 3D modeling. Tools like Meshy (a 3D asset generation service) or Edify leverage AI to rapidly generate realistic models for buildings, interiors, and landscapes, helping architects visualize concepts more efficiently and accurately (Meshy.ai, 2024; Nvidia et al., 2024). Additionally, AI-assisted design platforms allow architects to automate aspects of the building design process, such as room layout, facade generation, and environmental integration, using AI-driven algorithms (Onatayo et al., 2024).

Finally, in film production, AI-driven 3D scene generation is transforming the process of creating visual effects. Generative models are employed to create intricate 3D environments for films with ability for interactive human creativity augmentation (Zhang et al., 2024; Kazi et al., 2017). This is particularly valuable in film production, where the demand for detailed, customizable 3D models and scenes is often overwhelming.

In each of these industries, Large Language Models (LLMs) such as GPT are playing an increasingly important role in understanding and interpreting 3D environments. By combining LLMs with retrieval-augmented generation (RAG) techniques, systems are now capable of contextualizing text prompts in a 3D environment, allowing for better comprehension of spatial relationships and scene coherence. This makes it possible to generate more intuitive, contextually accurate 3D scenes based on natural language descriptions, thus accelerating content creation workflows across sectors.

2.3 Contribution

In this paper, inspired by advancements in generative artificial intelligence (Gen AI) and its application to creative industries, we examine how transformer-based and diffusion models can enhance 3D scene generation processes. Building on prior research into AI-assisted creativity and education technology, we explore how these tools can address the challenges of creating immersive and photorealistic environments. Specifically, we focus on leveraging AI for remote education systems and workforce onboarding, where hands-on, visual training is often critical.

Our work investigates how Gen AI systems can generate highly realistic and customizable virtual environments to simulate real-world scenarios, providing learners and professionals with interactive spaces that bridge theoretical knowledge and practical experience. By integrating findings from usability studies and adapting user-centric design principles, we aim to balance automation with creativity, enabling AI-driven systems to meet the demands of diverse educational and training contexts. Furthermore, our research highlights how these advancements contribute to reducing resource constraints, improving accessibility, and fostering collaboration in both creative and professional development domains. Taken together, this study emphasizes the transformative potential of Gen AI in creating scalable, efficient, and intuitive solutions for 3D content generation and practical education.

2.4 System Setup

The system setup for the AI-driven 3D scene generation platform includes a high-performance workstation equipped with an NVIDIA RTX 4090 GPU to handle intensive computational tasks related to generative modeling and real-time rendering. A dual-monitor setup provides one screen for user interaction through a graphical interface and another for displaying the generated 3D scenes.

Input device is a tablet for precision sketching and object manipulation. The workstation runs a custom software environment built on PyTorch, integrated with pre-trained diffusion and transformer-based models.

To streamline the user experience, the system employs voice recognition through a microphone, enabling natural language prompts to guide the generation process. This multi-modal setup ensures adaptability for various creative workflows, from architectural visualization to gaming environment design.

The software environment runs within NVIDIA Omniverse USD Composer, leveraging the powerful capabilities of the NVIDIA ecosystem. The system is built upon the following components:

NVIDIA Asset Management Server: This backend manages a vast library of 3D assets and associated metadata, supporting efficient storage and retrieval.

• Deep Search: A semantic search feature that allows users to find assets based on textual descriptions or keywords.

• Custom LLM: A Mixture of Experts (MoE) large language model, optimized for scene generation tasks. The model can be optionally quantized to Q4K for reduced storage requirements, albeit with slight degradation in output quality.

• RAG (Retrieval-Augmented Generation) Pipeline: The pipeline integrates with the LLM to provide contextually rich asset data. It retrieves and processes metadata, such as object names and specific properties, from the Asset Management Server, ensuring precise and efficient scene assembly.

This combination of advanced hardware and NVIDIA's Omniverse platform provides a robust, scalable environment for generating high-quality, interactive 3D scenes. We've initially built the demo inspired by NVidia's SIGGRAPH presentation (Nvidia, 2022).

Additionally, on Figure 1, the setup architecture is displayed which represents a practical evolution of the system described, incorporating advanced capabilities like RAG-based asset management, AI-driven scene assembly, and seamless cloud integration for deployment at scale.

To enhance scalability and meet enterprise requirements, this architecture provides an alternative approach for implementing the solution described earlier. By leveraging a cloud-based modular system with an integrated LLM and asset management pipeline, it offers a reliable and extensible framework for scaling 3D scene generation to support a growing number of users and complex scenarios.

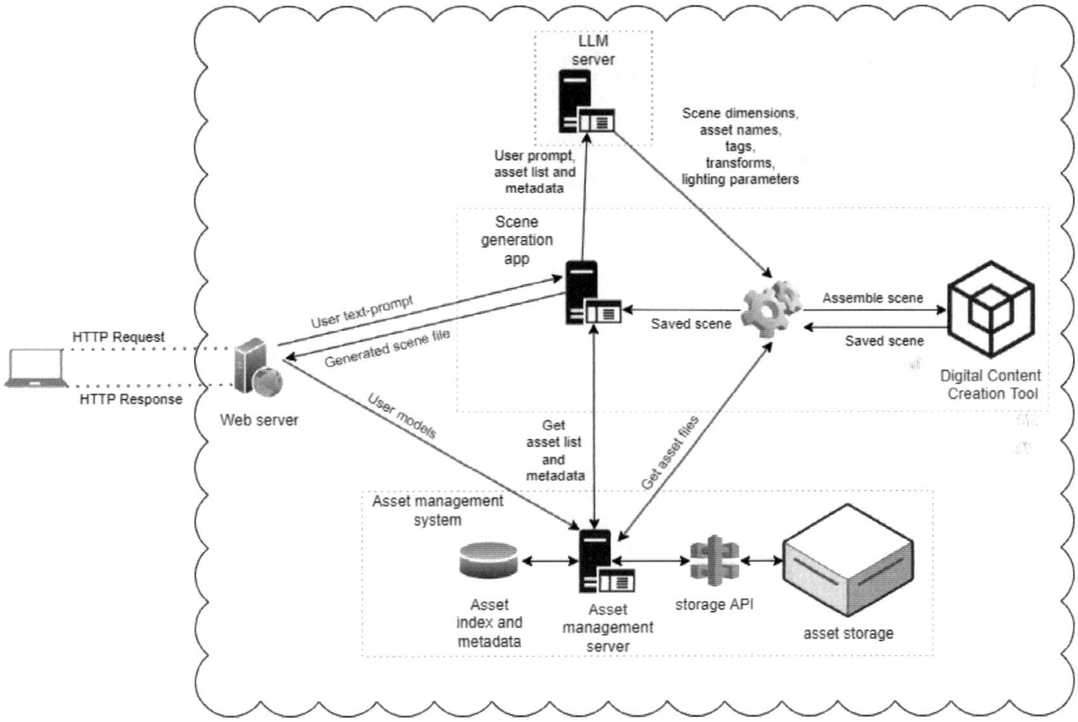

Figure 1. Proposed scalable system architecture

The workflow presented on Figure 2 illustrates the system's process for generating interactive 3D scenes based on user prompts. The experience begins when the user submits a text prompt describing the desired scene. The system generates a virtual ground plane where the assets will be placed. Next, the system retrieves metadata about required assets, including names and parameters, from a database.

This information is processed by a Retrieval-Augmented Generation (RAG) pipeline, which compresses and organizes asset data for efficient retrieval.

The RAG-enhanced data and user prompt are passed to a language model, which creates a detailed scene layout by interpreting the prompt and incorporating asset metadata. The system then identifies and downloads the necessary files for rendering the scene. After assets are gathered, they are positioned on the virtual ground plane according to the layout generated by the language model. Lighting parameters are applied to enhance realism.

Finally, the system renders a preliminary view of the scene, allowing users to preview it. The fully assembled scene file is made available for download, completing the interaction. This streamlined pipeline ensures the efficient generation of customized 3D environments while leveraging preexisting asset databases.

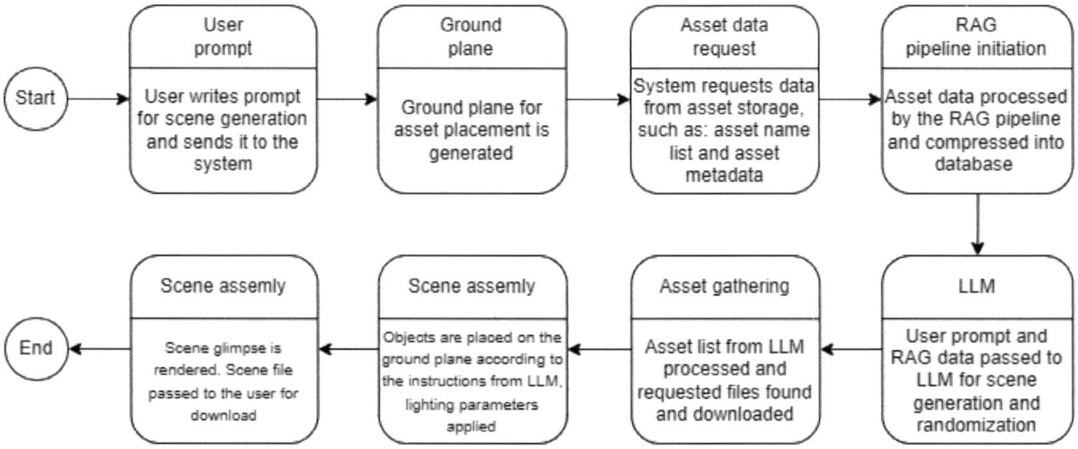

Figure 2. Flowchart of the interactive experience

2.5 Implementation

2.5.1 Architecture

The proposed system architecture, shown in Figure 1, consists of several interconnected components that facilitate scalable 3D scene generation using AI-based tools and asset management systems. The architecture integrates user interaction, asset indexing, and large language model (LLM) inference to automate the assembly and rendering of 3D environments. Further implementation details are described below.

Web Server (1): Acts as the central entry point for users, handling HTTP requests with user text prompts and returning the generated 3D scenes as responses.

Integrates with downstream components, ensuring seamless communication between the user interface and backend services.

Scene Generation Application (2): Orchestrates the scene creation workflow by processing user prompts and interfacing with other modules, such as the LLM Server and the Asset Management Server.

Sends user-generated prompts and asset metadata to the LLM Server (3) for processing.

Receives structured scene instructions, including asset names, positions, dimensions, and lighting parameters.

LLM Server (3): Runs a custom Mixture of Experts (MoE) LLM, which generates instructions for scene composition based on user prompts.

Integrates a Retrieval-Augmented Generation (RAG) pipeline to query the Asset Management Server for relevant asset metadata, ensuring contextual accuracy and optimized object placement.

Optionally supports model quantization to reduce computational overhead, enabling deployment in resource-constrained environments.

Asset Management System (4): Manages a database of 3D assets and their metadata, such as object dimensions, tags, and categories. Interfaces with a Storage API (5) to retrieve physical asset files for use in the generated scenes. The metadata, indexed for fast retrieval, enhances LLM scene composition efficiency.

Digital Content Creation Tool (6): NVIDIA Omniverse USD Composer to assemble, render, and finalize the generated 3D scenes. Receives structured scene parameters (e.g., asset placement, lighting configuration) from the Scene Generation App. Saves the final 3D scene for user access via the web server.

2.5.2 Detailed Workflow

The list below provides step by step workflow description.

1. User input and interaction:
   a. Users submit a text prompt describing the desired 3D scene through the web interface.
   b. The web server forwards this input to the Scene Generation Application for further processing.
2. Scene Composition with LLM and RAG:
   a. The Scene Generation Application queries the LLM Server with the user prompt and available asset metadata.
   b. The LLM Server, powered by a Mixture of Experts (MoE) model, generates structured outputs containing scene details (e.g., asset names, dimensions, positions, lighting).
   c. The RAG pipeline ensures accuracy by retrieving relevant asset metadata from the Asset Management System, enriching the LLM's responses.
3. Asset Retrieval and Assembly:
   a. The Scene Generation Application uses the generated instructions to query the Asset Management System for relevant assets.
   b. The Asset Management System retrieves asset files from the Storage API and sends them to the Scene Generation App.
   c. The Scene Generation App passes the assembled scene data to the 3D Software for final rendering.
4. Rendering and Output:
   a. The NVIDIA Omniverse USD Composer processes the scene data, applying object transformations, lighting parameters, and other visual effects.
   b. The finalized 3D scene is saved and returned to the web server for user access.

2.5.3 Detailed Workflow

This architecture is designed for scalability, enabling deployment in cloud-based environments or on local servers. Key considerations include following.

- Modular Design: Each component can be scaled independently to handle increased loads. For example, the LLM Server and Asset Management System can be hosted on separate instances for high availability.
- Efficient Retrieval: The use of a pre-indexed asset metadata database accelerates query times and reduces latency during scene generation.
- Optimized AI Models: The MoE LLM supports optional quantization (e.g., Q4K) to minimize resource usage, making the system adaptable for various deployment environments.
- Cloud Integration: The architecture supports integration with cloud-based storage APIs, enabling elastic scaling for asset retrieval and storage.

By following this implementation approach, the system provides an efficient, extensible, and scalable pipeline for AI-driven 3D scene generation at scale.

2.6 Discussion

The integration of advanced generative AI systems into 3D scene creation workflows marks a transformative shift in user experience (UX). While earlier generative models primarily focused on producing static assets or images, current approaches increasingly function as generative scene orchestration agents. These agents move beyond passive content creation to actively assist users in tasks such as object placement, stylistic adjustments, and scene configuration. Instead of viewing AI solely as a tool, this paradigm enables a more dynamic, collaborative relationship in which designers, educators, and other creative professionals guide and co-create with the AI.

A key facet of this evolution is the transition from traditional, manual inputs (e.g., mouse and keyboard) toward more intuitive, language-based interactions. By specifying desired outcomes through conversational prompts—such as requesting a hyper realistic nighttime setting with vintage-inspired textures – users can focus on conceptual and aesthetic decision-making. This approach aligns with broader trends in HCI research, where advancements in natural language processing and prompt-based interfaces lower technical barriers and facilitate rapid, iterative exploration. As a result, experts can devote their attention to high-level creative direction, while the AI efficiently generates variations and refines ideas.

Notably, the growing sophistication of these systems does not diminish the importance of human expertise. On the contrary, the role of the designer becomes even more critical for evaluating outputs, making nuanced creative judgments, and ensuring that generative results align with ethical and cultural values. Human oversight remains essential, especially given the expanding societal impact of automated systems. In tandem, developing industry guidelines, ethical frameworks, or professional certification programs can help ensure that these tools are deployed responsibly and inclusively.

Inclusivity and accessibility are likewise central to this new UX landscape. Future generative AI platforms should be designed to accommodate users with diverse abilities—such as those with visual, auditory, or motor impairments—through multimodal interfaces (e.g., voice commands, haptic feedback, or screen-reader compatibility). This inclusive approach can democratize 3D content creation, enabling a broad range of users to collaborate with AI systems and contribute meaningfully to creative workflows.

Finally, as designers learn to navigate this environment, they will cultivate a new hybrid skill set that blends prompt engineering techniques with established domain expertise. For instance, familiarity with relevant artistic principles enhances a user's ability to obtain desirable results from generative tools. At the same time, the iterative feedback loop between human and AI fosters mutual learning: users gain mastery over the capabilities and constraints of these tools, while the systems themselves improve from exposure to expert guidance.

In sum, this transformation in 3D scene generation reflects a broader trend where generative AI evolves into a creative partner, not merely a productivity tool. By simultaneously expanding creative possibilities, reinforcing the importance of human judgment, and emphasizing inclusivity, these generative scene orchestration agents set the stage for a future in which designers devote less time to technical minutiae and more effort to conceptual vision, narrative integrity, and socially responsible innovation.

3. CONCLUSION

We have reviewed the up-to-date capabilities in 3D scene generation, described our exploration, and outlined our contribution, the proposed system design optimizes workflows, democratizes access to immersive experiences, and bridges gaps in usability, scalability, and ethical design.

The approach and an implemented system are clearly showing speed-up and extension of the possibilities with GenAI for the creative process in 3D. The spatial awareness still of the LLM used still has some limitations, including misplacement and overlaps, the implications of the use of such systems are rather controversial, on one hand we have a speed-up, on the other we have not yet estimated potential social impact.

We invite you to discuss the current capabilities and promises of the research field.

REFERENCES

Abdellatif, A., Elsheikh, A.H. and Menke, H.P. (2024). 'Local Padding in Patch-Based GANs for Seamless Infinite-Sized Texture Synthesis', arXiv [cs.CV] [Preprint]. Available at: http://arxiv.org/abs/2309.02340.

Bahroun, Z. *et al.* (2023). 'Transforming Education: A Comprehensive Review of Generative Artificial Intelligence in Educational Settings through Bibliometric and Content Analysis', *Sustainability*, 15(17). Available at: https://doi.org/10.3390/su151712983.

Batista, J., Mesquita, A. and Carnaz, G. (2024). 'Generative AI and Higher Education: Trends, Challenges, and Future Directions from a Systematic Literature Review', Information, 15(11). Available at: https://doi.org/10.3390/info15110676.

Goodfellow, I. et al. (2014). 'Generative Adversarial Nets', in Z. Ghahramani et al. (eds) Advances in Neural Information Processing Systems. Curran Associates, Inc. Available at: https://proceedings.neurips.cc/paper_files/paper/2014/file/5ca3e9b122f61f8f06494c97b1afccf3-Paper.pdf.

Ho, J., Jain, A. and Abbeel, P. (2020b). 'Denoising Diffusion Probabilistic Models', arXiv [cs.LG] [Preprint]. Available at: http://arxiv.org/abs/2006.11239.

Huang, S. et al. (2023). 'Diffusion-based Generation, Optimization, and Planning in 3D Scenes', arXiv [cs.CV] [Preprint]. Available at: http://arxiv.org/abs/2301.06015.

Karras, T. et al. (2018). 'Progressive Growing of GANs for Improved Quality, Stability, and Variation', arXiv [cs.NE] [Preprint]. Available at: http://arxiv.org/abs/1710.10196.

Kazi, R.H. et al. (2017). 'DreamSketch: Early Stage 3D Design Explorations with Sketching and Generative Design', Proceedings of the 30th Annual ACM Symposium on User Interface Software and Technology (UIST 2017), pp. 401–414. Available at: https://doi.org/10.1145/3126594.3126662.

Kim, S.W. et al. (2023). 'NeuralField-LDM: Scene Generation with Hierarchical Latent Diffusion Models', arXiv [cs.CV] [Preprint]. Available at: http://arxiv.org/abs/2304.09787.

Meshy.ai (2024). 'Meshy.ai'. Available at: https://www.meshy.ai (Accessed: 27 November 2024).

Nvidia (2022). As Far as the AI Can See: ILM Uses Omniverse DeepSearch to Create the Perfect Sky. NVIDIA. Available at: https://blogs.nvidia.com/blog/ilm-omniverse-deepsearch/.

Nvidia et al. (2024). 'Edify 3D: Scalable High-Quality 3D Asset Generation', arXiv [cs.CV] [Preprint]. Available at: http://arxiv.org/abs/2411.07135.

Onatayo, D. et al. (2024). 'Generative AI Applications in Architecture, Engineering, and Construction: Trends, Implications or Practice, Education I& Imperatives for Upskilling—A Review', Architecture, 4(4), pp. 877–902. Available at: https://doi.org/10.3390/architecture4040046.

OpenAI et al. (2024). 'GPT-4 Technical Report', arXiv [cs.CL] [Preprint]. Available at: http://arxiv.org/abs/2303.08774.

Po, R. and Wetzstein, G. (2023). 'Compositional 3D Scene Generation using Locally Conditioned Diffusion', arXiv [cs.CV] [Preprint]. Available at: http://arxiv.org/abs/2303.12218.

Prakash, A. et al. (2020). 'Structured Domain Randomization: Bridging the Reality Gap by Context-Aware Synthetic Data', arXiv [cs.CV] [Preprint]. Available at: http://arxiv.org/abs/1810.10093.

Schnepf, A., Vasile, F. and Tanielian, U. (2023). '3DGEN: A GAN-based approach for generating novel 3D models from image data', arXiv [cs.CV] [Preprint]. Available at: http://arxiv.org/abs/2312.08094.

Sheremetieva, A. et al. (2023). 'What's my future: a Multisensory and Multimodal Digital Human Agent Interactive Experience', in Proceedings of the 2023 ACM International Conference on Interactive Media Experiences. New York, NY, USA: Association for Computing Machinery (IMX '23), pp. 40–46. Available at: https://doi.org/10.1145/3573381.3596161.

Shi, R. et al. (2023). 'Zero123++: a Single Image to Consistent Multi-view Diffusion Base Model', arXiv [cs.CV] [Preprint]. Available at: http://arxiv.org/abs/2310.15110.

Song, D. et al. (2024). 'MV-CLIP: Multi-View CLIP for Zero-shot 3D Shape Recognition', arXiv [cs.CV] [Preprint]. Available at: http://arxiv.org/abs/2311.18402.

Wang, Z., Li, D. and Jiang, R. (2024). 'Diffusion Models in 3D Vision: A Survey', arXiv [cs.CV] [Preprint]. Available at: http://arxiv.org/abs/2410.04738.

Zhang, L. et al. (2024). 'CLAY: A Controllable Large-scale Generative Model for Creating High-quality 3D Assets', arXiv preprint, arXi:2406.13897. Available at: https://doi.org/10.48550/arXiv.2406.13897.

AI-GENERATED VIDEO IS THE NEXT LANGUAGE FOR GAME PROTOTYPING: FOCUSING ON OPEN AI'S SORA

JaeJun Lee, Soyoun Eom and Joo-Eun Kang
Department of Game Design, School of Arts, Sungkyunkwan University, Seoul, Korea

ABSTRACT

Effective communication among diverse stakeholders is crucial in game development, particularly when creating games for specialized purposes such as therapy. In this paper, we present a case study of using AI-Generated video prototyping to facilitate communication between game designers and domain experts during the development of a therapeutic game based on Mindfulness-Based Cognitive Therapy (MBCT). Our research team employed a three-stage video prototyping pipeline using generative AI tools, such as OpenAI's ChatGPT and SORA, to create interactive video prototypes that effectively conveyed the game's design and intended player experience. Through interviews with domain experts, we evaluated the effectiveness of this approach in aligning the game design with MBCT theory, identifying differences in visual design direction, and promoting the expansion of game design ideas. Despite challenges in controlling specific aspects of the generated videos and the time-consuming nature of prompt engineering, we found that video prototyping served as an effective language for communicating game design ideas without loss of fidelity. This case study demonstrates the potential of AI-Generated video prototyping to enhance communication and collaboration between game designers and domain experts, particularly in the context of specialized game development projects.

KEYWORDS

Video Prototyping, Generative AI, Game Design Communication, Therapeutic Game, Mindfulness-Based Cognitive Therapy (MBCT), SORA

1. INTRODUCTION

Game development involves collaboration among various stakeholders, including designers, programmers, artists and project managers, from the initial design phase to the final product. During this process, a shared understanding of the game among project participants is crucial.

Our research team engaged in a project titled "Development of game-based digital Therapeutics technology for adolescent mental health management" to create a game called "Mind Trekking". Throughout this project, we communicated with a larger number of stakeholders compared to typical game development. Since the project aimed to develop a therapeutic game based on psychological theories and obtain FDA approval, psychologists providing the theoretical foundation, doctors conducting clinical trials, and medical device manufacturers overseeing the approval process were involved in the game design process.

The game was designed based on Mindful Based Cognitive Therapy (MBCT), and due to the goal of FDA approval, a precise understanding of the game by the psychologists and the research team managing the approval process was necessary before game production. However, communicating the anticipated play experience using game design documents centered around text, storyboards, and concept images proved to be extremely challenging for the research team, who had little to no experience with or understanding of games. Moreover, this project was conducted by university researchers, lacking the intensive development environment of professional game development companies.

Consequently, the environment required minimizing communication iterations by using high-resolution and high-fidelity prototypes. The prototyping method with the highest fidelity is working prototyping, which provides the highest level of understanding through direct interaction, surpassing explanations or observing gameplay (Buchenau et al, 2000). However, this approach is expensive, slow, and difficult to modify. This study focuses on the prototyping method we adopted in this context. Our research team noted the potential of generative AIs in generating videos, thus video-based prototypes to convey desired game play experiences.

The team's goals were aimed at building a video-based prototype that combines generated videos which richly demonstrate the game experience for communication with non-experts in games, and a visual novel engine to enable interaction, achieving a balance between fidelity and efficiency. The final playable prototype version is downloadable from URL found in the Appendix.

2. LITERATURE REVIEW

Despite the crucial role of prototyping in computer game design (Fullerton et al, 2006; Fullerton, Tracy, 2008), there is no specific methodology for prototyping (Manker, Jon, 2011). Research on the role of prototyping varies, including its purpose for communication (Otto et al, 2001; Camburn, 2017; Israel, Johann Habakuk, 2016; Lauff et al, 2018; Ulrich et al, 2016), allowing the experience of game ideas (Lee et al, 2021), confirming feasibility (Otto et al, 2001; Jessica et al, 2017), and establishing milestones (Otto et al, 2001; Ulrich et al, 2016). Game designers generally share the opinion that prototypes serve as sketches, communication of functionality, and the experience of an idea (Manker, Jon, 2011). Prototypes act as a language in the game development process and become the center of communicating the game experience (Manker, Jon, 2011).

Research on prototyping largely consists of the fidelity of prototypes and the efficiency of prototype production. Storyboarding game scenes are clear and efficient for explaining sequences, but it has low fidelity in describing interaction experiences through static screens. Paper prototyping is effective and fast (Snyder, Carolyn, 2003), but the facilitator can interfere with the player's experience (Bolchini et al, 2009). Interactive document methods that do not require a human facilitator have been studied (Signer et al, 2007). To increase fidelity and recreate the experience in combination with devices, papers are photographed and placed on devices (Bolchini, 2009), and animations are used to create prototypes to explain situations arising from interactions (Kultima et al, 2012). For efficiency, advancements in artificial intelligence and game production technology have led to the use of generative AI to create storyboards (Lee et al, 2023) and automatically generate prototypes for specific genres (Reyno et al, 2009).

Generative AI technology enables Text to Image and Image to Video, with Open AI's SORA capable of Text to Video (Sora, OpenAI). These technologies are used to innovate game design, efficiently produce game visual images (Lee, Lee, 2023), design characters (Ling et al, 2024), and manage game services (Riedl et al, 2013), thereby changing the game production process.

Therefore, our research team looks into enhancing efficiency of showcasing game experiences, employing generative AI to generate video-based prototypes.

3. VIDEO PROTOTYPING PIPELINE

The Video Prototyping Pipeline using Generative AI consists of three main stages (Figure 1). First, the game is designed based on theory and documented. Second, prompt engineering is performed to generate images and videos. Third, the generated videos are loaded into a visual novel engine to simulate the experience of making choices at critical points.

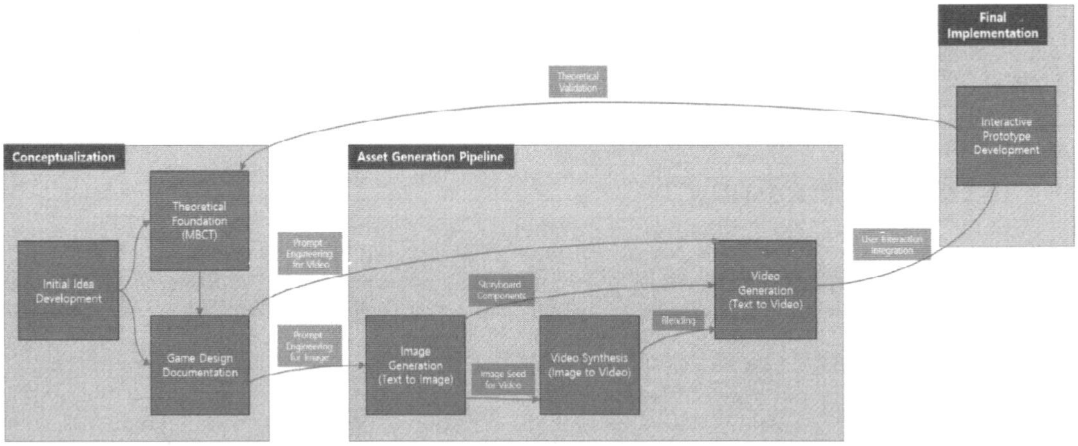

Figure 1. Pipeline Process

3.1 Conceptualization

In the first stage of the process, the MBCT theory and its mechanisms of action were organized into eight episodes based on an offline MBCT program in collaboration with theorists. The game design was developed to ensure that the offline MBCT mechanisms could also be effective in a digital environment (Table 1).

Table 1. MBCT sessions and corresponding video game design episodes

Episode	MBCT session	Video Game Design
1	Awareness and Automatic Pilot	An experience of focusing one's senses on birdsong amidst various natural sounds.
2	Living in our heads	An experience of perceiving and understanding the sensations of body parts displayed on the screen through one's own body.
3	Gathering the scattered mind	An experience of walking along a mountain trail, appreciating the surroundings, and inputting emotional responses.
4	Recognizing Aversion	While struggling on a difficult hike, participants are shown a bus, which they discover is actually on a return loop and does not ease their journey.
5	Allowing / Letting be	During the walk, participants encounter a very noisy group of hikers but are given the opportunity to show kindness to the group's dog.
6	Thought are not facts	A scene is staged where a squirrel, encountered during the walk, becomes angry when its acorn is taken away, only to realize that the acorn was rotten and feel relieved.
7	How can I best take care of myself?	An exercise in distinguishing between positive and negative activities experienced during the game.
8	Maintaining and Extending New learning	The provision of items and opportunities to decorate a "lake" that represents one's own mind or emotional state.

3.2 Asset Generation

To generate videos for the eight episodes, Open AI's Chat GPT pro version, SORA and Midjourney were used. Through prompt engineering, videos were generated directly using the text-to-video approach or by first going through the text-to-image process and then using the generated images as references for prompt engineering to create videos.

A total of 182 videos were iteratively generated using SORA, and after going through the remixing and blending process with SORA, 13 final videos were selected to compose the eight episodes (Figure 2). The process took approximately 35 hours. This work was carried out by one game designer who was not an expert in prompt engineering, and another game designer cross-checked whether the generated videos matched the intended design. Prompts were written under the aid of Open AI Chat GPT, results were generated in SORA and or used to generate images in Midjourney, which were then used as image prompts to be used in SORA. Initial prompt inputs made in SORA which led to final results are given in Appendix D. Designers have selected final results based on internal game design criteria, choosing those most effective in delivering desired game experience.

Due to the nature of generative AI, very specific aspects of the videos could not be controlled. In particular, it was impossible to control the specific facial expressions of characters, the movement paths of characters, animals, or objects, and the game's UI for Episodes 5, 6 and 3. In cases of Episode 7, where the generation of very specific photo panel designs was required, it was difficult to directly create videos using prompts in SORA. In such cases, images were generated through Midjourney and then used as seeds to create videos in SORA. For Episodes 3, 4, and 5, changes in actions and situations were needed while maintaining the composition and featuring the same characters. Therefore, to create Episodes 4 and 5, the video from Episode 3 was set as a seed, and the videos were generated by adjusting the remix intensity using SORA. When scenario changes over time were needed within a single video, such as in Episodes 2 and 6, SORA's storyboard feature was used. When blending elements of a video, such as the scene in Episode 2 where a cube transforms into an apple, the blend function was utilized. It was not possible to generate specific sections of Episode 1 that focused on training auditory sensations using SORA.

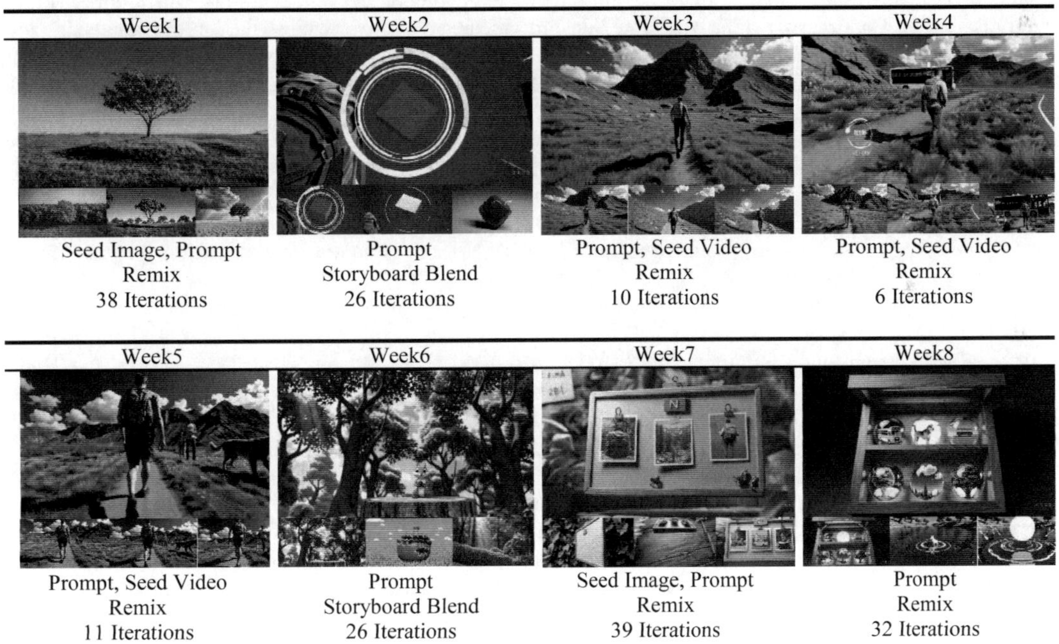

Figure 2. 1-8 Week's videos

3.3 Final Implementation

To reproduce the experience of making choices in a computer game within the prototype, player choices were made possible at critical points. Unity and the Utage Visual Novel Tool were used. When a single episode consisted of multiple videos, a choice function was added between the videos. Additionally, when transitioning from one episode to another, user input was received to handle branching, resulting in different videos being shown as outcomes (Figure 3).

Figure 3. Choice Function

4. FEEDBACK FROM THEORY EXPERTS

The feedback from domain experts provided valuable insights into the alignment between the game prototype and MBCT (Mindfulness-Based Cognitive Therapy) principles. To evaluate the effectiveness of the video prototyping method, we conducted written, unstructured interviews with two domain experts who have been advising the project and providing its theoretical foundation since April 2024. Their feedback was categorized into three major themes: alignment with theoretical expectations, differences in visual representation, and expansion of game design ideas. Notably, while the initial analysis focused predominantly on positive remarks, this refined evaluation incorporates more critical perspectives to capture the full depth and nuance of the expert insights. Full questions and feedback text are appended (Appendix B, Appendix C).

Experts generally acknowledged that the video prototype effectively communicated the theoretical principles of MBCT. Expert 2 noted, *"The video aligns almost perfectly with what I imagined."* Similarly, both experts agreed that video-based prototyping increased the fidelity of the prototyping process.

Strengths Identified:

- The video provided a more tangible and concrete representation of the theoretical framework.
- It allowed for the identification of gaps between the intended theory and its practical application.

Challenges and Limitations:

- While the video clarified many aspects of the theory, some nuances of MBCT, such as the subtle cognitive shifts necessary for mindfulness practice, were not explicitly represented.
- Certain elements, such as the implementation of decision-making processes, could be more deeply integrated to reflect MBCT's focus on mindful reactions versus automatic responses.

Expert 1 acknowledged this limitation, stating that while the prototype effectively showcased theory-to-practice translation, it could further refine its approach by considering *"whether the game truly encourages a mindful response or if it merely presents a pre-scripted experience."*

While the video prototype successfully communicated core ideas, Expert 2 pointed out differences between their expectations and the actual visual representation. *"It was checked whether we had the same thoughts. It's very similar to what I had in mind. However, I could see that the graphics, landscapes, people's appearances, and shapes were different from what I imagined."*

Strengths Identified:

- The visual representation helped experts verify their alignment with the development team's interpretation.
- It provided a basis for refining art direction to better fit the conceptual framework.

Challenges and Limitations:

- Differences in expectations regarding the aesthetic style created some cognitive dissonance.
- Expert 2 initially envisioned a more animated and stylized depiction, while the prototype leaned towards a documentary-like approach.

- The graphical design might influence the perceived target audience, as one expert mentioned the visuals seemed more suited for younger audiences rather than university students or adults.

This feedback suggests that visual alignment plays a critical role in how theoretical concepts are perceived and internalized. Further iterations could explore stylistic variations to ensure that the representation remains engaging while maintaining theoretical fidelity.

Experts also highlighted the potential of video prototyping in facilitating creative expansion and idea generation. Expert 1 remarked, *"Watching the video, I think it generates more expanded ideas about episode 2."* Similarly, Expert 2 noted that the interactive discussion was enriched because they could visually engage with the prototype, leading to more refined feedback.

Strengths Identified:

- Video prototyping encouraged deeper engagement and iterative refinement.
- It enabled domain experts to suggest improvements that might have been overlooked in a text-based or static-image prototype.

Challenges and Limitations:

- While video prototyping facilitated idea generation, it also risked constraining creativity by overly concretizing certain elements too early in the process.
- Some abstract elements of MBCT that rely on personal introspection may not be fully conveyed in a visual format, potentially limiting the interpretative flexibility of the game's design.

One expert suggested an alternative approach: incorporating more player-driven choices and emergent scenarios rather than relying on predefined sequences. This feedback highlights an important consideration—while video prototyping improves clarity, it may also inadvertently narrow the creative possibilities by cementing a specific design direction too soon.

5. DISCUSSION

Videos created using Sora cannot be precisely controlled. It was impossible to make the results of the game's interactions appear as if they were recorded gameplay footage. However, by showing the videos as if it were functioning, the experience was conveyed more intuitively and stimulated new imagination. Nevertheless, interaction is still not possible, falling short of the experience of actually doing. By simulating real-time input, a visual novel-style choice was provided at critical points to offer a doing experience. Through the video prototype, the results of the interaction can be sufficiently conveyed. While game designers can communicate without loss using generative images (Lee et al, 2023), videos have higher fidelity as they can confirm the specific implementation leading to user input.

High fidelity is important for prototypes, but game developers expect quick modifications and iterative testing during the prototyping process and use tools that facilitate this (Kasurinen et al, 2013; Schell, Jesse, 2008). In this regard, video prototyping requires engineering prompts and repeatedly generating videos until they match the intended vision. There were also many cases where the repeatedly generated videos had to be blended together. Acquiring the know-how for engineering prompts and the process of iterating videos demanded more time than initially anticipated. However, as prompt engineering time continues to decrease, its efficiency is hard to evaluate for now.

However, in our project, the game designer directly created the videos without loss of ideas or intentions, minimizing communication loss, and this process gradually became faster. When game episodes were explained using images, text, or examples of similar games, misunderstandings occurred. However, when shown through video, it became clear. Moreover, videos were excellent for showcasing not only the game mechanics but also the look and feel of the game art, indirectly presenting the experience.

6. LIMITATION

Interviews were conducted including two experts, out of the gaming industry, in order to assess the fidelity of the AI-powered video-prototyping process. However, as only two experts were interviewed, the collected insights, while valuable, may reflect a narrower scope of experience than would be ideal for broader generalization. Moreover, a written unstructured interview provides limited information, as feedback is given in a single-way, non-reflective manner. It is also to be noted that the effectiveness of the studied method should be interpreted with caution, regarding generalizing the research results within a game design professional group or industry.

7. CONCLUSION

This study demonstrates that AI-generated video prototyping serves as a powerful communication tool in game development, particularly when collaborating with experts who have limited familiarity with games. By providing a more immersive and clear visualization of game concepts than static images or written documents, this approach enables even non-experts to quickly grasp the design intentions and offer feedback. The high fidelity of video prototypes is especially effective when applying specialized theories such as MBCT, as it clarifies how abstract principles can be translated into tangible gameplay experiences, thereby reducing potential miscommunication.

Video-based prototypes also facilitate smoother interdisciplinary collaboration. Whereas traditional documentation often struggles to convey the essence of gameplay, the use of video prototypes gives psychologists and other non-game professionals an intuitive understanding of the intended player experience. This shared "visual language" allowed different stakeholders to engage in faster, more precise discussions about how to combine abstract theory with game mechanics, leading to more efficient and refined teamwork.

However, the current stage of AI video prototyping does have limitations. Generating the desired results requires iterative prompt adjustments and intricate fine-tuning, which can be time-consuming, and it remains challenging to control specific details such as character expressions, animations, or UI elements. These constraints make quick prototyping difficult, but considering the pace of technological advancement, it is reasonable to expect that more accurate and speedy video generation will become available in the future.

Considering these findings AI-generated video prototyping may have its value as a means of delivering design intentions with high fidelity, minimizing misunderstandings in the design process, and supporting more effective collaboration across different fields. As AI evolves to improve efficiency and potentially allow for interactive elements within video prototypes, its role in a broader range of game development scenarios is likely to grow, positioning video prototyping as additional methodology for communicating complex experiential designs.

ACKNOWLEDGEMENT

This research was supported by Culture, Sports and Tourism R&D Program through the Korea Creative Content Agency grant funded by the Ministry of Culture, Sports and Tourism in 2025 (Project Name: Development of game-based digital Therapeutics technology for adolescent mental health (psychological and behavioral control) management, Project Number: RS-2025-00344893, Contribution Rate: 100%).

REFERENCES

Bolchini, D., Pulido, D. and Faiola, A. (2009). FEATURE "Paper in screen" prototyping: an agile technique to anticipate the mobile experience. *interactions*, 16(4), pp.29–33. doi:10.1145/1551986.1551992

Buchenau, M. and Fulton Suri, J. (2000). Experience prototyping. In: *Proceedings of the 3rd Conference on Designing Interactive Systems: Processes, Practices, Methods, and Techniques*. New York City, USA, pp.424–433. doi:10.1145/347642.347802

Camburn, B., Viswanathan, V., Linsey, J., Anderson, D., Jensen, D., Crawford, R., Otto, K. and Wood, K. (2017). Design prototyping methods: state of the art in strategies, techniques, and guidelines. *Design Science*, 3, e13. doi:10.1017/dsj.2017.10

Fullerton, T. (2008). Game Design Workshop – A Playcentric Approach to Creating Innovative Games. 2nd ed. Elsevier, Burlington, MA, USA.

Fullerton, T., Chen, J., Santiago, K., Nelson, E., Diamante, V., Meyers, A., Song, G. and DeWeese, J. (2006). That cloud game: dreaming (and doing) innovative game design. In: *Proceedings of the 2006 ACM SIGGRAPH Symposium on Videogames*. Boston, MA, USA, pp.51–59. doi:10.1145/1183316.1183324

Israel, J.H., Bähr, B. and Exner, K. (2016). Perspectives on Future Prototyping—Results from an Expert Discussion. In: Springer International Publishing, Cham, pp.11–22. doi:10.1007/978-3-319-24439-6_2

Kasurinen, J., Strandén, J.-P. and Smolander, K. (2013). What do game developers expect from development and design tools? In: *Proceedings of the 17th International Conference on Evaluation and Assessment in Software Engineering*. Porto de Galinhas, Brazil, pp.36–41. doi:10.1145/2460999.2461004

Kent, L., Snider, C., Gopsill, J. and Hicks, B. (2021). Mixed reality in design prototyping: A systematic review. *Design Studies*, 77, 101046. doi:10.1016/j.destud.2021.101046

Kultima, A., Peltoniemi, M. et al. (2012). Games and Innovation Research Seminar 2011 Working Papers. Available at: https://urn.fi/urn:isbn:978-951-44-8705-7 (Accessed: 24 January 2025).

Lauff, C.A., Kotys-Schwartz, D. and Rentschler, M.E. (2018). What is a Prototype? What are the Roles of Prototypes in Companies? *Journal of Mechanical Design*, 140(6), 061102. doi:10.1115/1.4039340

Lee, J., Eom, S.-Y. and Lee, J. (2023). Empowering game designers with generative AI. *IADIS International Journal on Computer Science & Information Systems*, 18(2), pp.213–230.

Lee, J.J. and Lee, J. (2023). Generative AI for the Super Game Designer. In: *Proceedings of the International Conferences on Interfaces and Human Computer Interaction 2023 (IHCI 2023); Computer Graphics, Visualization, Computer Vision and Image Processing 2023 (CGVCVIP 2023); and Game and Entertainment Technologies 2023 (GET 2023)*, pp.203–212. Available at: https://www.scopus.com/inward/record.uri?eid=2-s2.0-85181821189&partnerID=40&md5=de31ebab30010675c438851e2ab3ceef (Accessed: 24 February 2025).

Ling, L., Chen, X., Wen, R., Li, T.J.-J. and LC, R. (2024). Sketchar: Supporting Character Design and Illustration Prototyping Using Generative AI. In: *Proceedings of ACM Human-Computer Interaction*, 8(CHI PLAY), Article 337, 28 pages. doi:10.1145/3677102

Manker, J. (2011). Game Prototyping – The Negotiation of an Idea. In: *Proceedings of DiGRA 2011 Conference: Think Design Play*. Tampere, Finland: DiGRA. Available at: https://dl.digra.org/index.php/dl/article/view/598 (Accessed: 24 February 2025).

Menold, J., Jablokow, K. and Simpson, T. (2017). Prototype for X (PFX): A holistic framework for structuring prototyping methods to support engineering design. *Design Studies*, 50, pp.70–112. doi:10.1016/j.destud.2017.03.001

OpenAI. (2024). Sora. Available at: https://openai.com/sora/ (Accessed: 24 January 2025).

Otto, K. and Wood, K. (2001). Design for the Environment, Product Design; Techniques in Reverse Engineering and New Product Development.

Reyno, E.M. and Carsí Cubel, J.Á. (2009). Automatic prototyping in model-driven game development. *Comput. Entertain.*, 7(2), Article 29, 9 pages. doi:10.1145/1541895.1541909

Riedl, M.O. and Zook, A. (2013). AI for game production. In: *2013 IEEE Conference on Computational Intelligence in Games (CIG)*, pp.1–8. doi:10.1109/CIG.2013.6633663

Schell, J. (2008). The Art of Game Design: A Book of Lenses. 1st ed. CRC Press, Boca Raton, USA. doi:10.1201/9780080919171

Signer, B. and Norrie, M.C. (2007). PaperPoint: a paper-based presentation and interactive paper prototyping tool. In: *Proceedings of the 1st International Conference on Tangible and Embedded Interaction*. Baton Rouge, LA, USA, pp.57–64. doi:10.1145/1226969.1226981

Snyder, C. (2003). Paper prototyping: The fast and easy way to design and refine user interfaces. Morgan Kaufmann, San Francisco, USA.

Ulrich, K.T. and Eppinger, S.D. (2016). Product design and development. McGraw-Hill, New York, USA.

APPENDIX

A. Playable Prototype (MindTrekking Demo)
https://1drv.ms/f/s!Ahutx5nfyiKuwJ0ksWGIGjNkoieH0w?e=61uun8

B. Interview Questions

Question 1:

Until now, we have explained the decisions made in our meetings using text and simple images. In comparison, does viewing the information in video form result in a different level of understanding?

Question 2:

After watching the video, were you able to assess whether we were all thinking along the same lines? Alternatively, if there were differences in perspectives, did the video provide an opportunity to offer more specific feedback?

Question 3:

If discrepancies between the development team's and the theory providers' views were not apparent from the text and image-based documents, did the video make these differences more noticeable

Question 4:

This paper is based on the hypothesis that video enhances the fidelity of prototyping. Please share your thoughts on this hypothesis.

Additional Comments:

Beyond the questions above, please feel free to provide any further insights or feedback.

C. Interview Feedback (Full Text)
Feedback from Professor Kim Min-A

"The visuals in the video were almost exactly what I had imagined. Previously, I could not know how the characters or landscapes would be implemented, so being able to see them in the video greatly enhanced my understanding.

It confirmed that we were thinking along the same lines—it was very similar to what I had envisioned. However, as mentioned in the first point, I noticed that the graphics, landscapes, and even the appearances of people differed from my expectations. I had seen many of the scenes outlined in our proposal and had imagined them as animated sequences, but the actual video had more of a documentary-like quality.

I believe that the video naturally increases the fidelity of the prototyping process. As someone without specialized knowledge in games, I initially had no clear sense of how the game's scenario would be realized in video form or which age group it might suit. After watching today's video, I felt that the content might be more appropriate for middle or high school students—or even children—rather than college students. This is because the scenario and graphics themselves do not seem to offer significant stimulation or appeal for adults. For example, as a parent of a first-grader, I think that even elements like reboarding a bus can help elementary school children reconsider their perspectives."

Feedback from Professor Yoon Sung-Min

"Watching the video, as opposed to reading text and viewing static images, provided a much higher level of understanding. Although not every detail described in the text and images was fully realized in the video, I believe that the underlying theoretical intentions were effectively communicated and could be applied to the video format. Additionally, the video stimulated more expansive ideas. For instance, the scene where an apple emerges from a bag seems to introduce the concept of encountering an object during a walk. The theory suggests that one should observe an object without immediate judgment—merely noting its attributes such as 'red', 'square', 'dotted', or 'with a stem'—and spend time perceiving it as it is, rather than instantly categorizing it. This approach allows for choices that may involve adding judgment or value, but the important point is to see the object as it truly is, rather than immediately assigning it a predetermined label. Such an approach could offer an opportunity to learn the mindful, automatic adjustment process inherent in human cognition.

In another example, the choice involving the bus represents a training scenario in mindfulness-based cognitive therapy, where one must decide between reacting automatically and responding skillfully. Although taking the bus to go faster might provide short-term relief, it could be counterproductive in the long run. Experiencing this scene may help illustrate that a more precisely designed game could serve as an effective mindfulness exercise. This concept is also explained in programs like 'Vicious Flower', where it is shown that when people face difficulties, they often resort to short-term behaviors—be it shopping, gaming, gambling, binge-watching, or oversleeping—to alleviate their distress, even though such actions rarely offer long-term benefits. Mindfulness, on the other hand, encourages individuals to pause these automatic reactions and instead respond in a more skillful manner.

Furthermore, viewing the video allowed me to more clearly discern the differences in understanding between theory providers and developers. The concrete implementations shown in the video help identify gaps between theoretical intentions and practical execution, thereby enabling a more advanced integration of the two. I accept the hypothesis that video prototyping enhances fidelity, as the video's tangible implementations allow us to assess whether the final product aligns with or deviates from the theoretical framework. While other methods may exist, since games are fundamentally visual, the video naturally serves as a preview of the game to be developed, providing a basis for feedback that can help ensure the prototype remains closely aligned with the underlying theory".

D. SORA Video generation prompts (Full Text)

Week	Image Seed	Video Seed	Prompt
1	○		The tree sways gently in the wind, with its branches and leaves moving fluidly and naturally, while the trunk remains rooted and stable. The camera remains fixed throughout the scene.
2			A collection of colorful 3D cubes slowly orbits around a hiking backpack placed at the center of the scene. Each cube moves smoothly in a circular path, creating a dynamic yet calm visual. Suddenly, a 3D red cube pops out from inside the hiking backpack, emerging with a gentle upward motion. As the red cube hovers in mid-air, a white circular marker briefly appears around it, highlighting the cube as if it has been selected. The marker remains visible for a moment, then fades away. After the marker disappears, the red cube begins to transform seamlessly into the shape of a 3D apple, retaining its position in mid-air. The camera remains fixed, capturing the entire sequence clearly, focusing on the movement of the cubes, the marker interaction, and the transformation.
3		○	Create a 5-second bright-themed 3D animation featuring a man hiking in a scenic mountainous environment. The camera starts with a full-body back view of the man and continuously follows him, keeping the man centered in the frame throughout the video. As the man progresses forward, the mountain in front of him gradually becomes more prominent and closer in view. At the 4-second mark, a sleek, interactive UI element appears on the screen, showing a touchable icon or indicator on the mountain. The animation emphasizes smooth character movement, realistic hiking gestures, and a visually engaging bright atmosphere. Maintain a consistent focus on the man, avoiding any shifts to other elements or locations in the scene.
4		○	*Strong remix prompt, based on result 'Week 3'* Create a 5-second bright-themed 3D animation featuring a man walking on a flat trail in a scenic mountainous environment. The camera starts with a full-body back view of the man and continuously follows him, keeping him centered in the frame at all times. The character's entire body remains visible throughout the video. As the man walks, a bus with 'RETURN' written on its front display approaches

			along the same flat trail from a distance. The bus gradually gets closer and comes to a stop in front of the man. At the moment the bus stops, two flat, 2D white circular UI markers dynamically appear on the bus, indicating that the bus is interactive and selectable. These markers should be touch-interactive UI elements. The animation emphasizes smooth movement of the bus and the character, a visually appealing bright atmosphere, and a clear focus on interactivity.
5		○	Create a 5-second bright-themed 3D animation featuring a man walking slowly on a flat trail in a scenic environment. The camera starts with a full-body back view of the man and continuously follows him, keeping him centered in the frame at all times. The character's entire body remains visible throughout the video. As the man walks slowly, several groups of people approach from the opposite direction, passing by him. Among them is a large retriever dog, initially walking alongside one of the groups. The dog begins to bark actively at the man while wagging its tail excitedly. After a moment, the dog breaks away from its group, running toward the man in an energetic and playful manner. The animation ends with the dog jumping up slightly as if trying to engage with the man, disrupting his peaceful walk. The focus remains on the man throughout, with the dog's playful yet disruptive behavior emphasized as a contrasting element. The animation should highlight the interaction between the man and the approaching groups while maintaining a bright and engaging atmosphere.
6			Create a 5-second bright-themed 3D animation featuring a squirrel in a forest environment. The scene shows the squirrel reacting angrily after noticing that the acorn it was about to eat has disappeared. The animation focuses on the squirrel's expressive body language and facial expressions, emphasizing frustration and anger. Maintain a bright and engaging forest setting, but keep the squirrel's reaction as the central focus of the animation.
7	○		Create a 5-second bright-themed 3D animation featuring a bulletin board with the title 'D' prominently displayed at the top. The animation begins with an empty bulletin board positioned for a clear, front-facing view. Three game-like, stylized photos fly in one by one from various directions and attach to the board in the following order: A 'RETURN' bus photo. People with a dog photo. A squirrel sitting on a stump photo. Each photo smoothly attaches to the board with a satisfying pin or stick motion, creating a dynamic and engaging animation. The animation should emphasize the vibrant, colorful, and stylized aesthetics, with the bulletin board and its title 'D' as the central focus throughout the sequence.
8			Create a 5-second bright-themed 3D animation featuring a wooden decorative display case housing seven crystal orbs. The orbs are arranged in a structured layout: three on the first row, three on the second row, and one on the third row, creating a balanced and visually pleasing composition. Each orb is uniquely colored and contains a stylized photo, representing: A dog. A bus. A squirrel. A tree. A backpack. A bird. A cloud. The wooden display case is polished, bright, and stylized to enhance a cheerful and natural aesthetic. Each orb glows faintly in its unique color, and the stylized photos inside are vivid and engaging. The camera remains stationary, focusing on the entire arrangement, emphasizing the layout of the orbs, their embedded photos, and the detailed wooden case. The overall tone is bright, natural, and visually appealing

CONTEXT STEERING AND AI FOR PERSONALIZED PLAYER EXPERIENCE IN VIDEO GAMES

Zachary Swensrude, Trevor Meester and Hossain Samar Qorbani
MacEwan University, Canada

ABSTRACT

The increasing demand for dynamic, responsive artificial intelligence AI in games necessitates lightweight alternatives to traditional pathfinding systems. The choice and implementation of AI solutions in video games are essential to the player experience. This paper overviews the context steering algorithm used in Lich's Lair, a roguelike top-down 2D action role-playing game developed in the Unity game engine. It offers insights into how implementing context steering agents can affect player experience through its impacts on the development process. An overview of the game mechanics is also provided to better understand how the research fits into the game. After development, a playtest with 37 participants was conducted, showing positive results. Players found the game fair, enjoyable, and easy to learn.

KEYWORDS

Game AI, Context Steering AI, User Experience

1. INTRODUCTION

Recognizing the limited academic research on context steering within game development, we aimed to explore its impact on player experience and assess its feasibility in a real-time gaming context. To evaluate player experience, we implemented a context-steering-based AI pathfinding solution in a roguelike game. We created enemy characters capable of responding to rapidly changing environments in a real-time 2D action game developed with Unity.

While classic methods like A* and Monte Carlo tree search (MCTS) dominate academic and commercial development, there is limited empirical analysis on lightweight steering alternatives like context steering, especially in commercial-style games. This work addresses that gap by implementing and evaluating such a system.

This paper explores a lesser-known AI technique called context steering, an approach initially designed for autonomous vehicle navigation (Bünger et al., 2021; Dockhorn et al., 2021), which uses real-time, short-range decision-making through dynamically updated interest and danger maps. Unlike more popular methods like A*, which rely on pre-calculated paths, context steering enables agents to respond fluidly to immediate environmental changes.

2. RELATED WORKS

Existing context-steering literature falls into two main categories:

- Describing and explaining context steering
- Discussing potential optimizations and improvements

While extremely important, these categories leave out a third key area— the implementation of steering algorithms within fully developed games. In this work, we have implemented context steering as the sole pathfinding method in Lich's Lair, a game we developed for this purpose and designed all AI systems around it.

We also completed one round of user testing with N = 37 players to determine how using context steering as the primary pathfinding system affects player experience.

As detailed in a study by Logofatu et al. (2019), other popular options for controlling AI movement and decision-making include:

- A-Star Pathfinding (A*): An efficient graph traversal algorithm that finds a path between two points using best-first search.
- Monte Carlo Tree Search (MCTS): A method for finding optimal decisions by taking random samples in the decision space and building a search tree.
- Genetic Algorithms: Methods that find the current fitness of an entity and mutate it to produce more optimized offspring, commonly used in AI pathfinding (Mitchell, 1996).

A* pathfinding, initially introduced for graph traversal, is widely used for autonomous vehicles and robots due to its speed and efficiency (Candra, Budiman, & Hartanto, 2020). Similarly, Monte Carlo Tree Search is frequently used in strategy games, particularly in complex decision-making scenarios such as Go (Browne et al., 2012). Genetic algorithms, originally proposed by Mitchell (1996), are useful for optimization problems by simulating evolutionary principles.

In contrast to these pathfinding algorithms, steering algorithms rely on less information, using only what is immediately available. Pathfinding algorithms can be referred to as long-range steering, whereas short-range steering, such as context steering, allows for more dynamic movement (Tomlinson, 2004).

Reynolds (1999) described this difference as following a script versus improvising lines in a play. Initially introduced by Fray (2015), context steering aimed to overcome limitations in traditional flocking behavior (Reynolds, 1999). Fray emphasized the need for AI to consider both movement goals and environmental hazards, introducing the multiple context maps approach.

A major challenge in context steering is handling multiple conflicting goals. Dockhorn et al. (2021) proposed a multi-objective solution using multi-criteria optimization, which allows AI to handle several priorities at once. Although this was not implemented in Lich's Lair, it provides insights for future improvements.

Beyond navigation, balancing gameplay and AI difficulty is crucial. Schell (2014) introduced core concepts such as Fairness, Challenge vs. Success, and Meaningful Choices, which we incorporated into Lich's Lair. For playtesting, we used Likert scale surveys, similar to studies by Andrade et al. (2006) and Pfau & Seif El-Nasr (2023), to evaluate user satisfaction and game balance.

3. CONTEXT STEERING IN PRACTICE

We adopted context steering as a lightweight alternative to traditional pathfinding solutions (Fray, 2015), avoiding the computational cost of A* for handling multiple enemies in Lich's Lair. Initially, we considered the A Pathfinding Project (Granberg, n.d.) but opted for context steering after discovering a Sunny Valley Studio (n.d.) tutorial.

Context steering uses interest and danger maps to track movement goals and obstacles. AI agents dynamically calculate movement by combining these maps, allowing adaptive enemy behavior. The system consists of multiple child behaviors generating movement vectors, which are combined into a final velocity.

Enemies track their surroundings through context maps, monitoring eight cardinal and ordinal directions. Each direction is weighted based on proximity to the target (interest map) and obstacles (danger map). The normalized sum of these weights determines movement, ensuring smooth obstacle avoidance and pursuit.

In Lich's Lair, an enemy's detection radius triggers movement when the player enters it. Once detected, the enemy marks the player's location, as illustrated in Figure 1a and 1b.

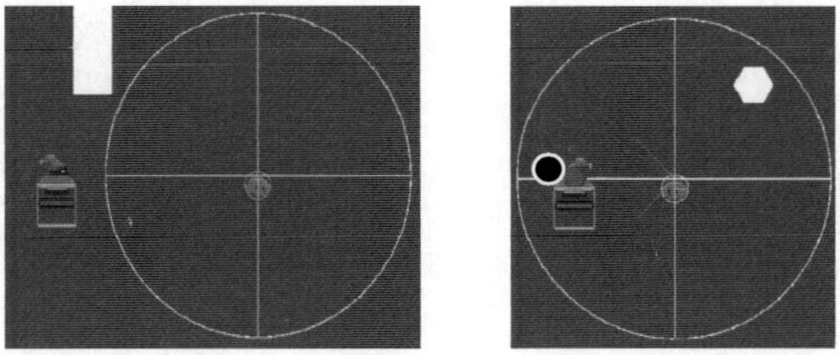

Figure 1a. Enemy detection radius (left) Figure 1b. Enemy detected player (right)

When the player is detected within this radius, the enemy begins generating its interest map, which points in the direction of the target. These directions are represented by light gray lines in Figure 2. As the enemy approaches an obstacle, the danger map comes into play, tracking the location and direction of nearby obstacles the enemy may need to avoid. Figure 2 also illustrates the danger map in action, with red lines pointing toward the obstacle and a red dot marking the obstacle itself.

By considering both maps, the context solver determines the optimal direction for movement. If there are no obstacles between the enemy and its target, the movement direction will always point directly toward the target. However, when obstacles are present, the context solver can shine. By simply summing the vectors from the danger and interest maps, the system calculates the best movement direction—one that avoids direct paths blocked by objects, allowing the enemy to "path find" around obstacles. This behavior is demonstrated in Figure 3, where the longer white line represents the movement direction chosen by the context solver after factoring in the interest and danger maps.

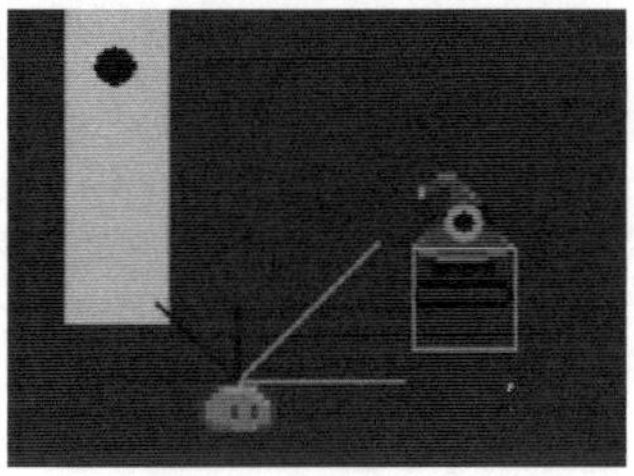

Figure 2. Interest map and danger map in action

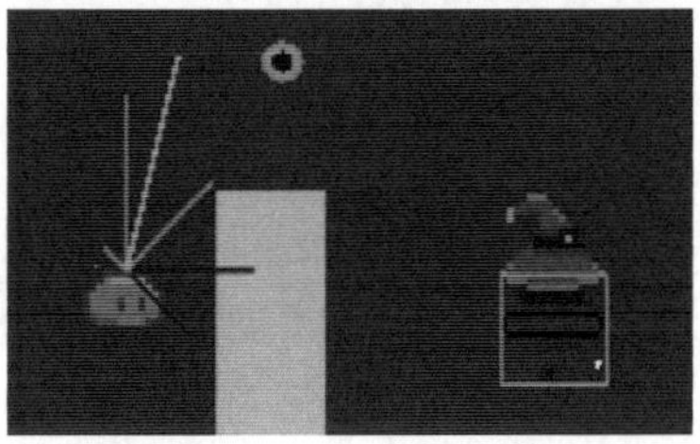

Figure 3. Context Solver steering around obstacles

With our implementation of context steering, the enemy moves directly toward the last visible detected position of the target, represented by the red dot at the top of Figure 3. This leads to interesting enemy interactions, allowing players to evade enemies by running behind objects and breaking the line of sight. We found this behavior particularly engaging because it simulates a realistic limitation—enemies only react to what they can see, rather than having omniscient knowledge of the player's location. This feels more natural to players than A* pathfinding, where enemies always know precisely where the player is.

By using existing context steering data, we could also implement the behavior of ranged enemies. This was achieved by adjusting the *targetReachedThreshold* in the ranged enemy's seek behavior, allowing it to stop at a predetermined distance from the player. Additionally, we took advantage of the fact that the context solver always points the enemy toward the player, using this direction as the ranged enemy's aim. This behavior is illustrated in Figure 4, where the long diagonal line represents the direction chosen by the context solver based on the interest and danger maps, also used as the ranged enemy's aim direction. Once the ranged enemy reaches the set threshold distance, it stops moving, aims at the player, and fires when neither advancing nor retreating.

A similar approach was applied to the Charging enemy type. This enemy follows the player until it reaches a specific distance, at which point it pauses to charge up before launching an attack in the solved direction. This behavior can also be seen in Figures 4a and 4b.

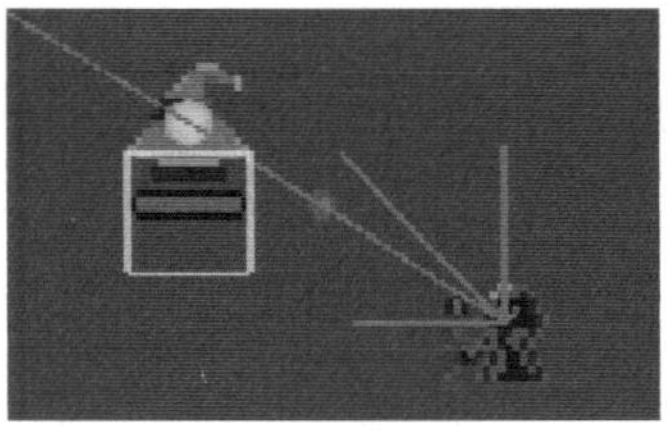

Figure 4a. Ranged

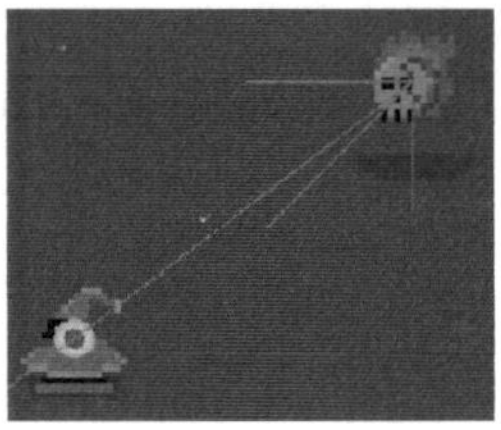

Figure 4b. Charging enemies using context solver for aim direction

Overall, context steering was crucial to our development and was the foundation for our enemy AI's behavior. From movement to attacking, all enemy actions were handled through context steering. Although every enemy type shared the same baseline context steering code, we used different flags at various points in their behavior to create distinct enemy types. The melee enemy relentlessly hunts down the player, attempting to get as close as possible. The ranged enemy approaches but stops early to shoot, retreating when the player gets too close. The Charging enemy follows the player until reaching a certain distance, then charges up an attack before rushing directly at the target.

In the final level of Lich's Lair, we introduced the Enchanted Shield enemy, which follows the player but stays just out of attack range, positioning itself to block the player's attacks and protect nearby ranged enemies. Despite their differences, all enemy types were controlled through flags and values using the same base scripts.

4. METHODOLOGY

As a student project, Lich's Lair was developed using only free and open-source software, including Unity (Unity Technologies, 2024) for game development and GitHub for version control. All art assets and sprites were created using Aseprite (Aseprite Community, 2022), while jsfxr and BeepBox (Nesky, 2023; Lavelle, 2011) were used to generate 8-bit sound effects. Background music was sourced from Marlon Silva on Itch.io under the Attribution-ShareAlike 4.0 International Creative Commons license, and typography included Old English Gothic Pixel and Kenney Mini Square, both licensed under the Attribution-ShareAlike 3.0 Unported Creative Commons license (Silva, 2021; ColorSwitchFan25, 2018).

4.1 Design/Prototype and Early Build

The concept and planning phase lasted one month, establishing the game's roguelike structure with randomized dungeon layouts and player upgrades for replayability. Context steering was chosen for AI design over alternatives like A* Pathfinding and Behavior Trees due to its more organic behavior. Early development focused on core systems, including player controls, AI agents, procedural upgrades, and dungeon generation, resulting in six room configurations, three player abilities, and two enemy archetypes. A small playtest confirmed the AI's effectiveness, leading to full-scale development.

The first two dungeon floors, boss encounters, and new enemy variants were implemented during mid-development. Ranged enemies received player-like abilities, AI balancing was refined, and a more extensive playtest used ISO 9241-11:2018 usability metrics to improve design. The final dungeon floor introduced ethereal enemies, new abilities, and structured enemy balancing using a weighted budget system. The Bee Swarm ability was added, affecting context steering to create unpredictable enemy behavior.

Context steering remained central to enemy AI and player interactions in *Lich's Lair*. The Fireball ability was introduced to counter enemy clustering and deal with area damage, followed by the Icicle ability, which pierced enemies in a straight line. Ranged enemies used interest vectors for aiming, allowing agile players to evade projectiles. Over time, enemies gained player-like abilities, enhancing strategic combat.

In the alpha phase, the Flamethrower was introduced, causing ranged enemies to stop advancing. This was resolved with context steering, making them approach before retreating at a threshold. Charging enemies combined ranged and melee behaviors, gaining speed within range but never retreating.

In beta, enemy interactions were refined with the Ghost Spear, which ignored walls, forcing players to adapt. The Tidal Wave ability countered this by blocking enemy movement. Bee Swarm added chaotic enemy behavior by randomizing avoidance patterns and enhancing strategy and visual effects.

4.2 Gameplay Mechanics and Design

Lich's Lair features an elemental weakness system, a randomly generated dungeon using premade rooms, a random orb upgrade system, and three levels, each with unique enemies and bosses. Randomization enhances replayability, while the elemental system allows players to specialize in one element or use a combination of all three.

4.2.1 Elemental Weakness System

Inspired by rock-paper-scissors mechanics, every ability and enemy belong to one of three elements: water, nature, or fire. Elemental interactions determine damage multipliers—1.5x for strengths, 1x for neutral, and 0.5x for weaknesses—encouraging strategic adaptability.

4.2.2 Random Dungeon Generation and Level Progression

Each playthrough randomizes the sequence of premade rooms, ensuring variety. The game has three themed levels:

Level 1: Cave, Level 2: Dungeon (introduces Charging enemies) , Level 3: Astral Plane (introduces Ghost enemies)

Enemies scale in difficulty, and each level concludes with a boss fight that rewards five upgrade orbs, reinforcing progression and escalating **challenges** (Schell, 2014).

4.2.3 Randomized Upgrade Orb System

Players receive an upgrade orb after each room, choosing from three random upgrades with rarity tiers (Common to Legendary).

Passive Upgrades enhance stats such as damage, health, speed, and elemental affinities.

Active Abilities introduce new element-based spells, scaling with rarity.

This system promotes strategic decision-making and playstyle customization.

4.3 User Testing

Following *The Lens of Fairness* (Schell, 2014), randomness ensures accessibility for all players. A 7-point Likert scale evaluated player experience based on six statements, assessing learning ease, control intuitiveness, difficulty, fairness, and enjoyment. Measuring human perception and enjoyment is inherently challenging. Drawing insights from psychology, we used a 7-point Likert scale to evaluate player feedback based on six key statements. Each player was asked to rate their experience according to the following:

1. The game is easy to learn.
2. I find the controls intuitive and easy to use.
3. The game provides clear instructions on how to play.
4. The game is too difficult (to complete).
5. The game is fair.
6. I enjoy playing the game.

The questionnaire was adapted from ISO 9241-11 usability metrics and tailored to our game's design focus. Although the questions prioritized user enjoyment and interface usability, future iterations will include more targeted items evaluating AI behavior perception.

5. RESULTS

In our questionnaire, in addition to the six Likert scale questions, we included demographic questions and inquiries about prior experience with similar games and how far each player progressed. This allowed us to assess each participant's skill level with their responses. Additionally, we asked four open-ended questions to gather qualitative feedback on specific game elements players liked or disliked, any bugs they encountered, and any additional comments they had.

With an emphasis on conducting playtests with a diverse range of players, our final (and largest) playtest involved students from an Introduction to Game Development class (N=37). This significantly expanded the variety of responses we received while also allowing participants who did not personally know us to provide unbiased feedback, free from any social pressure that could have influenced those with personal connections.

The general age range of participants was 18-24 years, with 27 males, 9 females, and 1 other. The majority (30 out of 37) had previously played similar roguelike action RPGs, indicating a high familiarity with the genre. Meanwhile, the seven participants who had not played similar games provided valuable insights from a fresh player perspective, creating a balanced mix of experienced and new players testing the game.

5.1 Data Analysis

Since we have one set of Likert scale responses for questions 2 through 7, we conducted a simple t-test (Table 1). While preliminary t-tests indicated significant differences from a neutral stance ($p < .0001$ for all questions), we acknowledge the limitations of this method on ordinal Likert scale data. Future work should include non-parametric analyses such as Kruskal-Wallis and report standard deviation and confidence intervals. The small p-values indicate that the mean of our Likert scale responses significantly differs from the neutral point (i.e., 4), assuming 4 represents neutrality on the scale. This suggests that participants' responses to these questions significantly deviate from a neutral stance.

Table 1. Likert Scale Feedback — Mean, Median, and P-Value for Each Question

Question	Mean	Median	P-Value
The game is easy to learn	6.13	7	$p < .001$
I find the controls intuitive and easy to use	5.70	7	$p < .001$
The game provides clear instructions on how to play	5.94	7	$p < .001$
The game is too difficult	2.89	2	$p < .001$
The game is fair	5.68	7	$p < .001$
I enjoy playing the game	6.08	7	$p < .001$

Balancing was a major challenge in *Lich's Lair*. Our primary approach was to implement an enemy or ability, then play the game and adjust character or ability stats based on what *felt* right, as this was the only method we were familiar with.

However, during our alpha playtest, we discovered issues with this approach. The responses to our question, *"The game's difficulty is well-balanced,"* resulted in a highly inconsistent distribution.

Following this playtest, we adopted a new balancing method. Rather than basing enemy statistics on *feel*, we assigned weighted health, damage, and speed values to each floor. We implemented a standardized budget from which each enemy could "purchase" their stats, with higher values costing more. This provided a more structured approach to balancing, replacing subjective adjustments with concrete numerical values. Our final balance budget table can be seen in Table 2.

Table 2. Lich's Lair Balance Budget Guide

Total Budget: 6 Points	
High	3
Medium	2
Low	1

By the time our final playtest took place, this system had been fully implemented, allowing us to test it with our largest and most diverse group of players. As shown in Table 3, this method proved significantly more effective. The statement *"The game is too difficult"* received a low average response (mean = 2.89, median = 2), while the statement *"The game is fair"* received a high average response (mean = 5.68, median = 7); both with a statistically significant difference from the neutral stance.

These results were promising. Additionally, 61% of players did not pass the first boss, indicating that the game remained as challenging as intended. However, the fact that players still found it *balanced and fair* demonstrated that this approach achieved the best possible outcome, maintaining difficulty while ensuring fairness.

Table 3. Lich's Lair Balance Budget Table

Range	Floor	HP	Damage	Speed
High Range	1	45	15	3
Mid Range	1	35	10	2.25
Low Range	1	25	5	1.5
High Range	2	120	20	3.5
Mid Range	2	60	15	2.75
Low Range	2	35	10	2
High Range	3	175	25	3.5
Mid Range	3	90	20	2.75
Low Range	3	60	15	2

However, the opposite could also occur. As such, our goal was to ensure that while the game could be extremely difficult, it still felt fair. Beyond fairness, making the game fun and accessible to all skill levels was a core priority in development, leading us to focus on three primary areas in our user testing.

6. DISCUSSION

There is potential to add several features to the project, particularly regarding accessibility improvements based on user feedback. Adding options to adjust the typeface and text size would enhance the user experience. Implementing alternative color schemes for players with Color Vision Deficiency (CVD) would make the game accessible to a broader audience. These visual enhancements could improve both readability and aesthetics.

We frequently describe the context steering system as 'lightweight' based on both runtime experience and our early testing with the A* Pathfinding Project. Implementing A* into our Unity project requires the integration of hundreds of additional files and tens of thousands of lines of code. In contrast, our context steering implementation consisted of fewer than 10 files and under 1,000 lines of code. While this is not a formal performance benchmark, it highlights the relative simplicity and ease of integration that made context steering significantly less resource-intensive during development. Future work should include CPU and memory profiling to support this claim with empirical data. Another interesting modification involves introducing "invisible targets" around the map. These targets would influence enemy movement, causing them to steer toward locations other than just the player. This adjustment would create more varied and less predictable enemy behaviors, making encounters more dynamic. While these are significant changes, our context steering algorithm allows for flexible modifications, making these improvements feasible. Although our primary playtest was conducted in a game development class, which ensured high genre familiarity and technical feedback, it does limit generalizability. Future work should involve broader player demographics to confirm results across a more varied skill and interest base

7. CONCLUSIONS

In summary, context steering had two significant impacts on the development of *Lich's Lair*:

1. Enhanced User Experience: Playtest results indicated that the game was enjoyable due to the player's direct interaction with context-steered enemies through various abilities.
2. Guided Game Design: Context steering significantly shaped enemy types and abilities, leading to emergent gameplay interactions that enriched the overall experience.

While *Lich's Lair* showed promising results in enjoyment, our findings are limited by the absence of an experimental version featuring an alternative enemy traversal and decision-making system. Additionally, the questions posed to participants focused more on user experience and overall enjoyment than on perceptions of enemy behavior and variety. Revising these questions—explicitly targeting enemy movement and interactions—would provide more insight into which aspects of context steering enhance the user experience.

Future studies could develop a second version of the game to address the experimental limitations using an alternative enemy behavior algorithm. This would allow for A/B testing, where different groups of participants playtest different steering algorithms to determine which approach provides the most enjoyable experience. Expanding the question to focus more on enemy behavior, combined with A/B testing, would help identify the strengths and weaknesses of context steering compared to traditional AI behavior models.

Implementing context steering in *Lich's Lair* proved an effective, lightweight alternative to traditional AI pathfinding, enabling real-time decision-making and dynamic enemy behavior. Playtesting confirmed that players found the AI fair and engaging, supporting diverse enemy types without performance issues.

However, limitations included the lack of direct comparisons with other AI methods. Future research could involve A/B testing different movement algorithms and refining enemy behaviors to reduce clustering. Additionally, context steering has broader applications in robotics, autonomous navigation, and crowd simulations, with video games serving as a valuable testing ground. It offers a scalable, efficient AI solution for enhancing gameplay and player engagement.

REFERENCES

Abiteboul, S. et al. (2000). *Data on the Web: From Relations to Semistructured Data and XML*. Morgan Kaufmann Publishers, San Francisco, USA.

Andrade, G., Ramalho, G., Gomes, A. S., & Corruble, V. (2006). Dynamic Game Balancing: An Evaluation of User Satisfaction. *Proceedings of the AAAI Conference on Artificial Intelligence and Interactive Digital Entertainment*, 2(1), 3-8.

Browne, C. B. et al. (2012). A Survey of Monte Carlo Tree Search Methods. *IEEE Transactions on Computational Intelligence and AI in Games*, 4(1), 1-43.

Bünger, N. M., Panjwani, S., Meghjani, M., Huang, Z., Ang, M. H., & Rus, D. (2021). Context and Orientation Aware Path Tracking. *2021 IEEE/RSJ International Conference on Intelligent Robots and Systems (IROS)*, Prague, Czech Republic, 5583-5589.

Candra, A., Budiman, M. A., & Hartanto, K. (2020). Dijkstra's and A-Star in Finding the Shortest Path: A Tutorial. *2020 International Conference on Data Science, Artificial Intelligence, and Business Analytics (DATABIA)*, Medan, Indonesia, 28-32.

Dockhorn, A., Mostaghim, S., Kirst, M., & Zettwitz, M. (2021). Multi-Objective Optimization and Decision-Making in Context Steering. *2021 IEEE Conference on Games (CoG)*, Copenhagen, Denmark, 1-8.

Fray, A. (2015). Context Steering: Behavior Driven Steering at the Macro Scale. In *Game AI Pro 2: Collected Wisdom of Game AI Professionals*. CRC Press.

Granberg, A. (n.d.). A* Pathfinding Project. Retrieved February 11, 2024, from https://arongranberg.com/astar/

Logofatu, D., Leon, F., & Muharemi, F. (2019). General Video Game AI Controller—Integrating Three Algorithms to Bring a New Solution. *2019 23rd International Conference on System Theory, Control and Computing (ICSTCC)*, Sinaia, Romania, 856-859.

Mitchell, M. (1996). *An Introduction to Genetic Algorithms*. MIT Press.

Pfau, J., & Seif El-Nasr, M. (2023). On Video Game Balancing: Joining Player- and Data-Driven Analytics. *arXiv preprint arXiv:2308.07576*.

Reynolds, C. W. (1999). Steering Behaviors for Autonomous Characters. *Proceedings of the Game Developers Conference 1999*, 763-782.

Schell, J. (2014). *The Art of Game Design: A Book of Lenses* (2nd ed.). A K Peters/CRC Press.

Tomlinson, S. L. (2004). The Long and Short of Steering in Computer Games. *International Journal of Simulation Systems, Science & Technology*, 5(1-2).

VIRTUAL REALITY TOUR FOR CULTURAL HERITAGE: A SYSTEMATIC MAPPING

Elinaldo Ribeiro de Azevedo[1], Ingrid Nery Mendes[2] and Otávio Noura Teixeira[1]
[1]*Programa de Pós-graduação em Computação Aplicada - PPCA, Núcleo de Desenvolvimento Amazônico em Engenharia - NDAE, Universidade Federal do Pará (UFPA) - Tucuruí, Pará, Brazil*
[2]*Programa de Pós-Graduação em Engenharia Elétrica - PPGEE , Instituto de Tecnologia - ITEC, Universidade Federal do Pará (UFPA) - Belém, Pará, Brazil*

ABSTRACT

This study conducts a systematic mapping (2017–2022) on Virtual Reality (VR) applications for preserving urban cultural heritage, focusing on historical education. It analyzes methodologies, tools, and outcomes, identifying gaps in current research. VR is highlighted as an immersive tool that transcends physical and temporal barriers, with applications like Unity 3D and Unreal Engine dominating development. The review, based on 372 studies from five databases, emphasizes educational potential and cultural preservation, using Belém, Pará, as a case study context, though no specific applications were found there. Key findings include high engagement and effective historical learning, with tools like photogrammetry and devices like HTC Vive widely used. Gaps include sample size, technological limitations, and the need for broader applicability. The study lays groundwork for future VR projects in culturally significant cities, promoting identity and historical understanding.

KEYWORDS

Virtual Reality, Cultural Heritage, City, Systematic Mapping

1. INTRODUCTION

The research presents a systematic mapping on the use of Virtual Reality (VR) in the preservation of a city's cultural heritage. The main objective is to analyze studies published between 2017 and 2022* that address the application of VR in recovering urban cultural aspects from specific historical periods. VR emerges as an innovative technological tool that enables immersive experiences, overcoming physical and temporal limitations in interacting with historical contexts.

The study aims to identify methodologies, approaches, and results from existing research, as well as gaps in current knowledge on the topic. In this way, it seeks to establish guidelines for the development of VR applications focused on the preservation and recovery of cultural heritage in specific locations during significant historical moments. The relevance of this study is based on the importance of cultural heritage in promoting identity and historical understanding within a society.

The literature provides a comprehensive analysis of the concepts of virtuality and its associated technologies. The term "virtual," as explained by Levy (2005), derives from the medieval Latin *virtualis*, meaning force or potential, representing a process of actualization and materialization of ideas.

Extended Reality (XR), according to Pinheiro and Pacheco (2023), encompasses three main technologies that connect the real and virtual worlds: Virtual Reality (VR), which transports users to digital environments through specialized headsets; Augmented Reality (AR), which overlays virtual elements onto the real world; and Augmented Virtuality (AV), which allows for the coexistence and interaction of real and virtual elements.

Tori and Hounsell (2020) characterize virtual environments as alternative realities that, although artificial, can stimulate sensory responses similar to those of the physical world. Arruda (2014) complements this perspective by defining simulation as a representation of reality that enables meaningful experiences, while Salen and Zimmerman (2012a) emphasize that each simulation derives its identity from specific real-life situations.

* This research was carried out between February and June 2023, as part of a course in the postgraduate program.

The effectiveness of these technologies is exemplified by Godulla et al. (2021) through the analysis of the simulation *1943 Berlin Blitz*, which demonstrated high immersive and narrative potential despite technical limitations. The impact of these technologies is further evidenced by Kolmar (2023), who records approximately 171 million virtual reality users worldwide.

The literature demonstrates the relevance of technology in cultural rescue and preservation, as Zaia et al. (2022) emphasize that cultural rescue is essential for preserving a society's history and identity, highlighting how virtual technologies can enrich experiences in historical environments.

In the context of digital games, Cole (2022) analyzes how "Assassin's Creed: Odyssey" provides an immersive experience of ancient Greece, creating "technocultural mashups" that renew cultural memory. De Ávila et al. (2021) expand this discussion, arguing that digital spaces offer new possibilities for preserving cultural heritage, considering the games themselves as cultural artifacts worthy of preservation.

Sukhov (2022) examines the game "Kingdom Come: Deliverance" as an educational tool, highlighting its external aspects (personal development) and internal aspects (in-game skills), as well as its ability to faithfully recreate the medieval architecture of the Kingdom of Bohemia.

In a specific historical context, Melo et al. (2021) and Chaves and Miranda (2016) analyze the urban transformations of Belém between 1940 and 1960, particularly on Presidente Vargas Avenue, noting how verticalization and modernization reflected external cultural influences and the progressive discourses of the time.

2. METHODOLOGY

The methodology of this research is grounded in the principles of Systematic Literature Review (SLR), following the approach of Kitchenham (2007), which establishes a rigorous framework for conducting reviews, encompassing planning, search, selection, critical analysis, and synthesis of results.

The PICOC methodology, as described by Camargo et al. (2021), is incorporated as a tool for precisely formulating research questions and identifying relevant selection criteria. This approach, adapted from disciplines such as Medicine and Social Sciences, provides a structured roadmap for defining the essential components of the investigation.

The methodological process utilizes the Escritha tool (SILVA, 2024) as the foundation for the review, aiming to ensure objectivity, replicability, and reliability. The detailed structure of the methodological plan, including research questions, search strategies, and inclusion and exclusion criteria, will be presented later, ensuring a robust investigation that will serve as a state-of-the-art guide for the development of VR applications in the context of cultural preservation.

2.1 Research Questions

At the beginning of the review, an investigation was conducted into VR applications focused on history education, specifically regarding historical and cultural recovery as a learning objective, with a particular emphasis on a specific city. In this study, the focus will be on Belém, Pará. The formulated research questions provide the foundation for a detailed exploration of this multifaceted topic.

- RQ1: What is the state of the art of VR applications for teaching historical-cultural rescue?
- RQ2: Which applications are set in Belém, Pará?
- RQ3: What game development engines were used?
- RQ4: Which applications are used for education?
- RQ5: What are the outcomes generated by these applications?

2.2 Strategies Used in Search Engines

The systematic search methodology was structured using five main scientific databases: ACM Digital Library, IEEE Digital Library, Science Direct, Scopus, and Periódicos CAPES. Google Scholar was deliberately excluded to prioritize peer-reviewed works, avoid result redundancy, and, primarily, to minimize grey literature.

The search strategy was developed considering two linguistic groups (English and Portuguese), with search strings (Table 1) adapted for each database. The fundamental structure of the strings incorporated terms related to Virtual Reality, historical-cultural aspects, education, and urban context. Some specific considerations were implemented: the term "Education" was retained without synonyms due to its universality; "Belém" was omitted from searches in English due to its regional specificity; and "Virtual Reconstruction" was included as a synonym for "Virtual Reality."

Specific refinements were applied through exclusion operators to ensure the precision of results. For example, terms such as "business," "game," "AR," and "smart" were excluded in the ACM Digital Library, while "health," "medicine," and "language" were removed in Science Direct.

The process resulted in a total of 372 studies: 206 from ACM, 9 from IEEE, 120 from Science Direct, 10 from Scopus, and 27 from CAPES.

The research was conducted between July and September 2023, using Google Sheets and the Escritha application for data organization and analysis.

Table 1. Search descriptors in Portuguese and English

Descriptors in Portuguese	Synonyms
Realidade Virtual	**Virtualidade, Ambiente virtual, Ambiente 3D**
Resgate cultural	**Reconstrução virtual, História**
Educação	–
Belém	**Cidade**

Descriptors in English	Synonyms
Virtual Reality	**Virtuality, Virtual Environment, 3D Environment**
Cultural Heritage	**Past,Virtual Reconstruction, Antique**
Education	–
City	**Urban**

2.3 Inclusion and Exclusion Criteria

The study selection methodology established specific inclusion and exclusion criteria to ensure rigor and relevance in the analysis. The inclusion criteria encompassed full articles published between 2017 and 2022, focusing on software development, educational applications, and historical preservation. Additionally, the presence of consolidated digital prototypes and measurable quantitative data was considered.

The exclusion criteria were defined to filter out studies lacking interactivity in the virtual environment, retaining only those that provide genuinely interactive user experiences. The analysis was limited to publications in Portuguese and English, establishing a linguistic scope appropriate for the research. It is worth noting that the inclusion criteria were applied flexibly to avoid excluding potentially relevant works, allowing for a more comprehensive analysis of the topic.

2.4 Criteria for selecting studies and identifying qualities

The quality analysis of the studies was structured based on specific criteria derived from the research questions. The evaluation process assigned scores to the studies according to three main criteria: use of Virtual Reality, focus on historical preservation, and presentation of application development methodology.

Following the PRISMA model (Haddaway et al., 2022), the results analysis revealed significant distributions within the inclusion criteria: 8.3% of the studies presented quantitative results, 25% consisted of full-text articles, and 66.7% included digital prototypes. Regarding the educational focus, 75% of the studies demonstrated an orientation toward educational purposes, while 58.3% presented specific development methodologies.

In the evaluation of exclusion criteria, it was identified that 12.5% of studies were rejected for focusing solely on modeling, 25% due to the absence of digital prototypes, and 37.5% for exclusively emphasizing object visualization. Notably, all accepted studies addressed historical recovery as a primary theme, highlighting the relevance of this topic within the analyzed dataset.

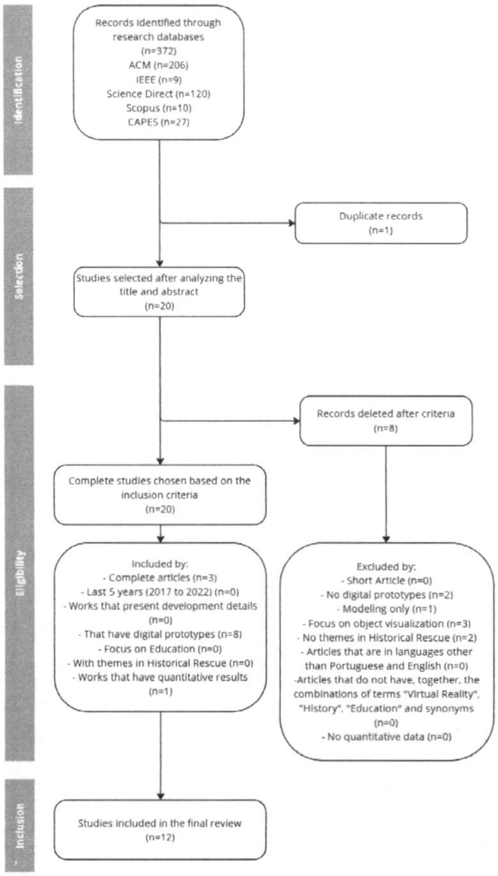

Figure 1. PRISMA flow for selection of works (CAMARGO et al., 2021)

2.5 Details of Selected Works

The methodology for analyzing the selected studies employed a systematic data extraction approach, identifying essential information such as the country of origin and the continent of affiliation. The analytical framework was organized into seven main categories: study objectives, methodology employed, presence of a prototype or digital application, game engine used, auxiliary programs, 3D modeling tools, and Virtual Reality devices.

For the evaluation of 3D modeling, the definition by Tori and Hounsell (2020) was followed, which characterizes it as the process of developing three-dimensional mathematical representations of objects. Additionally, as per Pavkov et al. (2017), the relevance of game engines as fundamental tools for developing user interactivity was considered. The analysis prioritized visual creation and interactivity tools that directly impact the end-user experience.

2.6 Data Extraction and Synthesis

The extraction and synthesis of data constitute an important stage in a systematic mapping, where information collected from selected studies is transformed into meaningful and useful knowledge. In the geographical distribution of the research, it was observed that 50% of the studies were conducted in Europe, 41.7% in Asia, and 8.3% in North America.

Regarding the tools used, it was identified that Unity 3D and Unreal Engine were the primary game engines employed (figure 2). For the development of the applications, various auxiliary programs were utilized, including Photoshop, Dreaming the Sphinx, Substance, and texture.com. In 3D modeling, the standout software included Maya, Blender, and 3D Studio, each featured in 4 studies, in addition to Zbrush, SketchUp, Lumion 3D, and AutoCAD.

Photogrammetry was a relevant technique mentioned in several studies, as described by Dezen-Kempter et al. (2015). For virtual reality visualization, the most commonly used devices were the HTC Vive, smartphones, and Oculus. Video mapping was also cited as a projection technology, as highlighted by Watier (2018). Augmented reality, according to Silva et al. (2022), was mentioned as a complementary technique, although it fell outside the main scope of the review.

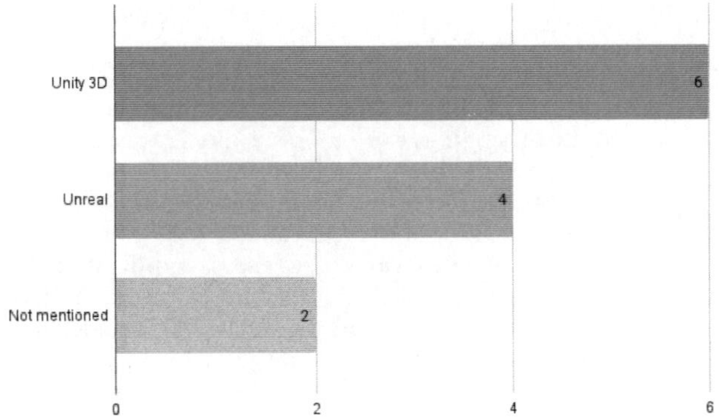

Figure 2. Distribution of game engines by studies

3. RESULTS AND ANALYSIS

The overall analysis of this study identified patterns, methodologies, characteristics, and educational impacts of these technologies, contributing to the advancement of knowledge and future research. Studies were evaluated according to three main criteria: use of VR (RQ1), focus on historical preservation (RQ2), and presentation of the application development methodology (RQ3). No study achieved a maximum score for the use of VR, but there was significant scoring for historical preservation and methodology.

Six methodologies were identified, highlighting practical projects present in 100% of the studies, which involved VR prototypes; the use of questionnaires in nine studies, which expanded the understanding of applications; bibliographic research in seven studies; case studies in three papers, some supported by specialists; interviews with experts in three studies; and technical visits to sites in two works. These approaches enabled both qualitative and quantitative evaluations, including statistical analyses to validate data and the reliability of instruments, such as the Shapiro-Wilk test (Andreoli et al., 2018), Cronbach's alpha (Andreoli et al., 2018; Selmanović et al., 2020), and the Chi-square test (Selmanović et al., 2020).

The results indicate that VR has proven effective in increasing engagement and raising awareness about cultural heritage, improving user experience and knowledge retention (Fu et al., 2020). Studies have shown that immersive environments can attract visitors and alter cultural perceptions, although variations exist depending on users' prior knowledge (Ch'ng et al., 2020). Serious games and gamification techniques were highlighted as strategies for measurable engagement and learning (Andreoli et al., 2018; Mendes et al., 2022). The integration of specialists and technical visits reinforced the accuracy and relevance of the developed virtual models (Ibrahim; Ali, 2018; López; Cruz, 2021; Walmsley; Kersten, 2019). Furthermore, combining VR with other technologies, such as augmented reality and mixed reality, expanded possibilities for interaction and learning (Remolar; Rebollo; Fernández-Moyano, 2021; Ribeiro et al., 2023; Zaia; Rose; Majewski, 2022).

Among the limitations identified, there is a need for VR experiences that are more pedagogically oriented, beyond purely exploratory environments, as well as the recommendation to compare VR and non-VR techniques to assess their educational value (Ch'ng et al., 2020). It is also suggested to explore different contents, audiences, and settings to maximize educational effectiveness, including the incorporation of animated physical elements, biometric measurements, and databases to enrich the experience (Selmanović et al., 2020). The expansion of VR use for cultural tourism and social engagement was also indicated as future opportunities (Abidin; Razak, 2019).

In summary, the studies analyzed highlight the potential of VR as an educational tool for teaching history and cultural recovery in urban areas, emphasizing its role in heritage preservation and promoting user engagement. The varied methodologies and results obtained provide a solid foundation for the development of future applications and research aimed at enhancing the integration of VR into heritage education.

Based on the studies analyzed, the research questions (RQs) answered in this systematic mapping are as follows:

RQ1 - What is the state of the art of VR applications for teaching historical-cultural rescue?: Between 2017 and 2022, studies predominantly originated from Asia and Europe, regions with greater digitized historical heritage, primarily using devices such as HTC Vive and smartphones for navigation (Fu et al., 2020; Walmsley; Kersten, 2019). Unity 3D and Unreal engines were the most used for development, while photogrammetry was the most common technique for 3D modeling.

RQ2 - Which applications are set in Belém, Pará?: This question remains open, as the work aims to serve as a basis for future implementations in the city and other locations of historical relevance.

RQ3 - What game development engines were used?: Unity 3D and Unreal stand out for their adaptability and ability to create interactive and updatable virtual environments.

RQ4 - Which applications are used for education?: Most studies focus on raising awareness for historical and cultural preservation, with potential for formal educational use.

RQ5 - What are the outcomes generated by these applications?: The studies present varied methodologies, including questionnaires, statistical tests, and gamification, indicating improvements in user experience, engagement, and knowledge acquisition, evaluated by instruments such as the Likert scale and the Virtual Reality Sickness Questionnaire (Fu et al., 2020; Deggim et al., 2017).

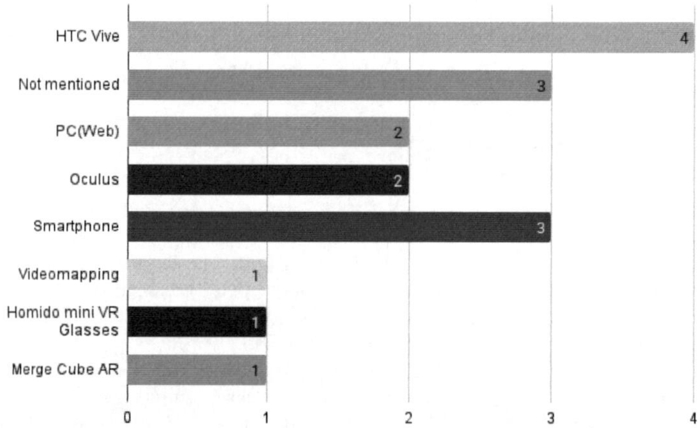

Figure 3. Distribution of 3D visualization devices and techniques by study

3.1 Existing Gaps

The analysis of the studies revealed that 3 works explicitly identified gaps or limitations, while 9 did not mention them directly, though they could be inferred. Fu et al. (2020) pointed out limitations such as system performance, operational design (e.g., use of a magnifying glass), generation of embedded knowledge, ambiguous interactions, unattractive design, and lack of a universal approach. Ch'ng et al. (2020) highlighted issues including sample size, cultural and historical inaccuracies, participants' prior knowledge, limited software/hardware configuration, and generalization of results. Selmanović et al. (2020) suggested improvements such as 360° sound and demographic segmentation.

Common gaps in studies with prototypes and questionnaires include sample size and diversity, technological limitations, and the applicability of results. Xingke and Yang (2020) did not explicitly state limitations, but these could involve questionnaire reliability, sample representativeness, digitization accuracy, and animation quality in virtual reality. Zaia, Rose, and Majewski (2022) cited difficulties in systematic data collection, financial resources, inadequate training, restricted sampling, and hardware/software limitations.

Walmsley and Kersten (2019) mentioned constraints in textures (4K resolution), LOD (Level of Detail) models, and visibility optimization within the environment.

4. CONCLUSION

There is strong evidence of a trend toward content assimilation through VR, as all studies that reported qualitative results from participants obtained positive data regarding the application of VR environments in the study of historical recovery. Therefore, based on this review, it is concluded that the proposed research questions (RQ1, RQ3, RQ4, and RQ5) were successfully answered, with the exception of one (RQ2), since it pertains specifically to the city of Belém, Pará, Brazil. This single unanswered question will be addressed through the continuation of this work, making it the foundation for the construction of a virtual reality environment characterized by this specific city.

It is concluded that VR is a promising tool for historical preservation, although gaps such as sample size and technological limitations remain to be overcome in future studies.

ACKNOWLEDGEMENT

I thank all the people who have contributed, directly or indirectly, to this project since it was conceived in 2016. I want to believe that it will not end here, as the concepts within it will serve as openings for future personal projects or those of others. However, I would like to specifically acknowledge the individuals who helped make this project a seed for new horizons:
Alan Hellyton Silva Pereira Júnior, Alexandre do Nascimento Alves, Amanda da Graça Brasil, Ana Alice da Silva Castro, André Dias Alves, Antônio Augusto Nogueira Neto, Bruno Brian Almeida, Bruno Caldas Lourenço, Caio Araujo Pereira, Caio Margalho Guerra, Daniel Lavareda Meireles, Emanuel Antonio de Melo Mesquita Neto, Francisco Felipe Gama da Silva, Gabriel Tele Jucá, Garbriel José Teixeira Monteiro, Genilson Lima Cardoso, Hugo Thomas de Souza Porfirio, Itamar Henrique Favacho Torres Brito, Jessé Cristiano Pacheco Monteiro, Joao Flavio Alencar de Souza da Serra, José Ricardo Sousa, José Victor da Silva Oeiras, Leonnardo Lair Tavares Gomes, Lucas Bernard Veloso Fagundes, Loan Victor Bastos da Silva, Luiz Edgar Medeiros da Silva, Marcos Pinheiro de Barros, Marcos Roberto Santa Maria Cardoso, Marlon Rodrigues da Silva, Mike Davis Rocha, Márcia Yasmin Filgueiras dos Santos, Patrick Campos Porto, Paulo Victor Rodrigues da Silva, Rafael Augusto de Sales Correa, Rafael de Amorim Bastos, Rosangela Rosa Souza, Samuel Victor de Arruda, Silva Trycia Isabele Pereira de Moraes e Yago Vasconcelos Machado.

REFERENCES

Andreoli, R., Corolla, A., Faggiano, A., Malandrino, D., Pirozzi, D., Ranaldi, M., Santangelo, G. and Scarano, V. (2018). A framework to design, develop, and evaluate immersive and collaborative serious games in cultural heritage. *Journal on Computing and Cultural Heritage*, [online] 11, pp.1–22. doi:https://doi.org/10.1145/3064644.

Arruda, E. P. (2014). *Fundamentos para o desenvolvimento de jogos digitais*. Bookman Editora.

Avila, C. de, Corso, A., & Fischer, G. D. (2021). Preservação e patrimônio em jogo na tecnocultura: a (re)construção da catedral de notre-dame em assassin's creed | journal of digital media & interaction. *Journal of Digital Media & Interaction*, *3*. https://doi.org/10.34624/jdmi.v3i7.15559

Camargo, C., Gonçalves, J., Conde, M. Á., Rodríguez-Sedano, F. J., Costa, P., & García-Peñalvo, F. J. (2021). Systematic literature review of realistic simulators applied in educational robotics context. *Sensors*, *21*, 4031. https://doi.org/10.3390/s21124031

Ch'ng, E., Li, Y., Cai, S., & Leow, F.-T. (2020). The effects of VR environments on the acceptance, experience, and expectations of cultural heritage learning. *Journal on Computing and Cultural Heritage*, *13*, 1–21. https://doi.org/10.1145/3352933

Chaves, C., & Miranda, L. (2016, February). *Avenida presidente vargas: onde belém foi mais moderna. Um estudo sobre a verticalização da avenida presidente vargas*. I SAMA - SEMINÁRIO de ARQUITETURA MODERNA NA AMAZÔNIA; Universidade Federal do Amazonas. https://arquiteturamodernanaamazonia.weebly.com/uploads/7/0/0/2/70024539/artigo_avenida_presidente_vargas_onde_bel%C3%89m_foi_mais_moderna__2_.pdf

Cole, R. (2022). Mashing up history and heritage in assassin's creed odyssey. *Games and Culture*, *17*, 915–928. https://doi.org/10.1177/15554120221115403

Deggim, S., P, Kersten T, Tschirschwitz, F., & Hinrichsen, N. (2017). SEGEBERG 1600 – RECONSTRUCTING A HISTORIC TOWN FOR VIRTUAL REALITY VISUALISATION AS AN IMMERSIVE EXPERIENCE. *The International Archives of the Photogrammetry, Remote Sensing and Spatial Information Sciences*, *XLII-2/W8*, 87–94. https://doi.org/10.5194/isprs-archives-xlii-2-w8-87-2017

Dezen-Kempter, E., Soibelman, L., Chen, M., & Müller, V. (2015). Escaneamento 3d a laser, fotogrametria e modelagem da informação da construção para gestão e operação de edificações históricas. *Gestão & Tecnologia de Projetos*, *10*, 113–113. https://doi.org/10.11606/gtp.v10i2.102710

Fu, X., Zhu, Y., Xiao, Z., Xu, Y., & Ma, X. (2020). RestoreVR: Generating embodied knowledge and situated experience of dunhuang mural conservation via interactive virtual reality. *Proceedings of the 2020 CHI Conference on Human Factors in Computing Systems*. https://doi.org/10.1145/3313831.3376673

Godulla, A., Planer, R., Wolf, C., Lück, A., & Vaaßen, F. (2021). An immersive journey through flawed technology: Users' perceptions of VR in journalism. *Journalism and Media*, *2*, 454–468. https://doi.org/10.3390/journalmedia2030027

Haddaway, N. R., Page, M. J., Pritchard, C. C., & McGuinness, L. A. (2022). PRISMA2020: An R package and Shiny app for producing PRISMA 2020-compliant flow diagrams, with interactivity for optimised digital transparency and Open Synthesis. *Campbell Systematic Reviews*, *18*. https://doi.org/10.1002/cl2.1230

Ibrahim, N., & Ali, N. M. (2018). A conceptual framework for designing virtual heritage environment for cultural learning. *Journal on Computing and Cultural Heritage*, *11*, 1–27. https://doi.org/10.1145/3117801

Kitchenham, B. (2007). *Guidelines for performing systematic literature reviews in software engineering*. https://cdn.elsevier.com/promis_misc/525444systematicreviewsguide.pdf

Kolmar, C. (2023, February). *25+ amazing virtual reality statistics [2023]: The future of VR + AR*. Zippia. https://www.zippia.com/advice/virtual-reality-statistics/#Virtual_Reality_Statistics_by_Devices

Lévy, P. (2005). *O que é o virtual?* (7th ed., pp. 15–18). Ed. 34.

Melo, I., Chaves, C., & Lima, G. (2021). Cartografias e contracartografias na documentação do patrimônio. Olhares sobre Belém entre 1940 e 1960. *Mouseion*, 1–1. https://doi.org/10.18316/mouseion.v0i39.9078

Mendes, Nery, Ingrid, Nogueira, Mendes, F.V., Teixeira, O.N. and Viviane, S. (2022). *The use of serious games for learning cardiopulmonary resuscitation procedures: A systematic mapping of the literature*. IntechOpen eBooks. [online] doi:https://doi.org/10.5772/intechopen.102399.

Pavkov, S., Franković, I., & Hoić-Božić, N. (2017). Comparison of game engines for serious games. *IEEE Xplore*, 728–733. https://doi.org/10.23919/MIPRO.2017.7973518

Pinheiro, J. V. de A. M. C., & Pacheco, P. (2023). *A Realidade Estendida E A Experiência Arquitetônica*. https://doi.org/10.17648/cics-2023-177813

Remolar, I., Rebollo, C., & Fernández-Moyano, J. A. (2021). Learning history using virtual and augmented reality. *Computers*, *10*, 146. https://doi.org/10.3390/computers10110146

Salen, K., & Zimmerman, E. (2012a). *Regras do jogo* (1st ed., Vol. 3, pp. 144–146). Editora Blucher.

Salen, K., & Zimmerman, E. (2012b). *Regras do jogo* (1st ed., Vol. 4, p. 25). Editora Blucher.

Selmanović, E., Rizvic, S., Harvey, C., Boskovic, D., Hulusic, V., Chahin, M., & Sljivo, S. (2020). Improving accessibility to intangible cultural heritage preservation using virtual reality. *Journal on Computing and Cultural Heritage*, *13*, 1–19. https://doi.org/10.1145/3377143

Silva, J. (2024). *Escritha — A ferramenta mais completa, eficiente e simples para produção científica*. Escritha.com. https://escritha.com/

Sukhov, A. A. (2022). Gamification of the middle ages: Educational discourse of "Kingdom come: Deliverance." *International Conference on Education and E-Learning*. https://doi.org/10.1145/3578837.3578846

Tori, R., & Marcelo (Eds.). (2020). *Introdução a realidade virtual e aumentada* (3rd ed., p. 11). Sociedade Brasileira de Computação. https://doi.org/10.5753/sbc.6654.2

Walmsley, A., & P, Kersten T. (2019). Low-cost development of an interactive, immersive virtual reality experience of the historic city model stade 1620. *The International Archives of the Photogrammetry, Remote Sensing and Spatial Information Sciences*, *XLII-2/W17*, 405–411. https://doi.org/10.5194/isprs-archives-xlii-2-w17-405-2019

Watier, M. (2018). Video mapping in audiovisual performances: Projecting the club scene onto the urban space. *DOAJ (DOAJ: Directory of Open Access Journals)*. https://doi.org/10.6092/issn.2280-9481/8363

Xingke, H., & yang, C. (2020). *Research on the display of material cultural heritage with the use of VR animation*. 65–70. https://doi.org/10.1145/3425577.3425590

Zaia, S. E., Rose, K. E., & Majewski, A. S. (2022). Egyptian archaeology in multiple realities: Integrating XR technologies and museum outreach. *Digital Applications in Archaeology and Cultural Heritage*, *27*, e00249. https://doi.org/10.1016/j.daach.2022.e00249

INTERACTIVE SOUNDSCAPE INSTALLATION URBAN GREEN SYMPHONY 4.0

Xin Yan[1], Takuro Shibayama[1] and Seiichiro Matsumura[2]
[1]Graduate School of Advanced Science and Technology
Tokyo Denki University, Japan
[2]Graduate School of Design
Tokyo University of Technology, Japan

ABSTRACT

This project introduces an experiential soundscape installation designed to promote public engagement with respect to the relationship between urban and green spaces. Using intuitive hand gestures, participants interact with site-specific field recordings, generate real-time musical expressions via machine learning, and experience responsive visual effects. Through playful, embodied exploration, they gradually develop awareness of the sonic contrasts between urban and green spaces. Version 4.0 focuses on the development of an immersive and interactive spatial sound system, marking a significant evolution of the project. It introduces a quadraphonic audio system based on Vector-Based Amplitude Panning (VBAP) and significantly refines the gesture-based interaction design to offer more fluid and intuitive control.

KEYWORDS

Interactive, Soundscapes, Gesture, Machine Learning, Vector Based Amplitude Panning

1. INTRODUCTION

Despite research showing that urban green spaces can mitigate noise pollution and enhance well-being, most studies have examined this topic from a quantitative and environmental engineering perspective, focusing on metrics such as green coverage, spatial distribution, and decibel reduction. Although these approaches are valuable, they often treat sound as an objective problem to be solved, neglecting how individuals perceive and interpret sound within specific contexts. Furthermore, few studies have investigated how interactive media can be employed to cultivate public awareness of the acoustic functions of green spaces (Yan and Matsumura, 2024(b); Yan and Matsumura, 2024(e)).

This project addresses these gaps by presenting an experiential installation that invites participants to actively engage with the sonic contrasts between urban and green spaces. Through embodied interaction and real-time audiovisual feedback, the installation transforms abstract environmental concepts into perceptible and emotionally resonant experiences. In contrast to conventional top-down evaluations, the installation emphasises subjective exploration and sensory immersion, offering a novel framework for sound-based environmental awareness. In doing so, it bridges the gap between soundscape ecology and interactive art, offering new insights into how individuals can understand and appreciate the functions of urban green spaces not only visually or spatially, but also sonically and intuitively.

2. TRANSITION OF DEVELOPMENT

The system developments as follows (Table 1):

1. Ver.1.0 was presented as the interactive installation ‘Urban Green Symphony’ at the ‘Intercollege Sonic Arts Festival 2023’ held at Aichi University of the Arts in Japan from 23 to 24 February 2024 (Yan and Matsumura, 2024(a)).

2. Ver.1.5 was presented at the 54th Research Meeting of the Japanese Society for Sonic Arts (JSSA) held at the Kunitachi College of Music in Japan on 1 June 2024 (Yan and Matsumura, 2024(b)).

3. Ver.2.0 and its evaluation experiments were presented at the 'NICOGRAPH2024' held at Tokyo City University in Japan from 9 to 10 November 2024 (Yan and Matsumura, 2024(c); Yan and Matsumura, 2024(d)).

4. Ver.3.0 was presented at the 'ADADA + CUMULUS 2024' International Conference held at National Cheng Kung University in Taiwan from 7 to 9 December 2024 (Yan and Matsumura, 2024(e)).

5. Ver.3.5 was presented as the interactive installation 'Urban Green Symphony Ver.3.5' at the 'Intercollege Sonic Arts Festival 2024' held at Doshisha Women's College of Liberal Arts in Japan from 23 to 24 February 2025 (Yan and Matsumura, 2025(f)).

Table 1. Transition of development

Version	Improvements	Remaining Issues
1.0		Complex two-hand gesture interactions. Insufficient sound effects.
1.5	Integrated the RAVE machine-learning model to transform noisy environmental sounds into therapeutic classical music.	Gesture interaction remains complex with both hands.
2.0 and its Evaluation	Simplified two-hand gesture interactions.	Overloaded experience content caused cognitive and operational fatigue.
3.0	Transitioned from two-hand to one-hand interaction; developed new user-friendly interaction modes; reduced the amount of experience content.	Lack of immersive sound design.
3.5	Attempted immersive sound design; increased the number of speakers.	Sound output was perceived as mechanical and unnatural.
4.0	Developed a dynamic sound trajectory system (e.g. using VBAP), enhancing spatial movement and auditory immersion.	

3. RESEARCH METHODS

3.1 Devices

This study presents the development and evaluation of Urban Green Symphony, an experiential interactive soundscape installation designed to deepen participants' interest in the balance between urban and green spaces. Developed on a 2023 MacBook Pro equipped with an M3 Max chip, this system operates using TouchDesigner by Derivative—a node-based visual programming environment for real-time multimedia interaction—and Pure Data (PD), an open-source platform for real-time sound synthesis and processing. Gesture-based interaction is enabled via Leap Motion 2 by Ultrahaptics, connected through USB.

Participants interact with the installation using intuitive hand gestures to switch between urban and green environments, trigger site-specific field recordings, and modulate the intensity of sound effects. This interactive framework transforms passive listening into a dynamic and expressive auditory experience, allowing users to 'conduct' the soundscape and engage with the acoustic environment in a participatory, embodied manner.

3.2 Selection of Cities

From 2016 to 2023, the 'Comprehensive Ranking of Global Cities' (2023, 11th Edition) prepared by the Global Power City Index (GPCI, 2023) consistently ranked London, New York, and Tokyo as the top three global cities. The GPCI rests on the assumption that a city's ability to attract people and businesses—its 'magnetism'—stems from its overall capabilities. This comprehensive ranking evaluates major cities worldwide across six dimensions: economy, research and development, cultural interaction, liveability, environment, and accessibility.

Because the author lives in Tokyo, this study focuses on cities within the Kanto metropolitan area, such as Tokyo, Yokohama, and Saitama.

3.3 Operation of the System

The system functions as follows (Figure 1):

1. Leap Motion captures the participant's hand positions (spatial coordinate data) and transmits them to the PC.
2. Touch Designer uses hand position data to control the target's position on the screen.
3. Simultaneously, hand coordinate data is transmitted to PD via OSC (Open Sound Control).
4. PD uses hand coordinate data to trigger the playback of soundscape audio.

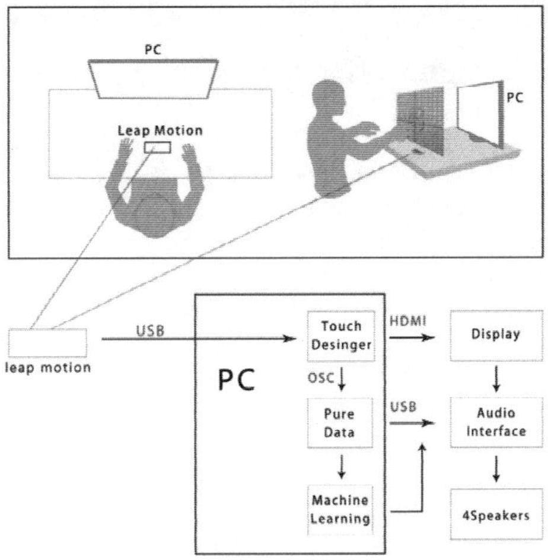

Figure 1. System

4. DEVELOPMENTS IN VER.4.0

After the Ver.3.0 presentation and Ver. 3.5 demo exhibition, participants and researchers suggested several technical improvements aimed at enhancing the immersive experience. Many of these suggestions focused on enhancing the auditory experience, emphasising the importance of creating a realistic spatial sound experience to deepen participants' engagement with the environment. In Ver.4.0, the following enhancements were made to improve the auditory spatial experience.

4.1 Preliminary Study on Spatial Sound Dynamics Design

Two commonly used methods for spatial sound control are Vector-Based Amplitude Panning (VBAP) and Higher-Order Ambisonics (HOA). HOA synthesises a full 360-degree sound field using spherical harmonic functions, enabling precise three-dimensional sound localisation. Unlike channel-based methods, HOA is not limited by a fixed number of loudspeakers; instead, the number of speakers depends on the Ambisonics order and practical implementation constraints (Gandemer et al., 2018).

However, human auditory perception is more accurate on the horizontal plane than on the vertical, due to anatomical features of the auditory system (Grantham, 1986; Perrott and Musicant, 1997; Lewald, 2013). Therefore, the present study adopts VBAP, which emphasises horizontal spatialisation and is particularly suitable for immersive installation environments.

To enhance spatial expressiveness, this study designs sound trajectories using geometric curves in polar coordinates. Compared to linear or fixed-point movements in Cartesian coordinates, polar trajectories enable smoother transitions and more dynamic spatial motion (Watanabe, 2024).

Version 4.0 adopts a four-speaker horizontal VBAP configuration, extending the standard three-speaker setup. This configuration offers two main advantages: it simplifies angle calculations during installation and enhances the fluidity of spatial sound movement. The integration of VBAP with polar trajectory design thus provides a robust technical foundation for creating immersive and exhibition-friendly spatial sound experiences.

5. SOUND TRAJECTORY SYSTEM CONFIGURATION

The system is primarily focused on two modes: Soundscape Mode and Symphony Mode. Each mode is described in detail below.

5.1 Sound Trajectory Design of the Soundscape Mode

The term 'soundscape' refers to an 'auditory landscape' that extends beyond mere physical sound. Soundscape studies examine how individuals perceive, interpret, and ascribe meaning to environmental sounds, which are shaped by cultural and social contexts. These sounds include not only music and anthropogenic noise but also natural elements such as wind, rain, birdsong, and insects (Schafer, 1993).

Such sounds—whether consciously perceived or not—can evoke emotional responses and memories, reconnecting individuals with specific times and places (McCartney, 2002).

Consequently, soundscapes are increasingly recognised not merely as noise or acoustic data, but as vital components that influence human well-being and environmental awareness (Schulte-Fortkamp and Dubois, 2006; Deng et al., 2009; Schulte-Fortkamp, 2013).

Building on this perspective, the present study introduces an interactive installation that uses real-world recordings from urban green spaces to investigate how ecological conditions shape acoustic environments. In Soundscape Mode, participants use hand gestures to interact with field recordings from Tokyo, Yokohama, and Saitama, generating personalised and spatially immersive auditory experiences.

Based on on-site surveys, the system investigates how variations in green space coverage and urban structure influence sound propagation and reflection. For each city, the system calculates the green coverage ratio within a five-kilometre radius of the city centre and uses these data to generate spatial sound trajectories. These trajectories represent the distribution and density of greenery, enabling participants to perceive how urban ecological differences shape acoustic textures.

When participants move their open right hand, a green particle circle appears on screen and follows the motion in real time. As the circle moves across different urban zones, its size dynamically adjusts according to each area's green coverage ratio. Entering a new urban zone triggers corresponding field recordings and sound layers, enabling users to explore in real time how variations in urban greenery influence the acoustic environment. This integration of gesture-based control, dynamic spatial audio, and responsive visuals creates a multisensory, embodied experience that deepens intuitive awareness of ecological and acoustic diversity across urban environments.

5.1.1 The Sound Trajectory of Tokyo

The cardioid trajectory, a heart-shaped curve generated by a circle rolling around another of equal size, is employed to simulate the green space distribution in central Tokyo. This pattern reflects the city's dense high-rise structures and intricate transport networks, creating a soundscape characterised by swift propagation and frequent reflections. The resulting auditory dynamics enhance the perception of motion and complexity, evoking Tokyo's fast-paced urban acoustics (Figures 2 and 3).

$x = 2r \cos\theta \, (1 - \cos\theta)$

$y = 2r\sin\theta \, (1 - \cos\theta)$

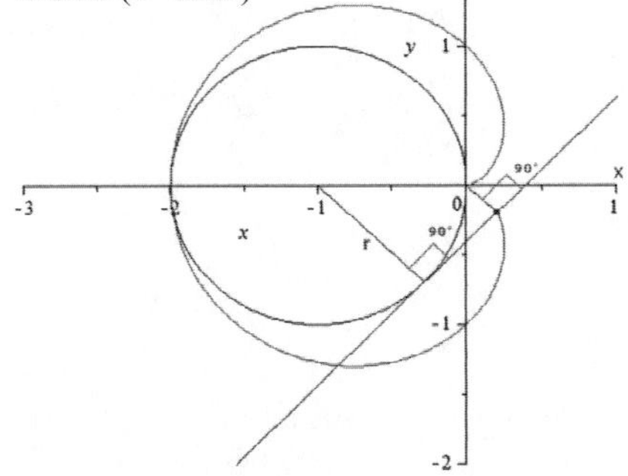

Figure 2. The Formula for Calculating a Cardioid Curve

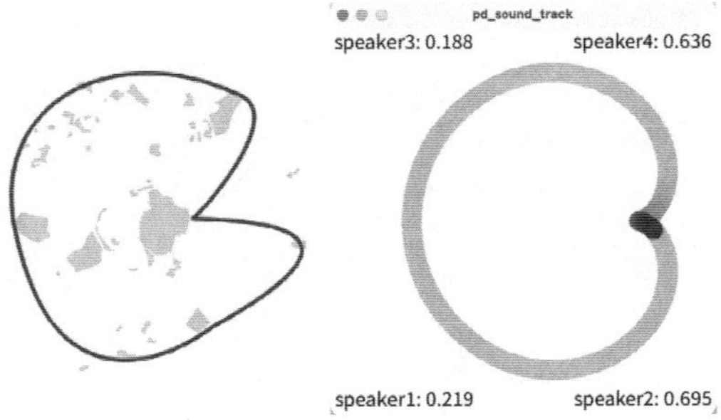

Figure 3. Simulation of Sound Cardioid Trajectories in Processing

5.1.2 The Sound Trajectory of Yokohama

The Tricuspid trajectory, or Steiner curve, formed by a circle rolling within another with three times its diameter, is applied to represent central Yokohama. As a coastal city with open waterfronts and vibrant port activity, Yokohama has a soundscape marked by transience and fluidity—sounds emerge and fade quickly across open spaces. The curve's three pronounced cusps evoke this ephemeral quality, creating a rhythm of dispersal and return that reflects the auditory dynamics of the city (Figures 4 and 5).

$x = (R - r) \cos\theta + r \cos\,(R - r\,/r\,{*}\theta),\ R = 3r$

$y = (R - r) \sin\theta + r \sin\,(R - r\,/r\,{*}\theta),\ \mathrm{R} = 3r$

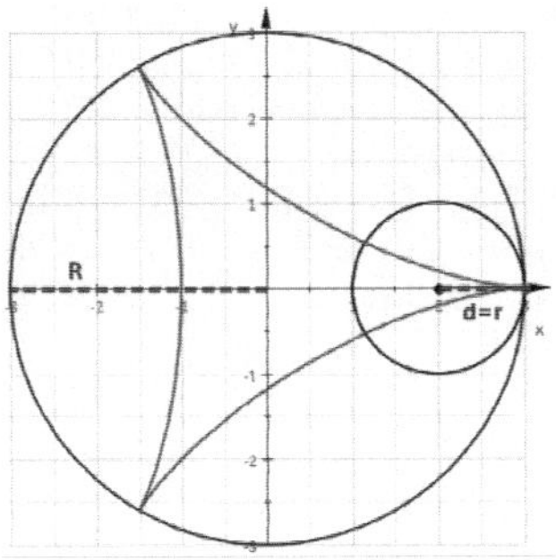

Figure 4. The Formula for Calculating a Tricuspid Curve

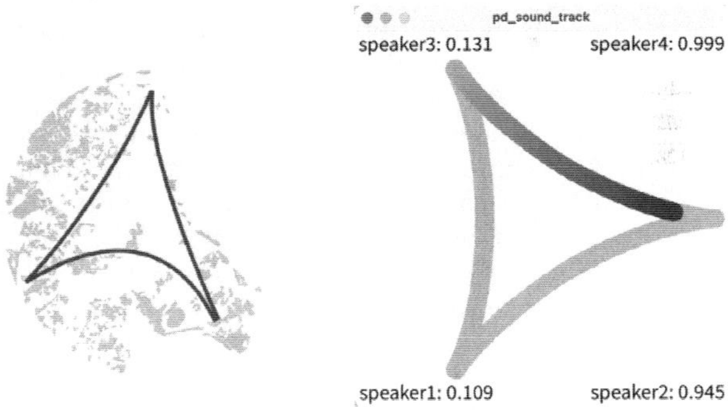

Figure 5. Simulation of Sound Tricuspid Trajectories in Processing

5.1.3 The Sound Trajectory of Saitama

The Epitrochoid trajectory, traced by a point on a circle rolling along the outside of a larger circle, is used for central Saitama. With its expansive farmland and low-rise landscapes, Saitama offers an auditory environment of slow, far-reaching sound propagation. The spiralling, outward-reaching form of the epitrochoid simulates this spaciousness, reinforcing a sense of tranquillity, openness, and gradual sonic diffusion (Figures 6 and 7).

$x = (R+r)\ \cos\theta - r\ \cos\ (R+r\ /r\ {*}\theta),\ R = 3r$

$y = (R+r)\ \sin\theta - r\ \sin\ (R+r\ /r\ {*}\theta),\ R = 3r$

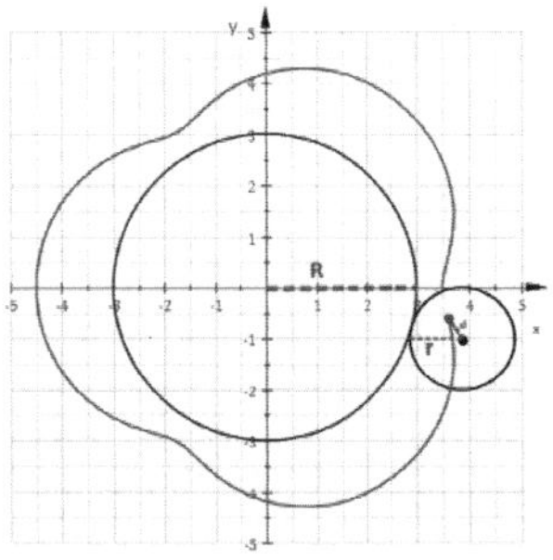

Figure 6. The Formula for Calculating an Epitrochoid Curve

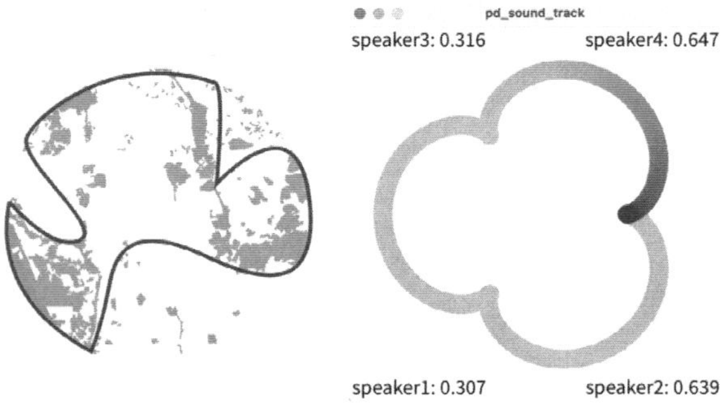

Figure 7. Simulation of Sound Epitrochoid Trajectories in Processing

5.2 Sound Trajectory Design of the Symphony Mode

In Symphony Mode, machine-learning techniques are employed to musically transform urban environmental sounds, enabling participants to 'conduct' the soundscape using hand gestures. This mode reimagines urban noise not as disruption but as creative material, offering an expressive and immersive musical experience that invites participants to reinterpret the acoustic environment from a performative perspective.

Machine-learning approaches are generally categorised into supervised, unsupervised, and reinforcement learning. For example, Support Vector Machines (SVMs), as a type of supervised model, learn from labelled data to classify or predict outcomes.

In the domain of music and sound synthesis, numerous models have been developed and creatively applied. The Realtime Audio Variational Autoencoder (RAVE), introduced by Caillon and Esling (2021), enables real-time timbral transformation and has been widely adopted in musical contexts. Other notable models include So-VITS-SVC (for singing voice conversion), Differentiable Digital Signal Processing (DDSP), and modified versions of BERT for symbolic music and audio understanding. Artistic applications of these technologies include transforming violin sounds into water-like textures using a texture-based model (Kumon, 2022) and generating real-time music from brainwave data via an SVM-based system (Inoue, 2022).

These examples underscore the creative potential of machine learning in expanding the expressive dimensions of sound. Building on this foundation, the present installation leverages RAVE to analyse and recompose environmental recordings into layered, symphonic textures. The source material derives from the field recordings used in Soundscape Mode but is algorithmically transformed to reveal novel sonic dimensions.

When participants close their right hand into a fist, Symphony Mode is activated for the currently selected city. The movement of the clenched hand then controls the trajectory of the sound layers, orchestrating their spatial dynamics and visual representations in real time.

The resulting auditory experience, delivered via a four-channel spatial audio system, is shaped in real time by the performer's gestures. Through this embodied act of 'conducting', participants engage with environmental sounds not merely as passive listeners, but as active interpreters. Familiar noises—once unnoticed—are reframed as expressive musical components. In this way, Symphony Mode fosters a renewed awareness of the urban soundscape, transforming listening into an act of creative discovery.

5.2.1 RAVE

The RAVE model (Caillon and Esling, 2021) is a variational autoencoder specifically designed for fast, high-quality audio synthesis. RAVE employs a unique two-stage training process:

1. Initial Training as a Variational Autoencoder (VAE): The model is initially trained as a standard VAE, focusing on representation learning.

2. Fine-Tuning with Adversarial Objectives: The model is further refined using adversarial generation objectives to achieve high-quality audio synthesis.

The RAVE model integrates multi-band decomposition of the original waveform with classical synthesis blocks, inspired by Engel et al. (2017), enabling high-quality audio synthesis at sampling rates up to 48 kHz without significantly increasing computational complexity. Analysing the latent space after training enables a controlled balance between reconstruction fidelity and representational compactness. This enables intuitive exploration and manipulation of latent trajectories. The model's compact architecture, low parameter count, and ability to converge on complex datasets enable real-time operation on standard laptop CPUs. RAVE demonstrates exceptional performance in automatic audio modelling and has applications in areas such as signal compression and timbral-style transformation.

5.2.2 The use of [nn~] in PD

The [nn~] object (Wesch, 2025) acts as a bridge between PD and the Libtorch C++ interface, enabling the integration of pre-trained deep-learning models—such as RAVE—into the PD environment. This intermediary layer allows real-time neural audio processing within PD, making advanced machine-learning capabilities accessible for interactive sound-based applications.

In this project, a pre-trained RAVE model developed by Antoine Caillon—originally trained on musical data—was integrated via [nn~] to enable real-time transformation of environmental field recordings into musical textures.

6. CONCLUSION AND FUTURE RESEARCH

This study explores the integration of urban green space distribution into soundscape art through the development of the Urban Green Symphony system. Evolving from Ver.1.0 to Ver.4.0, the latest iteration features a four-channel speaker configuration and trajectory designs informed by real-world green space distribution, significantly enhancing immersion and spatial perception.

The system presently includes only three trajectory types, which limits the range of spatial expression. Future work will involve user experience studies with Ver.4.0 to evaluate spatial localisation accuracy and immersive efficacy. Insights from these evaluations will inform the expansion and refinement of trajectory patterns, thereby improving the system's adaptability and expressive capacity. Additional efforts will focus on optimising user interaction and system responsiveness.

To further deepen immersion and personalisation, upcoming versions will incorporate a custom-trained RAVE model based on the project's environmental sound data. This will enable more context-sensitive and musically expressive transformations of urban noise into immersive spatial performances.

REFERENCES

Caillon, A., Esling, P. (2021). RAVE (Realtime Audio Variational Autoencoder), IRCAM - Sorbonne Université (online), https://arxiv.org/pdf/2111.05011.pdf.

Deng, Z., Wu, W., Shi, D. (2009). Two case studies on the soundscape in historical area and its subjective assessment from the local people. In INTER-NOISE and NOISE-CON Congress and Conference Proceedings, Vol. 2009, No. 4, pp. 2672–2680.

Engel, J., Hantrakul, L., Gu, C. and Roberts, A. (2019). DDSP: Differentiable Digital Signal Processing. Technical report. URL https://goo.gl/magenta/ ddsp-examples.

Engel, J., Resnick, C., Roberts, A., Dieleman, S., Norouzi, M., Eck, D., and Simonyan, K. (2017). Neural Audio Synthesis of Musical Notes with WaveNet Autoencoders. ISSN 2640-3498. URL https://proceedings.mlr.press/v70/engel17a.html.

Gandemer, L., Parseihian, G., Bourdin, C., et al. (2018). Perception of surrounding sound source trajectories in the horizontal plane: A comparison of VBAP and basic-decoded HOA. JActa Acustica united with Acustica, Vol. 104, No. 2, pp. 338–350.

GPCI (Global Power City Index). (2023). Institute for Urban Strategies the Mori Memorial Foundation (online), https://mori-m-foundation.or.jp/english/ius2/gpci2/index.shtml.

Grantham, D. W. (1986). Detection and discrimination of simulated motion of auditory targets in the horizontal plane. The Journal of the Acoustical Society of America, Vol. 79, No. 6, pp. 1939–1949.

Inoue, H., (2022). Music generation in real-time using SVM on EEG data. Japanese Society for Sonic Arts, Vol. 14, No. 3, pp. 24–30.

Kumon, T., Osaka, N. (2022). Creation of live electronics music using timber transfer with RAVE. Japanese Society for Sonic Arts, Vol. 14, No. 3, pp. 6–10.

LeapMotion2, Ultraleap, https://www.ultraleap.com/.

Lewald, J. (2013). Exceptional ability of blind humans to hear sound motion: Implications for the emergence of auditory space. Neuropsychologic, Vol. 51, No. 1, pp. 181–186.

McCartney, A. (2002). Circumscribed journeys through soundscape composition. Organised Sound, Vol. 7, No. 1, pp. 1–3.

Perrott, D. R., Musicant, A. D. (1997). Minimum auditory movement angle: Binaural localisation of moving sound sources. The Journal of the Acoustical Society of America, Vol. 62, No. 6, pp. 1463–1466.

PureData, Miller Puckette, https://puredata.info.

Schafer, R. M. (1993). The soundscape: Our sonic environment and the tuning of the world, San Francisco, Simon and Schuster.

Schulte-Fortkamp, B. (2013). Soundscape-A matter of human resources. In INTER-NOISE and NOISE-CON Congress and Conference Proceedings, Vol. 247, No. 3, pp. 4738–4742.

Schulte-Fortkamp, B., Dubois, D. (2006). Recent advances in soundscape research-Preface. Acta Acustica united with Acustica, Vol. 92, No. 6, pp. 5—8.

TouchDesigner, Derivative, https://derivative.ca/.

Watanabe, H. (2024). Controlling sound movement using geometric curves in “Anamnèse” for flute and electroacoustics. Japanese Society for Sonic Arts, Vol. 16, No. 2, pp. 7—12.

Wesch, B. (2025). Ircam: nn-tilde, GitHub-actions, https://acids-ircam.github.io/nn-tilde/.

Yan, X., Matsumura, S. (2024)(a). “Urban Green Symphony” Installation Exhibit, Intercollege Sonic Arts Festival 2023, Aichi University of the Arts, https://ic.jssa.info/.

Yan, X., Matsumura, S. (2024)(b). The interactive sound installation “Urban Green Symphony”. Japanese Society for Sonic Arts, Vol. 16, No. 2, pp. 14–19.

Yan, X., Matsumura, S., (2024)(c). Verification of the Interactive Soundscape Work “Urban Green Symphony” Ver. 2.0. The Society for Art and Science, NICOGRAPH2024, pp. P-2:1– P-2:2.

Yan, X., Matsumura, S. (2024)(d). “Urban Green Symphony” Ver. 2.0 Installation Exhibit, NICOGRAPH2024, Tokyo City University, https://www.art-science.org/nicograph/nico2024/.

Yan, X., Matsumura, S. (2024)(e). Interactive Soundscape Installation “Urban Green Symphony” Ver.3.0, Asia Digital Art and Design Association (ADADA) International Conference 2024, Taiwan, https://adada.info/2024/index.html.

Yan, X., Matsumura, S. (2025)(f). “Urban Green Symphony Ver.3.5” Installation Exhibit, Intercollege Sonic Arts Festival 2024, Doshisha Women’s College of Liberal Arts, https://ic.jssa.info/.

USING SENTIMENT ANALYSIS TO UNCOVER PLAYER RESPONSE TO GAME UPDATES VIA SOCIAL MEDIA

Niklas Böckmann and Neil Bretaña
IU International University of Applies Sciences
Bad Honnef, Germany

ABSTRACT

In this age of iterative game design, understanding player reactions to individual game updates is critical for improving player satisfaction and engagement. In this study, we introduce a novel methodology for analyzing sentiment of comments made on Reddit for League of Legends patch notes. Our approach utilizes the Reddit API and Google Natural Language API to generate sentiment and magnitude scores for comments on various patch updates. The analysis reveals distinct patterns in player sentiment across different patches, highlighting how updates influence player satisfaction. We used visualization tools, such as sentiment distributions and word clouds, to provide a comprehensive view of these reactions, emphasizing key trends and significant comments. Key findings include the identification of distinct sentiment patterns associated with each patch update and a nuanced understanding of player feedback through the most positive and negative comments. By bridging the gap between developer intentions and player experiences, our research offers actionable insights for game development and highlights the unique value of using Reddit discussions as a patch-labeled data source for sentiment analysis in gaming. This study addresses a significant gap in understanding sentiment surrounding game updates and provides a methodology that can be applied to assist in game development.

KEYWORDS

Games, Data Analytics, Sentiment Analysis

1. INTRODUCTION

Sentiment analysis is a method of evaluating words, phrases, or sentence structures within text to determine its emotional tone. It is widely used across various domains, including business, where it helps companies track customer satisfaction and brand reputation. Governments and organizations also leverage sentiment analysis to monitor public opinion on policies or events. As computational power and natural language processing techniques have advanced, sentiment analysis has become more accurate and sophisticated, turning qualitative data into actionable, quantitative insights (Liu, 2012).

Sentiment analysis is especially valuable in the gaming industry, where understanding player feedback can have a significant impact on game design and player engagement. Traditionally, game analytics has focused on internal game data, such as player behavior and gameplay metrics, to assess the player experience (El-Nasr et al., 2013). However, with the rise of external data sources, sentiment analysis is now increasingly being applied to social media and other platforms to gain insights into player sentiment, complementing traditional internal game data (Zagal et al., 2012).

Sentiment analysis of Reddit gaming content has been gaining traction in recent years. For instance, Balcıoğlu et al. (2025) recently did a large-scale study on mobile game reviews from Reddit, highlighting how player sentiment shifts with updates and gameplay elements. These findings illustrate how Reddit can effectively capture how players respond to games.

Most sentiment analysis in gaming so far has focused on aggregated reviews from platforms like Steam and Metacritic, which capture the general player sentiment over time (Yu et al., 2023; Strååt et al., 2017). However, these analyses fail to address player reactions to specific game updates. Player feedback about individual updates, such as changes in gameplay or content, is often lost in generalized reviews, making it difficult to analyze detailed reactions to game updates (Zagal et al., 2012; Lu et al., 2020; Yu et al., 2021).

Studies have shown that player performance and engagement can vary significantly before and after updates (Hyeong et al., 2020; Zhong et al., 2022; He et al., 2021). Yet, existing research has not fully addressed sentiment analysis targeted at game updates themselves. While some studies have recognized the need for this type of analysis, they continue to rely on more general data, leaving a gap in research that focuses on game updates.

This paper aims to address this gap by exploring sentiment analysis within game update discussions on the social media website Reddit, where players engage in real-time, in-depth discussions about the latest patches and changes to games. In this paper, we look at player feedback toward game updates for League of Legends. So-called "Games-as-a-service" or "Live-service games" like League of Legends, frequently releases updates or "patches" that adjust game mechanics, introduce new content, or balance gameplay elements. These updates can drastically alter the player experience, leading to a broad range of reactions from excitement to frustration. Such reactions are commonly expressed on Reddit, particularly in the subreddit r/leagueoflegends, which serves as a platform for players to discuss their experiences and opinions. These discussions are often highly specific, labeled according to the version of the game update, making them a rich source of real-time feedback. Yet, the potential of this data for sentiment analysis – especially in tracking player sentiment over time as new updates are rolled out – remains largely untapped.

2. METHODS

The analysis is divided into two primary phases: Data Collection and Data Analysis.

2.1 Data Collection and Pre-Processing

The data collection process is composed of the following: selecting Reddit game update subreddit URLs, game update comment collection via Reddit API, and sentiment analysis using Google Natural Language API.

2.1.1 Selecting the Reddit game update subreddit URLs

The process begins with the manual selection of relevant League of Legends subreddits that publish game update posts. Each post adheres to a specific URL structure, which is crucial for identifying and collecting the appropriate data. The typical URL format for these posts is composed of a submission ID and patch version. The URL "https://www.reddit.com/r/leagueoflegends/comments/" is the fixed prefix for all game update posts within the League of Legends subreddit. The "submission_id" represents a unique identifier for each specific post, which varies with every update and is randomly generated by Reddit. The "patchVersion" indicates the version of the patch being discussed, in this case patch 14.10.

To accurately collect and analyze data, the patch URLs were manually collected for each update. Since the "submission_id" values were not automatically generated, the process involved manually checking the subreddit for new posts each month and ensuring that each URL followed the described structure. While this approach worked for the scope of this study, future work could automate this process for scalability. For this analysis, only League of Legends Reddit subreddits for patches 14.10 up to 14.16 (patches from January until August 2024) were included.

2.1.2 Collecting Reddit Comments via Reddit's API

The Reddit API provides structured access to platform data, allowing developers to retrieve and process information programmatically (Reddit, 2025). For collecting comments from multiple threads within a specific subreddit, the API offers efficient methods to extract relevant data. The primary API endpoints utilized in this process include those for retrieving submissions and their associated comments.

Based on the parsed URLs and their submission IDs, the necessary data fields are extracted. The minimal required data fields for this analysis include: the comment text and the patch version. By collecting the patch version from the subreddit title or URL, each comment is labeled, enabling patch-specific sentiment analysis.

This is achieved using the "reddit.submission(submission_id)" method, which retrieves a submission object corresponding to the desired post. The "submission.comments.replace_more(limit=None)" method is then used to access all comments in the submission. This ensures that all nested comments are loaded by replacing MoreComments objects with actual comment data. Finally, the "submission.comments.list()" method retrieves all comments from the submission, including those across multiple threads. This was saved into a two-column CSV file, with columns for patch version and comment text as shown in table 1.

Table 1. Data structure of collected Reddit comments on patch update 14.10

Patch Version	Comment Text
1410	worst patch
1410	I love many things I see in this patch. Hopefully it will play out the way I think it will be.
1410	Not sure i like the mastery revamp. before when you were queued up with a 1mil pts lvl6 yasuo you at least knew what you were in for
1410	Sooo..why did they make lane Viego a thing again? Don't get me wrong, I'm having a blast picking it blind and listening to the whining of anyone who didn't expect it, but it does feel a little silly lol
1410	This Mastery system is straight up awful and needs to be removed/reverted back as soon as possible, i refuse to play with it in game.

2.1.3 Analyzing Sentiment with Google Natural Language API

The second step involves analyzing the sentiment of the comments using a sentiment analysis tool. In this case, we utilize the Google Natural Language API and store the results within the same table. Two new columns were added: Sentiment Score, which ranges from -1.0 (very negative) to 1.0 (very positive), and a magnitude score from 0 to infinity, which reflects the overall emotional strength of the comment, regardless of its positivity or negativity (Google Cloud, 2025). Deleted comments and very short replies, typically consisting of only one or two words, were excluded to avoid unnecessary API costs.

We loaded the comments into a Pandas DataFrame, providing a structured format for handling large datasets, which facilitates efficient manipulation and analysis, before individually processing each comment with the Google Cloud Natural Language API, adding the respective sentiment and magnitude score values to each row of the CSV file (table 2).

Table 2. Data structure of collected Reddit comments on patch update 14.10 including Google Natural Language API sentiment and magnitude score

Patch Version	**Comment Text**	**Sentiment Score**	**Magnitude Score**
1410	worst patch	-0,8	0,8
1410	I love many things I see in this patch. Hopefully it will play out the way I think it will be.	0.7	1.5
1410	Not sure i like the mastery revamp. before when you were queued up with a 1mil pts lvl6 yasuo you at least knew what you were in for	-0.4	0.9
1410	Sooo..why did they make lane Viego a thing again? Don't get me wrong, I'm having a blast picking it blind and listening to the whining of anyone who didn't expect it, but it does feel a little silly lol	0	1.2
1410	This Mastery system is straight up awful and needs to be removed/reverted back as soon as possible, i refuse to play with it in game.	-0.3	0.9

2.2 Data Analysis and Visualization

In the data analysis phase, sentiment scores and the corresponding text were thoroughly examined. This includes a semantic exploration to uncover the underlying meaning and context of user comments, ensuring a nuanced understanding of sentiment expression. Visualizations were then employed to illustrate sentiment scores across different patch versions, providing a clear overview of sentiment trends. Additionally, word clouds were generated to highlight frequently mentioned terms, and comments with the highest and lowest sentiment scores are identified to pinpoint areas of particular interest or concern.

2.2.1 Visualizing Sentiment Distribution per Patch

A key question is how players perceive a particular game update in comparison to previous ones. We answered this by visualizing the median sentiment distribution of patches in chronological order. To compute and visualize sentiment scores for each patch version, we first grouped the data based on the patch version. For each group, the median sentiment scores were calculated. Using the median instead of average reduces the impact of extreme values, providing a more accurate representation of typical sentiment. We then visualized the median sentiment scores using a bar plot. The x-axis represents the patch version and the y-axis shows the corresponding median sentiment score.

2.2.2 Creating Word Cloud of Most Frequently Used Words

To get a summary of the feedback, we displayed the most frequently used words in the most positive and negative comments using word clouds. The data were first grouped by patch version. Comments were filtered based on sentiment scores, with negative and positive feedback separated by predefined thresholds of -0.5 and 0.5. While the choice of threshold clearly influences the result, the ±0.5 cutoff was selected after experimenting with different values to find a balance that made the word clouds both meaningful and readable. The goal was to filter out noise without losing too much content. As the choice of thresholds significantly affects result interpretation, careful adjustment according to specific research objectives and dataset characteristics is recommended. The filtered comments were tokenized and preprocessed to remove punctuation and common stop words. Word frequencies were then counted, and the word cloud was created, with word size reflecting the frequency of each term.

2.2.3 Printing Comments with Highest and Lowest Sentiment

To fully interpret the underlying sentiments in the comments, we identified the raw comments that exhibit clearly positive or negative sentiments. To analyze Reddit sentiment data across all patch versions, the data was processed to identify the 10 comments with the lowest and highest sentiment scores for each patch version. For each patch version, the most negative and most positive comments were extracted.

3. RESULTS AND DISCUSSION

Reddit, as a platform, is uniquely suited for such analyzes, especially for popular games like League of Legends. Subreddits dedicated to specific games foster communities of highly engaged and knowledgeable players who have a deep understanding of the game's mechanics, lore, and community dynamics. These users often provide detailed, nuanced feedback that goes beyond superficial opinions, making their discussions an invaluable resource for developers and researchers. Players on these subreddits are not casual players; they tend to be invested in the game's progression and are vocal about how specific updates affect their experience. This makes Reddit a goldmine for feedback that is not only immediate but also often more insightful than reviews posted on traditional platforms. However, the findings may not be fully representative, as they primarily reflect the views of highly engaged players and cannot be generalized to casual or less active players.

Using the subreddit r/leagueoflegends, we collected a dataset consisting of 14,549 comments. Sentiment analysis results indicate that players predominantly perceive the League of Legends patch versions negatively, with sentiment scores typically ranging from -0.2 to -0.3 across most versions (Figure 1). The exception is patch version 14.9, which exhibits a notably more negative sentiment score of -0.4.

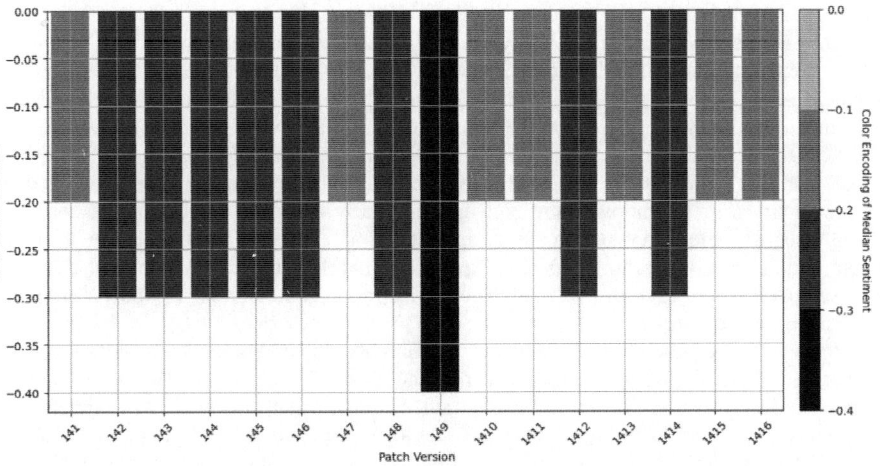

Figure 1. Median Sentiment Scores by Patch Version

The word clouds generated allow for the human interpretation of the most dominant themes (Figure 2). A particularly promising example is the word cloud for patch version 14.9, based on negative sentiment comments. Frequently occurring terms such as "nerf," "buff," "damage," and "item" indicate player dissatisfaction with game balancing, a critical aspect of live-service and esports-oriented games. Additionally, the word cloud highlights a focus on Riot's "Vanguard" – the newly introduced anti-cheat software. However, the word cloud also illustrates a key limitation: While recurring terms indicate areas of dissatisfaction, they alone do not provide sufficient context to interpret players' specific concerns. Without considering the full context of the comments, including their connections and nuances, a precise understanding of the issues is not possible. Additionally, the presence of irrelevant words often clutters the chart. Further tweaking of the analysis is necessary to improve the clarity of the results.

Figure 2. Word Cloud of Frequent Negative Terms in User Feedback for Patch 14.9 (Sentiment < -0.5)

The printed comments for patch version 14.9 allow closer inspection of the individual users' experience and feedback. Previously, the main topic "Vanguard" was already identified for this patch version. While the aggregated data left room for interpretation, these individual user comments have a clear message complaining about the forced installation of Riot's anti-virus. Users express concerns over security and fairness, highlighting the emotional impact of these changes. These comments illustrate the importance of directly examining user feedback, as sentiment analysis alone cannot fully capture the complexity of user concerns. Following the explanation of the data analysis methodology, it is valuable to transition to a broader examination of its significance within the context of game analytics and related research. The exploration of sentiment analysis in game update discussions is highly relevant for several reasons. First, the nature of live-service games like League of Legends, where regular updates are a key part of the gaming experience, makes understanding real-time player feedback critical for maintaining player satisfaction. Updates can introduce significant changes to gameplay mechanics, balance and player behavior. Player responses to these updates often provide essential feedback for developers seeking to iterate and improve their games. By analyzing sentiment, developers can better understand the impact of their updates, identifying areas of success or dissatisfaction that may not be captured in broader game reviews or by traditional game analytics.

Platforms like Reddit offer a unique structure that facilitates update-specific sentiment analysis. Each discussion thread is labeled by the version of the game update, providing an organized way to categorize feedback and track sentiment over time. This is particularly valuable for games like League of Legends, where frequent updates can lead to evolving player opinions as new features or balances are introduced. The ability to segment and analyze discussions based on specific updates allows researchers and developers to track how player sentiment changes with each patch, offering more granular insights into the factors driving player satisfaction or frustration.

Moreover, the Reddit community is made up of highly engaged players who are often experts in the games they discuss. These players possess an in-depth understanding of the mechanics and dynamics of the game, and their feedback tends to be more detailed and informed than that of casual players. This makes Reddit discussions especially valuable for developers seeking to understand the finer points of how an update affects gameplay. By focusing on these discussions, researchers can gain deeper insights into the expectations and concerns of the most dedicated player base, which is often the most vocal and influential in shaping community sentiment. Conversely, Reddit discussions may not fully represent the views of all players, as casual and infrequent players are less inclined to participate in detailed conversations regarding each patch version.

4. CONCLUSION

This study demonstrates an integration of the Reddit API for retrieving and aggregating comment data from various threads within specific subreddits. This approach has streamlined the extraction of comments, allowing for a comprehensive dataset that supports detailed analysis. The application of the Google Natural Language API for sentiment analysis has further enhanced this process by providing a clear overview of the emotional tone within the comments. The sentiment analysis, powered by advanced machine learning models, helps to quickly discern overall sentiment trends, making it easier to understand the general mood of the comment data.

Looking ahead, future research could focus on leveraging these AI tools to generate more coherent and insightful summaries that can assist game developers. By focusing on game update discussions, this research contributes to the growing body of work on game analytics by introducing a more granular approach to understanding player feedback. This analysis not only captures detailed player reactions to updates but also allows developers to track evolving sentiments of game updates over time.

Given the growing prevalence of live-service games, where regular updates are a core part of the game lifecycle, understanding real-time player sentiment is critical for iterative game design and community engagement. The analysis of update-specific discussions represents a relatively new opportunity in game analytics, offering actionable insights that can enhance player satisfaction and drive game improvement in a more dynamic and responsive manner.

REFERENCES

Balcıoğlu, Y. S. et al. (2025). Sentiment analysis of Reddit reviews on mobile gaming: Insights from the gaming community. *International Journal of Human–Computer Interaction.* https://doi.org/10.1080/10447318.2025.2464897

El-Nasr, M. et al. (2013). *Game analytics: Maximizing the value of player data.* Springer, London. https://doi.org/10.1007/978-1-4471-4769-5

Google Cloud (2025). *Cloud Natural Language API.* Google, Mountain View, USA. Retrieved from https://cloud.google.com/natural-language

He, Y. et al. (2021). Heterogeneous effects of software patches in a multiplayer online battle arena game. *Proceedings of the 16th International Conference on Foundations of Digital Games (FDG '21)*, Montreal, Canada, Article No. 11, pp. 1–9. https://doi.org/10.1145/3472538.3472550

Hyeong, J. H. et al. (2020). For whom does a game update? Players' status-contingent gameplay on online games before and after an update. *Decision Support Systems*, 139, 113423. https://doi.org/10.1016/j.dss.2020.113423

Liu, B. (2012). *Sentiment analysis and opinion mining*. Morgan & Claypool, San Rafael, USA. https://doi.org/10.1007/978-3-031-02145-9

Lu, C. et al. (2020). Patches and player community perceptions: Analysis of No Man's Sky Steam reviews. *Proceedings of the DiGRA 2020 Conference: Play Everywhere*, Tampere, Finland. Retrieved from https://dl.digra.org/index.php/dl/article/view/1303

Reddit (2025). *Reddit API*. Retrieved from https://www.reddit.com/dev/api/

Strååt, B. and Verhagen, H. (2017). Using user-created game reviews for sentiment analysis: A method for researching user attitudes. *Proceedings of GHITALY@CHItaly*, Italy.

Yu, Y. et al. (2023). Mining insights from esports game reviews with an aspect-based sentiment analysis framework. *IEEE Access*, 11, pp. 61161–61172. https://doi.org/10.1109/ACCESS.2023.3285864

Yu, Y. et al. (2021). Esports game updates and player perception: Data analysis of PUBG Steam reviews. *Proceedings of the 13th International Conference on Knowledge and Systems Engineering (KSE)*, Bangkok, Thailand, pp. 1–6. https://doi.org/10.1109/KSE53942.2021.9648670

Zagal, J. P. et al. (2012). Natural language processing in game studies research: An overview. *Simulation & Gaming*, 43(3), pp. 356–373. https://doi.org/10.1177/1046878111422560

Zhong, X. and Xu, J. (2022). Measuring the effect of game updates on player engagement: A cue from DOTA2. *Entertainment Computing*, 43, 100506. https://doi.org/10.1016/j.entcom.2022.100506

INTELLIGENT FROTH VELOCITY ESTIMATION THROUGH COMPUTER VISION TECHNIQUES

Abdullatif Al-Najim[1], Razan Al-Zannan[1], Erich Marko Lucic Oliva[2], Abrar Al-Amoudi[1], Mustafa Al-Naser[1] and Ayman Al-Mukahhil[1]

[1]*Yokogawa Saudi Arabia Company, Dhahran, Saudi Arabia*

[2]*Yokogawa America do Sul, Providencia, Chile*

ABSTRACT

The flotation process is one of the main mineral concentration technologies in the mining industry today. Therefore, effective monitoring and control of key froth parameters are important to maximize recovery and improve the quality of mineral concentrate. Operators and engineers adjust control decisions by observing various froth properties, with velocity being a key indicator of froth recovery. In this research, we introduce a computer vision-based algorithm to estimate froth velocity using images obtained from video recordings. The algorithm demonstrated a minimal mean absolute error (MAE) of less than 2 cm/s when compared to other system measurements, highlighting its accuracy. An advantage of the proposed method is its ability to provide a comprehensive analysis of the entire froth area, unlike alternating systems.

KEYWORDS

Flotation Process, Computer Vision, Froth Analysis, Froth Velocity, Mining, Image Analysis

1. INTRODUCTION

The mining industry is growing rapidly, with several investments, and advanced technologies have been developed in this business domain (Zmami et al., 2021). One of the most essential processes in the mineral industry is the froth flotation process, which is used as a solid-liquid separation method where the valuable ore minerals are separated from the less valuable materials based on differences in their hydrophobic properties, both natural and/or modified by means of reagents (Shean & Cilliers, 2011). In this process, air is injected into a flotation cell to generate bubbles that interact with hydrophobic mineral particles, allowing these particles to be separated by rising through the water medium to the surface (froth phase). The froth phase, which contains the valuable minerals, is then collected to produce a concentrate. This method is widely employed for extracting copper from sulfide ores, with 80% of the world's copper production relying on it (Yantén et al., 2023). However, the process is highly dependent on the quality of the froth, which is conventionally monitored through visual inspection of surface characteristics such as bubble size, froth color, and froth velocity. This manual inspection introduces subjectivity and inconsistency due to the reliance on operators' experience and judgment. The flotation process was introduced in the early 1900s, and although numerous research and development efforts have been made, it remains a complex process and is not fully understood. The complexity of froth flotation arises from the several variables that influence the process, including airflow, chemical reagents, froth depth, and feed conditions. These variables interact in complex patterns, making it challenging to accurately model the flotation process (Nakhaei et al., 2023). Conventionally, operators adjust the process setpoints based on a visual inspection of the froth phase, and this manual approach often results in delayed or incorrect adjustments, leading to inefficiencies such as mineral losses to tailings or suboptimal concentrate quality (Nakhaei et al., 2023; Guan et al., 2022). Currently, the level of automation in froth flotation remains low, with many flotation plants still relying on human observation, which is prone to errors and varies significantly between operators. Consequently, there is an increasing demand for advanced technologies that can provide metallurgical information about the flotation process, which can then be used to improve the accuracy of process control and reduce the need for manual intervention. Furthermore, increasing the level of automation in the flotation process is critical for improving performance, reducing operational costs, and ensuring consistent, high-quality concentrate production (Wang et al., 2018). Advanced process control (APC) has been implemented in the flotation process to eliminate input disturbances and maintain the process as close as possible to the steady state. These objectives are achieved by methods such as controlling mass pull, controlling recycling load, and controlling stream grade and/or recovery (Shean & Cilliers, 2011). Supomo et al. (2008) detailed a successful mass pull control strategy that uses machine vision to control the mass pull by measuring the velocity of the overflowing froth and then adjusting the froth depth. The second control strategy, re-circulating load control, reduces the residence time per flotation cell but enables valuable material to remain longer within the plant overall, thereby enhancing total recovery (Wills & Napier-Munn, 2006). In re-circulating load control, mass pull rates are measured and manipulated to eliminate input disturbances by regulating the recycled load rate. Furthermore, the grade and/or recovery control strategy has not been successfully implemented for advanced flotation control in industrial applications (Shean & Cilliers, 2011), and the reasons for this are, among other things, the complex behavior of the flotation process (Shean & Cilliers, 2011) and the lack of knowledge in control engineering required by operators and metallurgists (Wills & Napier-Munn, 2006; Hodouin et al., 2001; Thwaites, 2007). Other than APC, advanced technologies like computer vision have been introduced to quantify froth characteristics more accurately and objectively. These systems utilize images to extract froth features such as bubble size, froth velocity, and stability, and correlate them with key performance indicators like concentrate grade and recovery rate. With advancements in the dynamics of computer vision, it is possible to build better predictive flotation control models (Shean & Cilliers, 2011). For that purpose, this research utilizes computer vision techniques to propose an intelligent method for automated froth velocity estimation. The proposed method can assist operators in making accurate control decisions and reducing human error. The paper is organized as follows: Section 2 reviews previous methods in the literature for froth velocity estimation. Section 3 details the proposed method, and Section 4 validates it against other system measurements at a customer site. Finally, Section 5 summarizes the research outcomes.

2. LITERATURE REVIEW

Tang et al. (2009) discussed the relationship between froth velocity characteristics and froth flotation performance. The authors demonstrated a new fast template matching algorithm to calculate the froth velocity. The results in flotation production showed that decreasing the froth velocity turbulence degree can reduce the detachment ratio of the mineral particles on the bubbles, which in turn, improves the concentrate grade and decreases the ratio of minerals in the tailings. For that purpose, recent advances and technologies have been used in velocity estimation. These technologies can be categorized into three main groups: (a) classical statistical methods, (b) machine learning-based methods, and (c) image processing-based methods.

2.1 Classical Statistical Methods

In previous studies, several techniques were used to measure flow velocity. For example, Liu et al. (2013) proposed using the Scale-Invariant Feature Transform (SIFT) and Kalman filter to measure the velocity of froth flotation. This methodology can extract accurate velocity measurements under different conditions. Also, the research presented conclusive operational advice regarding the relationship between flotation performance and froth velocity.

2.2 Machine Learning-Based Methods

Froth velocity monitoring using machine learning has a positive impact on process performance. To maintain mass-pull stabilization rates between cells, an advanced camera system was developed by Williams and Oosthuizen (n.d.). The authors developed a system for monitoring the flotation cell using images from both boiling and non-boiling flotation cells. The dataset was trained using a Convolutional Neural Network (CNN). The results showed significant performance in detecting velocity, with an F1 accuracy of 94%. Jahedsaravani et al. (2023) proposed a pre-trained CNN model to measure froth velocity and bubble size from a froth flotation image dataset. As a result, this model proved to be a faster and more reliable approach compared to classical image preprocessing methods. Yang et al. (2023) proposed combining two deep learning methods—one is a cascade of unsupervised networks, and the other is a pre-trained supervised network. This approach showed accurate results in extracting froth velocity under high throughput conditions. Deep learning combined with a likelihood function was also used to extract froth velocity in the research by Lu et al. (2023). In addition, the SIFT algorithm was used to extract key features from froth images. This study demonstrated an efficient prediction model for extracting froth velocity.

2.3 Image Processing-Based Methods

Machine vision technologies were utilized by Moghadam et al. (2024), who proposed a model that used the Particle Image Velocimetry (PIV) technique for extracting froth velocity features. This research showed sufficient results with high accuracy for froth velocity. Zhang et al. (2021) used a new local feature-based method to measure velocity. The authors proposed a system integrating the new feature descriptor, Relative Position Information (RPI)-SURF, and the Local Image Correlation (LIC) from the nearest reference point. However, this method proved its efficiency after an extensive number of experiments.

While these methods may accurately estimate froth velocity, they also present certain limitations. For example, statistical methods (e.g., SIFT, Kalman filters) are often sensitive to image noise and lighting variations and can be computationally demanding, which limits their real-time applicability. Machine learning-based methods require large, labeled datasets and substantial computational resources, whereas training data may not be available in real scenarios. Meanwhile, image processing-based methods may struggle with accurate segmentation due to environmental changes and complex froth textures. These constraints highlight the importance of adopting adaptive approaches for reliable flotation monitoring.

3. METHODOLOGY

3.1 Data Collection & Processing

The objective of this research is to develop a method for calculating froth velocity. The dataset comprises video recordings of actual froth conditions obtained from the Chilean mining industry. To enhance the generalizability and robustness of the proposed method, the recordings were captured at various times of the day (08:27 and 17:10) across multiple flotation cells. Each video has a duration of approximately six minutes, providing diverse operating conditions and ensuring variability in the dataset.

3.2 Flotation Froth Image Processing

The proposed method analyzes the video by extracting sequential frames, which undergo several processing steps to determine froth velocity. The following sections detail the processing techniques used to estimate froth velocity at specific time frames.

3.2.1 Masking

The original images from the video capture the full cell. However, additional parts, such as the edges around the froth area, do not contribute to the analysis and may introduce noise. To achieve optimal analysis results, we first removed these parts by applying a masking technique, focusing only on the froth area. An example of the original image can be seen in Figure 1, while Figure 2 shows the image after applying the mask.

Figure 1. Original Image captured from the video

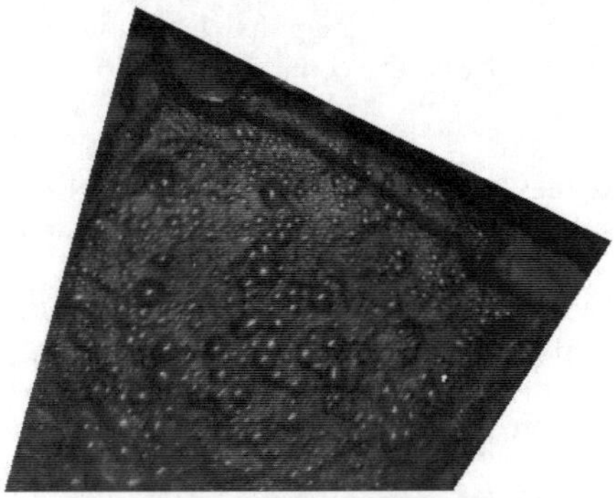

Figure 2. Image after applying the mask

3.2.2 Reference Area Selection

The velocity of froth is a key indicator of mineral recovery. Froth recovery occurs when it is poured from the edge of the cell, making velocity a variable that, together with other information, can be used to optimize ore recovery. However, it is possible to encounter situations where high velocity is directed away from the edge, indicating a lack of froth discharge into the concentrate trough, which reduces recovery. Therefore, estimating both the direction and magnitude of froth movement is crucial. To address this, we first identified the cell's top edge as a reference to determine whether the froth is moving toward it. It is possible to have more than one area of interest depending on the design and operation of the cell. However, we selected the top edge as the reference area because it is the edge of greatest interest from the point of view of cell operation in these cells.

3.2.3 Velocity Estimation

To measure froth velocity flow in a specific cell, the Optical Flow method has been applied. The Farneback method is used to demonstrate the flow of one cell, as shown in Figure 3. This method creates an optical flow object for estimating the direction and speed of moving objects.

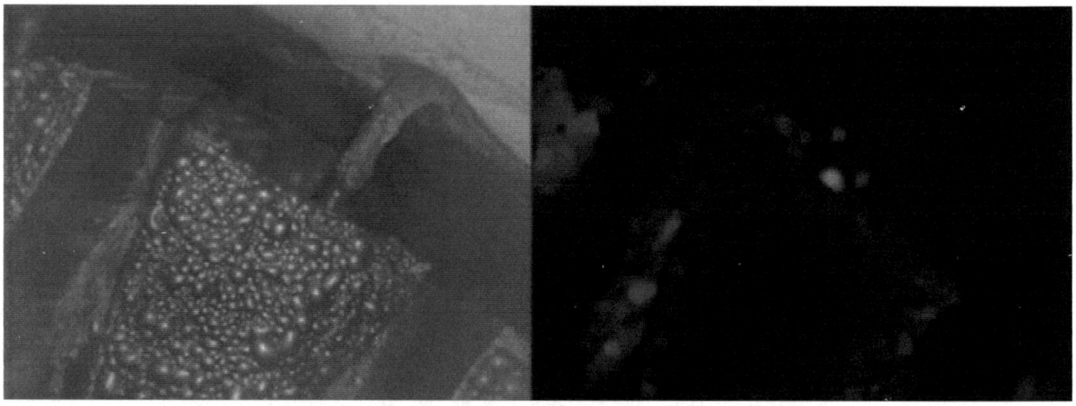

Figure 3. Opticalflow Farnback Method to measure velocity

3.2.4 Direction Estimation

The last step is to estimate the direction of the froth flow, which can determine the recovery state. If the froth flows toward the edge, it can be considered a desired condition. To estimate the direction, we first calculate the vector between the center point of the cell and the reference area. Then, we compute the dot product between this vector and the velocity vector obtained from the Optical Flow method. A positive result indicates that the angle between the vectors is ≤ 90 degrees, meaning they both point toward the cell's edge. Figure 4 visually represents the direction estimation process. The complete process is outlined in the following steps (see Figure 5 for a visual representation):

1. Read the video and extract two sequential frames.
2. Apply the identified mask to both frames to remove unrelated information.
3. Identify the edge of the cell as the reference area.
4. Calculate the vector from the center of the froth to the reference area.
5. Determine the flow vector using the Optical Flow method.
6. Calculate the dot product of these vectors to find the vector projection and the angle between them.
7. If the dot product ≥ 0, consider the flow to be toward the edge (indicating froth recovery).

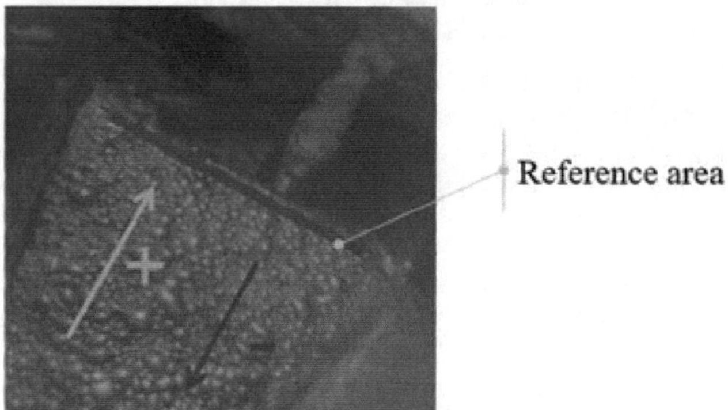

Figure 4. Flow direction and the reference area methodology

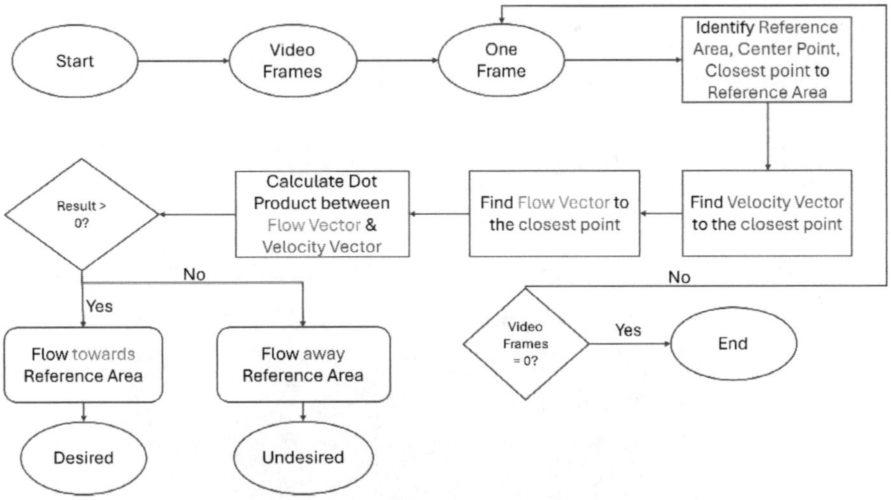

Figure 5. Extracting velocity steps diagram

4. RESULTS & DISCUSSION

To validate the froth velocity estimated by the proposed computer vision model, a comparative analysis was conducted against velocity measurements obtained from an alternative system. The data from both sources were collected over the same time periods corresponding to the video recordings. It is important to note that there is no universally accepted standard for measuring froth velocity; as such, each study typically employs its own estimation methodology. In this work, the accuracy of the proposed method is assessed through direct comparison with an existing measurement system. Prior to comparison, unit consistency was ensured. While the existing system reported velocity in centimeters per second (cm/s), the proposed computer vision method initially produced results in pixels per second (pixels/s). A conversion was applied using camera specifications, with a spatial resolution of 0.2 cm/pixel, allowing all outputs from the vision-based method to be transformed to cm/s by applying this ratio. The comparison was performed on three video recordings captured from flotation cells: cell03 at 08:27, cell03 at 17:10, and cell05 at 08:27. Evaluation metrics included Mean Squared Error (MSE), Root Mean Squared Error (RMSE), and Mean Absolute Error (MAE), as summarized in Table 1. For cell03 at both time intervals, the proposed method demonstrated strong agreement with the reference system, reporting MAE values of 2.0 cm/s and 1.7 cm/s, respectively. These low error margins indicate a reliable performance that is unaffected by varying lighting conditions. On the other hand, a higher error was observed for cell05, indicating a challenge in generalizing the method across different cells. The discrepancy arises from fundamental differences in how velocity is estimated. While the alternative system evaluates a small region near the top of the cell, where froth movement was minimal, the proposed method calculates velocity across the entire cell surface. Visual analysis of the cell05 video confirmed significant froth movement, which the other system failed to capture due to flow blockage near the top edge, as illustrated in Figure 6. To further assess the validity of the proposed approach, an additional test was conducted by restricting the analysis area to match the region used by the alternative system. Under this condition, the proposed method achieved a significantly lower MAE of 0.7 cm/s, confirming both its accuracy and reliability. This result also highlights the advantage of analyzing the entire froth surface. For example, in the case of cell05, full-area analysis revealed abnormal cell behavior, specifically, a "sunken state", where high froth motion occurred without mineral recovery, a situation not detectable through partial-area analysis. Moreover, systems that rely on segment-based analysis may suffer increased error when the distance between the camera and the region of interest varies, particularly near cell edges. Another advantage of the proposed method is its capability for real-time processing, addressing a common limitation of traditional statistical approaches. Additionally, the model is adaptable to diverse operational settings and camera configurations, as the reference area can be dynamically defined based on the camera angle. Nonetheless, some limitations remain, particularly the method's sensitivity to video quality, which could be addressed in future research. Overall, the proposed system demonstrated high efficiency and accuracy in froth velocity estimation, underscoring its potential to assist engineers and operators in monitoring and optimizing the flotation process.

Table 1. Error Margin with other system Data in Different Metrics

Cell & Time	Analysis Area	MSE (cm^2/s^2)	RMSE (cm/s)	MAE (cm/s)
Cell03 at 08:27	**Full Area**	**5.76**	**2.40**	**2.01**
Cell03 at 17:10	**Full Area**	**5.73**	**2.39**	**1.71**
Cell05 at 08:27	**Full Area**	**29.97**	**5.47**	**5.27**
Cell05 at 08:27	**Top Area**	**0.54**	**0.73**	**0.73**

Figure 6. Image of cell05 showing blockage at the top of the cell

5. CONCLUSION

In conclusion, monitoring the flotation process is crucial in the mining industry for mineral extraction from ores, with froth velocity being a key variable to maximize froth recovery. In this research, we proposed a computer vision-based algorithm to estimate froth velocity from images. By comparing the results with other system data, the proposed algorithm achieved a minimal MAE margin of around 2 cm/s across different froth cells at various times, demonstrating its ability to accurately estimate froth velocity. Additionally, the proposed method can evenly analyze the entire froth area, in contrast to alternative systems. This, when coupled with the ability to estimate more than one velocity of interest per cell, provides a system with a valuable capability to optimize the flotation process. In future work, computer vision or AI techniques could be used to estimate other froth features, such as froth color, froth load, or bubble size. Additionally, an integrated advisory system could be developed to support operators in decision-making within the mining industry. This method could eventually be incorporated into control systems to automate the process, leveraging velocity analysis for improved process management.

ACKNOWLEDGEMENT

The authors would like to acknowledge Yokogawa Saudi Arabia, Yokogawa America do Sul, and Yokogawa Electric Corporation in Japan for funding and supporting this research.

REFERENCES

Guan, C., Cai, G., Xu, F. and Li, X., (2022). Intelligent detection method for froth flotation based on YOLOv5. *IEEE Access*, 10, pp.120690–120701.

Hodouin, D., Jämsä-Jounela, S.-L., Carvalho, M. and Bergh, L., (2001). State of the art and challenges in mineral processing control. *Control Engineering Practice*, 9(9), pp.995–1005.

Jahedsaravani, A., Massinaei, M. and Zarie, M., (2023). Measurement of bubble size and froth velocity using convolutional neural networks. *Minerals Engineering*, 204, p.108400.

Liu, J., Gui, W. and Tang, Z., (2013). Flow velocity measurement and analysis based on froth image sift features and Kalman filter for froth flotation. *Turkish Journal of Electrical Engineering and Computer Sciences*, 21(8), pp.2378–2396.

Lu, F., Liu, H. and Lv, W., (2023). Prediction of clean coal ash content in coal flotation through a convergent model unifying deep learning and likelihood function, incorporating froth velocity and reagent dosage parameters. *Processes*, 11(12), p.3425.

Moghadam, H.S., Xiao, W., Dilek, Y., Ghorbani, G., Chiaradia, M., Santos, J.F., Ottley, C.J., Karsli, O., Khedr, M.Z. and Arai, S., (2024). Mineral, bulk rock, and isotope geochemistry of the Late Cretaceous Sabzevar Ophiolite in NE Iran and the magmatic and tectonic evolution of a continental back-arc basin oceanic crust in the Mesozoic Tethyan orogenic belt. *Geological Society of America Bulletin*.

Nakhaei, F., Irannajad, M. and Mohammadnejad, S., (2023). A comprehensive review of froth surface monitoring as an aid for grade and recovery prediction of flotation process. Part A: Structural features. *Energy Sources, Part A: Recovery, Utilization, and Environmental Effects*, 45(1), pp.2587–2605.

Shean, B. and Cilliers, J., (2011). A review of froth flotation control. *International Journal of Mineral Processing*, 100 (3-4), pp.57–71.

Supomo, A., Yap, E., Zheng, X., Banini, G., Mosher, J. and Partanen, A., (2008). PT Freeport Indonesia's mass-pull control strategy for rougher flotation. *Minerals Engineering*, 21(12-14), pp.808–816.

Tang, Z., Liu, J., Gui, W. and Yang, C., (2009). Froth bubbles speed characteristic extraction and analysis based on digital image processing. *Journal of Central South University (Science and Technology)*, 40(6), pp.1616–1622.

Thwaites, P., (2007). Process control in metallurgical plants—from an Xstrata perspective. *Annual Reviews in Control*, 31(2), pp.221–239.

Wang, Y., Sun, B., Zhang, R., Zhu, Q. and Li, F., (2018). Sulfur flotation performance recognition based on hierarchical classification of local dynamic and static froth features. *IEEE Access*, 6, pp.14019–14029.

Williams, B. and Oosthuizen, D., n.d. Using artificial intelligence to classify flotation froth conditions.

Wills, B. and Napier-Munn, T., (2006). *Wills' introduction to mineral processing technology*. 7th ed. Elsevier, Oxford, UK.

Yang, Y., Cao, S., Wang, X. and Yang, C., (2023). Froth velocity extraction method from froth image for flotation with large throughput based on composite deep learning network. *Measurement*, 223, p.113672.

Yantén, C., Kracht, W., Díaz, G., Lois-Morales, P. and Egaña, A., (2023). Froth images from flotation laboratory test in Magotteaux cell. *Data*, 8(4), p.69.

Zhang, H., Tang, Z., Xie, Y. and Gui, W., (2021). RPI-SURF: A feature descriptor for bubble velocity measurement in froth flotation with relative position information. *IEEE Transactions on Instrumentation and Measurement*, 70, pp.1–14.

Zmami, M., Ben-Salha, O., Almarshad, S.O. and Chekki, H., (2021). The contribution of mining sector to sustainable development in Saudi Arabia. *Journal of Sustainable Mining*, 20(2), pp.122–136.

EXPLAINABLE MODEL FOR FETAL PLANE CLASSIFICATION USING VISION TRANSFORMERS AND LAYERWISE RELEVANCE PROPAGATION

Sinchana S, Nisarga Kunder, Siri Gowri H and Shravani Hiremath
PES University, India

ABSTRACT

For prenatal diagnosis of anomalies and monitoring them, accurate classification of fetal anatomical planes from ultrasound images is essential because it allows clinicians to evaluate fetal development and administer treatment accordingly. However, manual classification of these planes is time-consuming and heavily dependent on the operator's expertise. In recent years, encoder-decoder-based Vision Transformers (ViT) have emerged as a better alternative to traditional convolutional neural networks (CNNs) in various natural language processing tasks like text prediction and image-based tasks like classification, achieving state-of-the-art performance. Despite these advancements, the use of ViTs within the medical domain, especially for MRI and Ultrasound images, remains relatively less due to its intricate architecture and relative difficulty in applying explainability techniques, as ViTs' attention-based mechanisms are more complex to interpret than those of CNNs. In clinical environments, model interpretability is essential; thus, explainability is crucial for delivering consistent and transparent decision support. This interpretability allows physicians to understand and verify model outputs, fostering trust in AI-driven diagnostic processes. Although CNN-based models frequently use explainability techniques like Grad-CAM, transformer-based models lack similar interpretability due to their distinct attention mechanisms and architectural structure.

In this work, there is the introduction of a novel approach using Layer-wise Relevance Propagation (LRP) to provide visual explanations for Vision Transformer (ViT) predictions on fetal ultrasound images. With LRP, we demonstrate the feasibility of deriving meaningful and interpretable insights from ViT models in medical imaging, paving the way for reliable and explainable AI applications in healthcare.

KEYWORDS

Fetal Ultrasound, Vision Transformer (Vit), Layer-Wise Relevance Propagation (LRP), Explain- Ability, Medical Image Analysis, Model Interpretability

1. INTRODUCTION

Prenatal ultrasound is an important procedure in obstetrics because of its utility in the monitoring of fetal growth and development as well as the identification of possible issues. Diagnosis of anatomical structures and their planes, in this case, the brain, thorax, abdomen, femur, and cervix, is critical, but in many situations is reliant on an ultrasound expert which introduces subjectivity and discrepancy.

This paper describes a new approach to automatically classify fetal ultrasound images into anatomical planes using a Vision Transformer (ViT) model with application specific fine-tuning. To improve interpretability further, the model is augmented with Layer-wise Relevance Propagation (LRP), making it possible to visualize the important regions of the image that impacted the model's output.

The contributions of this work are: (1) showing that with and without augmentation, ViTs are able to accurately classify the individual fetal planes, and (2) adding LRP facilitates explainability which makes it possible for doctors to evaluate the reasoning of the model. Such an intuitive framework may enhance the objective and accurate its use in clinical practice and improve the reliability and consistency of clinical decision making.

2. LITERATURE REVIEW

2.1 Role of Deep Learning in Fetal Ultrasound Classification

Deep learning models, particularly CNNs, have shown outstanding ability in identifying key features in fetal images. Bharati et al. (2024) reported high precision in detecting 12 out of 13 planes in fetal images, while Krishna and Kokil (2022) used a specialized CNN to identify subtle distinctions in brain images. Similarly, Kumar et al. (2016) employed models like MobileNetV2, VGG16, ResNet50, and InceptionV3 to detect brain abnormalities, with MobileNetV2 achieving an accuracy of 90.5%. However, CNNs often miss broader image patterns by focusing on local features, limiting their ability to capture the overall context essential in medical imaging. In fact, ViTs can recognize such large patterns by means of their attention mechanism. Such studies as Maurício et al. (2023) and Qu et al. (2020) prove that ViTs are efficient in complex analysis tasks.

2.2 Dataset Variability - Challenges in Classification

Fetal planes classification challenges arise due to the variability of the datasets. Imbalanced datasets can cause models to miss important details in less common images. Studies by Alam et al. (2022) and Men et al. (2023) discuss how small, imbalanced datasets often lead to models that don't generalize well. Multi-task learning is suggested by Krishna and Kokil (2022) as a strategy that will allow the model to learn and make the appropriate adjustments when faced with different planes. Men et al. (2023) also suggest applying domain adaptation techniques can reduce the impact of variations in ultrasound devices and users, enabling the model to perform reliably in diverse clinical settings.

2.3 Explainability of AI Models

AI must be explainable to be effectively adapted to healthcare, as transparency in a model's conclusions builds clinician trust. XAI methods enhance this transparency, with techniques like LRP and Grad-CAM (Alam et al., 2022; Bharati et al., 2024) highlighting image regions most relevant to predictions. For example, Alam et al. (2022) applied Grad-CAM in multi-label radiography to demonstrate how visual explanations improve robustness. However, these techniques often fall short in explaining complex cases. ViT-based models, with their native self-attention mechanisms, offer a promising alternative by providing built-in interpretability, making them suitable for fetal plane classification.

This study aims to address the said issues by optimizing a ViT-based explainable model for the classification of fetal planes and employing Layer-wise Relevance Propagation (LRP) to improve interpretability, making AI useful and more trustworthy for prenatal care.

3. METHODOLOGY

3.1 Dataset

The dataset consists of ultrasound images which are categorized into six different planes: brain, thorax, abdomen, cervix, femur and others. These images are divided into training and testing sub- sets, each with 6 classes ensuring balanced representation for each plane where possible. Each image is pre-processed to align with the input requirements of the ViT model, including resizing to 224x224 pixels.

3.2 Model Architecture

A pre trained Vision Transformer (ViT) model was utilized for feature extraction and fine-tuned on the fetal ultrasound dataset. ViTs employ self-attention mechanisms to capture long-range dependencies across an image. This ability is particularly beneficial for fetal plane classification, where anatomical structures extend across different regions. Extensive comparative studies indicate that ViTs outperform CNNs in medical imaging tasks requiring global spatial awareness. Their capability to dynamically focus on relevant regions enhances both classification accuracy and interpretability, particularly when integrated with Layer-wise Relevance Propagation (LRP). To tailor the ViT model for this task, the classification head was modified by incorporating a fully connected layer, ensuring optimized feature extraction and improved differentiation of fetal planes.

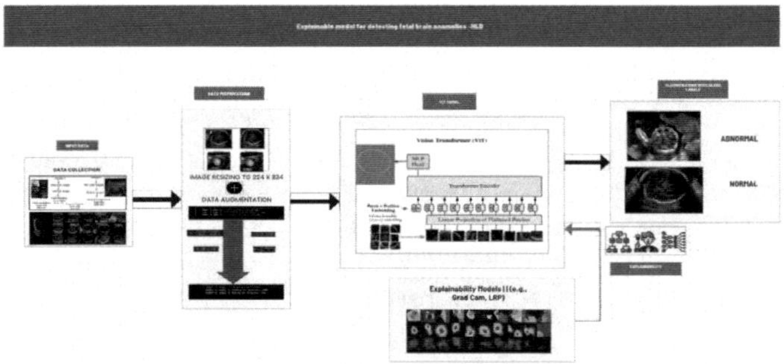

Figure 1. High-Level Design: Vision Transformer-Based Ultrasound Image Classification with Explainability

3.3 Training Strategy

To adapt the pretrained ViT model to the ultrasound dataset, transfer learning was employed. Fine tuned the entire model with a smaller learning rate (e.g., 1e-4) using the Adam optimizer, while adjusting the batch size based on available GPU memory. The loss function chosen was cross-entropy due to the multi-class nature of the problem. Early stopping was implemented to avoid overfitting, and class weights were used to address any class imbalance.

3.4 Explainability with Layer-wise Relevance Propagation (LRP)

Layer-wise Relevance Propagation (LRP) was applied to the fine-tuned ViT model to interpret its predictions and highlight relevant areas in each ultrasound image. LRP provides insight into which regions of an image are most influential in the model's classification decision, enhancing transparency and enabling a better understanding of how the model perceives distinct anatomical structures in each ultrasound plan.

3.5 Equations

3.5.1 Self-Attention Mechanism in ViT :

The core of ViT is the self-attention mechanism, where each token attends to other tokens in he sequence. Unlike CNNs, which rely on local responsive fields, self-attention allows each token to interact globally, capturing long-range dependencies. Self-attention is computed as:

$$Q = XWQ, K = XW_K, V = XW_V \quad \text{...(1)}$$

where W_Q, W_K , and W_V are learnable weight matrices that project the input X into query, key, and value representations.

The attention scores are computed using the scaled dot-product

$$Attention(Q, K, V) = softmax\left(\frac{QKT}{\sqrt{dk}}\right)V \quad \text{... (2)}$$

where dk is the dimension of the keys (often set to d/h, where h is the number of attention heads in multi-head attention).

3.5.2 Multi-Head Self-Attention:

To enhance the model's ability to focus on different parts of the input sequence, multi-head attention is applied by computing multiple independent self-attention mechanisms. Each attention head is defined as:

$$\text{head}_i = Attention(Q_i, K_i, V_i) \quad \ldots(3)$$

The multi-head attention output is then concatenated and linearly transformed:

$$\text{MultiHead}(Q, K, V) = \text{Concat}(\text{head } 1, \text{head } 2, \ldots, \text{head } h)W_o \quad \ldots(4)$$

Where W_o is a learnable projection matrix. This mechanism allows the model to attend to different features at multiple scales, improving feature representation, which is particularly advantageous in ultrasound image classification.

3.5.3 Layer Normalization and MLP:

Each transformer block includes layer normalization and a feed-forward MLP (multi-layer perceptron), applied as follows:

$$Z = LayerNorm(MultiHead(Q, K, V) + X) \quad \ldots(5)$$

$$\text{Output} = \text{LayerNorm}(MLP(Z) + Z) \quad \ldots(6)$$

The layer normalization ensures stability and faster convergence, while the MLP allows for non-linear transformations of the representations.

3.5.4 Classification Head:

For classification, ViT uses a CLS token, which serves as a global representation of the image. The final classification head is:

$$y = softmax(Wcls \cdot hcls) \quad \ldots(7)$$

where h_{CLS} is the representation of the CLS token after the final transformer layer, and WCLS is a learnable weight matrix.

By aggregating information from all tokens, the CLS token captures global dependencies in a way that is not possible with standard CNN architectures.

3.5.5 Theoretical Justification of ViTs vs CNNs:

CNNs process images through localized receptive fields, making them inherently limited in capturing global spatial relationships. The feature extraction process in a convolutional layer is given by:

$$h^{(l)}(x, y) = \sum_{i=-k}^{k} \sum_{j=-k}^{k} w_{ij} \cdot h^{(l-1)} \cdot (x + i, y + j) \quad (8)$$

where w_{ij} are the convolutional weights and k is the kernel size.

This operation restricts CNNs to local neighbourhood processing, which may not fully capture anatomical structures distributed across an ultrasound image. In contrast, the self-attention mechanism in ViTs considers all pixels simultaneously, ensuring that long-range dependencies are maintained, which is critical in fetal ultrasound classification.

3.5.6 Layer-wise Relevance Propagation:

For a fully connected layer, the relevance for neuron j in layer l is distributed to the lower layer as:

$$R^{(l-1)}{}_{i,j} = \sum_j \frac{x_i w_{ij}}{\sum_k x_k w_{kj}} \cdot R_j{}^{(l)} \quad \ldots(9)$$

where x_i is the activation of neuron i, w_{ij} is the weight connecting neurons i and j, and $R^{(l)}{}_j$ is the relevance at layer l.

For convolutional layers, LRP follows a similar approach but distributes relevance spatially:

$$R^{(l-1)}{}_{i,j} = \sum_{m,n} \frac{x_{i+m,j+n} w_{m,n}}{\sum_{p,q} x_{p,q} w_{p,q}} \cdot R_{i+m,j+n}{}^{(l)} \quad \ldots(10)$$

This ensures that the most relevant regions in the input image are highlighted, improving interpretability.

3.5.7 Conservation Principle in LRP:

The LRP method follows a relevance conservation principle, ensuring that the total relevance is preserved across layers .

$$\sum_i R^{(l-1)}{}_i = \sum_j R^{(l)}{}_j \quad \ldots(11)$$

This guarantees that the model's decision can be traced back to specific image regions, making it a more suitable explainability tool for ViTs.

4. EXPERIMENTS AND RESULTS

4.1 Model Training

The Vision Transformer (ViT) model was trained on a dataset of fetal ultrasound images divided into six anatomical planes which included brain, thorax, abdomen, cervix, femur and others US images. During training, a batch size of 32 was used, along with a learning rate of 1e-4 optimized using the Adam optimizer. The training process utilized early stopping to mitigate overfitting, resulting in a final training accuracy of 98%.

The ViT model was trained on a combination of local system CPU and Kaggle free GPU environment due to hardware constraints. Training on the local CPU was significantly slower and impractical for our model training, leading us to utilize Kaggle's GPU for improved efficiency.

4.2 Test Performance

The model achieved a test accuracy of 94%, indicating strong generalization capability across unseen ultrasound images. This result demonstrates the effectiveness of the ViT model in capturing the unique patterns of each anatomical plane in fetal ultrasound images.

4.3 Evaluation Metrics

To further validate the model's performance, calculated precision, recall, and F1-score for each class. The table below summarizes these metrics

Table 1. Performance Metrics for ViT Model on Fetal Ultrasound Image Classification

Class	Precision (%)	Recall(%)	F1-Score(%)
Brain	0.97	0.99	0.98
Thorax	0.93	0.94	0.94
Abdomen	0.92	0.91	0.92
Cervix	0.99	0.99	0.99
Femur	0.92	0.91	0.94
Others	0.92	0.92	0.92

Overall, the model achieved high precision and recall across all classes, with slight variations based on image characteristics and potential inter-class similarities.

5. DISCUSSION

The results of our ViT-based model demonstrate a strong performance, achieving a training accuracy of 98% and a test accuracy of 94% on fetal ultrasound image classification.

Furthermore, the implementation of Layer-wise Relevance Propagation (LRP) with ViT marks a unique application interpretability of our results.

Our approach also stands out due to the scarcity of research on topics like ViT and LRP in fetal ultrasound imaging. Limited work have been explored in this domain, positioning this study as an innovative contribution. While the results are promising, further exploration is warranted to validate these findings across different medical datasets and potentially enhance the model's robustness.

5.1 Explainability

This study employed Layer-wise Relevance Propagation (LRP) as our primary explainability approach to interpret the decisions made by the Vision Transformer (ViT) model. Generated visualizations for each of the six planes of fetal ultrasound images: brain, thorax, abdomen, cervix, femur and others. These visualizations illustrate the relevance scores assigned to each pixel in the ultrasound images, highlighting areas that the model focused on when making its classifications.

The following figures present the LRP visualizations for each plane:

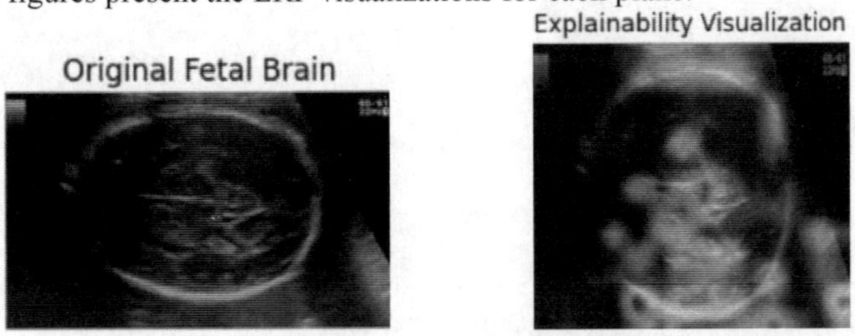

Figure 2. LRP Visualization for Brain Plane

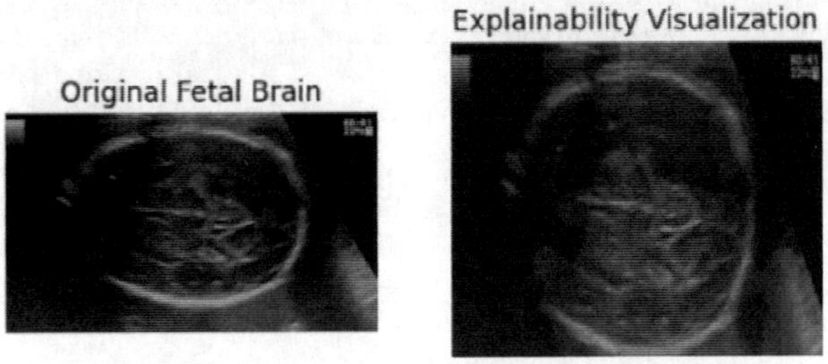

Figure 3. LRP Visualization for Brain Plane

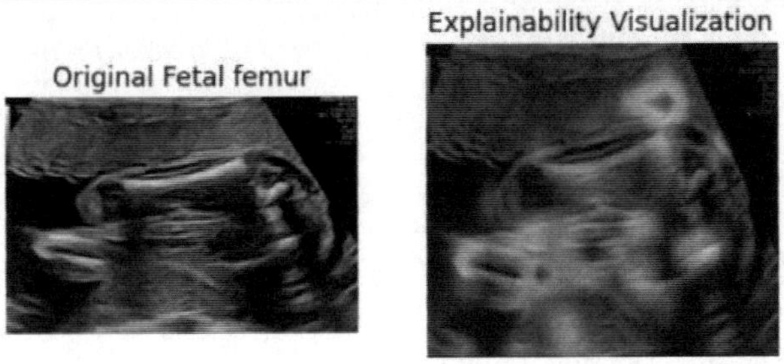

Figure 4. LRP Visualization for Femur Plane

Each visualization allows us to understand the model's decision-making process in a better way and highlights the areas of the ultrasound images that are most indicative of the corresponding classifications. This interpretability is crucial in the medical field, where understanding the rationale behind model predictions can lead to more informed clinical decisions.

6. CONCLUSION

This study presented a novel approach for classifying fetal ultrasound images using Vision Transformers (ViTs) and Layer-wise Relevance Propagation (LRP) for explainability. Our model achieved a training accuracy of 98% and a test accuracy of 94%, demonstrating its effectiveness in distinguishing between different planes of ultrasound scans. The use of ViTs in the medical domain, particularly for fetal ultrasound images, is still under-explored, and our findings contribute to this emerging area of research.

The LRP visualizations and heatmaps enhances the understanding some of the model's internal processes as its stress which features contributed to the decision making in a better sense than other interpretability methods such as GRAD-CAM, SHAP.

Overall, our work highlights the potential of leveraging advanced deep learning techniques for improving the accuracy and interpretability of medical image analysis

7. FUTURE WORK

As promising as the findings of our study have been, there are still several opportunities for further work. One of such possibilities is expanding the dataset to incorporate a wider variety of fetal ultrasound images, thus increasing robustness and generalization of the model.

Furthermore, one key limitation of this study was the use of Kaggle's free GPU for training, which imposed certain restrictions on batch size, memory, and computational speed. These constraints may have affected the model's ability to fully optimize and generalize across diverse fetal ultrasound images. In future work, we plan to utilize high-performance GPUs such as NVIDIA A100 or TPUs, which will allow for larger batch sizes, faster training, and better fine-tuning of the ViT model. This will not only improve training efficiency but also enhance model accuracy and generalizability across different datasets.

Lastly, exploring the application of ViTs in other areas of medical imaging could broaden the impact of this research, paving the way for further innovations in the intersection of artificial intelligence and healthcare.

REFERENCES

Bharati, S., Mondal, M. R. H. & Podder, P., (2024). A Review on Explainable Artificial Intelligence for Healthcare: Why, How, and When? *IEEE Transactions on Artificial Intelligence*, Vol. 5, No. 4, pp. 1429-1442.

Krishna, T. B. & Kokil, P., (2022). Automated Detection of Common Maternal Fetal Ultrasound Planes Using Deep Feature Fusion. *Proceedings of the 19th India Council International Conference (INDICON)*, Kochi, India, pp. 1-5.

Kumar, A. et al., (2016). Plane identification in fetal ultrasound images using saliency maps and convolutional neural networks. *Proceedings of the 13th International Symposium on Biomedical Imaging (ISBI)*, Prague, Czech Republic, pp. 791-794.

Maurício, J., Domingues, I. & Bernardino, J., (2023). Comparing Vision Transformers and Convolutional Neural Networks for Image Classification: A Literature Review. *MDPI Applied Sciences*. Available at: https://www.mdpi.com/2076-3417/13/9/5521.

Men, Q., Zhao, H., Drukker, L., Papageorghiou, A. T. & Noble, J. A., (2023). Towards Standard Plane Prediction of Fetal Head Ultrasound with Domain Adaptation. *Proceedings of the 20th International Symposium on Biomedical Imaging (ISBI)*, Cartagena, Colombia, pp. 1-5.

Alam, M. U., Baldvinsson, J. R. & Wang, Y., (2022). Exploring LRP and Grad-CAM Visualization to Interpret Multi-Label-Multi-Class Pathology Prediction Using Chest Radiography. *Proceedings of the 35th International Symposium on Computer-Based Medical Systems (CBMS)*, Shenzhen, China, pp. 258-263.

Qu, R., Xu, G., Ding, C., Jia, W. & Sun, M., (2020). Standard Plane Identification in Fetal Brain Ultrasound Scans Using a Differential Convolutional Neural Network. *IEEE Access*, Vol. 8, pp. 83821-83830.

DEVELOPMENT AND EVALUATION OF A LOW-COST STEREO AND MONO VISION-SYSTEM

Mahmoud Hussein and Bernard Durand
Laboratoire de Physique et Mécanique Textiles, Université de Haute Alsace, ENSISA, 11 rue des Frères Lumières, 68093 Mulhouse Cedex, France

ABSTRACT

This paper presents the development and evaluation of a low-cost, vision-based robotic grasping system using both monocular and stereo camera configurations. Integrated with a 6-DOF Mitsubishi industrial robot arm, the system performs object classification, dimensional verification, depth estimation, and autonomous grasping. In contrast to most vision-guided systems relying on expensive depth sensors or proprietary software, our solution emphasizes affordability and accessibility while maintaining competitive accuracy. Depth is estimated using a stereo triangulation pipeline and an artificial neural network (ANN)-based regression model trained on object features. Experimental results demonstrate that the ANN-based monocular setup achieves over 90% grasping success in dynamic environments with a processing time below 400 MS, while the stereo system offers enhanced precision. The system was tested in static and dynamic scenarios, with performance benchmarks including root mean square error (RMSE), classification accuracy, and real-time grasping success. This work contributes a complete, reproducible solution for affordable robotic grasping, with potential applications in flexible manufacturing and semi-structured environments.

KEYWORDS

Stereo Vision, Mono Vision, Sorting Objects, Vision System, Industrial Robot Arm, Quality Control

1. INTRODUCTION

Three-dimensional (3D) reconstruction from digital images is a fundamental challenge in machine vision, driving the development of numerous algorithms aimed at enhancing visual information interpretation and evaluation (Faugeras, 1993). These methods are broadly classified into two categories: active and passive techniques (Frauel et al., 2004). Active methods utilize external light sources to assist in constructing accurate 3D models, while passive techniques rely on ambient light, requiring precise control of lighting conditions. Among the passive methods, stereo vision stands out as one of the most effective and widely used approaches due to its superior performance when compared to techniques based on object shape, color, texture, or motion (Kriegman et al., 1989; Ballan & Cortelazzo, 2006).

In industrial automation, machine vision plays an increasingly vital role, offering solutions in fields such as textile quality control (Bahlmann et al., 1999), metal surface inspection (Tucker, 1989), glass manufacturing (Novini, 1990), component evaluation (Ker & Kengskool, 1990), print verification (Saxena et al., 2008), granite surface assessment (Gambardella & Versino, 1994), and semiconductor production (Corke, 2011). Robotic vision systems are generally categorized as 2D, 2.5D, or 3D systems. 2D systems are cost-effective and fast but are limited to planar detection. 2.5D systems provide partial 3D information through machine learning and single-camera setups. Full 3D vision systems employ multiple methods, including multi-camera arrays (Corke, 2011), RGB-D cameras (Jiang et al., 2011; Frank et al., 2017), or stereo vision, which estimates depth by matching features between two camera views, whether mounted on the robot or in fixed positions.

Several studies have applied mono and stereo vision systems to robotic applications such as object detection, depth estimation, and manipulation. For example, a stereo vision-based system is used for pose estimation in quality inspection (Yang et al., 2011). Kheng et al. (2010) present a service robot using color segmentation and stereo vision for object localization. A detailed stereo vision pipeline, including calibration, rectification, and triangulation, is outlined by Taryudi and Wang (2017). Similarly, Szabó and Gontean (2014) use stereo vision for 3D pose estimation, and Puheim et al. (2013) combine it with color segmentation to enhance object recognition. A neural-network-based tracking system using stereo vision is proposed by Hanh and Lin (2014), while Akhlaq et al. (2014) integrate stereo vision and fuzzy logic for robotic grasping. For cost-sensitive applications, Liaquat et al. (2015) propose a monocular depth estimation approach based on power fitting.

Depth estimation methods can be grouped into four principal approaches. The first is stereo vision, which uses horizontally-aligned cameras to calculate depth through triangulation (Koker et al., 2004). This method requires precise calibration and synchronization, with performance degradation possible if a camera fails. The second category involves hardware-assisted triangulation using laser pointers or LEDs, improving accuracy but increasing system complexity and cost (Davies, 1998). The third approach uses monocular image sequences and mathematical models (e.g., polynomial fitting) for approximate depth estimation (Liaquat et al., 2015). The fourth involves motion-based tracking from fixed cameras, where depth is inferred from object velocity, acceleration, and trajectory (Yurii, 2017), albeit at a high computational cost.

Object detection and robotic grasping have been extensively studied, with several state-of-the-art methods leveraging deep learning for object recognition and pose estimation. Models such as YOLOv7 (Saxena et al., 2008), EfficientDet (Saxena et al., 2008), and transformer-based detectors (Saxena et al., 2008) have demonstrated remarkable performance in detecting objects under varying lighting and occlusion conditions. In terms of depth estimation, modern approaches now include both supervised (e.g., DPT; Saxena et al., 2008) and self-supervised methods (Saxena et al., 2008), capable of generating dense depth maps from single RGB inputs.

For robotic grasping, tools like GraspNet (Saxena et al., 2008), GPD (Saxena et al., 2008), and Dex-Net (et al., 2008) offer robust grasp synthesis using RGB-D data. However, these approaches often require depth sensors like Intel RealSense or OAK-D, which, although more affordable than before, still increase For robotic grasping, tools like GraspNet (Saxena et al., 2008), GPD (Saxena et al., 2008), and Dex-Net (Saxena the overall system cost and complexity.

In contrast, our proposed system prioritizes cost and simplicity. It uses standard USB webcams, SURF-based feature matching, and shallow ANN architectures to approximate depth and enable object grasping. This trade-off makes our approach especially suitable for environments where budget constraints or hardware limitations preclude the use of advanced sensors or cloud-based inference pipelines.

The rest of this paper details the architecture of the proposed system, its camera modeling techniques, the experimental setup, and its integration with a Mitsubishi robot arm. Performance in terms of accuracy and processing time is evaluated, followed by a conclusion outlining findings and future research directions.

2. VISION SYSTEM

This section presents the architecture and functionality of the developed vision system, designed to perform object recognition, dimension verification, and robotic grasping using either monocular or stereo camera configurations. The system is optimized for real-time operation and is integrated with a 6-degree-of-freedom (DOF) Mitsubishi industrial robot arm.

An overview of the system architecture is shown in Figure 1. The setup includes a digital camera (mono or stereo), a personal computer for image processing, and Ethernet communication with the robot controller.

The vision system acquires images, processes them to extract object features, estimates the 3D coordinates of a point on the object's surface, classifies the object, and checks its dimensions. The final coordinates are sent to the robot controller, which calculates the required joint angles through inverse kinematics to execute grasping.

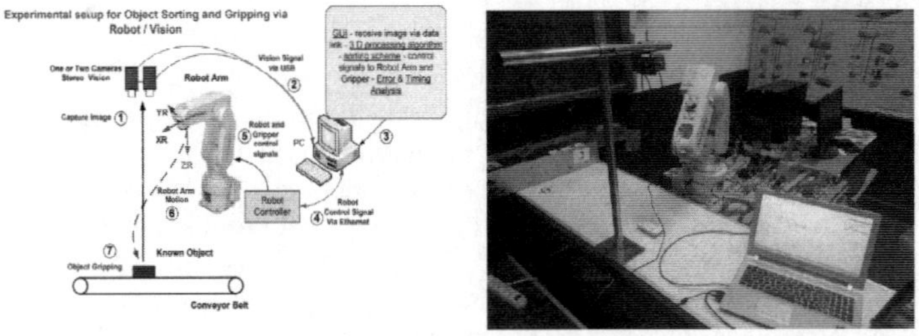

Figure 1. On the left, System overview and on the right experimental setup

2.1 Monocular Vision Approach

In the monocular configuration, a single camera is used to capture 2D images of the scene. Depth estimation is performed using two techniques: a polynomial regression model and an artificial neural network (ANN). Both methods are trained using datasets that correlate the apparent area of known objects with their distance from the camera. The ANN model provides higher accuracy and robustness, especially in variable lighting conditions.

To handle moving objects on a conveyor, the system incorporates motion compensation. It calculates the time delay introduced by image processing and adjusts the object's x-coordinate based on the conveyor speed. This allows the robot to successfully grasp the object without interrupting its motion. The overall process for object recognition and classification using monocular vision is illustrated in Figures 2, which depict the algorithm workflows using edge detection and SURF-based methods, respectively.

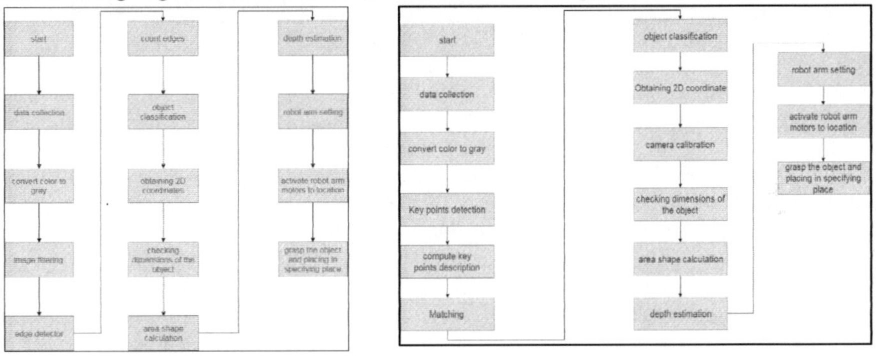

Figure 2. (Left) Edge detector object classification mono camera, (Right) surf object classification mono camera

The processing pipeline for monocular vision is illustrated in Figure 2 (left), which shows the workflow based on edge detection. After background subtraction, edges are extracted from the image, and geometric features such as corners are analyzed to classify the object and measure its dimensions. Figure 2 (right) presents an alternative workflow based on the SURF (Speeded-Up Robust Features) algorithm, which offers scale and rotation invariance. SURF detects keypoints and matches them with reference patterns to identify the object and estimate depth. Both methods conclude with a dimension-checking step, where the measured length in pixels is compared to known references to assess object conformity.

These flowcharts help visualize the sequence of operations involved in detection, classification, and dimensional analysis using a monocular camera, and they highlight the trade-offs between the two approaches in terms of accuracy and processing time.

2.2 Stereo Vision Approach

The stereo configuration utilizes two calibrated cameras placed side by side at a known baseline distance. These cameras simultaneously capture images of the scene from slightly different perspectives. Depth information is obtained by calculating the disparity between corresponding points in the left and right images. This disparity is then used to triangulate the 3D coordinates of a point on the object's surface. Unlike the monocular approach, stereo vision does not rely on prior knowledge of object size, making it suitable for identifying and measuring unknown or varying objects with higher precision. Figure 3(left) illustrates the stereo vision workflow using edge detection. In this approach, edges are extracted from both camera images, and the stereo correspondence is established to compute disparity. Once 3D coordinates are obtained through triangulation, object shape is analyzed by counting the number of detected edges, enabling classification. Dimensional measurements are then performed by calculating the Euclidean distance between two key 3D points. Figure 3 (right) shows an alternative stereo-based classification process using the SURF algorithm. SURF is applied to both stereo images to extract robust keypoints and match them with reference objects. The matched features are used for object recognition and 3D localization. The system then performs dimensional verification in all three spatial directions (X, Y, Z) by calculating distances between matched points.

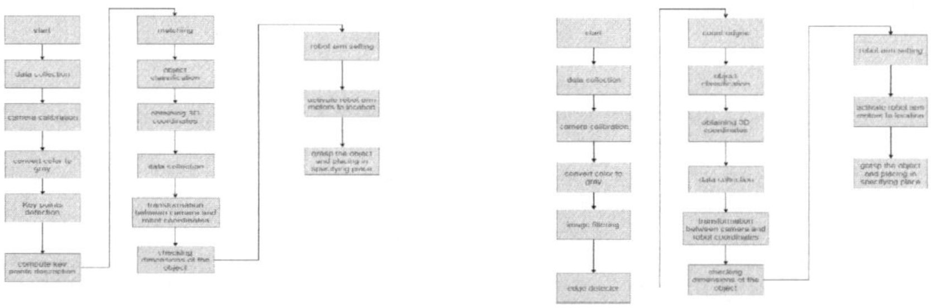

Figure 3. (Left) Edge detector object classification mono camera, (Right) surf object classification stereo camera

Figure 3 illustrates the versatility of the developed stereo vision system, which supports both shape-based and feature-based object recognition strategies. The edge detection approach offers a lightweight computational solution, ideal for recognizing regular geometries, while the SURF-based method provides greater robustness in scenarios involving complex textures or irregular shapes. Both methods are integrated with 3D coordinate extraction, object classification, and dimensional analysis, enabling the robot to perform accurate grasping and sorting based on geometric features.

Once a point on the object's surface is localized—whether via monocular or stereo vision—its 3D coordinates are computed in the camera's reference frame. For robotic manipulation, these coordinates must be accurately transformed into the robot's reference frame. While classical approaches like affine transformations or perspective-n-point (PnP) algorithms are widely used for camera-to-robot calibration, they often assume perfect pinhole camera models and ideal imaging conditions. To handle the nonlinear nature of this mapping, a neural network is trained using a dataset of known point correspondences between the camera and robot frames. This model enables real-time conversion of detected object positions into robot-understandable coordinates. The transformed coordinates are then transmitted to the Mitsubishi robot controller via Ethernet using the TCP/IP protocol. The controller performs inverse kinematics to compute the necessary joint angles, guiding the robot arm precisely to the object's position for grasping. The complete experimental setup depicted in Figure 1 includes the camera(s), conveyor platform, robot arm, and the control unit, illustrating the seamless integration of vision, computation, and actuation.

3. EXPERIMENTAL SETUP

To assess the effectiveness of the proposed vision-based robotic system, a fully integrated experimental platform was constructed, combining hardware, software, and communication components to perform real-time object detection, classification, depth estimation, and grasping. The robotic subsystem features a Mitsubishi 6-degree-of-freedom (DOF) industrial robot arm, selected for its precision and versatility in manipulation tasks. The processing unit consists of a Lenovo Z5170 laptop equipped with an Intel Core i7 processor and 8 GB of RAM, responsible for executing all vision and control algorithms. The vision system is configured in two modes: monocular and stereo. In the monocular setup, a single USB camera is mounted in a fixed position overlooking the conveyor belt. This camera captures 2D images used for object recognition and depth estimation. In the stereo configuration, two identical webcams are positioned with a fixed baseline 10 cm and aligned to ensure overlapping fields of view. The stereo cameras are calibrated using a standard checkerboard calibration procedure to determine their intrinsic and extrinsic parameters. Stereo rectification is applied to align image pairs for accurate disparity computation.

The cameras are directed toward a motorized conveyor belt system used to transport test objects. These objects include geometric shapes such as rectangular, triangular, and hexagonal profiles fabricated from lightweight materials, each with known dimensions. The goal is to simulate typical sorting and quality inspection tasks found in manufacturing environments. Images from the camera(s) are captured and processed using algorithms developed in C++ and implemented within the Visual Studio development environment. The OpenCV library is used extensively for tasks such as image acquisition, filtering, edge detection, keypoint extraction (using SURF), and contour analysis. Two depth estimation approaches are used for the monocular system: polynomial regression and artificial neural networks (ANN). The polynomial model is trained using a set of 97 reference images of objects at known distances, where the object's area in pixels is correlated to its real-world depth. The ANN is trained using the same dataset but offers improved generalization to varying object shapes and lighting conditions.

The system extracts the 2D pixel coordinates of the object's key features (e.g., center point, corners, or matched keypoints) in both vision modes and estimates the corresponding 3D coordinates. In the stereo case, this is done using triangulation based on the computed disparity. To allow the robot to act upon these coordinates, a coordinate transformation is required. A neural network model is trained to convert coordinates from the camera frame to the robot's base frame using a dataset of corresponding points. Once transformed, the coordinates are sent to the Mitsubishi robot controller via Ethernet using the TCP/IP protocol. The robot controller then computes the required joint angles using its built-in inverse kinematics engine and executes the grasping operation.

Testing was conducted in an indoor environment under stable lighting conditions to ensure consistent image quality. Both static and dynamic scenarios were evaluated. In the static scenario, objects were placed at fixed positions along the conveyor, while in the dynamic scenario, the conveyor was operated at controlled speeds to simulate continuous flow. For moving objects, the system compensated for image processing delay by predicting the object's future position based on the conveyor speed and the current timestamp. Multiple trials were performed to evaluate the system's accuracy in depth estimation, classification reliability, timing efficiency, and grasping success rate. The complete layout of the hardware setup, including the robot arm, vision components, and conveyor system, is shown in Figure 1. This platform enabled a direct performance comparison between monocular and stereo vision approaches, highlighting trade-offs in cost, complexity, and accuracy for real-world robotic applications.

4. EXPERIMENTAL RESULTS

A comprehensive set of experiments was conducted to evaluate the performance of the proposed vision-based robotic system in terms of depth estimation accuracy, processing speed, classification reliability, and grasping performance. Each configuration—monocular and stereo—was tested under static and dynamic conditions, with multiple trials (32 repetitions) per setup to ensure statistical reliability. Performance metrics are summarized in Tables 1–3, with Figure 4 illustrating robot trajectory tracking during a dynamic task.

4.1 Depth Estimation Accuracy

Depth estimation was first evaluated using monocular vision with polynomial regression and artificial neural networks (ANN). The ANN achieved the best accuracy, with a mean error of 0.0874 mm and a standard deviation of 0.0135 mm, significantly outperforming all polynomial models. Table 1 presents the complete RMSE in mm and standard deviation in mm values for each method. The 8th-degree polynomial model achieved a respectable RMSE of 0.216 mm, but was still less accurate and more sensitive to object shape and lighting variations compared to the ANN. The stereo vision system, based on triangulation, achieved the highest accuracy overall, with a mean error of 0.071 mm and a standard deviation of 0.0094 mm, confirming its robustness for precise depth measurements.

Table 1. Depth estimation error

Method	Poly1	Poly4	Poly8	Power1	Ration01	Sum of sine1	Stereo	ANN
RMSE	1.521	0.5253	0.216	1.4115	1.741	1.741	0.071	0.0874
Standard Deviation	0.131	0.065	0.0281	0.112	0.147	0.147	0.0094	0.0135

As seen in Table 1, lower-order polynomial models resulted in large errors and poor generalization. The ANN demonstrated high consistency and adaptability, while stereo vision, although more accurate, comes at a greater computational cost. But still ANN is difficult to apply for all the application because it needs training data for each position. However, this method indicate that it is possible apply ANN for estimating the depth. It could be useful for certain application.

4.2 Processing Time and Real-Time Constraints

Processing speed is critical for robotic systems operating in dynamic environments. Table 2 shows the Mean processing time and standard deviation for eight different algorithmic configurations. The fastest pipeline was monocular vision with shape detection and background subtraction, with an average time of 333.5 ms Stereo configurations had the highest processing times, especially when background subtraction was not used (2100 ms for SURF stereo), in addition to disparity computation and image rectification stages.

Table 2. consumed time and standard deviation for different methods

Vision Configuration	Mean Consumed time	Standard Deviation
Surf stereo vision	2100	41.7
Shape detection stereo vision	1750	38.9
Surf stereo + background subtraction	609	23.4
Shape stereo + background subtraction	507	21.2
Surf monovision	1650	36.2
Shape detection monovision	1150	32.1
Surf mono + background subtraction	478.5	19.6
Shape mono + background subtraction	333.5	15.4

4.3 Classification, Dimensional Verification and Grasping Performance

Object classification was evaluated using 120 known objects equally distributed among three shapes. Edge-based classification performed best overall, with the monocular system achieving 96.3% accuracy and the stereo system reaching 97.64%. SURF-based methods achieved slightly lower results due to inconsistent keypoint matching under varying lighting. Dimensional accuracy was also assessed by comparing estimated measurements to ground truth dimensions. The stereo system produced an average dimensional error of 1.84%

(SD: 0.93%), while the monocular ANN system reported 2.72% (SD: 1.21%). These results indicate that both systems are suitable for general industrial applications requiring moderate measurement accuracy.

The robotic grasping success was tested in both static and dynamic conditions. Results are summarized in Table 3, showing success rates, average completion time, and variability for each configuration. In static scenarios, the stereo system had a slight edge with 98% success, while the ANN-based monocular system followed closely at 96%. In dynamic scenarios with a conveyor speed of 0.2 m/s, success rates dropped slightly to 94% for stereo and 91% for mono, due to timing sensitivity and motion blur.

Table 3. Grasping performance

Vision Mode	Condition	Success Rate (%)	Mean Time (ms)	SD (%)
Stereo	static	97.73	5.1	0.429
Mono (ANN)	static	96.37	4.2	0.386
Stereo	Dynamic	93.86	5.6	0.502
Mono (ANN)	Dynamic	90.62	4.7	0.463

The slightly longer processing time of stereo vision was compensated by its higher accuracy, making it more robust for fast-moving targets.

To validate the system's real-time motion response, robot joint trajectories were recorded during object tracking using stereo vision. Figure 4 presents the variation of joint coordinates over time as the robot adjusted to a moving object's position. The smoothness and continuity of the trajectories demonstrate the system's stability and responsiveness, even in dynamic environments.

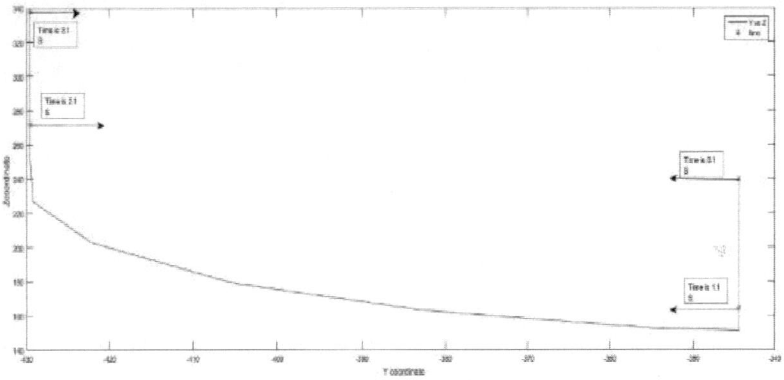

Figure 4. Robot Joint Trajectory during Object Tracking

5. CONCLUSION

This paper presented a low-cost, vision-guided robotic system for object detection, classification, dimensional analysis, and grasping using both monocular and stereo vision. Integrated with a 6-DOF Mitsubishi robot arm, the system was tested in static and dynamic environments. Two depth estimation methods for monocular vision—polynomial regression and artificial neural networks (ANN)—were evaluated, with ANN showing superior accuracy. A stereo vision system using disparity triangulation was also developed. Experimental results showed that the ANN-based monocular system achieved a depth error below 90 mm with 333 ms processing time, while the stereo system reached ~71 mm error but required over 500 ms to process. Both setups exceeded 97% classification accuracy and 90% grasping success in dynamic tests. Despite its performance, the system is limited by low-resolution webcams and CPU-based processing, which affect scalability and accuracy.

REFERENCES

Akhlaq, M. U., Izhar, U., & Shahbaz, U. (2014). Depth estimation from a single camera image using power fit. 2014 International Conference on Robotics and Emerging Technologies.

Ballan, L., & Cortelazzo, G. M. (2006). Multimodal 3D shape recovery from texture, silhouette and shadow information. In Proceedings of the Third International Symposium on 3D Data Processing, Visualization, and Transmission (3DPVT'06) (pp. 924–930).

Bahlmann, C., Heidemann, G., & Ritter, H. (1999). Artificial neural networks for automated quality control of textile seams. Pattern Recognition, 32, 1049–1060.

Corke, P. I. (2011). Robotics, Vision & Control: Fundamental Algorithms in Matlab. Springer.

Davies, E. R. (1998). Automated visual inspection. In Machine Vision (2nd ed., pp. 471–502). Academic Press.

Faugeras, O. (1993). Three-Dimensional Computer Vision: A Geometric Viewpoint. MIT Press.

Frank, D., Chhor, J., & Schmitt, R. (2017). Stereo-vision for autonomous industrial inspection robots. IEEE International Conference on Robotics and Biomimetics.

Frauel, Y., Tajahuerce, E., Matoba, O., Castro, A., & Javidi, B. (2004). Comparison of passive ranging integral imaging and active imaging digital holography for three-dimensional object recognition. Applied Optics, 43(2), 452–462.

Gambardella, L. M., & Versino, C. (1994). Robot motion planning integrating planning strategies and learning methods. In Proceedings of the 2nd International Conference on AIPS.

Hanh, L. D., & Lin, C.-Y. (n.d.). Combining stereo vision and fuzzy image-based visual servoing for autonomous object grasping using a 6-DOF manipulator. IEEE Conference on Robotics and Biomimetics.

Jiang, Y., Moseson, S., & Saxena, A. (2011). Efficient grasping from RGBD images: Learning using a new rectangle representation. International Conference on Robotics and Automation.

Ker, J., & Kengskool, K. (1990). An efficient method for inspecting machine parts by a fixtureless machine vision system. Vision'90 Conference.

Kheng, E. S., Hassan, A. H. A., & Ranjbaran, A. (2010). Stereo vision with 3D coordinates for robot arm application guide. IEEE Conference on Sustainable Utilization and Development in Engineering and Technology.

Koker, R., Oz, C., Cakar, T., & Ekiz, H. (2004). A study of neural network based inverse kinematics solution for a three-joint robot. Robotics and Autonomous Systems, 49, 227–234.

Kriegman, D. J., Triendl, E., & Binford, E. (1989). Stereo vision and navigation in buildings for mobile robots. IEEE Transactions on Robotics and Automation, 5(6), 792–803.

Liaquat, S., Khan, U. S., & Rehman, A.-U. (2015). Object detection and depth estimation of real-world objects using a single camera. 2015 Fourth International Conference on Aerospace Science and Engineering (ICASE).

Novini, A. R. (1990). Fundamentals of machine vision inspection in metal container glass manufacturing. Vision'90 Conference.

Puheim, M., Bundzel, M., & Madarasz, L. (2013). Forward control of robotic arm using the information from stereo-vision tracking system. IEEE 14th International Symposium on Computational Intelligence and Informatics.

Saxena, A., Driemeyer, J., & Ng, A. Y. (2008). Robotic grasping of novel objects using vision. The International Journal of Robotics Research, 27, 157–173.

Szabó, R., & Gontean, A. (2014). Robotic arm control in 3D space using stereo distance calculation. International Conference on Development and Application Systems.

Taryudi, & Wang, M.-S. (2017). 3D object pose estimation using stereo vision for object manipulation system. International Conference on Applied System Innovation.

Tucker, J. W. (1989). Inside beverage can inspection: An application from start to finish. Proceedings of the Vision'89 Conference.

Yang, Y. H., Xu, Y. L., & Li, X. (2011). Stereo vision-based arm control for service robot. Control and Decision Conference.

Yurii, V. (2017). Detection and dimension of moving objects using single camera applied to the round timber measurement. 2017 Federated Conference on Computer Science and Information Systems (FedCSIS).

OCR-GUIDED TEXT REMOVAL IN TECHNICAL DRAWINGS

Richard Martin, Elke Hergenröther* and Benjamin Meyer*
University of Applied Science Darmstadt, Dept. of computer science
Schöfferstraße 3, 64295 Darmstadt, Germany
**Prof. Dr.*

ABSTRACT

Technical drawings, such as architectural floor plans, often embed critical information as textual annotations alongside graphical elements. Accurately separating text from graphics is essential for automated processing but remains challenging, particularly when elements overlap and text varies widely in font, size, or orientation. We propose a method for precise text removal in technical drawings, leveraging modern Optical Character Recognition (OCR) outputs combined with pixel-level character localization. Our approach employs probabilistic character kernels and convolution-based matching to accurately assign pixels to recognized text, guided by an importance sampling strategy that improves sequential localization across text lines. A pixel-accurate masking process then selectively removes text while preserving adjacent graphical structures. Evaluation on real-world architectural plans demonstrates that the method achieves robust character localization, high resilience to structured occlusions, and effective preservation of drawing integrity, outperforming bounding-box-based removal techniques.

KEYWORDS

Text Removal, Image Segmentation, Convolutional Localization, Floor Plan Processing

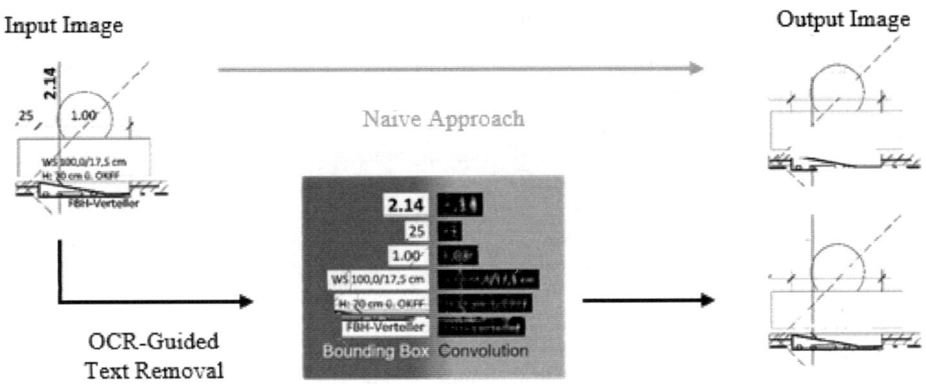

Figure 1. Complete overview of the (path above) a naive approach of removing text from a graphic and a refined approach, presented in this paper (path below)

1. INTRODUCTION

Technical drawings combine graphical elements with embedded semantic information in the form of text. Efficient separation of these components is crucial for automated processing and interpretation.

Text annotations often carry essential data such as dimensions, material specifications, or object labels, enabling advanced applications like semantic grouping and metric classification. However, the presence of text also complicates graphical analysis. Removing text is therefore a critical preprocessing step, as it simplifies the drawing and allows for cleaner recognition of geometric structures and relationships, provided that removal comes at minimal cost to the surrounding drawing elements. Difficulties arise when text overlaps graphical elements or when graphical elements are incorrectly classified as text. Both scenarios cause unintended removal of graphical details, leading to information loss in subsequent analyses. Traditional separation methods rely on heuristic approaches using connected component analysis, which frequently introduces classification errors. Modern OCR systems are robust against noise, distortions, and varied layouts, allowing direct text recognition without preliminary segmentation steps. Nevertheless, naive removal of entire detected regions often deletes underlying graphical content.

To address these challenges, we propose a method for text removal on the pixel level which leverages OCR outputs while mitigating the damage on overlapping graphical structures. Our approach employs convolution-based localization with robust, adaptable probabilistic character kernels, templates generated from a wide range of fonts, to enable accurate, low-loss removal of textual content and clean separation for downstream processing.

2. RELATED WORK

Early work on text and drawing separation in technical drawings is exemplified by the method proposed by Fletcher and Kasturi (1988), which remains widely implemented in floor plan analyzation pipelines. Their approach identifies potential text elements using connected component analysis (Rosenfeld and Pfaltz, 1966), without explicitly recognizing individual characters. These components are then filtered, grouped into text lines based on their collinearity via the Hough transform (Hough, 1962), and subsequently removed to generate a text-free drawing (Fletcher and Kasturi, 1988). However, pure connected component analysis often misclassifies small graphical elements as text (Tombre, 1998). Removing these falsely detected text regions can lead to the unintended deletion of parts of the drawing, impairing further processing. Although heuristic thresholds are commonly used to reduce such errors, manual correction by the user is frequently still required to achieve robust results (Dosch et al., 2000).

Overlapping between text and drawing elements presents another major challenge. In Fletcher and Kasturi's (1988) original method, such overlaps are typically assigned to the drawing layer and thus remain unremoved. Tombre et al. (2002) proposed an improved approach utilizing region categorization and subsequent segmentation via distance skeletons. However, their method still struggles with isolated characters and cases where entire words fully overlap graphical elements, both of which are common in architectural plans.

Ahmed et al. (2011) proposed a further improvement that targets overlapping elements by first removing wall structures and then identifying text regions through a smearing technique applied to connected components. This method improves text extraction even when annotations intersect with thin lines. However, it remains sensitive to diagonal text, where the smearing process fails to connect components properly, causing recognition performance to decline significantly.

Despite various improvements, earlier approaches still rely on separating text and graphics before applying OCR. This separation must be both complete and error-free to ensure accurate text recognition and an intact drawing, a condition that traditional methods frequently fail to meet.

Recent advances in artificial intelligence have transformed the analysis of technical drawings (Pizarro et al., 2022). Modern OCR engines now enable direct text recognition on architectural plans without requiring explicit prior separation of text and graphics (Ravagli et al., 2019). Ravagli et al. proposed a method that uses convolutional neural networks (CNNs) to recognize and classify text elements directly. However, in their approach, text removal is performed by overwriting the entire bounding box of each recognized element, resulting in the loss of all underlying graphical structures, even those not being part of the text.

In summary, while significant progress has been made in separating text from graphics in technical drawings, existing methods either rely on occasionally inaccurate pre-segmentation or cause substantial loss of graphical content during text removal. To overcome these limitations, we propose a refined approach that leverages OCR outputs combined with pixel-level character localization based on probabilistic templates, enabling precise and low-loss removal of text from complex technical drawings.

3. METHODOLOGY

Starting from OCR outputs, we refine the pixel-level localization of recognized characters to achieve precise text removal. Bounding boxes provided by the OCR engine are used only as rough guides; the final pixel assignments are determined through convolution-based matching against probabilistic character templates, minimizing the loss of underlying graphical structures.

While the OCR results supply character classification and their approximated localization, several challenges remain in mapping characters accurately to their corresponding pixels:

- Typical OCR output does not include information about the font type or font size being used.
- Fonts and font sizes often vary within a single technical drawing.
- Characters may exhibit significant variations in position or rotation.
- Text elements often overlap or partially obscure graphical features.

These challenges were identified through an analysis of approximately 2000 architectural plans, originally provided in vector format with embedded font information. The plans were rasterized at 300 dpi for later evaluation.

3.1 Character Kernel

Precise localization of individual characters within technical drawings requires a representation that is robust to font variations, sizes, and partial occlusions. To achieve this, we introduce the concept of probabilistic character kernels: two-dimensional templates that model the typical spatial structure of a character across a diverse set of 40 most common fonts used in technical drawings.

Each kernel is generated by rendering the same character in multiple fonts, centering the glyphs, and successively overlaying them to form an aggregate map. The resulting heatmap reflects the relative frequency with which each pixel is occupied by the character across all font variations: *pixels with high intensity* indicate *high probability*, corresponding to regions commonly covered by the character, while *pixels with low intensity* indicate *low probability*, corresponding to rarely occupied areas.

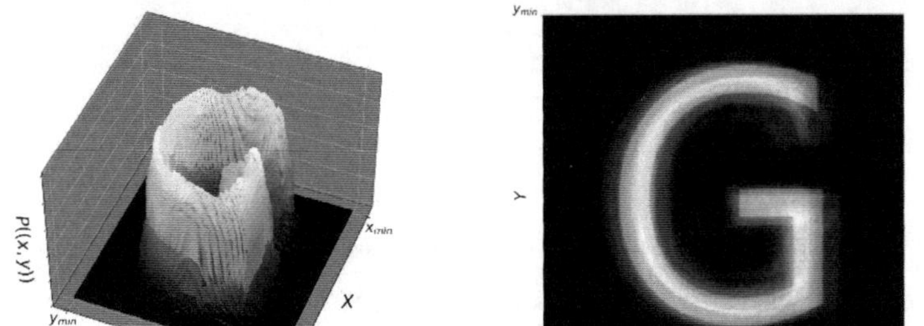

Figure 2. Probabilistic Character Kernel for the Letter 'G', as three-dimensional probability representation (left) and gray-scale two-dimensional probability representation (right)

An example kernel for the letter 'G' is shown in Figure 2. Frequent structural features, such as the left sided bowl or horizontal bar, appear prominently, whereas font-specific serifs or decorative variations are smoothed out. The kernels are normalized to form bivariate probability distributions, providing a flexible, font-agnostic model for pixel-level character localization during their later application.

For this work, a raster size of 300×300 pixels was chosen to accommodate the largest observed font size in the dataset, balancing localization accuracy and computational efficiency.

Scaling down a kernel can introduce minor discretization errors, but it is generally more reliable than scaling up, which causes uncertainty due to interpolation artifacts; thus, generating kernels at the maximum expected size is recommended. To further prevent error regions from extending into adjacent characters in the detection step, particularly important for non-monospace fonts, the kernels were slightly truncated at the edges.

All fonts were weighted equally during kernel construction to ensure a generalizable model. However, the framework allows for later specialization by adjusting font contributions, for example, to prioritize certain font families commonly used in specific technical drawing styles.

The resulting kernels provide a robust, font-agnostic basis for subsequent convolution-based character localization.

3.2 Convolution-Based Character Localization

Once probabilistic character kernels are generated, they can be used to localize text at the pixel level through convolution. For each OCR-provided bounding box, a convolution is performed between the binarized drawing and the corresponding character kernel, seeking the position with the highest match probability.

Prior to convolution, each bounding box is geometrically normalized to a standard reading direction to account for possible rotation of the bounding box in the original drawing. To account for variability in character scale, the character kernel is resized incrementally over a range of plausible sizes inferred from the bounding box dimensions.

At each scale, the character kernel is normalized using the Z-transformation to have zero mean and unit variance, ensuring comparability across scales.

The Z-transformation applied to the kernel is defined as:

$$Z(x) = \frac{x-\mu}{\sigma} \quad (1)$$

where x denotes the pixel intensity, μ is the mean, and σ is the standard deviation of all pixel values within the kernel.

This normalization not only aligns the magnitude of the kernel for the convolution but also implicitly integrates an error measure: the subtraction of the mean amplifies deviations, allowing the convolution to capture both the structural match (hit probability) and the mismatch (error) within a single response. After normalization, a discrete convolution is performed between the scaled kernel and the binarized input region resulting in a two-dimensional heat map $C(u,v)$, where each pixel value is defined as:

$$C(u,v) = K * I_{u,v} = \sum_{i,j} K_{i,j} \cdot I_{u+i,v+j} \quad (2)$$

Here, $C(u,v)$ represents the convolution score at position (u,v), $K(i,j)$ is the normalized kernel, and $I(u+i, v+j)$ denotes the binarized input image at offset positions. In the heatmap, a high value indicates for strong correspondence between kernel and image.

Figure 3. Convolution of a text sample (left) with the character kernel of the letter 'A'. The results of the convolution (right) are displayed as a normalized gray scale image. The local maximum (here a clearly visible white spot) indicates the position

Figure 3 shows an example of a localized character, where the convolution heatmap reveals a clear match as a distinct bright region.

To further ensure consistency across different kernel scales, the convolution result is additionally normalized by the sum of the positive values in the kernel. This second normalization bounds the resulting convolution scores between zero and one, making them comparable across different character sizes.

For each tested kernel scale, the maximum value within the convolution heatmap is recorded. The global maximum across all scales identifies both the most likely center position, because all kernels were generated centered, and the optimal size of the character within the bounding box.

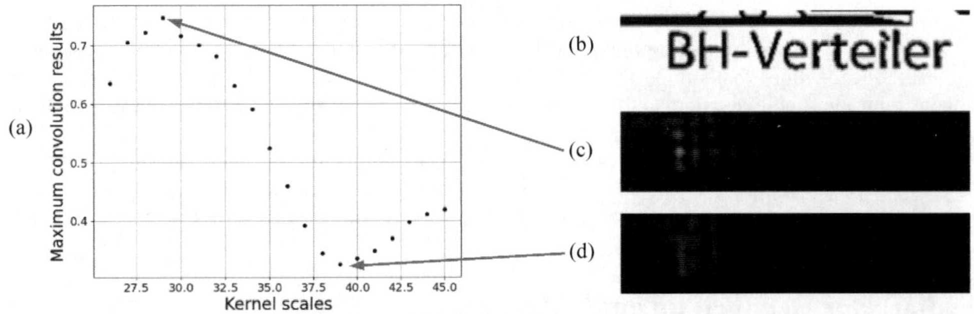

Figure 4. Convolution of the 'B' kernel at different scaling sizes: (a) the maximum convolution values for different kernel sizes, (b) the text sample, (c) the convolution result using a 30 px kernel size (showing the best maximum), and (d) the convolution result using a 39 px kernel size (showing the lowest maximum)

Figure 4 illustrates the relationship between kernel scale and maximum convolution response, highlighting the process of selecting the best-matching character size through multi-scale evaluation. This process robustly captures character locations even under font variations, minor distortions, or partial occlusions, and serves as the foundation for the subsequent text removal step.

3.3 Importance Sampling for Focused Character Localization

While convolution effectively locates characters, relying solely on the global maximum within a bounding box can lead to mislocalizations. This is due to repeated or similar character shapes within a word, causing a match of the wrong instance, particularly when identical or visually similar letters occur multiple times, such as 'm' and 'n' or 'i' and 'l'. Without additional guidance, the convolution process may prematurely focus on a later occurrence of a similar character, disrupting the intended left-to-right reading sequence.

To address these challenges, we introduce an importance sampling strategy which modifies the convolution response prior to selecting the character location. Rather than evaluating the raw convolution heatmap, it is reweighted by a positional heuristic that emphasizes regions near the expected character position and attenuates distant areas. The importance weighting function $\omega(x)$ is defined piecewise based on the relative offset x from the current expected character position o:

$$\omega(x) = \begin{cases} \frac{2}{1+\exp(-s^{-1}(x-o))} & if\ x < o \\ 2 - \frac{2}{1+\exp(-s^{-1}(x-o))} & if\ x \geq o \end{cases} \tag{3}$$

where s is a slope parameter controlling the sharpness of the focus.

In practice, s is dynamically adapted based on the width of the OCR bounding box and the number of recognized characters, according to

$$s = \frac{\text{image width}}{\text{text length}} \cdot s_{\text{base}} \tag{4}$$

where $s_{\text{base}} = 2$ is fixed for all experiments.

This formulation creates a smooth, asymmetric weighting centered at the expected position, promoting consistent localization while allowing some flexibility for variations in character spacing. After each successful character localization, the expected position is updated by shifting o by the width of the localized character. At each step, the convolution heatmap is multiplied elementwise by $\omega(x)$ after convolution is performed, dynamically guiding the search toward the next expected character location.

Figure 5. Convolution of a text sample (a) and the resulting heatmap for the letter 'a' without importance sampling, highlighting all matches (b) and with importance sampling, keeping emphasis on the first match (c)

Figure 5 illustrates the effect of importance sampling. Without importance sampling, the convolution heatmap exhibits multiple competing maxima corresponding to visually similar characters, increasing the risk of incorrect localization. With importance sampling applied, the search is sharply focused on the correct character, improving both accuracy and consistency and allowing to keep accurate track of which characters are already removed.

Having established precise character localization through convolution and importance sampling, we proceed to the removal phase. The goal is to eliminate recognized text pixels from the drawing with minimal impact on adjacent graphical structures, enabling a clean separation of text and graphics for subsequent analysis.

3.4 Character Removal through Masking

Once a character has been localized, the next step is its removal from the drawing in a pixel-precise manner. Rather than deleting entire bounding boxes, the method generates a binary mask for each recognized character, based on its associated probabilistic kernel scaled to the detected size and positioned at the localized center. All pixels corresponding to nonzero entries in the scaled kernel are considered text pixels and can be removed from the drawing. This approach ensures that only the actual text is eliminated, while graphical structures that overlap or are adjacent to text regions remain intact. By successively accumulating the removed pixels inside a buffer image, a masks for all detected characters within a line of text can be obtained.

After processing all recognized characters within a bounding box, the accumulated mask is applied to the input image, effectively removing only the text while leaving overlapping or nearby graphical elements untouched.

4. EVALUATION

To evaluate the effectiveness and robustness of the proposed text removal method, we consider three core aspects: (1) the consistency of character localization, (2) robustness to graphical overlap, and (3) the degree to which non-textual elements are preserved. These tests were designed to simulate real-world challenges present in technical drawings and to quantify the improvements achieved by our approach compared to standard bounding-box-based removal proposed by Ravagli et al.

4.1 Character Matching Consistency

To evaluate character matching consistency, we generated a convolution matrix (Figure 6), visualizing the maximum convolution scores between character kernels (rows) and templates (columns). White cells indicate strong matches (high convolution scores), and black cells indicate weak matches. A clear white diagonal shows robust self-matching reliability. However, off-diagonal white spots also appear, notably between visually similar characters (e.g., 'l' and '1'), due to structural font similarities. Since our approach targets pixel-level localization rather than symbolic accuracy, such overlaps do not hinder text removal effectiveness. Characters like 'J' exhibit weaker self-matches due to font variability, slightly reducing convolution scores. Nevertheless, our masking approach remains effective, as it utilizes all non-zero convolution results.

4.2 Overlap Robustness

To evaluate the system's resilience to structured graphical interference, such as lines typically found in architectural or technical plans, we conducted a controlled occlusion experiment using synthetic line overlays. This test quantifies how reliably individual characters can be matched and localized when partially obscured, simulating real-world plan elements such as walls, dimensions, or electrical lines.

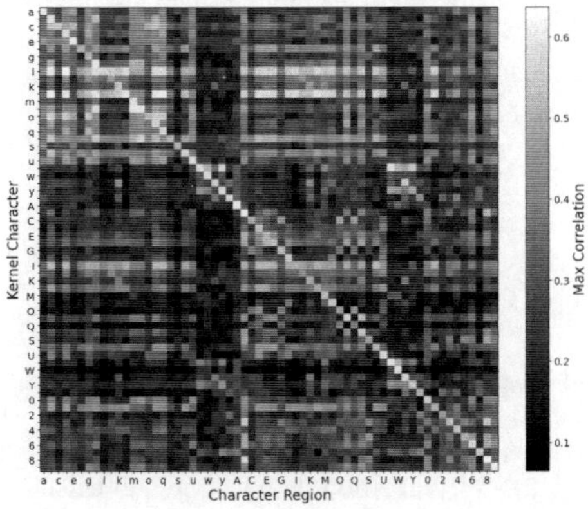

Figure 6. Character-to-Character Convolution Matrix. White indicates high convolution scores (strong matches), black indicates low scores. The white diagonal illustrates consistent self-matching

We define robustness $\mathcal{R} \in [0,1]$ as the ratio between the match score under occlusion, S_{occluded}, and the match score of the clean character template, S_{clean}:

$$\mathcal{R} = \frac{S_{\text{occluded}}}{S_{\text{clean}}} \quad (5)$$

A robustness score close to 1 indicates minimal impact from occlusion, while lower values reflect sensitivity to interference.

Each alphanumeric character (A–Z, a–z, 0–9) was overlaid with a single line at controlled angles $\theta \in \{0°, 10°, \dots, 170°\}$ and the thickness $t \in \{1, 3, 5, 7, 9\}$. Then the proposed convolution algorithm was performed for each combination of (θ, t) and the resulting robustness values were aggregated across characters.

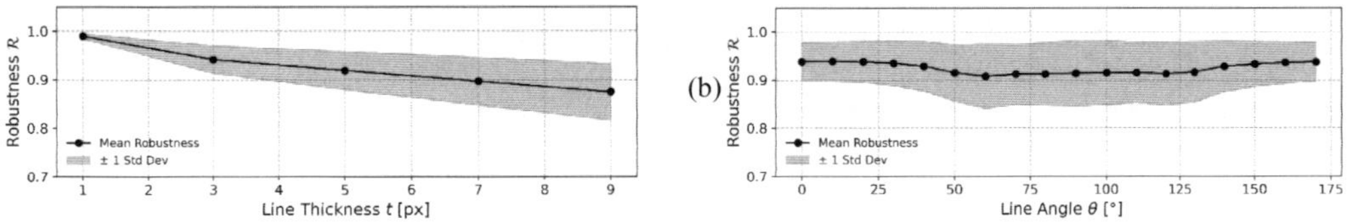

Figure 7. Average normalized robustness (y-axis) for varying line thickness in pixel (x-axis) (a) and average normalized robustness (y-axis) for varying line angles (x-axis) (b)

As shown in Figure 7 (a), robustness declines progressively with increasing line thickness, but even at maximum interference levels, the system maintains an average robustness near 0.88. Thin lines (1–3 px) have negligible impact, indicating a resilience to typical technical linework such as thin architectural guides. The observed increase in variance at higher thicknesses reflects character-specific vulnerabilities, where certain glyphs lose critical stroke information. Despite this, the overall robustness values remain consistently high, underscoring the system's ability to preserve recognition confidence under significant structured occlusion.

Angle-dependent behavior, summarized in Figure 7 (b), remains stable across most directions, with a slight dip near vertical occlusions ($\theta = 90°$), where ascenders, descenders, or central stems are most likely overlapped.

Characters like 'I', 'l', '1', and 'E' show reduced robustness and minor localization drift under vertical interference, though robustness typically remains above 0.85.

4.3 Drawing Preservation

An important objective of text removal is to minimize unintended damage to graphical structures. To assess this, we calculate the proportion of non-textual drawing elements that were incorrectly removed during the cleaning process, by comparing the original plan graphics with the cleaned output.

Evaluation results show that the proposed method achieves a low median drawing removal rate of 3.5%, indicating that the algorithm preserves the integrity of architectural plans while effectively eliminating text. This highlights the system's ability to operate conservatively in affected regions, maintaining a high level of graphical detail.

5. CONCLUSION AND FUTURE WORK

This work presented a method for pixel-accurate text removal in technical drawings, leveraging OCR outputs combined with convolution-based character localization using probabilistic kernels. The approach achieves robust text extraction across varying fonts, sizes, and overlapping structures, while preserving underlying graphical elements with minimal loss. Evaluation demonstrated consistent character localization, resilience to structured occlusions, and effective separation of text and graphics, outperforming naive bounding-box removal strategies.

Future work will explore integrating generative inpainting techniques to reconstruct graphical content in regions previously occupied by removed text and overlapping elements. We plan to investigate edge-aware methods such as EdgeConnect (Nazeri et al., 2019), originally developed for natural images, and assess their applicability to technical drawings. Depending on the outcomes, alternative approaches specifically addressing the sparse, high-contrast nature of technical graphics may be considered.

Beyond inpainting, we anticipate that reliable text removal with minimal disruption to surrounding drawing elements will directly benefit downstream tasks such as line detection and template matching, improving both robustness and accuracy. By eliminating overlapping adjacent text artefacts, the drawing becomes cleaner, structurally more consistent, and accessible for computational processing.

REFERENCES

Ahmed, S. et al, (2011). Text/graphics segmentation in architectural floor plans. *2011 International Conference on Document Analysis and Recognition*. IEEE, pp. 734–738.

Dosch, P. et al, (2000). A complete system for the analysis of architectural drawings. *International Journal on Document Analysis and Recognition*, Vol. 3, No. 2, pp. 102–116.

Fletcher, L.A. and Kasturi, R., (1988). A robust algorithm for text string separation from mixed text/graphics images. *IEEE Transactions on Pattern Analysis and Machine Intelligence*, Vol. 10, No. 6, pp. 910–918.

Hough, P.V.C., (1962). *Methods and means for recognizing complex patterns*. Patent, US.

Nazeri, K. et al., (2019). EdgeConnect: Generative image inpainting with adversarial edge learning. *arXiv preprint arXiv:1901.00212*.

Pizarro, P.N. et al, (2022). Automatic floor plan analysis and recognition. *Automation in Construction*, Vol. 140, 104348.

Ravagli, J. et al, (2019). Text recognition and classification in floor plan images. *2019 International Conference on Document Analysis and Recognition Workshops (ICDARW)*. IEEE, pp. 1–6.

Rosenfeld, A. and Pfaltz, J.L., (1966). Sequential operations in digital picture processing. *Journal of the ACM*, Vol. 13, No. 4, pp. 471–494.

Tombre, K., (1998). Ten years of research in the analysis of graphics documents: Achievements and open problems. *Proceedings of the 10th Portuguese Conference on Pattern Recognition*. Lisboa, Portugal, pp. 11–17.

Tombre, K. et al, (2002). Text/graphics separation revisited. *Document Analysis Systems V*. Springer Berlin Heidelberg, Berlin, Heidelberg, pp. 200–211.

STANDARDISED OBJECT DETECTION AND HUMAN ACTION RECOGNITION IN COMBAT SPORTS

Evan Quinn and Niall Corcoran
Technological University of the Shannon: Midlands Midwest, Limerick, Ireland

ABSTRACT

This study introduces a standardised methodology for object detection and human action recognition (HAR), designed for combat sports. The research examines the challenges posed by rapidly changing, high-intensity environments through the integration of advanced computer vision (CV) techniques and machine learning models. A comprehensive framework was established using YOLO-based detection for accurate localisation of athletes and equipment, in conjunction with Transformer architectures for efficient temporal sequence analysis of intricate fighting movements. The system uses generative models to create interpretable narratives, thereby improving the practical application of analytics for coaches and athletes. The methodology underwent rigorous validation through the use of annotated video datasets obtained from training sessions and competitive matches, showcasing high accuracy and real-time performance. Significant contributions encompass the application of modular design principles for scalable deployment, the development of adaptive processing pipelines to address data variability, and the incorporation of explainability features to enhance user trust and understanding. The integration of these components enhances action detection and classification while offering essential insights into tactical execution and movement efficiency. The findings demonstrate that the proposed system can substantially enhance conventional performance analysis, minimising dependence on manual video review and subjective evaluations. This study establishes a framework for a combat sports analytics platform that improves training protocols, supports injury prevention, and enhances athletes' competitive advantage through data-driven decision-making.

KEYWORDS

YOLO, Object Detection, Combat Sports, Computer Vision, Human Action Recognition, Transformers

1. INTRODUCTION

Recent advancements in artificial intelligence (AI) and computer vision (CV) are having an impact across a range of industries, and sports analytics has become a focus for innovation (Host and Ivašić-Kos, 2022; Van Zandycke et al., 2022). Combat sports involve swift movements and dynamic interactions, posing distinct challenges that require real-time, accurate, and context-sensitive analytical solutions. Conventional approaches that depend on manual video analysis and subjective scoring are labour-intensive and susceptible to human bias (Kasiri-Bidhendi et al., 2015; Ishac and Eager, 2021). Deep learning (DL) frameworks, especially convolutional neural networks (CNNs) and object detection architectures such as YOLO (You Only Look Once), have shown significant enhancements in speed and reliability for sports video analytics (Redmon et al., 2016; Bochkovskiy et al., 2020). YOLO processes complete images in one pass, producing bounding boxes and class probabilities efficiently, which is advantageous for tracking athletes, strikes, and defensive manoeuvres in dynamic settings (Yin et al., 2020; Veit et al., 2016). Object detection serves as a foundational element. However, comprehending the temporal dynamics of combat sports necessitates models that can effectively capture sequential action patterns. Methods such as optical flow integration and temporal attention mechanisms have demonstrated efficacy in analysing complex movements, including transitions between offensive and defensive postures (Sevilla-Lara et al., 2019; Kong and Fu, 2022). Transformer architectures, using self-attention mechanisms, improve temporal modelling by concentrating on contextually significant segments of action sequences, facilitating detailed performance assessments (Vaswani et al., 2017; Sun et al., 2022). These advancements are essential for producing actionable insights, including the identification of tactical weaknesses and the optimisation of training regimens (Kim, 2022; Bernick et al., 2021).

This study integrates YOLOv5 and Transformer models with a generative AI component based on GPT to transform raw action data into interpretable textual insights. Although YOLO has been used in sports contexts, this framework uniquely standardises data pipelines, facilitates modular optimisation, and delivers actionable narrative analytics specifically designed for combat sports. The system converts raw spatial-temporal data into comprehensible narrative summaries, effectively linking algorithmic outputs with practical coaching requirements (Jaiswal et al., 2020; Liu and Liu, 2021). Modularity facilitates scalability: the YOLO component concurrently processes multiple video streams, while the transformer module adjusts to different action complexities (Fang et al., 2020; Tavara, 2019). This flexibility facilitates deployment across various contexts, ranging from regulated training environments to actual competitions (Van Zandycke et al., 2022; Coswig et al., 2016). The principles of the framework are real-time detection, robust temporal modelling, and user-centric interpretability which extend beyond combat sports to team sports, such as tracking player formations in football, and individual disciplines, such as refining techniques in tennis (Chaquet et al., 2013; Weinstein, 2018). The incorporation of multimodal data, including inertial sensors, enhances its applicability in healthcare and security sectors (Brezov et al., 2023; Gan and Liu, 2024). This work addresses the limitations of manual analysis and advances automated interpretable solutions.

1.1 YOLO Models

The YOLO architecture transformed object detection by conceptualising it as a single regression task, facilitating real-time performance via grid-based predictions of bounding boxes and class probabilities (Redmon et al., 2016). In contrast to conventional multi-stage detectors, YOLO employs a unified methodology that reduces computational overhead, rendering it suitable for high-speed applications such as combat sports (Yin et al., 2020). Later versions, including YOLOv4, incorporated improvements such as the DarkNet framework and sophisticated feature extraction methods, attaining leading accuracy while maintaining speed (Bochkovskiy et al., 2020). YOLOv4 integrates spatial pyramid pooling and path aggregation networks, enhancing the detection of small-scale objects, including gloves and footwork patterns in martial arts (Pang et al., 2022; Kasiri-Bidhendi et al., 2015). Pretraining on extensive datasets such as COCO-text, enhanced the generalisability of YOLO. The diverse annotations of COCO-text for text and objects in natural scenes established a strong basis for fine-tuning sport-specific models (Veit et al., 2016; Jaderberg et al., 2014). Recent innovations, such as attention modules and deformable convolutions, have enhanced the utility of YOLO.

Attention mechanisms emphasise prominent areas (e.g., a boxer's fists during a punch), whereas deformable convolutions adjust to non-standard object shapes, such as grappling postures in Mixed Martial Arts (MMA) (Gao et al., 2020; Vaswani et al., 2017). In combat sports, the speed-accuracy trade-off of YOLO is essential. Yin et al. (2020) demonstrated that Faster-YOLO achieves 98% precision in strike detection at 120 frames per second (FPS), surpassing earlier models such as Region-based CNN (R-CNN). Bochkovskiy et al. (2020) demonstrated that YOLOv4 can localise athletes in crowded environments, achieving a mean average precision (mAP) of 92%, which is crucial for the analysis of sparring sessions. Synthetic data augmentation techniques complement these advancements by addressing dataset limitations in specialised areas such as martial arts (Perez and Wang, 2017; Taylor and Nitschke, 2018). Future iterations may incorporate multimodal inputs, such as depth sensors or inertial data, to improve 3D pose estimation and tackle challenges such as occlusions during clinches (Ishac and Eager, 2021; Sigurdsson et al., 2016). Leveraging YOLO's adaptability, combat sports analytics can attain significant precision in real-time performance evaluation.

2. RESEARCH DESIGN

This study employs a systematic and modular methodology for the development of an automated combat sports analysis system. The design incorporates an optimised codebase and a corresponding dataset to accurately monitor and assess training performance in combat sports. The framework comprises three essential components: object detection, temporal sequence analysis, and narrative generation. A YOLOv5-based object detector is employed to efficiently and precisely identify fighters, equipment, and critical actions in video frames. This component establishes the system's foundation by accurately capturing spatial information in real time. A custom Transformer model was developed to analyse temporal sequences and identify patterns in combat actions based on the detected objects.

This allows the system to track athletes' movements over time and interpret complex sequences, identifying transitions between offensive and defensive manoeuvres. The integration of these models facilitates thorough data collection and efficient training, ensuring the monitoring of six distinct categories of actions and objects. The system was developed using Python and employs established libraries, including PyTorch for DL, OpenCV for image processing, and Streamlit for interactive web interfaces. This technology enables scalable development and enhances real-time analytical capabilities. The modular design facilitates the independent optimisation and scaling of each component, thereby enabling the system to adapt to diverse research requirements and practical applications in high-intensity training environments. This research design offers a strong and flexible framework for the analysis of automated combat sports. This establishes a robust basis for future improvements and integration with additional sports technologies, ensuring the system can adapt to emerging technological advancements while fulfilling the stringent requirements of real-time performance monitoring.

2.1 Dataset Collection and Pre-processing

A comprehensive dataset was used to cover various combat sports scenarios, including boxing, MMA, and kickboxing. The dataset contains 9,412 images across six classes: person, boxing-bag, low-guard, punch, high-guard, and kick-knee. It includes a total of 31,019 annotations, resulting in an average of approximately 3.3 annotations per image. The dataset is divided into 70% for training, 15% for validation, and 15% for testing. The images exhibit varying resolutions, averaging 0.41 megapixels, with a maximum of 2.07 megapixels, and a standardised median resolution of 640×640 pixels. The data collection process included the uploading, organisation, and storage of raw image and video data for later annotation. Pre-processing steps were essential for maintaining consistency and improving image quality. Automated orientation correction was used to standardise image alignment, and all images were resized to dimensions of 640×640 pixels. Contrast enhancement techniques enhanced visual clarity, while various data augmentation methods were used, including rotation, cropping, shearing, brightness adjustments, exposure modifications, and partial greyscale conversion, to replicate diverse real-world conditions and strengthen model robustness. Transfer learning was employed by fine-tuning pre-trained YOLO models on a custom dataset, which accelerated convergence and improved generalisability. The training pipeline was developed in Python, utilising PyTorch for DL, OpenCV for image processing, and Streamlit for interactive user interfaces. The hardware requirements specify the need for an NVIDIA A100 GPU to enable efficient training on platforms such as Google Colab. The dataset is divided into training, validation, and test sets, with split information detailed in the appendix. The pre-processing and systematic data structure establish the basis for the effectiveness of the combat sports analysis system.

2.2 Implementation Overview

The combat sports analysis system is structured using a modular architecture consisting of three main components. The YOLOv5 model detects six distinct elements of combat sports in individual frames: person, boxing bag, low guard, punch, high guard, and kick-knee. It employs bounding-box annotations and Intersection over Union (IoU)-based logic to ensure accurate action counting while preventing double counting. The Transformer module concurrently processes sequences of YOLO detections, using a standard PyTorch Transformer encoder to capture temporal context and predict higher-level events, including combinations of actions. The system was developed using Python and uses essential libraries such as PyTorch for DL, OpenCV for image and video processing, and Streamlit for creating an interactive user interface. The code structure is systematically arranged to facilitate efficient operation, commencing with checks for the environment and dependencies, followed by the configuration of a Streamlit user interface that enables users to upload data, initiate training, and execute inference. Utility functions facilitate tasks including the verification of internet connectivity, the cloning of the YOLOv5 repository, and the updating of configuration files. YOLOv5 is trained using a dataset specified in a 'data.yaml' file, with outcomes recorded as model checkpoints and logs. Subsequently, YOLO inferences on video data are transformed into per-frame multi-hot vectors, which act as input for the Transformer model. This model employs an early-stopping mechanism to enhance performance and is used to produce advanced statistics and a GPT-based textual summary of combat actions. The framework consists of three modules: YOLO detection, Transformer temporal sequence analysis, and generative AI narrative generation. Each module can be optimised and interchanged independently. Figure 1 shows the modular flowchart of interactions of the system.

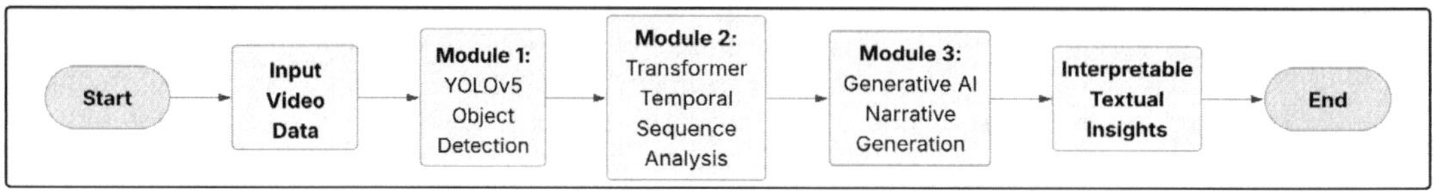

Figure 1. Modular Framework for Combat Sports Analysis

2.3 Computational Efficiency

The system's computational efficiency was assessed through the measurement of key performance indicators, including average inference time per image and memory usage during model execution. This evaluation was important for assessing the real-time applicability of this approach in combat sports settings. A comparative analysis was conducted on several YOLO models to evaluate their storage requirements and assess their performance across different hardware configurations, including high-performance GPUs, to determine the impact of computational resources on overall efficiency. This experimental framework enabled the benchmarking of YOLOv5 in three primary domains: object detection, tracking, and HAR. The capacity of each model to accurately identify and localise athletes and combat-related equipment across various scenarios in the context of object detection was examined.

mAP was used as the principal metric for in-depth performance analysis. Through the recording and analysis of computational metrics, the model configurations that exhibited the highest efficiency across various deployment scenarios were identified. This analysis elucidated the trade-offs between model size, inference speed, and accuracy, thereby guiding the decisions on hardware utilisation and scalability. These insights inform the choice of a model that satisfies demands for real-time performance and optimisation in combat sports analysis. YOLOv5 was used for its flexibility and ease of customisation, facilitating precise tuning of detection parameters for combat sports analytics. The latest YOLO models were not compatible with the modular framework.

3. RESULTS

3.1 Model Training Results

The evaluation dataset comprises 9,412 images and 31,162 annotations, resulting in an average of 3.3 annotations per image across six distinct classes. The dataset includes 113 null examples, with image resolutions varying from 0.41 MP to 2.07 MP, and a median image size of 640x640 pixels in square format. The evaluation of the dataset and model performance involves the recording of the following key metrics: Precision (%): Quantifies the ratio of accurately predicted positive instances to the total predicted positives. The highest precision attained is 96.27%. Recall (%): Assesses the ratio of accurately predicted positive instances to the total actual positive instances. The achieved recall is 96.87%. The F1 Score represents the harmonic mean of precision and recall, thereby offering a balance between these two metrics. The following acronyms are used: True Positive (TP) and False Positive (FP), and False Negative (FN). The calculation can be expressed as follows:

$$Precision = \frac{TP + FP}{TP} \quad Recall = \frac{TP + FN}{TP} \quad F1 = 2 \times \frac{Precision \times Recall}{Precision + Recall}$$

The performance of the model was assessed using established object detection metrics. The Mean Average Precision at an Intersection over Union (IoU) threshold of 0.5 (mAP@0.5) indicates the model's detection accuracy, achieving a maximum value of 98.14%. The mAP@0.5:0.95 metric provides a comprehensive evaluation by averaging precision across multiple IoU thresholds from 0.5 to 0.95, with the highest recorded value being 83.15%. The inference time, defined as the duration needed for a single forward pass in the model's inference phase, was not explicitly reported; however, it can be derived from validation logs or by evaluating the model on a representative dataset. Table 1 presents a summary of the training results for YOLOv5.

Table 1. YOLOv5 Training Results

Class	Images	Instances	Precision	Recall	mAP@50	mAP@50-95
All	564	1816	0.963	0.969	0.981	0.83
Boxing-bag	564	268	0.977	0.993	0.994	0.921
High-guard	564	186	0.978	0.968	0.992	0.841
Kick-knee	564	41	0.904	0.922	0.927	0.664
Low-guard	564	235	0.958	0.974	0.99	0.833
Person	564	860	0.983	0.982	0.993	0.885
Punch	564	226	0.976	0.973	0.992	0.837

The dataset comprises 564 images, featuring detected instances for each class, accompanied by key evaluation metrics: Precision (P), Recall (R), mAP@50, and mAP@50-95. The model demonstrates high performance, achieving an average precision of 96.3% and a recall of 96.9%, which reflects its effectiveness in object detection and classification. The mAP@50 score of 98.1% indicates superior detection performance at an IoU threshold of 0.5, whereas the mAP@50-95 score of 83% illustrates the model's robustness across various IoU thresholds. In the individual classes, "person" and "boxing-bag" demonstrate the highest precision and recall, whereas "kick-knee" presents the lowest mAP@50-95 at 66.4%, highlighting potential areas for enhancement. Figure 2 illustrates the breakdown of the dataset classes, indicating the total instances for each class. The significant disparity in class totals for individuals, relative to other classes, may result in performance issues in commercial applications. However, within the context of research testing, this phenomenon illustrates the model's capacity to learn from under-represented classes. Future research should focus on balancing dataset classes, which is expected to enhance model performance in analysing combat sports.

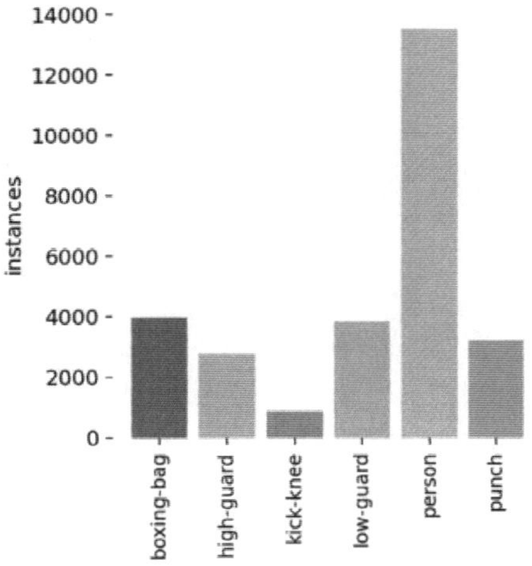

Figure 2. Dataset Classes

Figures 3 and 4 illustrate the model's classification accuracy by contrasting true and false predictions across all classes, emphasising areas of misclassification. Visualising the distribution of correctly and incorrectly classified instances aids in diagnosing model performance, identifying biases, and determining which categories contribute most to errors. This facilitates focused enhancements in training data or model architecture to improve predictive accuracy. The F1-Confidence Curve demonstrates the fluctuation of the F1 score at different prediction confidence thresholds, aiding in the determination of an optimal equilibrium between precision and recall. Analysing this curve allows practitioners to identify the optimal confidence threshold that maximises the F1 score, thereby ensuring a robust balance between false positives and false negatives in the model. This is especially beneficial in contexts where precision and recall are essential, such as in medical diagnosis or fraud detection.

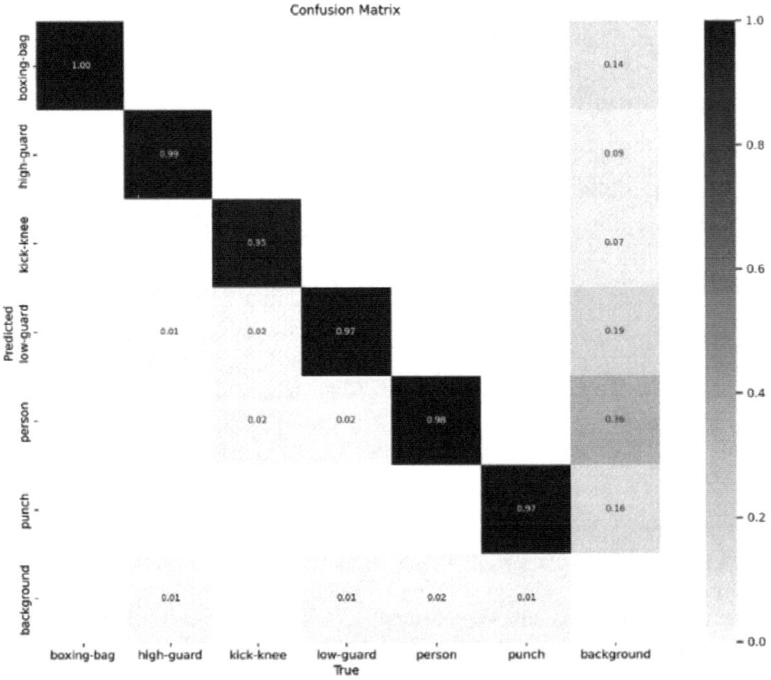

Figure 3. Confusion Matrix

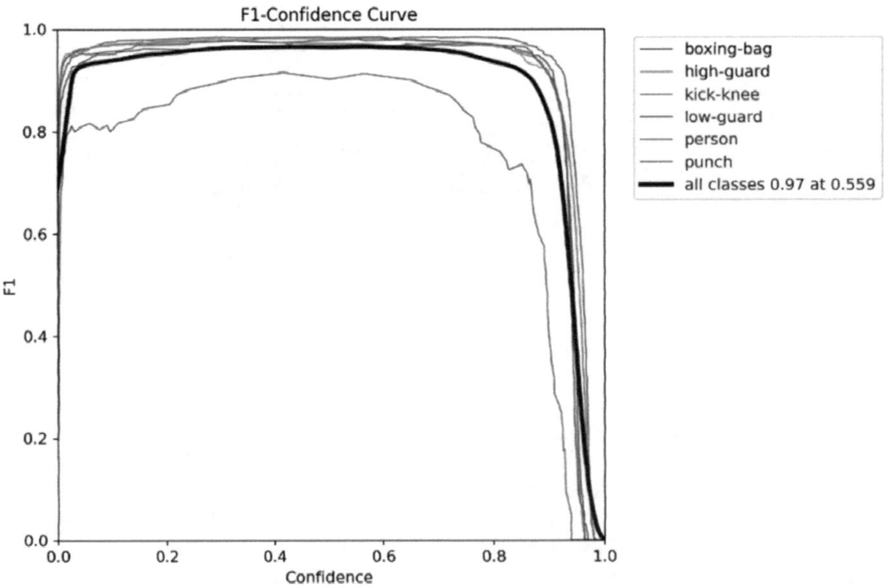

Figure 4. F1-Confidence Curve

3.2 Model Validation

Figure 5 depicts the validation batch produced by the model, showing the augmentations included. This visualisation highlights augmentation techniques, including rotation, cropping, and contrast enhancement, in diversifying the training data and enhancing the model's performance across different conditions.

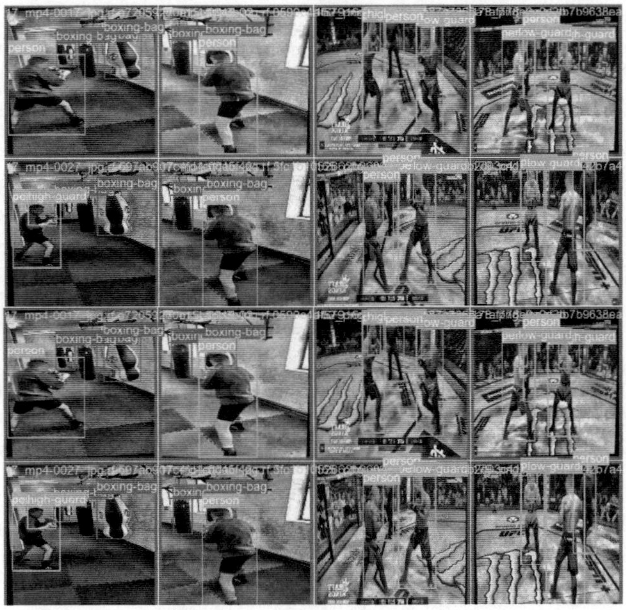

Figure 5. Validation Batch Sample

All participants had substantial expertise in movement and performance analysis, ensuring reliable and informative feedback on the model's outputs. Their thorough understanding of biomechanical principles allowed for the assessment of subtle variations in motion patterns, see Table 2 for participant's overview.

Table 2. Participants information used for model analysis.

Expert ID	Background	Experience
Expert A	Professional Kickboxing/Boxing Coach. Kickboxing Record (77 wins, 5 losses); Boxing Record (31 wins, 15 losses)	24+ years
Expert B	Muay Thai (2 exhibition bouts). Boxing (4 competitive bouts winning 2 and losing 2, 2 exhibition matches). Winner of the Celtic warrior box cup. Amateur Kickboxing Record (8 wins, 1 loss)	5+ years
Expert C	ICO and WKO Irish champion; Pro Muay Thai Fight (1 win). Amateur Boxer (6 wins, 4 losses)	5+ years
Expert D	Sport & Exercise scientist with a MSc degree in High Performance, specializing in field sports. The reviewer has not previously worked in combat sports, but his knowledge of human physiology and biomechanics provide good insight.	5+ years

Furthermore, their previous experience with analogous analytical tasks allowed them to offer constructive and informed critiques. The procedure followed by the experts includes: Experts conducted a structured evaluation process for each of the three video clips; Manual enumeration of identified actions: punches, kicks, and defensive capabilities; Model-Annotated Video Evaluation. The expert's assessment of the sample videos was compared with the models' detections to enhance the understanding of accuracy.

3.3 Expert Evaluations

Tables 3, 4, and 5 show the comparison of video analysis between the experts and the YOLO model. The results for the model count were gathered by the transformer model after run-time.

Table 3. Expert Count vs. Model Count (Video One – 15 seconds long)

	Experts					
Action Type	**A**	**B**	**C**	**D**	**Model Count**	**Agreement (%)**
Punches	38	34	36	36	36	50%
Kicks	5	5	5	5	5	100%
Total Strikes	43	39	41	41	41	50%

Table 4. Expert Count vs. Model Count (Video Two – 15 seconds long)

	Experts					
Action Type	**A**	**B**	**C**	**D**	**Model Count**	**Agreement (%)**
Punches	22	19	20	22	22	50%
Kicks	7	7	8	7	7	75%
Total Strikes	29	26	28	29	29	50%

Table 5. Expert Count vs. Model Count (Video Three – 15 seconds long)

	Experts					
Action Type	**A**	**B**	**C**	**D**	**Model Count**	**Agreement (%)**
Punches	16	15	16	16	16	75%
Kicks	0	0	0	0	0	100%
Total Strikes	16	15	16	16	16	75%

Figure 6 shows sample frames extracted from the combat sports videos from a user study, providing an insight into model performance in real-world scenarios. Frames 1 to 3 are samples from Video One. Frames 4 to 6 are samples from Video Two. Frames 7 to 9 are samples from Video Three. To assess the practical value of the proposed approach, an expert evaluation was conducted. The goal was to determine how accurately the model's inferences align with domain-expert opinions and whether its outputs could meaningfully inform real-world decision-making (e.g., coaching strategies, athlete feedback, etc.). This evaluation provides important feedback on the model's usability, interpretability, and potential areas for improvement.

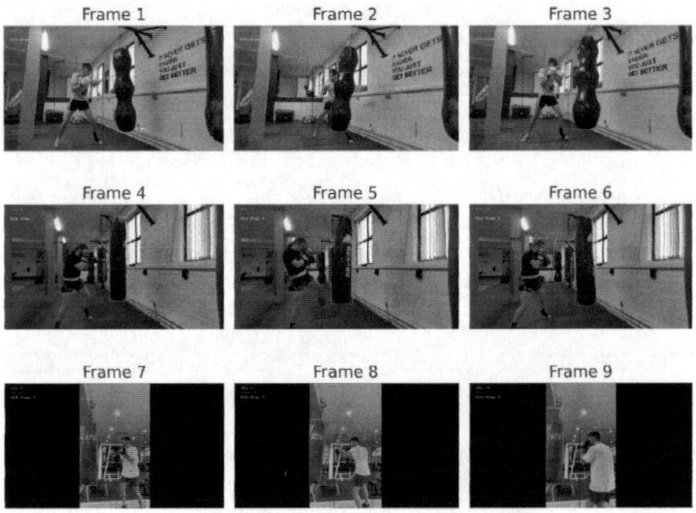

Figure 6. Sample Frames from Videos

4. DISCUSSION

The findings reveal both the potential and difficulties of implementing advanced CV techniques in combat sports. The initial system performance evaluation demonstrated that this integrated framework produced promising results. The GPT insights are shown in Figure 7 and should be compared to the results in Table 3. The YOLOv5 model demonstrated accuracy in real-time processing by detecting actions such as "punch," "high-guard," and "low-guard." The Transformer model demonstrated its ability to capture the sequential flow of actions, which is essential for understanding complex combat sequences. Iterative enhancements, including the incorporation of duration tracking and overlap analysis, facilitated a more accurate assessment of fighter performance. Hit detection and efficiency calculations were refined to distinguish between successful and unsuccessful strikes, providing additional metrics crucial for performance evaluation. This iterative optimisation process has improved the detection accuracy of frequent actions.

```
0 : "Active 55.56% of the time, resting 44.44%."
1 : "36 punch."
2 : "5 kick-knee."
3 : "Punch => 87.80% of total."
4 : "Single athlete with bag."
```

Figure 7. GPT Insights from Video One

Data augmentation is essential to address various challenges associated with dataset curation. The application of augmentation techniques, including rotation, cropping, brightness, and contrast adjustments, enhanced the model's exposure to diverse scenarios, thereby improving its generalisability. The capacity for real-time analysis and interpretation of combat actions presents opportunities for improving training methods, performance assessment, and referee assistance in competitive contexts. The system offers data-driven insights that minimise dependence on subjective human judgement. The modular nature of this approach allows for the independent optimisation or replacement of components as new technologies develop; ensuring the system's adaptability to changing dynamics in combat sports and its capability to integrate with other sensor-based data sources. This approach has highlighted challenges in detecting rare movements and the necessity for greater diversification of datasets.

5. CONCLUSIONS

This study presents a CV system employing techniques to analyse combat sports in real time. This system uses YOLOv5 for rapid object detection and a Transformer model for temporal sequence modelling, creating a framework for analysing combat actions. This method seeks to improve video analysis by precisely identifying techniques, such as guard positions and striking movements, while offering real-time feedback. The system identifies common actions but struggles with uncommon movements due to dataset limitations. Iterative optimisations, including duration tracking and overlap analysis, have improved accuracy and provided deeper analytical insights. The modular architecture allows for independent updates of components, ensuring adaptability to new technologies and enabling integration of additional data streams from wearable sensors or other sources. This research applies a generative model to transform detections into coherent textual summaries. This feature links algorithmic outputs to the practical needs of coaches and athletes, offering immediate insights to inform training adjustments. Future research will focus on enhancing and diversifying the dataset and refining temporal modelling to capture increasingly complex action sequences.

REFERENCES

Bernick, C., et al. (2021). Concussion Occurrence and Recognition in Professional Boxing and MMA matches: Toward a Concussion Protocol in Combat Sports. *The Physician and Sportsmedicine*, Vol. 49, No. 4, pp. 469-475.

Bochkovskiy, A., et al. (2020). Yolov4: Optimal Speed and Accuracy of Object Detection. *arXiv preprint*, Vol. 1, No. arXiv:2004.10934, pp. 1-17.

Brezov, D., et al. (2023). Predicting the Rectal Temperature of Dairy Cows Using Infrared Thermography and Multimodal Machine Learning. *Applied Sciences*, Vol. 13, No. 20, pp. 1-10.

Chaquet, J.M., et al. (2013). A Survey of Video Datasets for Human Action and Activity Recognition. *Computer Vision and Image Understanding*, Vol. 117, No. 6, pp. 633-659.

Coswig, V.S., et al. (2016). Biochemical Differences Between Official and Simulated Mixed Martial Arts (MMA) Matches. *Asian Journal of Sports Medicine*, Vol. 7, No. 2, pp. 1-10.

Fang, S., et al. (2020). Meta-MSNet: Meta-learning based multi-source data fusion for traffic flow prediction. *IEEE Signal Processing Letters*, Vol. 28, No. 1, pp. 6-10.

Gan, J. & Liu, J. (2024). Applied Research on Face Image Beautification Based on a Generative Adversarial Network. *Electronics*, Vol. 13, No. 23, pp. 4780-4780.

Gao, X., et al. (2020). Data Augmentation in Fault Diagnosis Based on the Wasserstein Generative Adversarial Network with Gradient Penalty. *Neurocomputing*, Vol. 396, No. 1, pp. 487-494.

Host, K. & Ivašić-Kos, M. (2022). An Overview of Human Action Recognition in Sports Based on Computer Vision. *Heliyon*, Vol. 8, No. 6, pp. 1-25.

Ishac, K. & Eager, D. (2021). Evaluating Martial Arts Punching Kinematics Using a Vision and Inertial Sensing System. *Sensors*, Vol. 21, No. 6, pp. 1-25.

Jaderberg, M., et al. (2014). Synthetic Data and Artificial Neural Networks for Natural Scene Text Recognition. *arXiv preprint*, Vol. 1, No. 1, pp. 1-10.

Jaiswal, A., et al. (2020). A Survey on Contrastive Self-Supervised Learning. *Technologies*, Vol. 9, No. 1, pp. 1-22.

Kasiri-Bidhendi, S., et al. Combat Sports Analytics: Boxing Punch Classification Using Overhead Depth Imagery. *IEEE International Conference on Image Processing (ICIP)*, 2015, Québec City, Canada. IEEE, pp. 1-5.

Kim, B.-M. (2022). The Structural Relationship between Exercise Passion, Sports Confidence, and Exercise Continuation Intention for Taekwondo Players: Moderating the Effect of the Coach's Support. *International journal of environmental research and public health*, Vol. 19, No. 23, pp. 1-10.

Kong, Y. & Fu, Y. (2022). Human Action Recognition and Prediction: A Survey. *International Journal of Computer Vision*, Vol. 130, No. 5, pp. 1-37.

Liu, S. & Liu, Y. (2021). Application of Human Movement and Movement Scoring Technology in Computer Vision Feature in Sports Training. *IETE Journal of Research*, Vol. 1, No. 1, pp. 1-7.

Pang, Y., et al. (2022). Analysis of Computer Vision Applied in Martial Arts. 2nd International Conference on Consumer Electronics and Computer Engineering (ICCECE). Guangzhou, China: IEEE.

Perez, L. & Wang, J. (2017). The Effectiveness of Data Augmentation in Image Classification Using Deep Learning. *arXiv preprint*, Vol. 1, No. 1, pp. 1-8.

Redmon, J., et al. (2016). You Only Look Once: Unified, Real-Time Object Detection. IEEE Conference on Computer Vision and Pattern Recognition. Las Vegas, NV, USA: CVPR.

Sevilla-Lara, L., et al. (2019). On the Integration of Optical Flow and Action Recognition. *Lecture Notes in Computer Science (including subseries Lecture Notes in Artificial Intelligence and Lecture Notes in Bioinformatics)*, Vol. 11269 LNCS, No. 1, pp. 281-297.

Sigurdsson, G.A., et al. Hollywood in Homes: Crowdsourcing Data Collection for Activity Understanding. *14th European Conference on Computer Vision*, 2016, Amsterdam, The Netherlands. Springer, Cham, pp. 510-526.

Sun, Z., et al. (2022). Human Action Recognition From Various Data Modalities: A Review. *IEEE Transactions on Pattern Analysis and Machine Intelligence*, Vol. 1, No. 1, pp. 1-20.

Tavara, S. 2019. Parallel Computing of Support Vector Machines. *ACM Computing Surveys*, Vol. 51, No. 6, pp. 1-38.

Taylor, L. & Nitschke, G. Improving Deep Learning with Generic Data Augmentation. *IEEE Symposium Series on Computational Intelligence (SSCI)*, 2018, Nanyang Technological University, Singapore. IEEE, pp. 1542-1547.

Van Zandycke, G., et al. (2022). DeepSportradar-v1: Computer Vision Dataset for Sports Understanding with High Quality Annotations. *MMSports '22: 5th International ACM Workshop on Multimedia Content Analysis in Sports*, Vol. 5, No. 5, pp. 1-8.

Vaswani, A., et al. (2017). Attention is All You Need. Proceedings of the 31st International Conference on Neural Information Processing Systems. Long Beach, California, USA: Curran Associates Inc.

Veit, A., et al. (2016). Coco-text: Dataset and Benchmark for Text Detection and Recognition in Natural Images. *arXiv preprint*, Vol. 1, No. 1, pp. 1-10.

Weinstein, B.G. (2018). A Computer Vision for Animal Ecology. *Journal of Animal Ecology*, Vol. 87, No. 3, pp. 533-545.

Yin, Y., et al. (2020). Faster-YOLO: An Accurate and Faster Object Detection Method. *Digital Signal Processing*, Vol. 102, No. 1, pp. 1-11.

SEEING THE UNSEEN: AI-POWERED CAMOUFLAGED PEST DETECTION

Henry O. Velesaca[1,3] and Angel D. Sappa[1,2]
[1]*Escuela Superior Politécnica del Litoral, ESPOL, Campus Gustavo Galindo Km. 30.5 Vía Perimetral, Guayaquil, 090902, Ecuador*
[2]*Computer Vision Center, Campus UAB, 08193 Bellaterra, Barcelona, Spain*
[3]*Software Engineering Department, Research Center for Information and Communication Technologies (CITIC-UGR), University of Granada, 18071, Granada, Spain*

ABSTRACT

This paper presents an innovative approach for detecting camouflaged agricultural pests using YOLOv11, a state-of-the-art deep learning architecture, and SINet-v2. The research focuses specifically on cotton bollworm detection, a significant threat to agricultural productivity. Our methodology leverages advanced neural networks to identify subtle patterns distinguishing concealed pests from their surrounding environment. Using a comprehensive dataset of 1,073 cotton bollworm images, the YOLOv11 and SINet-v2 architectures are evaluated against an existing approach. The results obtained by YOLOv11 demonstrate superior performance in the Average Precision metric for detection of 71.3% and segmentation of 60.3%. Compared to recently presented methods, like Mask R-CNN+PVT, our approach shows improved detection capabilities while requiring fewer computational resources. This work contributes to advancing automated pest management systems in agriculture, offering a more efficient and accurate solution for early pest detection.

KEYWORDS

Camouflaged Object Detection, Pest Detection, YOLO

1. INTRODUCTION

Agricultural pests pose a significant threat to global food security, causing substantial crop losses estimated at billions of dollars annually (https://www.fao.org/plant-production-protection/about/en) (Oerke, 2016). The challenge of detecting these pests is further complicated by their evolutionary adaptations, particularly camouflage mechanisms that make them nearly invisible to conventional detection methods (Skendžić et al., 2021).

In recent years, the emergence of deep learning technologies has revolutionized computer vision applications, offering unprecedented capabilities in automated pest detection and monitoring systems (Karar et al., 2021; Ullah at al., 2022). These advances have transformed traditional agricultural practices by introducing sophisticated neural network architectures like Convolutional Neural Networks (CNNs) (Venkatasaichandrakanthand et al., 2023), Region-based CNNs (R-CNN) (Rong et al., 2022), and You Only Look Once (YOLO) variants (Liu at al., 2020), which have demonstrated remarkable accuracy in identifying and classifying various pest species. The integration of these technologies has enabled real-time monitoring, early detection of pest infestations, and more precise application of pest control measures, leading to significant improvements in crop protection strategies and reduced pesticide usage.

The importance of this work lies in its potential to transform pest management practices, enabling early detection and targeted intervention strategies (Chen at al., 2020). This advancement could substantially reduce pesticide usage while improving crop protection efficiency, thereby contributing to more sustainable agricultural practices. Our approach not only addresses the immediate challenge of pest detection but also provides a scalable framework for future developments in agricultural monitoring systems.

This research presents an innovative approach for detecting camouflaged agricultural pests using state-of-the-art deep learning techniques. Our methodology leverages advanced convolutional neural networks (CNNs) and feature extraction algorithms to identify subtle patterns and characteristics that distinguish concealed pests from their surrounding environment. By combining high-resolution imaging with sophisticated neural network architectures (Peng et al, 2022).

To address this work in detail, the manuscript is organized as follows. Section 2 introduces the background on the use of pest detection techniques based on deep learning and addresses the problem as a camouflaged object detection approach. Section 3 presents the proposed approach to carry out the identification of pests using deep learning techniques. Then, section 4 shows the experimental results taking as a reference a case study for the camouflage detection of cotton bollworm. Finally, conclusions are presented in Section 5.

2. BACKGROUND

As described above, this document presents a deep learning-based approach to camouflaged agricultural pest detection. This section summarizes some of the most relevant techniques related to the present work. First, approaches based on Deep Learning are reviewed, followed by approaches based on Camouflaged Object Detection.

2.1 Deep Learning Approaches

Deep learning approaches, particularly CNN techniques, have demonstrated superior performance in pest detection. As is the case, the work proposed by Rivadeneira et al. (2023), which presented a novel approach that is especially valuable for camouflage scenarios, as it integrates super- resolution techniques with object detection methods like YOLOv8 (Jocher et al., 2023) to address the problem of very low-resolution thermal images. The most relevant feature of the camouflage area is that it allows the detection of objects that could remain undetected in visible spectrum images since it uses improved thermal images through a guided super-resolution strategy that is supported by a high-resolution image of the visible spectrum. This makes the system particularly useful for identifying camouflaged objects that will be difficult or impossible to detect using conventional images alone.

However, there are certain limitations and problems, such as the work presented by Fuentes et al. (2017) identified that these systems require massive amounts of labeled training data and significant computational resources. Their study on tomato disease detection showed that while achieving 96% accuracy under controlled conditions, performance dropped significantly when dealing with new or unseen pest varieties.

2.2 Camouflaged Object Detection Approaches

Recent research has specifically addressed the challenge of detecting pests as a Camouflaged Object Detection (COD) problem. Remarkable work by Wang et al. (2023) shows a camouflaged insect segmentation system using a Progressive Refinement Network that employs an innovative multi- stage approach to accurately detect and segment insects that blend into their environment. This architecture implements a hierarchical process that gradually refines visual features, starting with coarse features and progressing to fine details, achieving significant accuracy in detecting camouflaged insects. However, the system faces limitations such as dependence on large and well- labeled data sets, difficulties with variable lighting conditions, and extremely complex camouflage patterns, in addition to requiring considerable computational power for real-time processing.

Finally, the work recently presented by Meng at al. (2024) shows a segmentation system for camouflaged bollworm instances, which combines the Pyramid Vision Transformer (PVT) architecture with Mask R-CNN, creating a hybrid approach that improves detection and segmentation of this pest in agricultural environments. This integration leverages PVT's ability to capture global relationships and hierarchical features, while Mask R-CNN provides accurate segmentation at the instance level, achieving superior results in identifying cotton bollworms even when they are camouflaged in foliage. However, the system presents limitations in terms of required computational resources, sensitivity to varying environmental conditions, and the need for an extensive and diverse training dataset to maintain its effectiveness in different field scenarios.

3. PROPOSED APPROACH

This section details the different stages followed to carry out the proposed approach. First, the dataset is detailed, then the techniques used, and finally, the metrics needed for the quantitative evaluation.

3.1 Dataset Description

The cotton bollworm dataset represents a specialized collection of images focused on one of the most destructive agricultural pests affecting cotton crops worldwide. This dataset has been specifically created by Meng et al. (2024) to address the challenges in detecting these pests in various scenes and environmental conditions. The dataset is available at the following URL: https://www.kaggle.com/datasets/kexinmeng1/the-dataset-of-cotton-bollworms.

3.2 Deep Learning Techniques

For the segmentation task, YOLOv11 (Jocher et al., 2024) is selected as the first neural network architecture. This choice is driven by several key advantages: its exceptional processing efficiency and real-time detection capabilities, coupled with its ability to identify multiple objects simultaneously in a single forward pass. YOLOv11's sophisticated architecture offers remarkable flexibility, allowing for fine-tuned optimization to handle varying environmental conditions, including diverse lighting scenarios, and viewing perspectives. Furthermore, its open-source nature and robust community support ensure both straightforward implementation and sustainable long-term maintenance, making it an ideal choice for this application.

On the other hand, based on the state of the art, a comparison is made with the work proposed by Meng et al. (2024), which uses the Pyramid Vision Transformer (PVT) architecture with Mask R-CNN to detect camouflaged cotton bollworm instances. The dataset proposed by the same authors' team is used and compared with the metrics presented in the original paper.

Finally, it is also chosen to use SINet-v2 (Fan et al., 2021) which is a neural network used for COD tasks in two stages: search and identification. It uses EfficientNet as a backbone and incorporates two modules, neighbor connection decoder (NCD) and group-reversal attention (GRA) that allow it to excel in detecting camouflaged objects. This architecture is chosen because it has demonstrated state-of-the-art results on major reference datasets and is available as open source.

3.3 Metric Evaluation

For the evaluation of the proposed work, Average Precision (AP) (e.g., for bounding boxes and segmentation tasks), Recall, F1-score, and Pixel Accuracy metrics will be calculated to establish the performance of the proposed approach. Table 1 shows the details of the metrics to be calculated as well as a description of each of them.

Table 1. Metrics used to evaluate proposed work. TP, FP, TN, and FN represent True Positive, False Positive, True Negative, and False Negative, respectively \cite{meng2024camouflaged}

Metric	Description
AP^B	Average Precision for predicted bounding boxes, calculated across multiple IoU thresholds from 0.5 to 0.95 in steps of 0.05
AP_{B50}	Average Precision for predicted bounding boxes, evaluated at an IoU threshold of 0.5
AP_{B75}	Average Precision for predicted bounding boxes, evaluated at an IoU threshold of 0.75
AP^S	Average Precision for predicted masks, calculated across multiple IoU thresholds from 0.5 to 0.95 in steps of 0.05
AP_{S50}	Average Precision for predicted masks, evaluated at an IoU threshold of 0.5
AP_{S75}	Average Precision for predicted masks, evaluated at an IoU threshold of 0.75
Pixel Accuracy	PA = (TP + TN) / (TP + TN + FP + FN)
Recall	R = TP / (TP + FN)
F1-Score	F1 = 2 x P x R / (P + R); P = TP/ (TP + FP)

4. CASE STUDY

This section presents the case study experimental results obtained with the proposed framework. For the performance evaluation of the proposed approach, the metrics described in Table 1 are used.

4.1 System Implementation

All experiments are conducted on a high-performance workstation configured with an Intel Core i9 processor (base clock: 3.3 GHz, 16 cores/24 threads) and an NVIDIA Titan XP GPU (12GB GDDR5X, 3840 CUDA cores). This hardware configuration provided the computational resources required for efficient training, validation, and testing of the tested architectures in the context of COD tasks. The system's specifications are chosen to ensure optimal processing of complex neural network operations and handling of large-scale dataset operations.

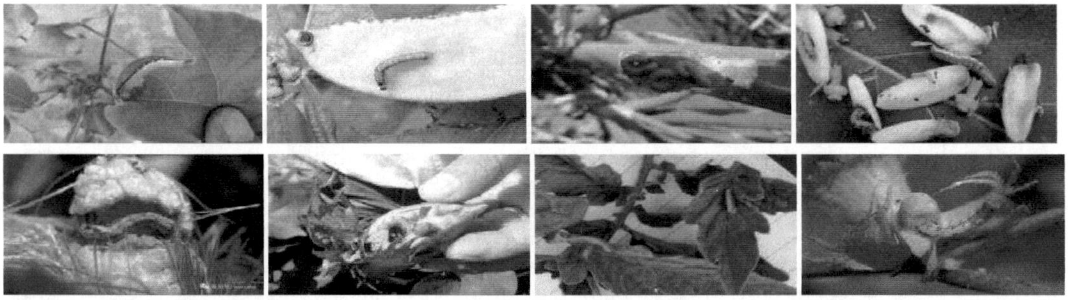

Figure 1. Example of images from the cotton bollworm dataset presented by Meng et al. (2024)

4.2 Dataset

The dataset used for the different experiments carried out is obtained from (Meng et al., 2024). This dataset consists of 1080 images, but inconsistencies are found in 7 of these images, which are removed. Table 2 shows the distribution of the dataset for each of the subsets. Additionally, Figure 1 shows examples of the images that are part of the dataset.

Table 2. Distribution of dataset

Task	Cotton bollworm	
	# of Images	# of Instances
Training	856	932
Validation	161	172
Testing	56	69
Total	1073	1176

4.3 YOLOv11 Implementation

To enhance the model's training capabilities, the initial step involved expanding the training dataset through data augmentation techniques. This is accomplished using the Albumentations library (Buslaev et al., 2020), a powerful tool specifically designed for computer vision applications, including the development of object detection models like YOLOv11. The library provides a comprehensive suite of image transformation operations, encompassing techniques such as random cropping, rotational adjustments, brightness modifications, contrast alterations, and various other transformations. These modifications can be systematically applied during the data preprocessing phase, creating additional training samples that maintain realistic characteristics while introducing controlled variations to the original images. This approach effectively enriches the training dataset, promoting better model generalization and robustness. The model "*yolo11m-seg.pt*" with training epochs of 500, batch size of 8, and image size of 640 × 640 pixels are used as execution parameters.

4.4 SINet-v2

The SINet-V2 implementation is used for the detection of cotton bollworm camouflage. This architecture has been designed for the COD task and is considered for this work because it is a state-of-the-art architecture that has obtained very good results. The implementation uses PyTorch and features a custom loss function that combines weighted BCE (Binary Cross Entropy) and IoU (Intersection over Union). Training is carried out for 100 epochs with a batch size of 16 and an image size of 352×352 pixels, using the Adam optimizer with an initial learning rate of 0.0001 that is adjusted every 25 epochs.

4.5 Experimental Results

As a last stage to evaluate the performance of the proposed approach 56 test images are considered for the calculation of the metrics. Table 3 shows the result of the calculation of the metrics for each of the techniques. The values of the Mask R-CNN+PVT (Meng et al., 2024) technique are obtained from the original paper. In addition, Figure 2 (*3rd column*) uses the images of the results of the article proposed by Meng et al. (2024) for qualitative comparison in this work.

Table 3. Evaluation of metrics for each technique---notation as presented in Table 1

Technique	Detection			Segmentation			PA	R	F1
	AP^B	AP_{B50}	AP_{B75}	AP^S	AP_{S50}	AP_{S75}			
Mask R-CNN+PVT	62.5	89.7	72.9	59.5	89.2	72.9	**98.61**	**99.12**	**98.95**
YOLOv11	**71.3**	**92.3**	**73.8**	**60.3**	**90.3**	**73.1**	98.34	96.47	97.79
SINet-v2	54.5	71.3	59.8	44.5	56.3	49.2	90.07	65.61	47.70

Table 3 shows that YOLOv11 architecture achieved notable metrics with an AP^B of 71.3% for detection and an AP^S of 60.3% for segmentation, significantly outperforming the Mask R-CNN+PVT model which achieved 62.5% and 59.5% respectively. This improvement in accuracy is particularly relevant considering the inherent complexity of detecting camouflaged pests and a notable aspect of YOLOv11 is its computational efficiency. The proposed model requires substantially fewer resources, operating at 123.0 GFlops compared to the 154.78 GFlops of the Mask R-CNN+PVT while maintaining a smaller number of parameters (22.34M vs 41.78M) (see Table 4). This optimization in computational resources makes the system more viable for practical implementations in real agricultural environments. These results are particularly impressive considering the complex nature of the test images including various camouflage patterns and varying environmental conditions.

Table 4. Comparison between GFlops and the number of parameters

Technique	Input size (px)	GFlops	#Param. (M)
Mask R-CNN+PVT	800 x 640	154.78	41.78
YOLOv11	640 x 640	123.00	22.34
SINet-v2	352 x 352	144.48	26.98

On the other hand, Figure 2 shows the qualitative evaluation of the results obtained by each technique, in which better obtaining of bounding boxes and segmentation masks can be obtained using YOLOv11; these results are consistent with the quantitative metrics obtained for the detection and segmentation tasks. In addition, Figure 3 shows more challenging images when finding the cotton bollworm camouflaged in the different scenarios where they blend in with the environment, and it is more difficult to visualize them with the naked eye. These qualitative results demonstrate the robustness of YOLOv11 in complex scenarios, and this can equal or improve the results of state-of-the-art techniques specialized for COD tasks. Also, SINet-v2 does not obtain good results and is limited to detecting and segmenting salient objects in this particular dataset (see Table 2 *1st row, 2nd column*).

Although the presented dataset is an excellent contribution, it also presents certain inconsistencies in the labeling, for example, Table 2 (*5th row, 2nd column*) shows a labeling error where the GT does not contain the mask of the small worm located on the right side but Mask R-CNN+PVT and YOLO can detect it. Likewise, Table 3 (*1st row, 2nd column*) shows a labeling error where the GT does not show the mask of the small worm located on the left side, but YOLO also detects it (*1st row and 4th column green mask*). This is one reason why the PA, R, and F1 metrics do not present higher values.

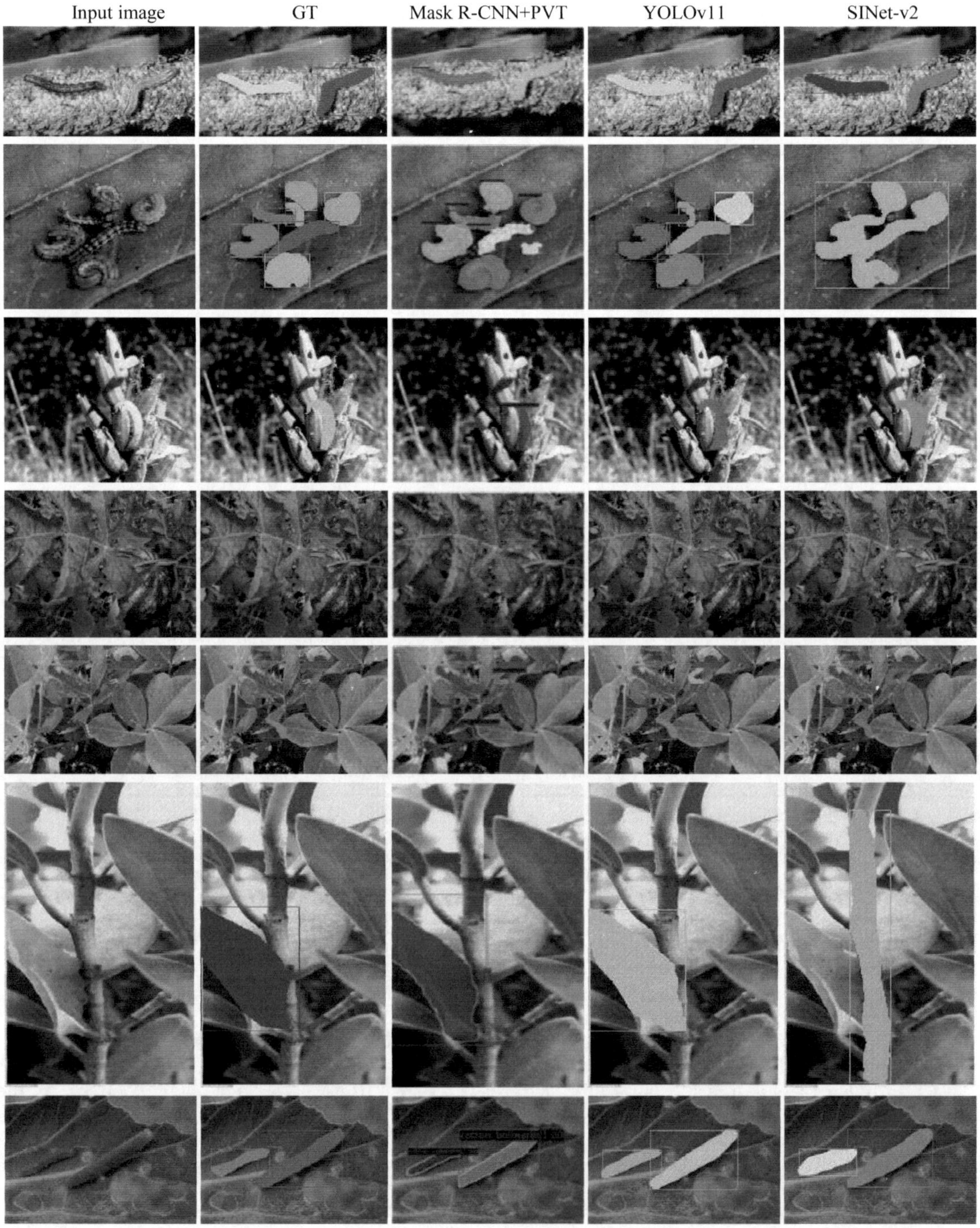

Figure 2. Prediction results using Mask R-CNN+PVT, YOLOv11, and SINet-v2

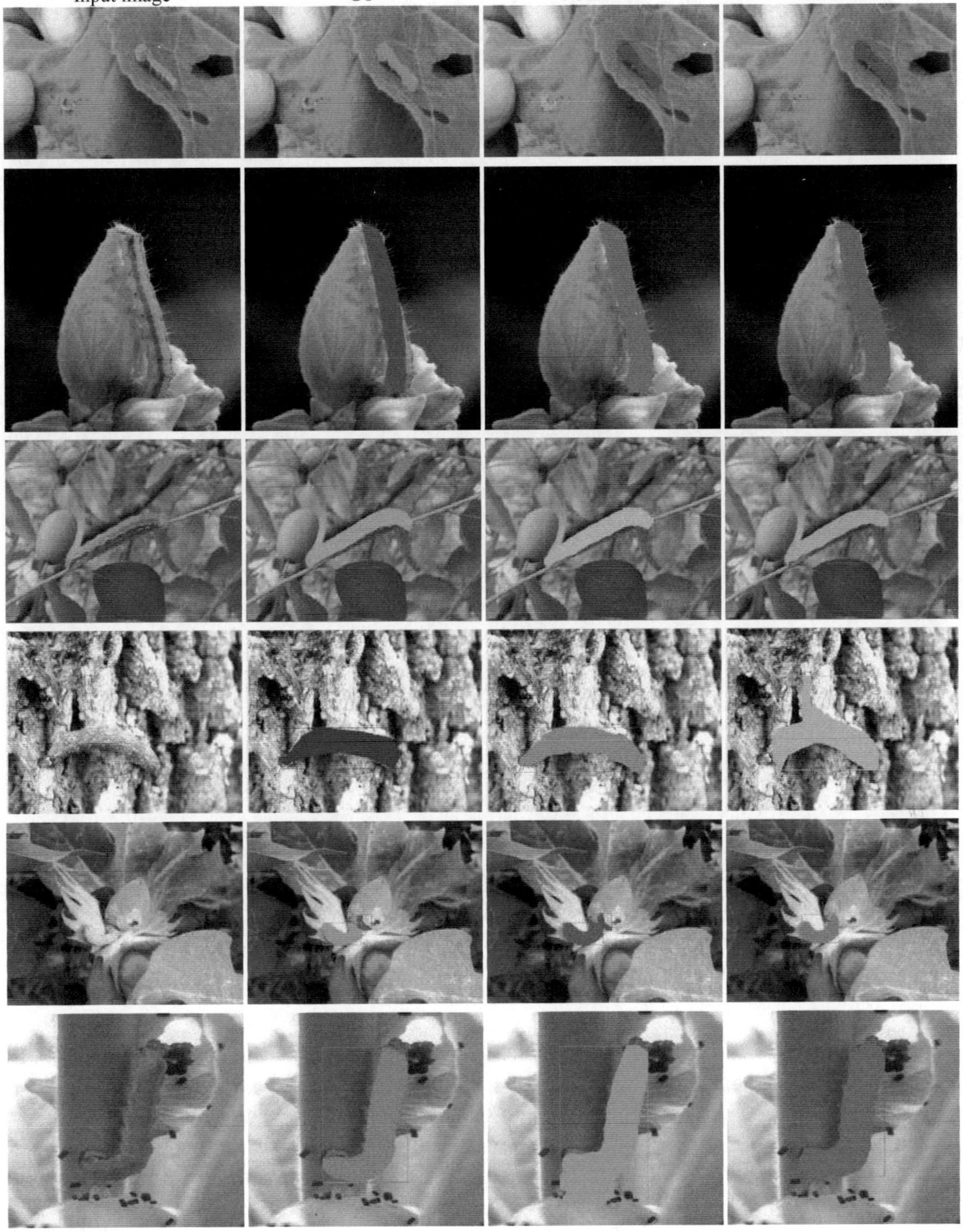

Figure 3. Prediction results using YOLOv11 and SINet-v2 on challenging camouflage images

5. CONCLUSION

This research demonstrates the effectiveness of the YOLOv11-based approach for camouflaged agricultural pest detection, significantly outperforming recent methods such as Mask R-CNN+PVT in both performance and computational efficiency. Another finding is that SINet-v2 exhibits lower performance than YOLOv11, despite SINet-v2 being a specialized architecture for COD tasks. The YOLOv11 evaluation architecture not only achieves better pest detection and segmentation but also requires fewer computational resources, making it more practical for deployments in real agricultural environments. Systems based on these types of technologies not only promise to reduce herbicide use but also offer more precise and environmentally friendly weed control solutions. The robustness of the system is evidenced by its ability to maintain high performance under various challenging scenarios with different camouflage patterns and varying environmental conditions, thus establishing a solid foundation for future developments.

ACKNOWLEDGEMENT

This material is based upon work supported by the Air Force Office of Scientific Research under award number FA9550-24-1-0206; in part by the ESPOL project CIDIS-003-2024-T; and in part by the University of Granada.

REFERENCES

Buslaev, A., Iglovikov, V.I., Khvedchenya, E., Parinov, A., Druzhinin, M. & Kalinin, A.A., (2020). Albumentations: fast and flexible image augmentations. Information, 11(2), p.125.

Chen, C.J., Huang, Y.Y., Li, Y.S., Chang, C.Y. & Huang, Y.M., (2020). An AIoT based smart agricultural system for pests detection. IEEE Access, 8, pp.180750-180761.

Fan, D.P., Ji, G.P., Cheng, M.M. & Shao, L., (2021). Concealed object detection. IEEE Transactions on Pattern Analysis and Machine Intelligence, 44(10), pp.6024-6042.

Fuentes, A., Yoon, S., Kim, S.C. & Park, D.S., (2017). A robust deep-learning-based detector for real-time tomato plant diseases and pests recognition. Sensors, 17(9), p.2022.

Jocher, G., Chaurasia, A. & Qiu, J., (2023). Ultralytics yolov8. Available at: https://github.com/ultralytics/ultralytics

Jocher, G. & Qiu, J., (2024). Ultralytics yolo11. Available at: https://github.com/ultralytics/ultralytics

Karar, M.E., Alsunaydi, F., Albusaymi, S. & Alotaibi, S., (2021). A new mobile application of agricultural pests recognition using deep learning in cloud computing system. Alexandria Engineering Journal, 60(5), pp.4423-4432.

Liu, J. & Wang, X., (2020). Tomato diseases and pests detection based on improved Yolo V3 convolutional neural network. Frontiers in Plant Science, 11, p.898.

Meng, K., Xu, K., Cattani, P. & Mei, S., (2024). Camouflaged cotton bollworm instance segmentation based on PVT and Mask R-CNN. Computers and Electronics in Agriculture, 226, p.109450.

Oerke, E.C., (2006). Crop losses to pests. The Journal of Agricultural Science, 144(1), pp.31-43.

Peng, Y. & Wang, Y., (2022). CNN and transformer framework for insect pest classification. Ecological Informatics, 72

Rivadeneira, R.E., Velesaca, H.O. & Sappa, A., (2023), November. Object detection in very low-resolution thermal images through a guided-based super-resolution approach. In: 2023 17th International Conference on Signal-Image Technology & Internet-Based Systems (SITIS), IEEE, pp.311-318.

Rong, M., Wang, Z., Ban, B. & Guo, X., (2022). Pest Identification and Counting of Yellow Plate in Field Based on Improved Mask R-CNN. Discrete Dynamics in Nature and Society, 2022(1), p.1913577.

Skendžić, S., Zovko, M., Živković, I.P., Lešić, V. & Lemić, D., (2021). The impact of climate change on agricultural insect pests. Insects, 12(5), p.440.

Ullah, N., Khan, J.A., Alharbi, L.A., Raza, A., Khan, W. & Ahmad, I., (2022). An efficient approach for crops pests recognition and classification based on novel deeppestnet deep learning model. IEEE Access, 10, pp.73019-73032.

Venkatasaichandrakanthand, P. & Iyapparaja, M., (2023). Pest detection and classification in peanut crops using CNN, MFO, and EViTA algorithms. IEEE Access, 11, pp.54045-54057.

Wang, J., Hong, M., Hu, X., Li, X., Huang, S., Wang, R. & Zhang, F., (2023). Camouflaged insect segmentation using a progressive refinement network. Electronics, 12(4), p.804.

UNDERWATER IMAGE ENHANCEMENT USING TRANSFORMER-BASED GENERATIVE ADVERSARIAL NETWORKS

Kai-Hsun Chen and Jin-Jang Leou
Department of Computer Science and Information Engineering
National Chung Cheng University, Chiayi 621, Taiwan, ROC

ABSTRACT

In this study, an underwater image enhancement approach using transformer-based generative adversarial networks is proposed, which consists of feature extraction module, enhanced channel-wise multiscale attention module, mixed attention module, image reconstruction module, and discriminator. Feature extraction module captures and represents related patterns and structures from underwater images. In both enhanced channel-wise multiscale attention and modified mixed attention modules, various attention mechanisms are utilized to enhance various types of underwater image features. Image reconstruction module will generate the final processed underwater image. Additionally, discriminator is employed to compute score S for cGAN loss computations. Based on the experimental results obtained in this study, in terms of six objective performance metrics and subjective evaluation, the performance of the proposed approach is better than those of five comparison approaches.

KEYWORDS

Underwater Image Enhancement, Generative Adversarial Network, Vision Transformer, Feature Extraction, Taylor Expanded Multi-Head Self-Attention, Manhattan Self-Attention

1. INTRODUCTION

Underwater image enhancement was an important research topic in image processing and computer vision applications, such as ocean engineering and underwater exploration and archaeology (Jain and Deo, 2006). The scattering and absorption of light in underwater environments differ significantly from those in natural light environments. Underwater light scattering and the varying absorbance of water molecules at different wavelengths may degrade severely the quality of underwater images.

Underwater image enhancement approaches can be roughly classified into two categories: traditional and learning-based approaches. Traditional approaches for underwater image enhancement usually used handcrafted features and predefined algorithms, which can be further classified into six sub-categories: spatial domain-based, transform domain-based, color constancy-based, optical imaging-based, polarization-based, and prior knowledge-based approaches. Spatial domain-based approaches (Fu et al., 2014) adjusted image pixel values by redistributing image histograms and performed image color, saturation, and intensity enhancement in different color spaces. Transform domain-based approaches (Agaian et al., 2001) used mathematical transforms, such as Fourier and wavelet transforms, to perform underwater image enhancement in transformed domains. Color constancy-based approaches (Zhang et al., 2019) tackled color distortion and blurriness in underwater images by using color constancy algorithms. Optical imaging-based approaches (Wen et al., 2013) improved underwater image clarity and realism using Jaffe-McGlamery model. Polarization-based approaches (Treibitz et al., 2009) captured underwater images with reduced noise via some passive imaging techniques. Prior knowledge-based approaches (Zhang et al., 2022) utilized prior knowledges, such as dark channel and maximum intensity priors, to restore degraded underwater images.

Learning-based approaches can be further classified into three sub-categories: convolutional neural network based (CNN-based), diffusion-based, and transformer-based. CNN-based approaches (Li et al., 2020; Li et al., 2024; Zhou et al., 2024) used extracted underwater image features, such as intricate details and structures, to enhance color fidelity, contrast, and overall visual clarity. Diffusion-based approaches (Tang et al., 2023; Guan et al., 2024) iteratively denoised and enhanced underwater images by simulating diffusion processes. Transformer-based approaches (Peng et al., 2023; Khan et al., 2024) leveraged some self-attention mechanisms of vision transformers (ViTs) to capture long-range dependencies and global contextual information in underwater images. Additionally, Liu et al. (2025) proposed an underwater image enhancement approach using cascaded contrastive learning. In this study, an underwater image enhancement approach using transformer-based generative adversarial networks is proposed.

This paper is organized as follows. The proposed underwater image enhancement approach is described in Section 2. Experimental results are shown in Section 3, followed by conclusions.

2. PROPOSED APPROACH

2.1 System Architecture

As shown in Figure 1, based on conditional generative adversal network architecture (cGAN) (Isola et al., 2017), the proposed approach consists of five main modules, namely, feature extraction module, enhanced channel-wise multiscale attention module, modified mixed attention module, image reconstruction module, and discriminator. Feature extraction module captures and represents related patterns and structures from underwater images. In both enhanced channel-wise multiscale attention and modified mixed attention modules, various attention mechanisms are utilized to enhance various types of underwater image features. Image reconstruction module will generate the final processed underwater image. Additionally, discriminator is employed to compute score *S* for cGAN loss computations.

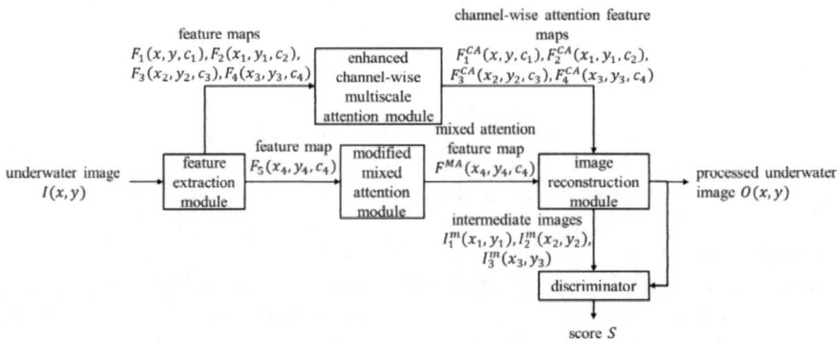

Figure 1. Framework of the proposed approach

In this study, $I(x,y)$, $F_1(x,y,c_1)$, $F_2(x_1,y_1,c_2)$, $F_3(x_2,y_2,c_3)$, $F_4(x_3,y_3,c_4)$, and $F_5(x_4,y_4,c_4)$ denote the input underwater image and various scaled feature maps, respectively, where $I(x,y) = \big(I_R(x,y), I_G(x,y), I_B(x,y)\big)$ consists of three (red, green, blue) component images, $0 \le I(x,y) \le 255$, $-1 \le F_1(x,y,c_1), F_2(x_1,y_1,c_2), F_3(x_2,y_2,c_3), F_4(x_3,y_3,c_4), F_5(x_4,y_4,c_4) \le 1, 1 \le x \le W, 1 \le x_1 \le W/2, 1 \le x_2 \le W/4, 1 \le x_3 \le W/8, 1 \le x_4 \le W/16, 1 \le y \le H, 1 \le y_1 \le H/2, 1 \le y_2 \le H/4, 1 \le y_3 \le H/8, 1 \le y_4 \le H/16, c_1 = 1,2,\dots,32, c_2 = 1,2,\dots,64, c_3 = 1,2,\dots,128$, $c_4 = 1,2,\dots,256$, and H and W denote the height and width of underwater images, respectively. $F_1^{CA}(x,y,c_1)$, $F_2^{CA}(x_1,y_1,c_2)$, $F_3^{CA}(x_2,y_2,c_3)$, $F_4^{CA}(x_3,y_3,c_4)$, and $F^{MA}(x_4,y_4,c_4)$ denote four scaled channel-wise attention feature maps and mixed attention feature map, respectively. To compute score S of discriminator, intermediate underwater images $I_1^m(x_1,y_1)$, $I_2^m(x_2,y_2)$, and $I_3^m(x_3,y_3)$ are fed into discriminator, along with the processed underwater image $O(x,y)$.

2.2 Feature Extraction Module

As shown in Figure 2, the proposed feature extraction module consists of convolution layers (*conv*'s), depth-wise separable and deformable convolution layers (DSDCNs) (Qiu et al., 2023), Taylor expanded multi-head self-attention transformer blocks (T-MSAs) (Qiu et al., 2023), depth-wise convolution layers (*dwconv*'s) (Chollet, 2017), and the inverse operation of pixel shuffle (*PixelUnshuffle*) (Shi et al., 2016). DSDCN and hard sigmoid-weighted linear unit activation function (*HardSwish*) (Howard et al., 2019) are utilized to enhance feature representation by accommodating various scales and flexible receptive fields. The proposed feature extraction module can effectively extract informative features for underwater image quality. T-MSA applies self-attention over the entire feature map using Taylor expansion on softmax activation function ($softmax$), which can effectively model long-range pixel dependencies and enable fine-grained feature processing. To reduce computational complexity, *dwconv*, *conv*, and *PixelUnshuffle* are together utilized to downsample the feature maps. In this study, the proposed feature extraction module extracts five feature maps at different scales.

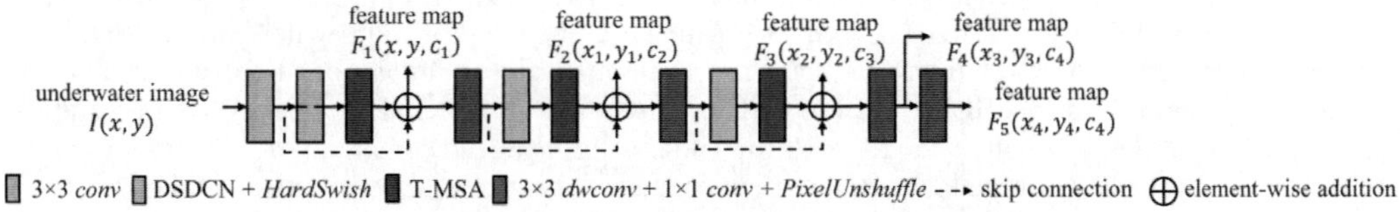

Figure 2. Framework of the proposed feature extraction module

$F_1(x, y, c_1)$, $F_2(x_1, y_1, c_2)$, $F_3(x_2, y_2, c_3)$, and $F_4(x_3, y_3, c_4)$ with different sizes and different numbers of channels are fed into the proposed enhanced channel-wise multiscale attention module for channel-wise multi-head attention. $F_5(x_4, y_4, c_4)$ has the same number of channels as $F_4(x_3, y_3, c_4)$ with smaller in size, which is fed into the proposed modified mixed attention module to obtain more detailed image features. Additionally, skip connections are employed to directly connect the input and output layers with same resolutions, which will reserve image features and prevent gradient vanished during training.

2.3 Modified Mixed Attention Module

As shown in Figure 3, the proposed modified mixed attention module consists of four consecutive modified mixed attention blocks, which will effectively extract global and local features from underwater images.

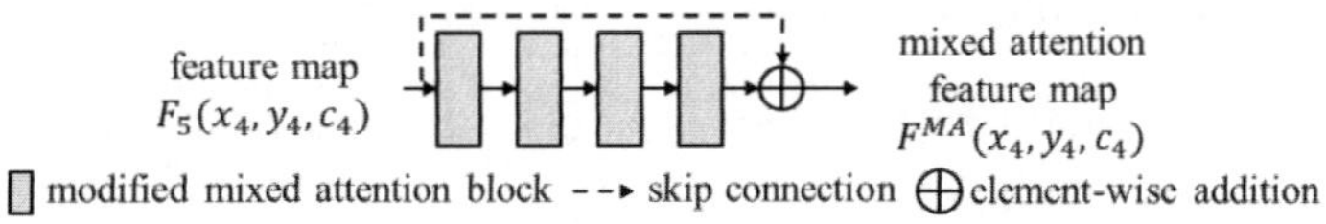

Figure 3. Framework of the proposed modified mixed attention module

As shown in Figure 4, the proposed modified mixed attention block consists of linear projection operation, two attention mechanisms (Li et al., 2023; Liu et al., 2021), namely, anchored stripe attention and window attention, three operations (Yang et al., 2020), namely, global context embedding (GCE), channel normalization (CN), and gate adaptation (GA), and a gated depth-wise convolution feed-forward network (GDFN) (Zamir et al., 2022). Multi-layer perceptron (MLP) in transformer layer is replaced by GDFN in the proposed modified mixed attention module.

Anchored stripe attention is utilized to effectively model long-range pixel dependencies and comprehensively capture global features in underwater images. By partitioning the feature map into windows of different sizes, window attention is utilized to capture diverse spatial information. GCE, CN, and GA are together employed to model channel relationships in various feature maps. Finally, through element-wise addition, two generated feature maps are combined with the previous feature map via skip connections. The resulting feature map is then fed into GDFN to generate the processed feature map.

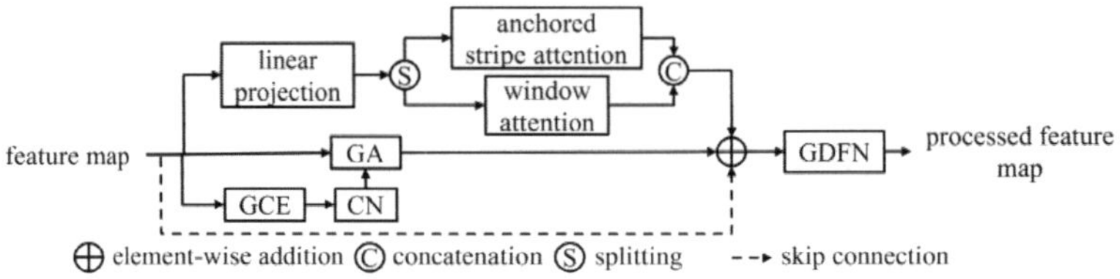

Figure 4. Framework of the proposed modified mixed attention block

2.4 Enhanced Channel-Wise Multiscale Attention Module

As shown in Figure 5, the proposed enhanced channel-wise multiscale attention module consists of four parallel positional encoding generators (PEGs) (Chu et al., 2021) and linear projection operations, four consecutive enhanced channel-wise multi-head attention blocks (enhanced CHMAs), and four parallel feature mapping operations. Four PEGs are utilized to extract positional embedding of multiscale feature maps, which may better preserve positional relationships between pixels after linear projection. Four consecutive enhanced CHMAs are employed to enhance different channel features in underwater images, while parallel feature mapping operations are employed to perform underwater image reconstruction. The proposed enhanced CHMA consists of layer normalization, modified enhanced channel-wise attention, and GDFNs.

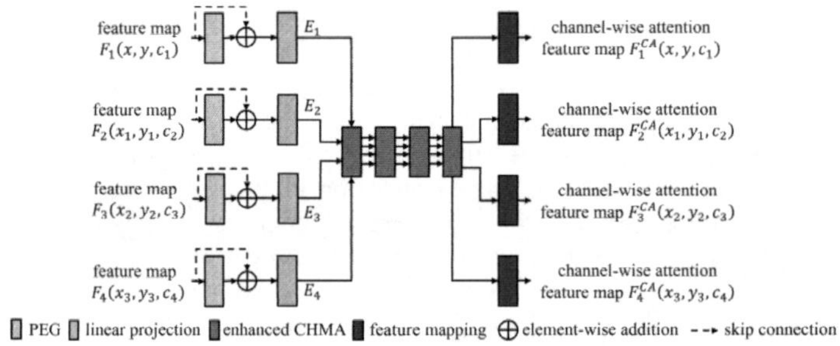

Figure 5. Framework of the proposed enhanced channel-wise multiscale attention module

2.5 Image Reconstruction Module

In this study, in image reconstruction module, the feature maps generated by enhanced channel-wise multiscale attention and modified mixed attention modules are utilized to reconstruct enhanced underwater images. As shown in Figure 6, the proposed image reconstruction module consists of *conv*'s, leaky rectified linear unit function (*LeakyReLU*), Gaussian error linear unit function (*GELU*), Manhattan self-attention blocks (MaSAs) (Fan et al., 2023), spatio-spectro fusion-based attention blocks (SSFBs) (Khan et al., 2024), and upsampling operation (bilinear interpolation). SSFB is utilized to integrate frequency and spatial information. In this study, mixed attention feature map and channel-wise attention feature maps are processed through four MaSAs, SSFBs, and concatenation operations to generate the final processed underwater image.

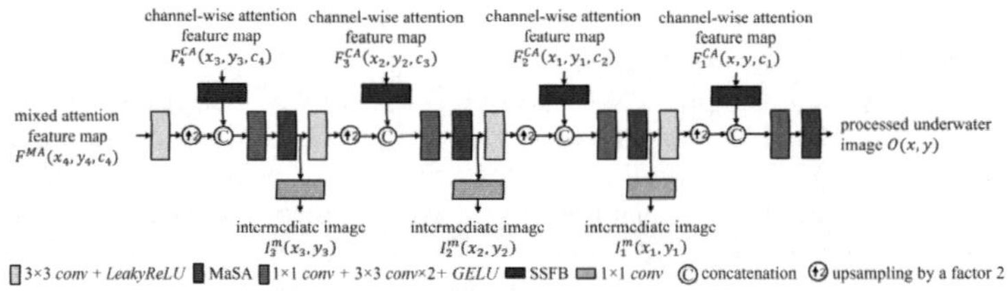

Figure 6. Framework of the proposed image reconstruction module

2.6 Discriminator

In this study, discriminator in Peng et al. (2023) is employed, in which three intermediate images $I_1^m(x_1, y_1)$, $I_2^m(x_2, y_2)$, and $I_3^m(x_3, y_3)$, the processed underwater image $O(x, y)$, and ground-truth images at different scales are together employed to compute score S for cGAN loss computations.

2.7 Loss functions

To generate more realistic and visually appealing underwater images, cGAN loss L_{cGAN} (Isola et al., 2017) is employed, in which score S and $L_{cGAN}(G, D)$ are defined as

$$S = \mathbb{E}\left[\log\left(1 - D\left(G(I(x, y))\right)\right)\right], \tag{1}$$

$$L_{cGAN}(G, D) = \mathbb{E}\left[\log\left(D(GT(x, y))\right)\right] + S, \tag{2}$$

where $\mathbb{E}[\cdot]$ denotes the expectation operator, $G(\cdot)$ and $D(\cdot)$ denote generator and discriminator, respectively, and $GT(x, y)$ denotes ground-truth image. To ensure accuracy in multiple scales by minimizing the difference between the processed and ground-truth images, pixel-wise loss L_{pixel} is employed. To balance low-level pixel accuracy, in terms of structural similarity index measure (SSIM) $SSIM$, SSIM loss L_{SSIM}, and perceptual loss L_{per} (Johnson et al., 2016) are employed and defined as

$$L_{SSIM} = 1 - SSIM, \tag{3}$$

$$L_{per} = \sum_{k=1}^{n} \left\| \phi_k(O(x, y)) - \phi_k(GT(x, y)) \right\|_1, \tag{4}$$

where $\phi_k(\cdot)$ and n denote the k-th layer feature extractor and number of layers in pretrained VGG-19 network (Simonyan et al., 2014), respectively, and $\|\cdot\|_1$ denotes L_1 norm. To ensure accurate color representation and better perceptual quality, LAB color loss L_{LAB} and LCH color loss L_{LCH} (Peng et al., 2023) are employed.

The total loss L_{total} is defined as

$$L_{total} = \lambda_1 \cdot \arg\min_G \max_D L_{cGAN}(G, D) + \lambda_2 \cdot L_{pixel} + \lambda_3 \cdot L_{SSIM} + \lambda_4 \cdot L_{per} + \lambda_5 \cdot L_{LAB} + \lambda_6 \cdot L_{LCH}, \tag{5}$$

where λ_1, λ_2, λ_3, λ_4, λ_5, and λ_6 denote six weighting coefficients (empirically set to 0.2, 0.02, 1.1, 1.1, 10^{-5}, and 0.01, respectively).

3. EXPERIMENTAL RESULTS

3.1 System Setup and Datasets

In this study, the proposed approach is implemented on Microsoft Windows 10 (64-bit) platform with Intel Core i7-13700 5.20 GHz (CPU), 64 GB main memory (RAM), Nvidia GeForce RTX 4090 (GPU), python version 3.8.17, PyTorch version 2.0.1, CUDA version 11.8, and cuDNN version 8.9.7.

To show the effectiveness of the proposed approach, full-reference UIEB (Li et al., 2020) and LSUI (Peng et al., 2023) datasets, and no-reference U45 (Li et al., 2019) and underwater color cast set (UCCS) (Liu et al., 2020) datasets are employed. UIEB contains 890 images (800 images for training and 90 images for testing). LSUI contains 4279 images (3879 images for training and 400 images for testing). U45 and UCCS contains 45 and 300 real-world underwater images for testing. All the images in datasets are resized to 256×256 for training and testing. In this study, Adam optimizer (Kingma et al., 2014) is employed for training. The initial learning rate is set to 5×10^{-4}, which is decreased with cosine annealing.

3.2 Performance Metrics and Experimental Results

To evaluate the performance of the proposed approach, peak signal-to-noise ratio (PSNR) and structural similarity index measure (SSIM) are employed for full-reference evaluation metrics, while blind/referenceless image spatial quality evaluator (BRISQUE) (Mittal et al., 2012), natural image quality evaluator (NIQE) (Mittal et al., 2013), underwater image sharpness measurement (UISM) (Panetta et al., 2016), and underwater image quality measurement (UIQM) (Panetta et al., 2016) are employed for no-reference evaluation metrics.

To evaluate the performance of the proposed approach, five comparison approaches, namely, MMLE (Zhang et al., 2022), DM (Tang et al., 2023), U-shape (Peng et al., 2023), HCLR-Net (Zhou et al., 2024), and Spectroformer (Khan et al., 2024) are employed. In this study, in terms of average PSNR (dB), SSIM, UISM, and UIQM, performance comparisons between five comparison approaches and the proposed approach on UIEB and LSUI datasets as well U45 and UCC datasets are shown in Tables 1 and 2, respectively. For subjective quality evaluation, some experimental results of five comparison approaches and the proposed approach on UIEB, LSUI, U45, and UCCS are shown in Figures 7-10.

Table 1. In terms of average PSNR (dB), SSIM, UISM, and UIQM, performance comparisons between five comparison approaches and the proposed approach on UIEB and LSUI datasets

datasets	UIEB				LSUI			
metrics / approaches	PSNR (dB)	SSIM	UISM	UIQM	PSNR (dB)	SSIM	UISM	UIQM
MMLE	21.37	0.859	6.23	**3.29**	19.68	0.785	6.49	2.64
DM	28.64	0.929	6.34	3.06	29.31	0.913	6.63	3.03
U-shape	22.91	0.910	6.49	2.89	24.16	0.930	6.65	2.97
HCLR-Net	24.99	0.925	6.59	3.03	23.57	0.886	6.82	3.01
Spectroformer	24.96	0.917	6.71	3.08	24.36	0.905	**6.91**	3.06
Proposed	**29.09**	**0.931**	**6.88**	3.18	**32.67**	**0.944**	6.87	**3.13**

Table 2. In terms of average BRISQUE, NIQE, UISM, and UIQM, performance comparisons between five comparison approaches and the proposed approach on U45 and UCCS datasets

datasets	U45				UCCS			
metrics / approaches	BRISQUE	NIQE	UISM	UIQM	BRISQUE	NIQE	UISM	UIQM
MMLE	23.928	4.95	6.54	2.68	25.110	4.90	6.35	3.02
DM	19.401	3.80	7.27	3.24	26.600	4.16	6.47	3.12
U-shape	21.566	4.31	6.87	3.10	23.549	4.40	6.58	3.14
HCLR-Net	**18.109**	3.86	7.32	3.10	27.800	4.02	6.44	3.05
Spectroformer	19.957	3.84	7.35	3.24	23.258	3.98	6.56	3.21
Proposed	19.165	**3.77**	**7.38**	**3.27**	**23.182**	**3.97**	**6.59**	**3.24**

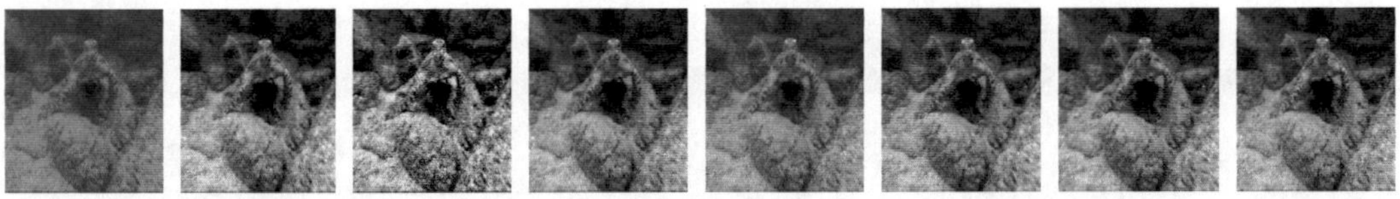

(a) (b) (c) (d) (e) (f) (g) (h)

Figure 7. Some experimental results on UIEB dataset: (a) underwater image, (b) ground-truth, (c)-(h) processed images by MMLE, DM, U-shape, HCLR-Net, Spectroforme, and the proposed approach, respectively

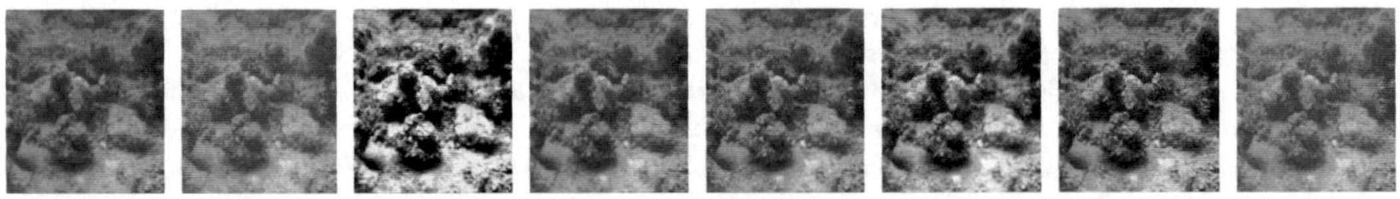

(a) (b) (c) (d) (e) (f) (g) (h)

Figure 8. Some experimental results on LSUI dataset: (a) underwater image, (b) ground-truth, (c)-(h) processed images by MMLE, DM, U-shape, HCLR-Net, Spectroformer, and the proposed approach, respectively

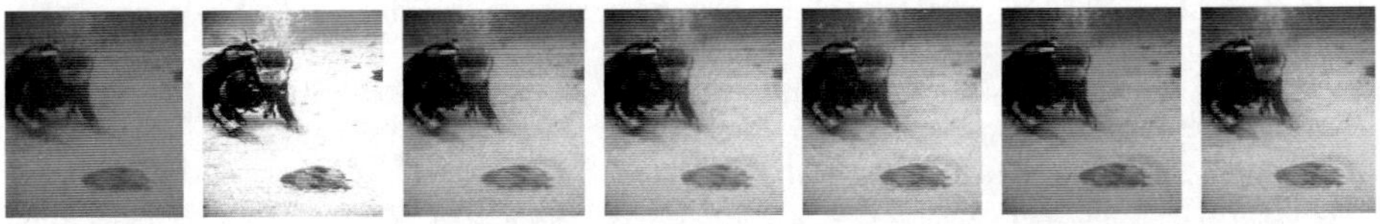

(a) (b) (c) (d) (e) (f) (g)

Figure 9. Some experimental results on U45 dataset: (a) underwater image, (b)-(g) processed images by MMLE, DM, U-shape, HCLR-Net, Spectroformer, and the proposed approach, respectively

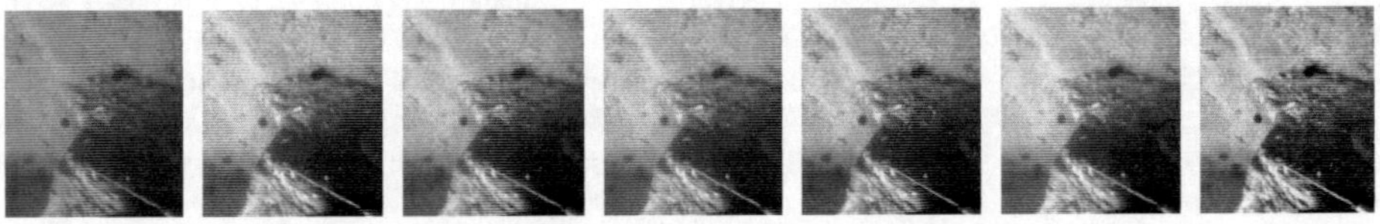

(a) (b) (c) (d) (e) (f) (g)

Figure 10. Some experimental results on UCCS dataset: (a) underwater image, (b)-(g) processed images by MMLE, DM, U-shape, HCLR-Net, Spectroformer, and the proposed approach, respectively

4. CONCLUSIONS

In this study, an underwater image enhancement approach using transformer-based generative adversarial networks is proposed, which consists of feature extraction module, enhanced channel-wise multiscale attention module, mixed attention module, image reconstruction module, and discriminator. Based on the experimental results obtained in this study, in terms of six objective performance metrics and subjective evaluation, the performance of the proposed approach is better than those of five comparison approaches.

ACKNOWLEDGEMENT

This work was supported in part by National Science and Technology Council, Taiwan, ROC under Grant NSTC 113-2221-E-194-037.

REFERENCES

Agaian, S. S., Panetta, K. and Grigoryan, A. M., (2001). Transform-Based Image Enhancement Algorithms with Performance Measure. *In IEEE Trans. on Image Processing*, Vol. 10, No. 3, pp. 367-382.

Chollet, F., (2017). Xception: Deep Learning with Depthwise Separable Convolutions. *Proc. of 2017 IEEE/CVF Conf. on Computer Vision and Pattern Recognition (CVPR)*, pp. 1251-1258.

Chu, X. et al., (2021). Conditional Positional Encodings for Vision Transformers. *In arXiv:2102.10882v3*.

Fan, Q. et al., (2023). RMT: Retentive Networks Meet Vision Transformers. *In arXiv:2309.11523v5*.

Fu, X. et al., (2014). A Retinex-Based Enhancing Approach for Single Underwater Image. *Proc. of 2014 IEEE Int. Conf. on Image Processing (ICIP)*, pp. 4572-4576.

Guan, M. et al., (2024). DiffWater: Underwater Image Enhancement Based on Conditional Denoising Diffusion Probabilistic Model. *In IEEE Journal of Selected Topics in Applied Earth Observations and Remote Sensing*, Vol. 17, pp. 2319-2335.

Howard, A. et al., (2019). Searching for MobileNetV3. *Proc. of 2019 IEEE/CVF Int. Conf. on Computer Vision (ICCV)*, pp. 1314-1324.

Isola, P. et al., (2017). Image-to-Image Translation with Conditional Adversarial Networks. *Proc. of 2017 IEEE/CVF Conf. on Computer Vision and Pattern Recognition (CVPR)*, pp. 5967-5976.

Jain, P. and Deo, M. C., (2006). Neural Networks in Ocean Engineering. *In Ships and Offshore Structures*, Vol. 1, pp. 25-35.

Johnson, J., Alahi, A. and Fei-Fei, L., (2016). Perceptual Losses for Real-Time Style Transfer and Super-Resolution. *Proc. of 2016 European Conf. on Computer Vision (ECCV)*, pp. 694-711.

Khan, R. et al., (2024). Spectroformer: Multi-Domain Query Cascaded Transformer Network for Underwater Image Enhancement. *Proc. of 2024 IEEE/CVF Winter Conf. on Applications of Computer Vision (WACV)*, pp. 1454-1463.

Kingma, D. P. and Ba, J., (2014). Adam: A Method for Stochastic Optimization. *In arXiv:1412.6980v9.*

Li, C. et al., (2020). An Underwater Image Enhancement Benchmark Dataset and Beyond. *In IEEE Trans. on Image Processing*, Vol. 29, pp. 4376-4389.

Li, H., Li, J. and Wang, W., (2019). A Fusion Adversarial Underwater Image Enhancement Network with a Public Test Dataset. *In arXiv:1906.06819.*

Li, K. et al., (2024). TCTL-Net: Template-Free Color Transfer Learning for Self-Attention Driven Underwater Image Enhancement. *In IEEE Trans. on Circuits and Systems for Video Technology*, Vol. 34, No. 6, pp. 4682-4697.

Li, Y. et al., (2023). Efficient and Explicit Modelling of Image Hierarchies for Image Restoration. *Proc. of 2023 IEEE/CVF Conf. on Computer Vision and Pattern Recognition (CVPR)*, pp. 18278-18289.

Liu, R. et al., (2020). Real-World Underwater Enhancement: Challenges, Benchmarks, and Solutions under Natural Light. *In IEEE Trans. on Circuits and Systems for Video Technology*, Vol. 30, No. 12, pp. 4861-4875.

Liu, Y. et al., (2025). Underwater Image Enhancement with Cascaded Contrastive Learning. *In IEEE Trans. on Multimedia*, Vol. 27, pp. 1512-1525.

Liu, Z. et al., (2021). Swin Transformer: Hierarchical Vision Transformer Using Shifted Windows. *Proc. of 2021 IEEE/CVF Int. Conf. on Computer Vision (ICCV)*, pp. 10012-10022.

Mittal, A., Moorthy, A. K. and Bovik, A. C., (2012). No-Reference Image Quality Assessment in the Spatial Domain. *In IEEE Trans. on Image Processing*, Vol. 21, No. 12, pp. 4695-4708.

Mittal, A., Soundararajan, R. and Bovik, A. C., (2013). Making a "Completely Blind" Image Quality Analyzer. *In IEEE Signal Processing Letters*, Vol. 20, No. 3, pp. 209-212.

Panetta, K., Gao, C. and Agaian, S., (2016). Human-Visual-System-Inspired Underwater Image Quality Measures. *In IEEE Journal of Oceanic Engineering*, Vol. 41, No. 3, pp. 541-551.

Peng, L., Zhu, C. and Bian, L., (2023). U-Shape Transformer for Underwater Image Enhancement. *In IEEE Trans. on Image Processing*, Vol. 32, pp. 3066-3079.

Qiu, Y. et al., (2023). MB-TaylorFormer: Multi-Branch Efficient Transformer Expanded by Taylor Formula for Image Dehazing. *Proc. of 2023 IEEE/CVF Int. Conf. on Computer Vision (ICCV)*, pp. 12802-12813.

Shi, W. et al., (2016). Real-Time Single Image and Video Super-Resolution Using an Efficient Sub-Pixel Convolutional Neural Network. *Proc. of the 2016 IEEE/CVF Conf. on Computer Vision and Pattern Recognition (CVPR)*, pp. 1874-1883.

Simonyan, K. and Zisserman, A., (2014). Very Deep Convolutional Networks for Large-Scale Image Recognition. *In arXiv:1409.1556v6.*

Tang, Y., Kawasaki, H. and Iwaguchi, T., (2023). Underwater Image Enhancement by Transformer-Based Diffusion Model with Non-Uniform Sampling for Skip Strategy. *Proc. of 2023 the 31st ACM Int. Conf. on Multimedia*, pp. 5419-5427.

Treibitz, T. and Schechner, Y. Y., (2009). Active Polarization Descattering. *In IEEE Trans. on Pattern Analysis and Machine Intelligence*, Vol. 31, No. 3, pp. 385-399.

Wen, H. et al., (2013). Single Underwater Image Enhancement with a New Optical Model. *Proc. of the 2013 IEEE Int. Symposium on Circuits and Systems (ISCAS)*, pp. 753-756.

Yang, Z. et al., (2020). Gated Channel Transformation for Visual Recognition. *Proc. of 2020 IEEE/CVF Conf. on Computer Vision and Pattern Recognition (CVPR)*, pp. 11794-11803.

Zamir, S. et al., (2022). Restormer: Efficient Transformer for High-Resolution Image Restoration. *Proc. of 2022 IEEE/CVF Conf. on Computer Vision and Pattern Recognition (CVPR)*, pp. 5728-5739.

Zhang, W. et al., (2019). Single Image Defogging Based on Multi-Channel Convolutional MSRCR. *In IEEE Access*, Vol. 7, pp. 72492-72504.

Zhang, W. et al., (2022). Underwater Image Enhancement via Minimal Color Loss and Locally Adaptive Contrast Enhancement. *In IEEE Trans. on Image Processing*, Vol. 31, pp. 3997-4010.

Zhou, J. et al., (2024). HCLR-Net: Hybrid Contrastive Learning Regularization with Locally Randomized Perturbation for Underwater Image Enhancement. *In Int. Journal of Computer Vision*, Vol. 132, pp. 1-25.

MULTIRESOLUTION DWT-2D VERSUS LAPLACIAN PYRAMID FOR FACIAL RECOGNITION USING SFA SKIN DATABASE

Ouarda Soltani[1] and Souad Benabdelkader[2]
[1,2] Batna 2 University, Electronics Department, Batna - Algeria
LEA (Laboratoire d'Électronique Avancée) Laboratory

ABSTRACT

Facial recognition technology has become a critical component in biometric identification systems, making the best use of advanced image processing techniques to identify or verify individuals on the basis of their facial features. The work presented here proposes a performance evaluation study between the multiresolution discrete wavelet transform (2D-DWT) and the Laplacian Pyramid (LP) in the conception of a comprehensive facial recognition system based upon the Principal Component Analysis (PCA) technique. Both of the two pyramidal representations contributed to a reduction in the dimensionality of the feature vectors, and their associated face recognition systems were assessed on SFA and FEI color facial databases using SFA skin samples. Recognition rates achieved through LP are particularly remarkable.

KEYWORDS

Face Recognition, Face Identification, Laplacian Pyramid, 2D-DWT, Eigenfaces

1. INTRODUCTION

The world, methods and technology are changing rapidly, making the traditional security measures increasingly viewed as inadequate in the digital era. Passwords, identification cards, and badges based on knowledge or possession are prone to loss, forgetfulness or misuse. In response to these limitations, technological advancements have introduced biometric systems as a more secure method of access control and identification, thus taking a big step forward in security practices. According to Roethenbaugh (Roethenbaugh, 1998) biometrics involve the application of unique, measurable human characteristics for the automatic recognition or verification of identity. The primary aim of employing biometric features is to enhance convenience in daily activities while mitigating the risk of fraud (Nuh and al, 2020). Among the most recent and widely adopted biometric technologies is facial recognition, whose central purpose is to develop computer systems that adapt specifically to individuals. Facial recognition (Muhtahir and al, 2020), (Qinjun and al, 2023), (Sadi and al, 2023), (Jiaqi and al., 2022), (Chen and al, 2023), (Nguyen and al, 2023), (Sana and al, 2024), (Bandari and al, 2023) offers several advantages over other biometric security technologies, including its natural aspect and discretion, its ease of use and non-intrusive nature, without forgetting its efficiency. In this context, the work presented here proposes giving an automatic facial recognition system that is both simple and effective. Therefore, it is crucial to work at each level of the system: detection, attributes extraction and recognition, while contributing to various aspects of the processing chain.

The paper is organized as follows: Section 2 gives a brief overview of the proposed methods. Section 3 details the system methodology. Section 4 presents the simulation results along with the performance assessment. Finally, the conclusion is provided in Section 5.

2. OVERVIEW OF THE PROPOSED METHODS

2.1 Pyramid Decompositions

These representation models lead to the creation of images pyramid, ranging from the original image to a coarser one, which may help reduce numerical complexity in terms of data volume and processing time by operating at both large and fine scales. Additionally, algorithms are simplified and processing results become more concise since the problem can be examined at different scales. Another significant advantage is the ability to reconstruct signals with a minimal number of samples derived from such decompositions. The models adopted here concern both the Laplacian Pyramid and the multiresolution 2D-Discrete Wavelet Transform.

2.1.1 Laplacian Pyramid (LP)

LP proposed in (Burt and al, 1983), (Wahyuni and Sabre, 2016), (Weiyi and al, 2023), (Jianguo and al, 2018), (Sumiya and al, 2022), aims to represent an image at multiple scales by separating the details of the image from its basic components. LP is achieved in two main steps (Figure 1).

1. ***Gaussian Pyramid Generation***: generates the Gaussian pyramid $\{G_0, G_1, \ldots, G_n\}$ as a sequence of smoothed copies of the original image at different scales through a series of weighted low-pass filtering process executed by convolution with the kernel ***W*** on a 5×5 window. The parameter ***a*** in ***W*** is chosen so that the unimodality condition is best achieved.
2. ***Laplacian Pyramid Generation:*** leads to the formation of a pyramid $\{L_1, L_2, \ldots, L_n\}$ of images that contains the details as one goes from one resolution to another.

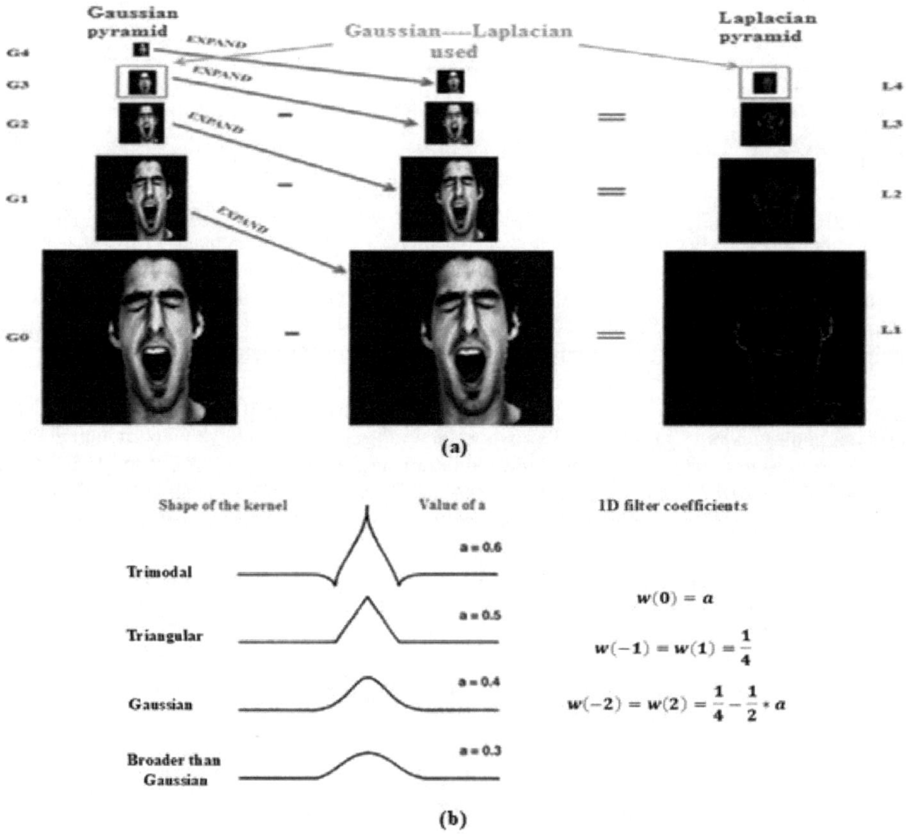

Figure 1. LP representation model. (a) Four level decomposition.
(b) Appearance of the weighting kernel as a function of the parameter a

2.1.2 Multiresolution Analysis

Multiresolution analysis using Two-Dimensional Orthogonal Discrete Wavelet Transform (DWT-2D) allows for the decomposition of an image into components at various levels of detail. This method captures both the spatial and frequency information of the image, making it particularly useful for analyzing the texture and finer details of facial features (Mallat, 1989), (Abdulelah, 2021), (Silvester and al, 2018), (Tiantian and al., 2016), (Bader and al, 2022), (MAmeen and al, 2017). Multiresolution analysis of an image can be described as a decomposition into a set of frequency bands with preferred spatial orientations, as it provides at each scale the following four sub-images (Figure 2):

- Approximation or Low-Resolution Sub-band;
- Horizontal Detail Sub-band;
- Vertical Detail Sub-band;
- Diagonal Detail Sub-band.

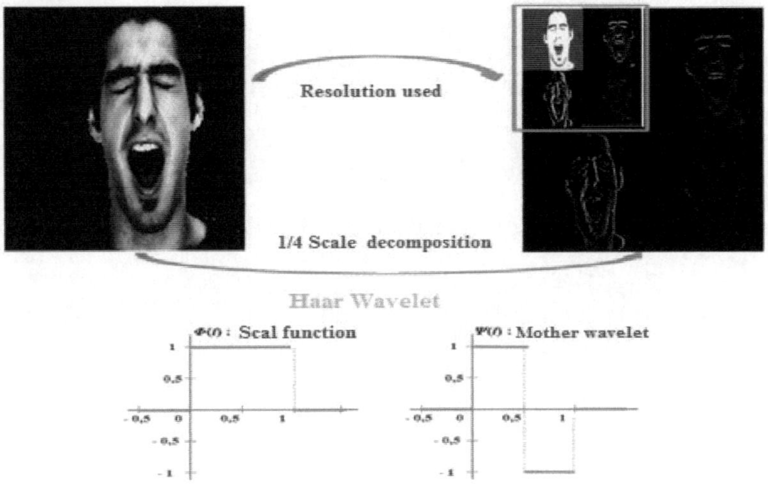

Figure 2. DWT-2D model: Two level decomposition using Haar wavelet

2.2 Principal Component Analysis (PCA)

PCA (Turk and al, 1991), (Ian and al, 2016), (Khawla and al, 2023), (Peng and al, 2021) operates on the basis of preserving the most significant variations of the face while eliminating redundancies. These major variations, so-called principal parameters, are retained as eigenvectors of a covariance matrix and are referred to as eigenfaces. The latter shall be used to identify or verify individuals.

The procedure for extracting distinctive parameters using PCA is described in the following steps:

1. Formation of the training set S with M faces images, having each the same dimensions (N rows and N columns).
2. Compilation of each image I_i **(N×N)** as a column vector Γ_i of size (N×N) ×1 (Figure 3)

$$S = \{\Gamma_1, \Gamma_2, \Gamma_3, \dots, \Gamma_M\} \tag{1}$$

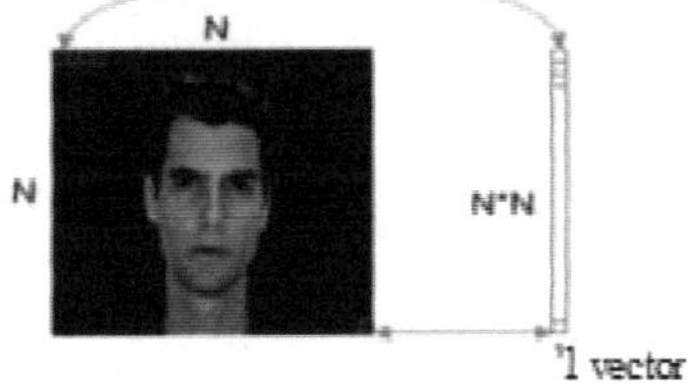

Figure 3. Compilation of an image as a vector

3. Calculation of the average face image (Ψ), using the vectors Γ_i as follows:

$$\Psi = \frac{1}{M}\sum_{i=1}^{M}(\Gamma_i) \quad (2)$$

4. Calculation of a new set of column vectors Φ_i, (i=1, 2, …, M), by subtracting the average face image from each of the images Γ_i, as follows:

$$\Phi_i = \Gamma_i - \Psi \quad (3)$$

Assembling vectors Φ_i into the matrix A = [Φ_1, Φ_2, …, Φ_M] of dimension ($N^2 \times M$).

5. Calculation of the covariance matrix C as follows:

$$C = A.A^T \quad (4)$$

The size of the matrix C ($N^2 \times N^2$) makes the computations time and memory consuming, even for images of relatively small sizes. Therefore, the calculation will be limited to finding an approximation of the eigenvectors.

6. Reduction of the covariance matrix C ($N^2 \times N^2$) to a matrix L of dimension M×M:

$$L = A^T.A \quad (5)$$

7. Calculation of the eigenvectors, y of L ($A^T.A$).
8. Calculation of the eigenvectors, x, of C using the relation:

$$y = A^T x \quad (6)$$

Let V be the matrix of eigenvectors of L. The matrix U of eigenvectors of C is then obtained by:

$$U = AV \quad (7)$$

9. Representation of each face in the training set as a linear combination of its eigenvectors u_i such as:

$$\emptyset_i = \sum_{j=1} w_j u_j \quad (8)$$

The row vectors, u_i of U represent the eigenfaces of the facial images in the training set. Images with the highest eigenvalues contribute more significantly to the formation of the eigenface space. These weights can be calculated as follows:

$$w_j = u_j^T \emptyset_i \quad (9)$$

10. Construction of the matrix W (M×M) of the feature vectors for each image in the training set such as:

$$W_i = [w_1, w_2 \dots\dots.. w_M] \quad (10)$$

2.3 Recognition Process

The eigenface space formed earlier in the learning phase is meant to help determine or verify a person's identity. Therefore, the recognition process adopts the same strategy of PCA followed by a comparing step (Figure 4). In particular, for a facial image (N×N) to be processed for recognition:

1. Form the column vector image Γ_T (N^2x1), then calculate the average face image, Ψ, using of Γ_T. Generate the column vector Φ_T as follows:

$$\Phi_T = \Gamma_T - \Psi \quad (11)$$

2. Specify the feature vector through a projection into the eigenface space, as a column vector w_T of dimension (N×1):

$$w_T = U.\Phi_T \quad (12)$$

3. The person's identity in the considered facial image is established through an assessment of some similarity score between the vector w_T and each of the feature vectors w_i in the matrix W constituted previously by formula (10). This is essentially a classification procedure based on calculating a preset distance metric.

3. METHODOLOGY

The architecture of the proposed recognition system is displayed by the detailed flowchart in Figure 5.

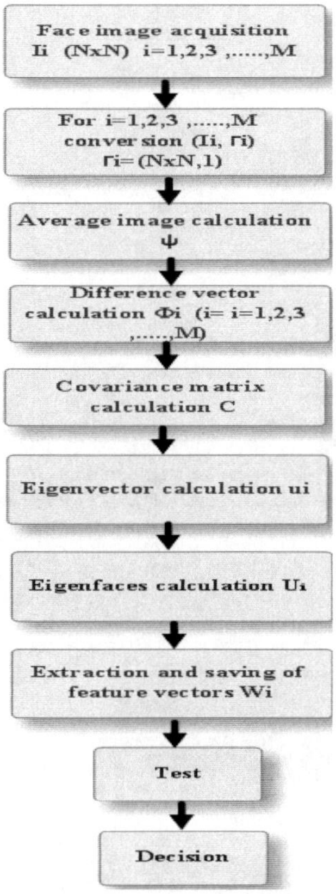

Figure 4. Face recognition based PCA method

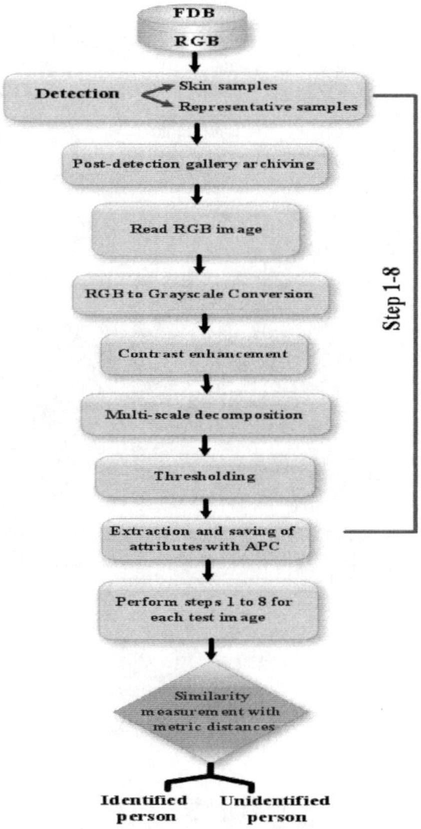

Figure 5. The face recognition system architecture

3.1 Detection

The face detection process-based skin color segmentation has been examined in detail within two methods in (Soltani and Benabdelkader, 2022), (Soltani and Benabdelkader, 2021). Both approaches execute the well-known Euclidean distance (ED) and Manhattan distance (MD) as skin color similarity measures together with either the human skin samples provided by SFA database or the new representative (min, max, mean, median) ones constituted out according to the four rules of minimum, maximum, mean and median.

As a reminder, SFA (Casati, and al, 2013) is composed of four distinct sets of images structured in folders as shown in Figure 6. Each original image (**ORI**) has its ground truth (**GT**) version, in which every pixel but the skin was manually painted in black (RGB 0, 0, 0). A total of three skin (**SKIN**) and five non-skin (**NS**) samples were randomly retrieved from each original image. Every sample consists of a set of square sample masks collected from the same central pixel, and varying in sizes by two pixels, from the smaller of 1 pixel to the largest of 35x35 pixels.

After the detection process is completed, two new collections of segmented facial images are stored in Ground Truth (GT) color format, where each skin detected region is RGB coded while each non-skin detected region is black. The first collection is generated through a detection procedure by means of original SFA skin samples (Soltani and Benabdelkader, 2022) whereas the second derives from using the generated representative skin samples of the minimum, maximum, average, and median rules (Soltani and Benabdelkader, 2021). These new GT post-detection galleries will serve as data entry for facial recognition purposes (Figures 7 and 8).

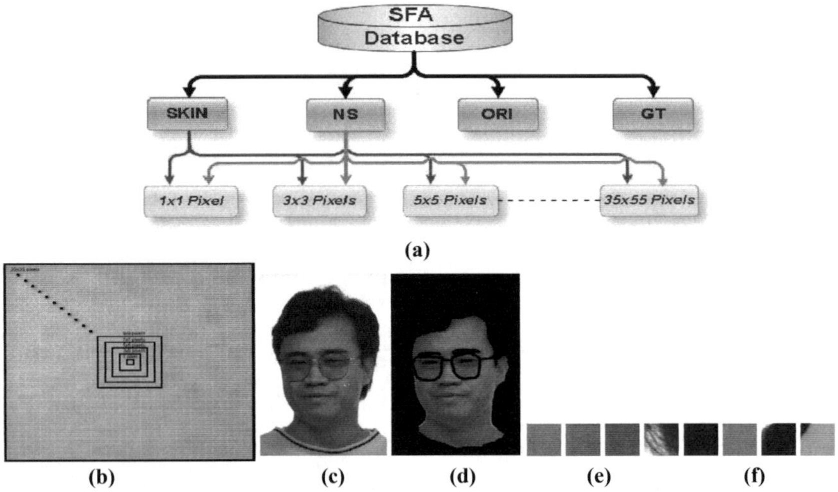

Figure 6. An example of SFA database content. (a) Folder-like structure of SFA. (b) Example of skin samples creation. (c) ORI: img(163). (d) GT: img(163). (e) Three SKIN samples of size 35×35. (f) Five NS samples of size 35×35

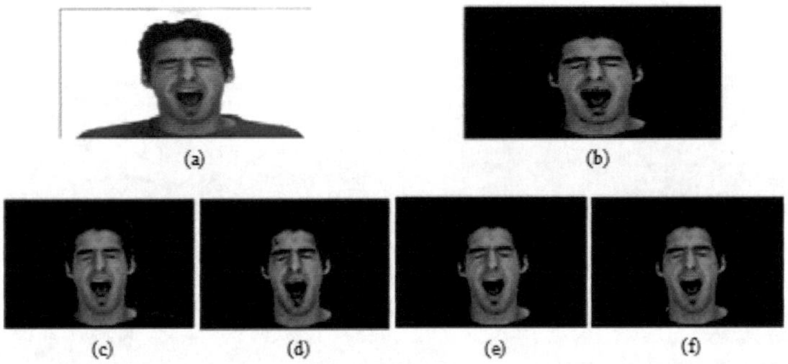

Figure 7. Example of SFA post-detected GT image. (a) Original RGB SFA image. (b) GT SFA image. (c)-(f) GT post-detected images using masks of minimum, maximum, mean and median rule respectively

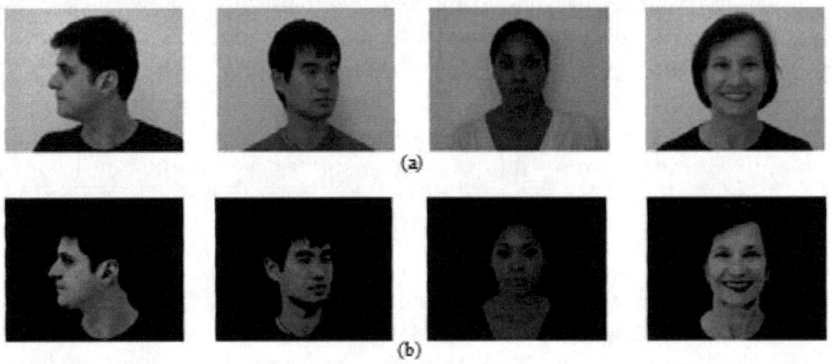

Figure 8. Examples of post-detection FEI images. (a) Original RGB FEI images. (b) GT post-detected images

3.2 RGB to Grayscale Conversion

Most facial recognition systems perform a grayscale (GS) conversion to facilitate processing. In this work, we conducted an RGB to GS conversion for all GT images in the post-detection galleries.

3.3 Contrast Enhancement

This step is performed to address the issue of lighting variation by bringing all facial images of the same person to a uniform contrast level. Moreover, contrast enhancement improves the appearance of facial images and significantly highlights facial features (Figure 9). The method used, known as Brightness Bi-Histogram Equalization (BBHE), is a histogram equalization approach based on the principle of image average brightness preservation.

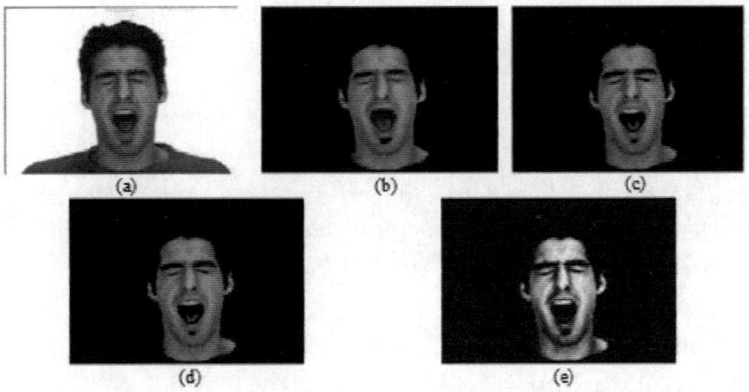

Figure 9. Graphical illustration of the contrast enhancement process. (a) Original RGB SFA image. (b) GT SFA image. (c) Post-detection GT image. (d) GS version from (c). (e) Enhanced GS image

3.4 Pyramid Decompositions

At this stage, the recognition system carries on with a multiscale decomposition of each GS enhanced image. The models adopted are:

1. LP with dyadic Gaussian and Laplacian Pyramids with (see Figure 1):
   — Trimodal weighting kernel (a = 0.6);
   — Gaussian and Laplacian bands of the third level of decomposition (G3 + L4).
2. Dyadic Multi-Resolution Analysis of DWT-2D with (see Figure 2):
   — Haar wavelet;
   — Approximation and detail sub-bands at scale ¼.

3.5 Thresholding of Detail Sub-bands and Laplacian Images

Thresholding of detail sub-bands from the DWT-2D as well as the Laplacian image from the Laplacian pyramid is crucial as it eliminates all low-amplitude coefficients, retaining only the significant ones since they are used as input data for the feature extraction process. Indeed, their reduced volume results in attribute vectors of minimal size. Additionally, sought after attributes will be more precise as they are obtained through the processing of coefficients that describe facial features at different scales. After thresholding, the resulting images (approximations, details, Gaussian, and Laplacian) are archived in two new data galleries.

The thresholding process is conducted such that any coefficient in a sub-band B^k of size M×N, with amplitude below a predefined threshold *T*, is set to zero:

$$B_{ij}^{k} = \begin{cases} B_{ij}^{k} & \text{if } \left|B_{ij}^{k}\right| \geq |T| \\ 0 & \text{if } \left|B_{ij}^{k}\right| < |T| \end{cases} \qquad i = 1, 2, \mathrm{K}, M \; ; \; j = 1, 2, \mathrm{K}, N \qquad (13)$$

3.6 Parameters Extraction

This critical phase involves applying the PCA technique to all output images from the above selected pyramidal models followed by thresholding, for the purpose of getting the required attributes to describe adequately each analyzed face.

3.7 Classification and Decision

The face models obtained in terms of feature vectors enable the classification of each face subject to identification or verification. This implies a comparison between two feature vectors by calculating a similarity measure, the value of which can lead to one of two classifications: 1) known identity (information that is as similar as possible within the same category), or 2) unknown identity (information that is as distinct as possible), (Fabbri and al, 2008), (Liand Bao, 2009), (Hasnat and al, 2013), (Sharma and al, 2012), (Indra and Hayati ,2019).

3.8 Measures Used

Four metric distances have been considered to perform the features comparison task, namely Euclidean distance (ED), Manhattan distance (MD), Canberra distance (CD), and Chebyshev distance (ChD).

Given two feature vectors $H = (H_1, H_2, \ldots, H_M)$ and $H_T = (H_{T1}, H_{T2}, \ldots, H_{TM})$, the distances used are defined as follows:

Euclidean: $ED(H, H_T) = \sqrt{\sum_{k=1}^{M}(H_k - H_{Tk})^2}$ (14)

Manhattan : $MD(H, H_T) = \sum_{k=1}^{M}|H_k - H_{Tk}|$ (15)

Canberra : $CD(H, H_T) = \sum_{k=1}^{M}\frac{|H_k - H_{Tk}|}{|H_k| + |H_{Tk}|}$ (16)

Chebyshev: $ChD(H, H_T) = max|H_k - H_{Tk}|$ (17)

3.9 Facial Recognition

The recognition score is expressed by:

$$Recognition\ Rate = \frac{Number\ of\ Recognized\ Faces}{Total\ Number\ of\ Test\ Images} \quad (18)$$

4. SIMULATION RESULTS

4.1 Simulations with SFA Facial Images

After carrying out the training procedure of the SFA post-detection galleries, several face images (JPEG format, 512×768 pixels), representing both women and men, various skin tones, different types of emotions and variations in lighting, have undergone a complete testing process according to the following scheme:

- Training Phase: 48 images;
- Testing Phase: 16 images;
- Each person examined in the testing phase has three prototypes in the training phase.

Table 1 reports the facial recognition rates associated with each of the multi-scale models, on the basis of the four distances ED, MD, CD and ChD. The numerical values vary from one model to another and from one metric distance to another, regardless of the post-detection gallery used. However, overall, they are very satisfactory, reaching up to 100%. For more details, the main observations can be summarized as follows:

- The post-detection gallery using representative samples ensures better performance regardless of the metric used.

— LP consistently shows the highest performance across all metrics for both skin and representative samples, making it the most effective among all models. It may be more robust in distinguishing between different facial features under varying conditions.
— DWT-2D also performs very well, particularly with representative samples, but slightly less so with skin samples compared to LP.
— PCA is less effective in comparison, ranking third with both types of samples. However, its performance is markedly increased when combined to representative samples.

Table 1. Recognition Rates with SFA

Samples	Model	ED (%)	MD (%)	ChD (%)	CD (%)
Skin	DWT-2D	93.75	100	81.25	100
	LP	100	100	93.75	93.75
	PCA	87.50	81.25	87.50	75
Representative	DWT-2D	100	100	93.75	100
	LP	100	100	93.75	93.75
	PCA	93.75	93.75	93.75	81.25

4.2 Simulations with FEI Facial Images

Similarly to SFA, the facial images selected from the FEI post-detection galleries (JPEG format, 640×480 pixels) for a potential identification or verification were used as follows:
— Training Phase: 99 images;
— Testing Phase: 9 images;
— Each person studied in the testing phase has eleven prototypes in the training phase.

Based on numerical percentages corresponding to the FEI database in table 2, the same comments apply as those made on SFA database regarding the classification of the multi-scale models adopted as well as the type of skin samples used in the implementation of the detection process. Not forgetting to mention, of course, the variations in rate values due to the different metrics. Nevertheless, two important comments should be made:
— The recognition rates obtained with original SFA skin samples generally appear lower than those in table 1. This could be attributed to the fact that SFA Faces are better detected by means of skin samples from the same database, therefore giving the best candidates to perform the attributes extraction procedure.
— More interesting, however, is to recognize that representative skin samples allow improving noticeably the recognition rates in table 2, often reaching 100% with LP and DWT-2D.

Table 2. Recognition Rates with FEI

Samples	Model	ED (%)	MD (%)	ChD (%)	CD (%)
Skin	DWT-2D	88.88	77.77	100	77.77
	LP	88.88	100	99.99	88.88
	PCA	88.88	77.77	55.55	66.66
Representative	DWT-2D	100	100	100	88.88
	LP	100	100	88.88	100
	PCA	88.88	88.88	88.88	77.77

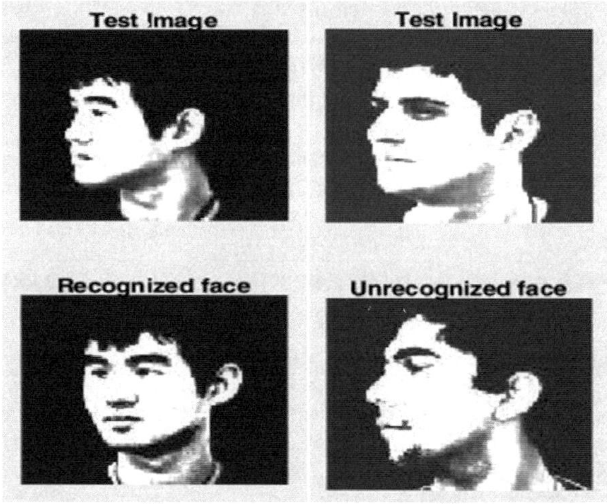

Figure 10. Example of face recognition with FEI database. (a) Recognized face. (b) Unrecognized face

5. CONCLUSION

The work presented above provides a performance comparison between the models of LP, DWT-2D and PCA for the purpose of face recognition. These models have been associated to both SFA skin samples and those skin representative constituted out using the initial SFA. The final recognition scores are outcomes of a classification carried out by calculating some similarity measure using the various metrics of ED, MD, CD and ChD. Results have been derived using simulations run on both SFA and FEI color faces databases.

The findings reveal that LP consistently delivers high recognition rates and maintains strong performance across almost all metrics with both skin and representative samples in SFA and FEI databases. The DWT-2D model demonstrates its strength in ranking second. However, the scores achieved with the representative samples, in SFA or FEI, are fully comparable to those of LP, making this model very reliable.

Finally, it is important to emphasize that the scores of all models improve with the representative skin samples whichever the faces database used, making these new skin samples very reliable with respect to the face recognition issue.

REFERENCES

Abdulelah, A. (2021). Face recognition using enhancement discrete wavelet transform based on MATLAB. *Indonesian Journal of Electrical Engineering and Computer Science*, 23(2), 1128–1136. https://doi.org/10.11591/ijeecs.v23.i2.pp1128-1136

Bader, M. A., Alshraideh, H., & Alhaddad, M. (2022). Face recognition system based on the multi-resolution singular value decomposition fusion technique. International Journal of Data and Network Science, 6(4), 1249–1260. https://doi.org/10.5267/j.ijdns.2022.6.009

Bandari, S. D., Kavitha, P., & Priya, S. (2023). A survey on face recognition monitoring attendance system. *International* Journal of Advanced Research in Science, Communication and Technology, 3(10), 369–401. https://doi.org/10.48175/IJARSCT-10482

Burt, P. J., & Adelson, E. H. (1983). The Laplacian pyramid as a compact image code. IEEE Transactions on Communications, 31(4), 532–540. https://doi.org/10.1109/TCOM.1983.1095851

Casati, J. P. B., Moraes, D. R., & Rodrigues, E. L. L. (2013). SFA: A human skin image database based on FERET and AR facial images. In Proceedings of the IX Workshop de Visão Computacional (pp. …). Rio de Janeiro.

Chen, L., Hu, W., & Wang, L. (2023). A survey of face recognition. Journal of Image Processing, 45(2), 123–145. https://doi.org/10.1016/j.impr.2023.06.004

Fabbri, R., da Silva, L. R., & Borges, F. S. (2008). 2D Euclidean distance transform algorithms: A comparative survey. ACM Computing Surveys, 40(1), 1–44. https://doi.org/10.1145/1322432.1322434

Hasnat, A., Ibraheem, K., & Aljunid, S. A. (2013). Comparative study of distance metrics for finding skin color similarity of two color facial images. Advances in Computer Engineering and Robotics, 3(2), 99–108.

Indra, D., & Hayati, L. (2019). Skin detection using color distance measurement and thresholding. International Journal of Engineering *and Advanced Technology*, 8(C5), 1441–1443.

Jianguo, S., Li, Y., & Wang, S. (2018). Multi-focus image fusion algorithm based on Laplacian pyramids. *Journal of the Optical Society of America A*, 35(3), 120–130. https://doi.org/10.1364/JOSAA.35.000480

Jiaqi, Q., Zhang, H., & Li, X. (2022). Review on facial-recognition-based applications in disease diagnosis. *Bioengineering (Basel),* 9(7), 273. https://doi.org/10.3390/bioengineering9070273

Khawla, A., & Rabie, T. (2023). Survey of face recognition using eigenfaces. *In Proceedings of the International Conference on Robotics and Computer Vision* (ICRCV) (pp. 169–174).

Li, J., & Lu, B.-L. (2009). An adaptive image Euclidean distance. *Pattern Recognition*, 42(2), 349–357. https://doi.org/10.1016/j.patcog.2008.07.006

Mallat, S. (1989). A theory for multiresolution signal decomposition: The wavelet representation. *IEEE Transactions on Pattern Analysis and Machine Intelligence*, 11(7), 674–693. https://doi.org/10.1109/34.192463

Mameen, M., & Al-Shammari, E. (2017). Wavelet transform based face recognition using SURF descriptors. *International Journal of Electronics and Electrical Engineering*, 5(1), 94–98. https://doi.org/10.18178/ijeee.5.1.94-98

Muhtahir, O., Khan, S., & Ali, B. (2020). Review on face recognition systems: Recent approaches and challenges. *Multimedia Tools and Applications*, 79(37–38), 27511–27533. https://doi.org/10.1007/s11042-020-09261-2

Nguyen, T., & Lee, S. (2023). Past, present, and future of face recognition. *Electronics*, 12(8), 987. https://doi.org/10.3390/electronics12080987

Nuh, Y., Ahmed, F., & Chaudhry, S. R. (2020). A survey of biometric approaches of authentication. *International Journal of Advanced Computer Research*, 10(47), 96–104. https://doi.org/10.19101/IJACR.2019.940152

Peng, P., Huang, X., & Gao, Y. (2021). A face recognition software framework based on principal component analysis. *PLoS ONE*, 16(7), e0254965. https://doi.org/10.1371/journal.pone.0254965

Qinjun, L., Wei, Z., & Hua, Y. (2023). Facial recognition technology: A comprehensive overview. *Academic Journal of Computing & Information Science*, 6(7), 15–26. https://doi.org/10.25236/AJCIS.2023.060703

Roethenbaugh, G. (1998). An introduction to biometrics and general history. *In Biometrics Explained* (Section 1).

Sharma, M. K., & Kaur, A. (2012). Skin infection identification using color and Euclidean distance algorithm. *In Proceedings of the International Conference on Advances in Computing, Communications and Informatics* (pp. 471–480). Springer. https://doi.org/10.1007/978-3-642-30931-7_49

Silvester, T., & Amin, A. (2018). Face recognition based on discrete wavelet transform and Euclidean distance. *Computer Science and Engineering*. (Conference paper – DOI not found)

Siniya, Y., & Kumar, P. (2022). Gaussian Fourier pyramid for local Laplacian filter. *IEEE Signal Processing Letters*, 29(6), 1115–1119. https://doi.org/10.1109/LSP.2022.3154679

Sumiya, Y., Iida, M., & Nakano, T. (2022). Gaussian Fourier pyramid for local Laplacian filter. *IEEE Signal Processing Letters*, 29(6), 1111–1115. https://doi.org/10.1109/LSP.2022.3154679

Soltani, O., & Benabdelkader, C. (2021). Euclidean distance versus Manhattan distance for new representative SFA skin samples for human skin segmentation. *Journal de Traitement du Signal*, 38(6), 1843–1851. https://doi.org/10.18280/ts.380624

Soltani, O., & Benabdelkader, C. (2022). Euclidean distance versus Manhattan distance for skin detection using the SFA database. *International Journal of Biometrics*, 14(1), 46–60. https://doi.org/10.1504/IJBM.2022.10039416

Sundaran, U., Ou, J., Xiong, Y., & Tian, W. (2024). Facial expression recognition (FER) survey: A vision, architectural elements, and future directions. *PeerJ Computer Science*, 1, 1–35. https://doi.org/10.7717/peerj-cs.1019

Tiantian, G., Zhang, Y., & Li, J. (2017). A review of wavelet analysis and its applications: Challenges and opportunities. *IEEE Access*, 5, 1–36. https://doi.org/10.1109/ACCESS.2017.2700919

Turk, M., & Pentland, A. (1991). Eigenfaces for recognition. *Journal of Cognitive Neuroscience*, 3(1), 71–86. https://doi.org/10.1162/jocn.1991.3.1.71

Wahyuni, I., & Sabre, R. (2016). Wavelet decomposition in Laplacian pyramid for image fusion. *International Journal of Signal Processing Systems*, 4(1), 37–44.

Weiyi, K., Zhisheng, Y., & Xuebin, L. (2023). 3D face recognition algorithm based on deep Laplacian pyramid under the normalization of epidemic control. *Computer Communications*, 199, 30–41. https://doi.org/10.1016/j.comcom.2022.12.011

Short Papers

DRAWING CLOSER: DESIGNING HAPTIC MIXED REALITY INTERFACES FOR INDIVIDUALS WITH INCOMPLETE LOCKED-IN SYNDROME TO ENHANCE EXPRESSION AND COMMUNICATION

Pedro Amado[1], Eliana Penedos-Santiago[2], Bruno Giesteira[2], Andreia de Sousa[3], Cláudia Lima[4] and Sílvia Simões[1]
[1]Faculty of Fine Arts, University of Porto / i2ADS Research Unit, Porto, Portugal
[2]Faculty of Fine Arts, University of Porto / ID+ Research Unit, Porto, Portugal
[3]Lusófona University, HEI-Lab, Porto, Portugal
[4]Lusófona University, ID+, Porto, Portugal

ABSTRACT

This paper presents a human-centered, mixed-reality design that enables non-verbal communication for individuals with Incomplete Locked-In Syndrome (LIS) through a haptic co-creation. Traditional augmentative and alternative communication tools frequently overlook affective and relational dimensions, focusing on functional outputs. We propose a novel haptic drawing system developed for an XR headset to address this gap. The system supports embodied and multisensory interactions, enabling patients and caregivers to communicate by drawing in a proprioceptive approach, simultaneously mirrored in a digital augmented reality space. Patients interact through accessible input interfaces tailored for minimal motor capabilities, using eye tracking, head movement, or limited hand control. This tactile-dialogic approach enriches emotional expression, enhances relational presence, and prioritizes emotional well-being alongside functionality. The paper proposes a system that integrates different interaction modes in the specific context of LIS, merging physical touch with digital augmentation, opening valuable pathways for inclusive and affective computing within immersive healthcare contexts.

KEYWORDS

Incomplete Locked-In Syndrome (LIS), Mixed Reality (MR), Drawing, Non-Verbal Communication, Affective Computing, Human-Computer Interaction (HCI)

1. INTRODUCTION

Locked-In Syndrome (LIS) is a rare and severe neurological condition resulting from brain stem damage, while cognitive functions remain fully intact. In its classic form, patients retain vertical eye movements and blinking as their only means of interaction with the outside world. The seminal clinical definition of the syndrome was established by Plum and Posner (1982), later refined by Bauer et al. (Bauer et al., 1979), who categorized LIS into classic, incomplete, and total forms based on preserved motor function and communication ability. Common etiologies may include neurodegenerative disorders such as Amyotrophic Lateral Sclerosis (ALS) (Laureys et al., 2005). ALS is a progressive neurodegenerative disease that often leads to LIS as it advances. In late-stage ALS, patients may experience complete paralysis, including the loss of eye movement, resulting in a state known as Complete Locked-In Syndrome (CLIS) (Khalili-Ardali et al., 2021). This progression underscores the importance of developing communication systems tailored to the needs of ALS patients. Research is being conducted in collaboration with APELA, a Portuguese ALS care association, which has been instrumental in supporting ALS patients and contributing to research aimed at improving their quality of life. Despite these significant motor constraints, patients with LIS commonly express a persistent desire for emotional connection, social interaction, and creative self-expression (Amado et al., 2024; Penedos-Santiago et al., 2025) as observed in previous participatory design studies with ALS patients. For instance, Vella et al. (2022) employed a participatory design process involving therapists, researchers, and a small sample of ALS patients to iteratively define user needs and requirements for a web-based Augmentative and Alternative Communication (AAC) platform. Their study highlighted the value of interdisciplinary collaboration in identifying functional gaps, particularly in understanding the low usability scores of an existing AAC communication solution. While their sample size was limited, the emphasis on need discovery and therapist insights underscores the importance of involving all stakeholders in the co-design of accessible communication tools, as we do in our digital drawing system. Similarly, Peters et al. (2020) conducted an in-depth study with two ALS participants with advanced motor constraints, exploring the use of BCI-based communication systems. Although their technical approach—relying on steady-state visual evoked potentials—differs from our non-invasive MR system, their findings emphasize the critical importance of adapting interaction techniques to the specific motor and cognitive abilities of each user. Their work reinforces our commitment to ensuring that the proposed system accommodates diverse levels of control and offers meaningful, affective interaction opportunities even for users with the most severe physical limitations.

Traditional non-invasive AAC systems for LIS, such as textual matrices and symbol boards, primarily support functional communication like letter selection or binary responses (Jeunet et al., 2020; Käthner et al., 2015; Kübler, 2020a, 2020b; Kübler & Botrel, 2019; Larradet et al., 2020; Vidal, 2020). While effective for basic needs, they often neglect emotional and eudaimonic dimensions vital for long-term well-being, such as joy, personal meaning, and creative expression (Hassenzahl, 2010; Mekler et al., 2016; Voity et al., 2024).

To address this gap, we propose a human-centered MR haptic drawing system using the HTC Vive Focus XR headset and non-invasive sensors (eye-tracking, facial recognition, motion). Drawing is reimagined as a relational, affective interface combining tactile and digital interaction (Hassenzahl, 2004; Lyons, 2012; Rachmad, 2017). Studies show that affective computing in immersive environments enhances engagement and emotional regulation through adaptive, real-time feedback (Lampropoulos et al., 2024; Reidy et al., 2020).

Our proposed interaction scenario enables synchronous and asynchronous co-creation, where caregivers trace gestures on the patient's body using VR controllers, mirrored in an augmented reality space. Patients respond via adaptive inputs like gaze or head tracking, with an optional "ghost mode" for replaying and extending sessions independently. Informed by workshops with ALS patients and design students, the system emphasizes proprioceptive and emotional engagement through collaborative drawing. These insights shaped requirements such as multimodal input, gesture amplification, and therapeutic tools. This work advances embodied and affective computing by reframing AAC systems to support emotional well-being and relational presence alongside core functionality, offering new paths for inclusive and therapeutic immersive design.

2. HAPTIC DRAWING AND EMBODIED COMPUTING

Haptic drawing has long played a communicative role in therapeutic and artistic contexts, as seen in Morgan O'Hara's *Live Transmission* (O'Hara, 2014), which captures micro-movements as records of embodied presence, and Dennis Oppenheim's *Two Stage Transfer Drawing* (1971), which frames drawing as a relational, tactile act. In LIS contexts, where typical non-verbal cues are limited, digital interfaces must enable alternative expressions of presence and emotion through embodied computing and tactile interaction.

Research highlights the effectiveness of haptic and gesture-based systems in supporting sensory communication with minimal motion (Aparicio, 2015; Köpsel et al., 2016; Larradet et al., 2020). Simulated or delayed somatosensory feedback can still foster strong perceptions of connection and intention (van Erp & Toet, 2015), reinforcing its value not only in assistive settings but in broader human connection contexts (Price et al., 2021). For individuals with severe motor impairments, mark-making—whether direct or assisted—can be psychologically transformative, offering a way to reclaim agency, express emotion, and reduce anxiety (Czamanski-Cohen & Weihs, 2016). Drawing, viewed as a language of embodiment (Massironi, 2001), becomes a trace of presence when speech and gesture are unavailable. Artists such as Hunt and Quintas highlight how generative drawing systems can act as proxies for user agency, particularly relevant for LIS patients with limited control. Research by Larradet et al. (2020) and Köpsel et al. (2016) shows haptic and gesture-based systems can support embodied interaction even with minimal motion.

This shift toward embodied computing, where system feedback is informed by physical properties like resistance or amplitude, aligns with findings by Price et al. (2021), who demonstrate that somatosensory feedback—simulated or delayed—can evoke strong feelings of connection. Haptic prompts, vibration, or spatialized audio can simulate proximity and foster co-presence. VR and MR further contribute by supporting perceptual vastness and relational interaction (Giesteira & Alves, 2025), promoting autonomy and engagement (Köpsel et al., 2016). Our system integrates these principles to enable real-time haptic co-drawing, framing drawing as both therapeutic and expressive interaction.

3. PILOT STUDY AND PRELIMINARY FINDINGS

A pilot study is planned with four ALS patients experiencing incomplete LIS. Sessions will include the following procedures: 1) Calibration & Familiarization (e.g. Interface walkthrough, sensitivity settings); 2) Drawing Tasks (asking to complete focused haptic drawing activities based on actions, responses and co-creation); 3) Continuous and final user evaluation (e.g.: using observational notes and adapted user experience metrics such as UEQ+, following the approval from the association and university ethics committees. In an initial exploratory phase using analogue drawing exercises (Giesteira, et. al), participants reported emotionally rich experiences—ranging from autobiographical resonance to joy in co-creation—despite varied physical and emotional starting points. One participant, initially anxious, responded positively after guided support, underscoring the value of onboarding. Functionally, the sessions revealed key needs: gesture stabilization for tremors, tools to separate cognitive ability from motor constraints, and structured prompts. All participants described the activity as innovative, intuitive, socially engaging, and meaningful, reinforcing the system's potential to support relational expression and well-being.

4. CONCEPT AND SYSTEM OVERVIEW

Our digital mixed reality system, developed specifically for the HTC Vive Focus XR headset, supports a range of interaction options designed to accommodate varying degrees of motor control and promote expressive, relational communication between patients and caregivers. The system offers multiple interaction modes to support expressive co-creation between patients and caregivers, including tactile tracing (Co-Creation Mode), accessible input responses (Drawing Co-Creation Option), and asynchronous engagement through replayable traces (Ghost Mode). Additionally, patients can take creative control through direct manipulation (Author Mode) or guide semi-autonomous agents for playful, indirect outputs (Director Mode), aligning with Shneiderman & Maes's (1997) principles of interface design. Drawings are represented digitally as expressive visual ribbons imbued with physical properties such as elasticity, inertia, and friction, enhancing their affective and creative potential.

In the context of drawing, this opens the possibility for shared AR canvases, ghost tracing, and reactive environments where users can express, reflect, and interact with others asynchronously or in real time. These approaches shift communication from a utilitarian mode (answering questions, spelling) to an affective and expressive dimension, enabling users to be seen, felt, and understood beyond words. The application will be developed incrementally through iterative phases and tested with a voluntary group of 4 incomplete LIS patients with varying degrees of physical constraints. Beginning with basic drawing capabilities and gradually adding advanced multimodal features. Each iteration will undergo rigorous usability evaluations with LIS patients, driving continuous refinement based on user feedback and performance metrics. Accessibility assessments will also be considered. This approach aligns with the user-centered Spiral Model (Boehm, 1988), an iterative, risk-driven methodology particularly suited for participatory design in digital health contexts. It also follows the principles outlined by Preece, Sharp, and Rogers (2023), emphasizing iterative prototyping and evaluation closely tailored to users' health-related needs. This structured roadmap ensures technical feasibility and sensitivity to LIS patients' cognitive and physical constraints, establishing a flexible foundation for ongoing research and scalable therapeutic implementations.

5. CONTRIBUTION AND OUTLOOK

This paper presents a novel communication system for individuals with Incomplete Locked-In Syndrome (LIS), blending physical and digital touch to enable expressive, non-verbal interaction. Moving beyond functional AAC tools, it emphasizes emotional well-being, relational presence, and creative agency through modes that support co-creation, personalized visuals, and shared artifacts. Grounded in analogue trials and workshops with students and ALS patients, the system aims to enhance agency and foster emotional connection, aligning with Newcomb's ABX model (Brewer, 1968) to facilitate triadic meaning-making between patient (A), caregiver (B), and artifact (X). By embedding hedonic and eudaimonic values, including serendipitous discovery via agent-driven or direct drawing, the interface promotes joy and creative fulfillment. Ongoing development focuses on usability, scalability, and adaptability across LIS profiles, contributing to inclusive, affective healthcare design. Broader implications include informing universal design and accessibility strategies through customizable inputs, embodied co-creation, and empathetic interaction design principles.

REFERENCES

Amado, P., Penedos-Santiago, E., Lima, C., Simões, S., Giesteira, B., & Peçaibes, V. (2024). Challenges and Opportunities for Designing Digital Communication Interfaces for Persons with Partial Locked-in Syndrome. *13th EAI International Conference Proceedings*. 13th EAI International Conference: ArtsIT, Interactivity & Game Creation, Abhu Dhabi.

Aparicio, A. (2015). Immobilis in mobili: Performing arts, BCI, and locked-in syndrome. *Brain-Computer Interfaces*, *2*(2–3), 150–159. https://doi.org/10.1080/2326263X.2015.1100366

Bauer, G., Gerstenbrand, F., & Rumpl, E. (1979). Varieties of the locked-in syndrome. *Journal of Neurology*, *221*(2), 77–91. https://doi.org/10.1007/BF00313105

Brewer, R. E. (1968). Attitude Change, Interpersonal Attraction, and Communication in a Dyadic Situation. *The Journal of Social Psychology*. https://www.tandfonline.com/doi/abs/10.1080/00224545.1968.9712482

Czamanski-Cohen, J., & Weihs, K. L. (2016). The bodymind model: A platform for studying the mechanisms of change induced by art therapy. *The Arts in Psychotherapy*, *51*, 63–71. https://doi.org/10.1016/j.aip.2016.08.006

Giesteira, B., et al. (2025). Towards the Requirements of VR Drawing for Patients with Partial to Complete Locked-In Syndrome. AditGames 2025 (In Press).

Giesteira, B., Alves, T. (2025), Towards the Design of Transformation: a Review of Transformative VR Experiences. International Conference on Human Interaction and Emerging Technologies (IHIET). (In Press)

Hassenzahl, M. (2004). The Thing and I: Understanding the Relationship Between User and Product. In M. A. Blythe, K. Overbeeke, A. F. Monk, & P. C. Wright (Eds.), *Funology: From Usability to Enjoyment* (pp. 31–42). Springer Netherlands. https://doi.org/10.1007/1-4020-2967-5_4

Hassenzahl, M. (2010). *Experience Design: Technology for All the Right Reasons*. Springer International Publishing. https://doi.org/10.1007/978-3-031-02191-6

Jeunet, C., Bernaroch, C., Cabestaing, F., Chavarriaga, R., Colamarino, E., Corsi, M. C., Coyle, D., De Vico Fallani, F., Enriquez-Geppert, S., Figueiredo, P., Grosse-Wentrup, M., Kleih, S., Kober, S., Kubler, A., Lotte, F., Maby, E., Mattia, D., Mattout, J., Muller-Putz, G., … Wriessnegger, S. (2020, September 29). *A user-centred approach to unlock the potential of non-invasive BCIs: An unprecedented international translational effort: CHIST-ERA CONFERENCE 2020*.

Käthner, I., Kübler, A., & Halder, S. (2015). Comparison of eye tracking, electrooculography and an auditory brain-computer interface for binary communication: A case study with a participant in the locked-in state. *Journal of NeuroEngineering and Rehabilitation*, *12*(1), 76. https://doi.org/10.1186/s12984-015-0071-z

Khalili-Ardali, M., Wu, S., Tonin, A., Birbaumer, N., & Chaudhary, U. (2021). Neurophysiological aspects of the completely locked-in syndrome in patients with advanced amyotrophic lateral sclerosis. *Clinical Neurophysiology: Official Journal of the International Federation of Clinical Neurophysiology*, *132*(5), 1064–1076. https://doi.org/10.1016/j.clinph.2021.01.013

Köpsel, A., Majaranta, P., Isokoski, P., & Huckauf, A. (2016). Effects of auditory, haptic and visual feedback on performing gestures by gaze or by hand. *Behaviour & Information Technology*, *35*(12), 1044–1062. https://doi.org/10.1080/0144929X.2016.1194477

Kübler, A. (2020a). The history of BCI: From a vision for the future to real support for personhood in people with locked-in syndrome. *Neuroethics*, *13*(2), 163–180. https://doi.org/10.1007/s12152-019-09409-4

Kübler, A. (2020b). The history of BCI: From a vision for the future to real support for personhood in people with locked-in syndrome. *Neuroethics*, *13*(2), 163–180. https://doi.org/10.1007/S12152-019-09409-4/FIGURES/11

Kübler, A., & Botrel, L. (2019). The Making of Brain Painting—From the Idea to Daily Life Use by People in the Locked-in State. In A. Nijholt (Ed.), *Brain Art: Brain-Computer Interfaces for Artistic Expression* (pp. 409–431). Springer International Publishing. https://doi.org/10.1007/978-3-030-14323-7_15

Lampropoulos, G., Fernández-Arias, P., Antón-Sancho, Á., & Vergara, D. (2024). Affective Computing in Augmented Reality, Virtual Reality, and Immersive Learning Environments. *Electronics*, *13*(15), Article 15. https://doi.org/10.3390/electronics13152917

Larradet, F., Barresi, G., & Mattos, L. S. (2020). Affective communication enhancement system for locked-in syndrome patients. *Lecture Notes in Computer Science (Including Subseries Lecture Notes in Artificial Intelligence and Lecture Notes in Bioinformatics)*, *12188 LNCS*, 143–156. https://doi.org/10.1007/978-3-030-49282-3_10/FIGURES/10

Laureys, S., Pellas, F., Van Eeckhout, P., Ghorbel, S., Schnakers, C., Perrin, F., Berré, J., Faymonville, M.-E., Pantke, K.-H., Damas, F., Lamy, M., Moonen, G., & Goldman, S. (2005). The locked-in syndrome: What is it like to be conscious but paralyzed and voiceless? *Progress in Brain Research*, *150*, 495–511. https://doi.org/10.1016/S0079-6123(05)50034-7

Lyons, L. (2012). Drawing your way into understanding. *Drawing Knowledge. Tracey Journal.*

Massironi, M. (2001). *The psychology of graphic images: Seeing, drawing, communicating.* Psychology Press.

Mekler, E., on, K. H.-P. of the 2016 chi conference, & 2016, undefined. (2016). Momentary pleasure or lasting meaning? Distinguishing eudaimonic and hedonic user experiences. *Dl.Acm.Org*, *2016-January*, 4509–4520. https://doi.org/10.1145/2858036.2858225

O'Hara, M. (2014). Live Transmission/Performative Drawing. *PAJ: A Journal of Performance and Art*, *36*(2 (107)), 2–5. https://doi.org/10.1162/PAJJ_a_00188

Penedos-Santiago, E., Simões, S., Amado, P., & Giesteira, B. (2025). Drawing for Social Re-Connectivity Through Collaborative and Digital Environments. Preliminary Drawing Activities. In A. Abreu, J. V. Carvalho, A. Mesquita, A. Sousa Pinto, & M. Mendonça Teixeira (Eds.), *Perspectives and Trends in Education and Technology* (pp. 242–247). Springer Nature Switzerland. https://doi.org/10.1007/978-3-031-78155-1_23

Peters, B., Bedrick, S., Dudy, S., Eddy, B., Higger, M., Kinsella, M., McLaughlin, D., Memmott, T., Oken, B., Quivira, F., Spaulding, S., Erdogmus, D., & Fried-Oken, M. (2020). SSVEP BCI and Eye Tracking Use by Individuals With Late-Stage ALS and Visual Impairments. *Frontiers in Human Neuroscience*, *14*. https://doi.org/10.3389/fnhum.2020.595890

Plum, F., & Posner, J. B. (1982). *The diagnosis of stupor and coma* (Vol. 19). Oxford University Press, USA.

Price, S., Jewitt, C., Chubinidze, D., Barker, N., & Yiannoutsou, N. (2021). Taking an Extended Embodied Perspective of Touch: Connection-Disconnection in iVR. *Frontiers in Virtual Reality*, *2*. https://doi.org/10.3389/frvir.2021.642782

Rachmad, Y. E. (2017). *Digital Empathy Theory.*

Reidy, L., Chan, D., Nduka, C., & Gunes, H. (2020). *Facial Electromyography-based Adaptive Virtual Reality Gaming for Cognitive Training* (No. arXiv:2005.05023). arXiv. https://doi.org/10.48550/arXiv.2005.05023

Rogers, Y., Sharp, H., & Preece, J. (2023). *Interaction design: Beyond human-computer interaction* (6th ed.). https://www.wiley.com/en-us/Interaction+Design%3A+Beyond+Human+Computer+Interaction%2C+6th+Edition-p-9781119901099

Shneiderman, B., & Maes, P. (1997). Direct manipulation vs. Interface agents. *Interactions*, *4*(6), 42–61. https://doi.org/10.1145/267505.267514

van Erp, J. B. F., & Toet, A. (2015). Social Touch in Human–Computer Interaction. *Frontiers in Digital Humanities*, *2*. https://doi.org/10.3389/fdigh.2015.00002

Vella, F., Clastres-Babou, F., Vigouroux, N., Truillet, P., Calmels, C., Mercadier, C., Gigaud, K., Issanchou, M., Gourinovitch, K., & Garaix, A. (2022). *User Centred Method to Design a Platform to Design Augmentative and Alternative Communication Assistive Technologies* (No. arXiv:2211.13079). arXiv. https://doi.org/10.48550/arXiv.2211.13079

Vidal, F. (2020). Phenomenology of the Locked-In Syndrome: An Overview and Some Suggestions. *Neuroethics*, *13*(2), 119–143. https://doi.org/10.1007/S12152-018-9388-1/FIGURES/1

Voity, K., Lopez, T., Chan, J. P., & Greenwald, B. D. (2024). Update on How to Approach a Patient with Locked-In Syndrome and Their Communication Ability. *Brain Sciences 2024, Vol. 14, Page 92*, *14*(1), 92. https://doi.org/10.3390/BRAINSCI14010092

BREAKING BARRIERS: GAMIFICATION IN RECRUITING TO OVERCOME COMMUNICATION CHALLENGES – PSYCHOLOGICAL, SOCIAL AND CULTURAL DIFFERENCES IN PERCEPTION AND PARTICIPATION –

Manuela Sachse and Jessica Melzer
Westsächsische Hochschule Zwickau, Germany

ABSTRACT

Traditional application procedures present significant barriers for candidates with diverse communication styles. Classical interviews and standardized assessments can systematically disadvantage neurodivergent individuals and others with specific communicative needs. Gamified selection processes offer a more objective, interactive, and stress-reducing alternative. This paper investigates the extent to which gamification in recruitment can help overcome existing communication barriers and enable more inclusive talent assessment. Drawing on current research, the paper highlights mechanisms behind gamified assessments and discusses implementation challenges. Particular focus is placed on bias reduction, candidate experience, and long-term impacts on labor market diversity. The findings indicate that gamification represents a promising approach toward fairer and more objective personnel selection. Given limited empirical evidence—especially for neurodivergent applicants—this paper provides a conceptual foundation for future research on inclusive, gamified recruitment.

KEYWORDS

Gamification, Recruitment, Game-Based Assessment, Inclusive Hiring, Cognitive Diversity

1. INTRODUCTION

Digitalization and automation have fundamentally changed how organizations recruit talent.

Traditional methods emphasize standardized interviews and interpersonal skills but can pose barriers for candidates with different communication needs. Research shows that conventional selection can disadvantage certain applicants, despite their professional competence. (Sasson et al., 2017; Proft et al., 2016).

Modern recruitment increasingly uses digital tools in pre-selection and decision-making to improve efficiency and objectivity. Yet many assessments test cognitive and social skills in ways not equally accessible to all candidates. (Georgiou, Nikolaou & Gouras, 2019).

In response to these challenges, "gamification" has gained growing attention in both academic and professional contexts. The term refers to the application of game-like elements—such as points, levels, challenges, and reward systems—in non-game settings, with the aim of promoting motivation, interaction, and performance (Dahm & Dregger, 2018). Huotari and Hamari (2012) define gamification as "enhancing a service with affordances for gameful experiences to support users' value creation" (p. 19). This perspective broadens the understanding of gamification beyond technical features, framing it as a strategic design approach embedded in user experience. While gamification is already applied in fields like professional training and digital marketing, its theoretical foundation within recruitment remains underdeveloped.

This paper examines how gamification can reduce bias and promote inclusion, particularly for neurodivergent candidates. It synthesizes interdisciplinary research, compares gamified and traditional assessments, and outlines criteria for inclusive design. Rather than offering a systematic review, it presents a conceptual framework linking communicative barriers to game-based mechanisms. The aim is to foster dialogue and lay a foundation for future research on fairer, communication-sensitive recruitment practices.This paper does not aim to provide a systematic literature review, but rather presents a conceptual argument grounded in selected examples from current research. Its goal is to initiate a research dialogue and to identify critical gaps that warrant further empirical investigation—emphasizing the urgent need for more inclusive recruitment approaches, particularly those that leverage gamification to reduce communicative barriers.

Despite growing interest, empirical evidence on its recruitment effectiveness remains limited. This lack of research is particularly striking with respect to neurodivergent candidates, whose specific challenges in traditional assessment contexts are well-documented. This paper addresses these gaps by offering a conceptual framework that explicitly links communicative barriers to specific gamified mechanisms. It outlines key areas—such as fairness perceptions, task validity, and candidate experience—that require empirical exploration to validate the inclusive potential of gamified approaches.

2. CHALLENGES OF TRADITIONAL RECRUITMENT PROCESSES FOR INDIVIDUALS WITH DIVERSE COMMUNICATION NEEDS

Application processes often reflect implicit social norms optimized for neurotypical candidates Key selection phases—from screening to in-person assessments—involve intensive verbal and non-verbal interaction (Voß & Würtemberger, 2023). For neurodivergent applicants, this can cause structural disadvantages, as their communication often diverges from recruiters' expectations. Studies show that individuals with autism, ADHD, or high introversion struggle with spontaneous conversation, eye contact, and social cues (Ellestad et al., 2023). Yet these abilities often serve as proxies for social competence in interviews, disadvantaging candidates despite their qualifications (Reich & Dalferth, 2023). High-stress interview settings can further impair performance in already disadvantaged groups. Under stress, social interaction worsens for many, distorting perceptions of job suitability (McKnight-Lizotte, 2018). These challenges raise the question whether alternative methods—especially gamified assessments—can enable more objective and inclusive evaluation.

3. COMPARISON OF TRADITIONAL INTERVIEWS AND GAMIFIED ASSESSMENTS

Traditional interviews are often shaped by subjective factors like personal affinity, nonverbal cues, or cultural fit (Georgiou et al., 2019), whereas gamified assessments follow standardized, data-driven procedures that enhance objectivity and reduce judgment bias (Landers & Sanchez, 2022). While interviews demand verbal fluency and social performance—challenges for neurodivergent candidates—gamified formats emphasize cognitive and analytical abilities in system-based environments, minimizing interpersonal pressure. If thoughtfully designed, they can accommodate diverse communication styles, though accessibility depends on clear instructions, adaptable interfaces, and inclusive formats (Willis et al., 2021). Gamified methods also improve engagement, particularly among younger applicants, and reduce anxiety through narrative elements and feedback (Baah et al., 2024; Dichev et al., 2015). In sum, gamification offers a structured, inclusive alternative to traditional hiring—provided its implementation aligns with sound pedagogical and ethical standards..

4. GAMIFICATION AS AN ALTERNATIVE APPROACH IN RECRUITMENT

Gamification refers to the integration of playful elements into non-game contexts with the goal of increasing motivation and engagement (Deterding et al., 2011). In HR, gamification is used in onboarding, training, and performance evaluation (Latz & Koob, 2024). HR gamification uses badges, points, leaderboards, challenges, and tangible rewards (Mahat et al., 2022). These elements aim to boost engagement, performance, and training outcomes (Mohanty & Christopher B, 2024 It can be implemented via platforms, hybrid approaches, or in-person formats (Mahat et al., 2022). Applying game-based mechanisms to recruitment may help address challenges faced by neurodivergent applicants and others with diverse communication needs.

Studies suggest that game-related assessments (GRAs) - i.e., assessments based on interactive, game-like tasks—can positively influence candidate selection (Ohlms et al., 2024). GRAs show strong convergent validity with personality and cognitive ability tests, while reducing test anxiety (Hilliard et al., 2022; Leutner et al., 2023). They also show promise for assessing cognitive flexibility and fairness for candidates with special communication needs (Hommel et al., 2021; Willis et al., 2021). The next section explores how these strategies can help reduce communicative barriers in recruitment..

4.1 Advantages of Gamified Selection Procedures for Candidates with Special Communicative Requirements

Gamified selection procedures offer significant advantages for candidates with special communicative requirements, highlighting the inclusive potential of game-based recruitment assessments (GRAs). By utilizing simulation-based scenarios or avatars, these assessments can be conducted in low-stress, controlled environments that minimize social pressure. Brunzini et al. (2022) demonstrated that simulation-based assessments reduce stress significantly compared to traditional interviews: in a trial with 120 candidates, those assessed in a mixed-reality setting showed 28% lower physiological and 48% lower subjective stress levels. Neurodivergent candidates in particular rated gamified assessments as fairer and more pleasant. Furthermore, GRAs enable a more objective evaluation by relying on data-driven indicators such as problem-solving and analytical reasoning. Landers and Sanchez (2022) found that gamified assessments exhibit higher predictive validity ($r = .67$) than traditional interviews ($r = .42$), while also reducing socially desirable responses and unconscious bias toward neurodivergent individuals. Finally, gamified assessments promote alternative communication modes by allowing candidates to demonstrate their skills through interactive challenges and simulation-based tasks. This fosters a more equitable evaluation environment. As shown by Altomari et al. (2023), neurodivergent applicants particularly benefit from such approaches, with a significantly higher success rate and a 25–40% reduction in stress, underlining the inclusive potential of gamified recruitment practices.

4.2 Existing Research Gaps

Despite their potential for inclusive recruitment, gamified methods still face challenges. Implementing such formats raises fundamental questions about validity, fairness, technical feasibility, and ethical responsibility. These aspects must be critically examined to ensure gamification is not just innovative but also responsible.

While many studies confirm reduced stress and greater engagement, some warn against overrelying on digital proxies for social skills. Few studies compare experiences across neurotypes—a key blind spot in current research. Despite these advantages, gamified recruitment also poses challenges—discussed in the next section.

5. CHALLENGES AND OPEN QUESTIONS REGARDING THE IMPLEMENTATION OF GAMIFICATION IN RECRUITMENT

While gamification presents an innovative pathway toward inclusive recruitment, its implementation involves several challenges that require careful and deliberate attention. First, the validity and job relevance of gamified tasks must be ensured—activities should not merely appear playful but must accurately measure competencies that are truly required for the position. Misaligned game mechanics can distort outcomes and compromise interpretability. Additionally, the technical infrastructure poses accessibility concerns, as not all candidates have equal access to reliable devices, internet connectivity, or digital literacy. Assessments must also be designed inclusively for individuals with visual or motor impairments. Data protection and ethics present another major issue: gamified tools often collect sensitive behavioral and emotional data, raising concerns about transparency, algorithmic influence, and secure data handling. Establishing clear ethical guidelines and robust data infrastructure is essential. Some candidates may view gamified methods as unprofessional. Clear communication of purpose and evaluation logic is essential to build trust Cultural coding of game mechanics must be addressed early to prevent exclusion (Fernandes et al., 2022).

6. CONCLUSION

This paper shows that traditional interviews often disadvantage individuals with diverse communication needs, whereas gamified assessments offer a more inclusive alternative by reducing social pressure and enabling objective evaluation. However, successful implementation requires valid, ethically sound, and target group-sensitive design. Gamification is not a replacement, but a useful complement to conventional methods, provided it addresses candidate experience, fairness, and technical feasibility.

Despite its promise, empirical studies on gamification's effects across neurotypes remain scarce. This paper helps close that gap by linking communicative barriers—especially among neurodivergent candidates—to specific game-based mechanisms and proposing inclusion-oriented design strategies.

Future research should compare traditional and gamified formats across neurotypes, assess performance equity and anxiety reduction via design features (e.g., avatars, narratives), and investigate data ethics, fairness, and cross-cultural acceptance in gamified recruitment.

REFERENCES

Ajayi, F. A., & Udeh, C. A. (2024). Innovative recruitment strategies in the IT sector: A review of successes and failures. Magna Scientia Advanced Research

Altomari, L., Altomari, N., & Iazzolino, G. (2023). Gamification and soft skills assessment in the development of a serious game: Design and feasibility pilot study. JMIR Serious Games, 11, e45436. https://doi.org/10.2196/45436

Baah, C., Govender, I., & Subramaniam, P. R. (2024). Enhancing Learning Engagement: A Study on Gamification's Influence on Motivation and Cognitive Load. *Education Sciences*, *14*(10), 1115. https://doi.org/10.3390/educsci14101115

Brunzini, A., Papetti, A., Messi, D., & Germani, M. (2022). A comprehensive method to design and assess mixed reality simulations. Virtual Reality, 26, 1257–1275. https://doi.org/10.1007/s10055-022-00632-8

Burtscher, S., & Gerling, K. (2024). Neurodivergence and work in human-computer interaction: Mapping the research landscape. Proceedings of the 3rd Annual Meeting of the ACM SIGCHI Symposium on HCI Research. https://doi.org/10.1145/3663384.3663386

Dahm, M., & Dregger, A. (2018). Der Einsatz von künstlicher Intelligenz im HR: Die Wirkung und Förderung der Akzeptanz von KI-basierten Recruiting-Tools bei potenziellen Nutzern. Arbeitswelten der Zukunft. Springer.

Deterding, S., Dixon, D., Khaled, R., & Nacke, L. (2011). From game design elements to gamefulness: Defining "gamification". *Proceedings of the 15th International Academic MindTrek Conference: Envisioning Future Media Environments*, 9–15.

Dichev, C., Dicheva, D., & Angelova, G. (2015). From gamification to gameful design and gameful experience in learning. *Cybernetics and Information Technologies, 15*(3), 20–34. https://doi.org/10.1515/cait-2014-0007

Dugyala, R., Gaddam, V. K., & Eroju, H. (2024). Smart recruitment system. Proceedings of the 15th International Conference on Emerging Trends in Human Resource Management.

Ellestad, A. I., Beymer, L. L., & Villegas, S. (2023). The lived experiences of individuals with high-functioning autism during the job interview process: A phenomenological study. Journal of Employment Counseling, 60(2), 78–96. https://doi.org/10.1002/joec.12186

Fernandes, A., Melo, M., & Machado, C. F. (2022). *The use of gamification in training and socialization processes in a multicultural context*. In The Human Side of Service Engineering (pp. 45–57). Springer. https://doi.org/10.1007/978-3-030-98040-5_4

Norton, E. S. (2022). Neurobiology of communication disorders: The state of the science and new insights from social EEG. Journal of the American Academy of Child & Adolescent Psychiatry, 61(10 Suppl.), S137. https://doi.org/10.1016/j.jaac.2022.07.545

Georgiou, K., Nikolaou, I., & Gouras, A. (2019). Gamification in employee selection: The development of a gamified assessment. International Journal of Selection and Assessment, 27(4), 1–13. https://doi.org/10.1111/ijsa.12240

Georgiou, K., & Nikolaou, I. (2020). Are applicants in favor of traditional or gamified assessment methods? Exploring applicant reactions towards a gamified selection method. Computers in Human Behavior, 109, 106356. https://doi.org/10.1016/j.chb.2020.106356

Hilliard, A., Kazim, E., Bitsakis, T., & Leutner, F. (2022). Measuring personality through images: Validating a forced-choice image-based assessment of the Big Five personality traits. Journal of Intelligence, 10(1), 12. https://doi.org/10.3390/jintelligence10010012

Hommel, B. E., Ruppel, R., & Zacher, H. (2021, November 8). Assessment of cognitive flexibility in personnel selection: Validity and acceptance of a gamified version of the Wisconsin Card Sorting Test. PsyArXiv Preprints. https://doi.org/10.31234/osf.io/kcp85

Huotari, K./Hamari, J. (2012): Defining gamification: a service marketing perspective, in: Association for Computing Machinery (Hrsg.): Proceedings of the 16th International Academic MindTrek Conference - International Conference on Media of the Future, Tampere, Finland/New York, USA, S. 17 - 22.

Karmadonova, T. (2024). Modern information-measurement technologies: Transforming talent selection in the digital age. Journal of Digital HR Innovations, 18(2), 112–125.

Landers, R. N., & Sanchez, D. R. (2022). Game-based, gamified, and gamefully designed assessments for employee selection: Definitions, distinctions, design, and validation. International Journal of Selection and Assessment, 30(1), 1–16. https://doi.org/10.1111/ijsa.12376

Latz, A., & Koob, D. (2024). Optimierung der Kompetenzentwicklung von Berufseinsteigern und Auszubildenden mithilfe von gamifizierten Prozessen. Proceedings of the Jahrestagung der Gesellschaft für Informatik.

Lee, J., & Ko, Y. (2024). Comparing metaverse and face-to-face instruction for enhancing English skills and attitudes among EFL adolescents. Education and Information Technologies. https://doi.org/10.1007/s10639-024-13162-4

Leutner, F., Codreanu, S.-C., Brink, S., & Bitsakis, T. (2023). Game-based assessments of cognitive ability in recruitment: Validity, fairness and test-taking experience. Frontiers in Psychology, 13, 942662. https://doi.org/10.3389/fpsyg.2022.942662

Mahat, J., Alias, N., & Yusop, F. D. (2022). Systematic literature review on gamified professional training among employees. Interactive Learning Environments, 31, 6747–6767. https://doi.org/10.1080/10494820.2022.2146783

McKnight-Lizotte, M. (2018). Work-related communication barriers for individuals with autism: A pilot qualitative study. The Australian Journal of Rehabilitation Counselling, 24(1), 12–26. https://doi.org/10.1017/jrc.2018.4

Mohanty, S., & Christopher, B. P. (2024). The role of gamification research in human resource management: A PRISMA analysis and future research direction. SAGE Open, 14(2). https://doi.org/10.1177/21582440241243154

Ohlms, M. L., Melchers, K. G., & Kanning, U. P. (2024). Playful personnel selection: The use of traditional versus game-related personnel selection methods and their perception from the recruiters' and applicants' perspectives. International Journal of Selection and Assessment, 32, 381–398. https://doi.org/10.1111/ijsa.12466

Proft, J., Gawronski, A., Krämer, K., Schoofs, T., Kockler, H., & Vogeley, K. (2016). Autismus im Beruf. Zeitschrift für Psychiatrie, Psychologie und Psychotherapie, 64(4), 277–285. https://doi.org/10.1024/1661-4747/a000264

Ramos-Villagrasa, P. J., & Fernández-del-Río, E. (2022). Game-related assessments for personnel selection: A systematic review. Frontiers in Psychology, 13, 812900. https://doi.org/10.3389/fpsyg.2022.812900

Reich, K., & Dalferth, M. (2023). Vom Vermittlungsparadigma hin zur nachhaltigen Unterstützung von Unternehmen bei der Eingliederung von Menschen mit hochfunktionalem Autismus – Ergebnisse einer Arbeitgeberbefragung. Die Rehabilitation, 62(4), 289–298.

Salvetti, F., Bertagni, B., Contardo, I. (2023). Intelligent Digital Humans for Bias-Free Recruitment Interviews: A Diversity & Inclusion Training Program. In: Guralnick, D., Auer, M.E., Poce, A. (eds) Creative Approaches to Technology-Enhanced Learning for the Workplace and Higher Education. TLIC 2023. Lecture Notes in Networks and Systems, vol 767. Springer, Cham. https://doi.org/10.1007/978-3-031-41637-8_36

Shankar, C. S. U., Ganesan, J., & Yeo, S. F. (2024). Examining the role of gamification in enhancing candidate engagement and experience through gamified selection processes.

Sasson, N. J., Faso, D. J., Nugent, J., Lovell, S., Kennedy, D. P., & Grossman, R. B. (2017). Neurotypical peers are less willing to interact with those with autism based on thin slice judgments. Scientific Reports, 7, 40700. https://doi.org/10.1038/srep40700

Spoor, J. R., & Walkowiak, E. (2024). Enabling neurodiversity in organisations: Leveraging the HRM and digital technology nexus. In E. Patton & A. M. Santuzzi (Eds.), Neurodiversity and work (pp. 255–274). Palgrave Macmillan. https://doi.org/10.1007/978-3-031-55072-0_11

Veglianti, E., Trombin, M., Pinna, R., De Marco, M. (2023). Customized Artificial Intelligence for Talent Recruiting: A Bias-Free Tool?. In: Dal Zotto, C., Omidi, A., Aoun, G. (eds) Smart Technologies for Organizations. Lecture Notes in Information Systems and Organisation, vol 60. Springer, Cham. https://doi.org/10.1007/978-3-031-24775-0_15

Voß, E., & Würtemberger, S. (2023). Recruiting: Selektionsprozesse objektiv und durchlässig für Vielfalt gestalten. In Vielfalt im Employee Lifecycle (pp. 45–63). Springer Gabler. https://doi.org/10.1007/978-3-658-39841-5_3

Willis, C., Powell-Rudy, T., Colley, K., & Prasad, J. (2021). Examining the use of game-based assessments for hiring autistic job seekers. Journal of Intelligence, 9(4), 53. https://doi.org/10.3390/jintelligence9040053

THAT'S ANCIENT HISTORY: HERITAGE AND VIDEOGAMES IN A BLENDED INTENSIVE PROGRAMME

Bárbara Barroso[1], Rita Costa[2], Thibaud Hulin[3], Jens Nilsson[4], Stefan Tidlund[4] and Tanja Korhonen[5]
[1]Research Center in Digitalization and Intelligent Robotics (CeDRI), Instituto Politécnico de Bragança, Portugal
[2]Transdisciplinary Research Center in Education and Development (CITeD), Instituto Politécnico de Bragança, Portugal
[3]Université Marie et Louis Pasteur, France
[4]University West, Sweden
[5]Kajaani University of Applied Sciences, Finland

ABSTRACT

The integration of cultural heritage into video game design is an innovative approach to fostering engagement and learning. This paper examines a Blended Intensive Programme (BIP) that explores the intersection of heritage and video games, providing students with hands-on experience in designing and developing games that interpret and preserve cultural heritage. The BIP aims to balance historical accuracy with engaging gameplay, fostering interdisciplinary collaboration and critical thinking. This study evaluates the pedagogical framework, learning outcomes, and implications for digital heritage education.

KEYWORDS

Heritage, Videogames, Game Design, Blended Intensive Programme, Digital Humanities

1. INTRODUCTION

Cultural heritage constitutes a core element of individual and collective identity. According to the United Nations Educational, Scientific and Cultural Organization (UNESCO) (2003), it encompasses both tangible (monuments, artifacts) and intangible (traditions, rituals, knowledge) expressions passed through generations. As societies evolve, so too must the methods through which heritage is preserved and communicated. Digital technologies – particularly video games – have emerged as powerful tools for cultural mediation and dissemination. Recent systematic reviews demonstrate that video games not only reproduce and transmit cultural knowledge but also generate new cultural representations and participatory frameworks for identity construction (Cerezo-Pizarro et al., 2023). Games enable immersive and interactive engagements with history and memory, making them particularly relevant in contemporary educational settings (Chapman, 2016; Anderson et al., 2010), providing an interactive and immersive medium that allows players to engage with historical narratives, artifacts, and traditions (Schrier, 2014; Majewski, 2015).

Beyond entertainment, games function as cultural artifacts that reflect and shape our understanding of the world (Bogost, 2007). In the context of education, they can promote critical thinking, empathy, and participation (Schrier, 2014; Tavinor, 2009). This paper explores the application of these ideas in a higher education setting, analysing how a Blended Intensive Programme (BIP) on Heritage and Videogames enabled students to collaboratively develop games that represent diverse cultural heritages while engaging in multidisciplinary, multicultural teamwork, highlighting its pedagogical and technical challenges.

2. CONTEXT AND RATIONALE

The Heritage in Videogames BIP was designed as an interdisciplinary initiative involving multiple European universities. Hosted by Bragança Polytechnic University (Instituto Politécnico de Bragança – IPB, Portugal), with participation from University West (Sweden), Kajaani University of Applied Sciences (Finland), and Université Marie & Louis Pasteur (France), as institutional partners, the programme combined virtual and physical learning experiences. The primary goal was to equip students with skills in game design while instilling an appreciation for historical accuracy and cultural representation, focusing on cultural and natural heritage as the foundation for creative processes. The programme sought to bridge digital transformation and cultural education by engaging students in the challenge of preserving and/or communicating heritage through interactive digital media.

Recent research affirms the pedagogical value of incorporating game design into heritage education. Liarokapis et al. (2020) highlight the growing role of visual computing and immersive technologies in both preserving and interpreting cultural assets. Øygardslia and Aarsand (2018) emphasize the importance of artifacts as epistemic tools in the classroom, noting that designing games on historical topics facilitates knowledge construction through material and digital means. Likewise, Majewski (2015) and Salazar (2018) argue that games allow for the reimagining of heritage in ways that resonate with contemporary audiences, while raising questions about authorship, accuracy, and cultural sensitivity. Schrier (2014) discusses how historical games can serve as a medium for experiential learning.

In this light, the BIP not only intended to promote skill development in game design and digital storytelling, but also foster critical awareness of heritage politics, representation, and authenticity. As Champion (2019) argues, games can function as archaeological arguments or experiential simulations, raising critical questions about authorship and interpretive agency in digital heritage contexts. The students were challenged to research, interpret, and creatively express local heritage elements, translating them into interactive experiences that could communicate meaning across cultural boundaries.

3. STRUCTURE AND IMPLEMENTATION OF THE BIP

3.1 Pedagogical Framework

The programme was structured around key learning objectives:

- Understanding Heritage: definitions, classifications (tangible vs. intangible), authenticity and historical accuracy.
- Game Design Principles: game and level design, narrative development, interactivity, and user experience.
- Multicultural Collaboration: working in diverse teams to develop heritage-based games.

Students engaged in iterative design, following an agile development model (Healy & Cullen, 2022). The curriculum included case studies, prototyping sessions, and expert-led discussions on game-based heritage representation. The programme included participants from a diverse range of academic backgrounds, bringing together students from both bachelor's and master's degree courses. This interdisciplinary cohort enriched the collaborative dynamic, fostering a variety of perspectives in the design process. The prototyping sessions were structured around concrete, day-to-day goals that allowed teams to apply insights gained during earlier theoretical modules. These practical activities built progressively on prior learning, enabling students to translate conceptual understanding into meaningful design decisions.

3.2 Digital Tools and Methods

Participants employed a range of digital tools, including game engines, 3D modelling and photogrammetry software, 2D image editors, audio workstations, and collaborative platforms to support conceptualization, asset creation, modelling and implementation. This toolset enabled the production of accurate digital representations of heritage elements, in line with best practices in visual computing for cultural heritage (Liarokapis et al., 2020).

4. LEARNING OUTCOMES AND IMPACTS

This programme produced six prototypes of five different genres, including educational, action, arcade, and simulation games, each designed to enhance the audience's connection to cultural heritage and develop interdisciplinary skills.

The project "A Tayū's Nightmare," designed based on a temporary exhibition at the Museu do Oriente (Portugal), combines procedurally structured dungeon crawler mechanics with narrative conventions and aesthetics inspired by Kabuki theatre. In this game, players navigate a narrative about a young girl who is escaping a manipulative yokai.

Another project, titled "Echoes of the Great War," was developed in partnership with the Musée de la Grande Guerre (France). This immersive experience places players in World War I, allowing them to explore soldiers' experiences through interactive gameplay and a low-poly art style.

"Biolens" is a survival and simulation game set on an alien planet, where players document diverse flora and fauna while avoiding various dangers. This game features a solarpunk aesthetic and incorporates ideas gathered in collaboration with Mirandela's Ecoteca (Portugal), fostering a deeper understanding of human interaction with natural heritage.

Designed with Le Pavillon des Sciences (France), "Quiziverse" encourages players to analyse scenarios to identify genuine scientific mistakes, fostering an understanding of how errors impact innovation and progress in science, as well as how science has its own history.

"Fast Harvest" considered Museu da Oliveira e do Azeite (Portugal) exhibitions showcasing the processes involved in olive oil production, to put the players in the role of Uncle Alberto, who must harvest olives while outsmarting pests, combining dexterity-based gameplay with real-time resource allocation mechanics.

In a 3D exploratory game set on the hill of Notre-Dame-du-Haut, the players are guided by a virtual avatar of the architect Le Corbusier, whose commentary facilitates a deeper understanding of the site's architectural and historical significance. Solving environmental puzzles players progressively unlock new areas of the site, reconstructing Le Corbusier's sketchbook.

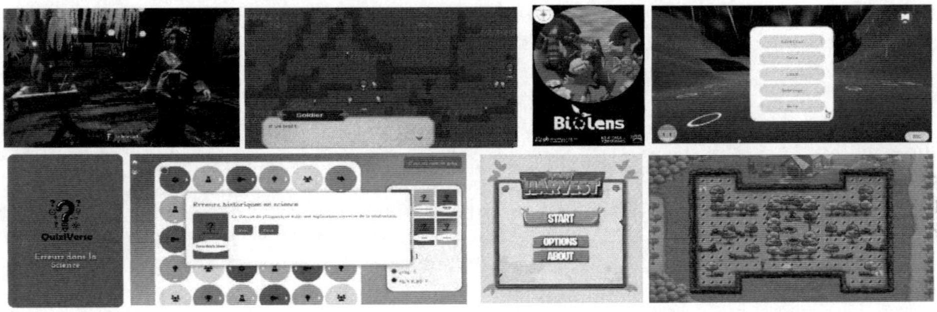

Figures 1 - 8. From top left to bottom right: (1) Gameplay of "A Tayū's Nightmare", (2) Gameplay of "Echoes of the Great War", (3,4) "Biolens" poster and UI (5, 6) Gameplay of "Quiziverse" (7, 8) UI and gameplay of "Fast Harvest"

On the whole, these projects collectively showcase the intersection of entertainment, education, and innovation in game design, offering players engaging and thought-provoking experiences. The projects were presented at Bragança Gaming TakeOver, an event that emphasized both gaming and education. In partnership with IPB, the event featured workshops tailored for students of all ages. Students had the opportunity to showcase their prototypes alongside informative posters, allowing them to receive diverse feedback on their work.

The evaluation of student projects and feedback revealed several key findings:

- Enhanced Historical Awareness: Participants demonstrated improved knowledge of natural and cultural heritage concepts and ethical considerations in digital representation.
- Game Design Competencies: The programme fostered skills in game design, narrative construction, UI/UX design, and technical development.
- Interdisciplinary Collaboration: Students reported greater understanding about teamwork across disciplines, crucial for heritage-based digital projects.

5. DISCUSSION AND CHALLENGES

5.1 Balancing Fun and Fidelity

One of the primary challenges encountered in the programme was balancing historical fidelity with engaging gameplay. While previous research emphasizes the importance of accuracy in educational games (Øygardslia & Aarsand, 2018), making historical content accessible and enjoyable to broad audiences often necessitated simplifying complex narratives or incorporating fictionalized elements. Students grappled with how much creative license they could take without compromising cultural integrity and/or processes authenticity.

Recent theoretical contributions suggest that heritage experiences in digital environments should not be limited to factual accuracy but must consider epistemological frameworks that support critical engagement and co-creation (Bonacchi & Krzyzanska, 2021). This aligns with the BIP's goal to treat heritage not as a fixed set of truths but as a domain for participatory interpretation. Projects were encouraged to provoke reflection and dialogue rather than serve as definitive historical accounts.

Furthermore, the development of immersive experiences proved particularly effective in encouraging players to emotionally engage with the content. Drawing from research on immersive virtual museums, games in this programme leveraged environmental storytelling and spatial narratives to increase player presence and emotional connection (Ferdani & Pagano, 2022). Such design choices enabled players to navigate reconstructed heritage environments and interact with contextualized elements that deepened their learning experience.

5.2 Remote Collaboration and Intercultural Dynamics

Another challenge was facilitating effective remote collaboration among students from different institutions and cultural backgrounds. The programme required coordination across languages, time zones, and levels of digital literacy. According to Cagiltay et al. (2015), successful multicultural virtual teamwork relies on clearly defined roles, shared communication norms, and sustained facilitation. These findings were confirmed in the BIP context, where structured project management tools and asynchronous feedback cycles proved essential.

Students also had to navigate intercultural differences in communication styles and interpretations of cultural norms. In group discussions, what was seen as a respectful representation by one participant might be interpreted differently by another, leading to productive exchanges about intent, meaning, and audience expectations. These moments became critical learning opportunities for negotiating meaning in collaborative design. By foregrounding empathy and dialogue in the creative process, teams were able to arrive at representations that were inclusive and respectful of diverse perspectives.

6. CONCLUSION

The student-developed prototypes suggest that digital games can be powerful tools for engaging with cultural heritage in interpretive, emotional, and experiential ways. Rather than simply transmitting historical information, these projects appeared to encourage players to form personal and narrative connections with heritage material. Participants approached heritage as a dialogic and dynamic space – one in which they could act as interpreters and storytellers. Through iterative design, they explored tensions between accuracy, representation, and user engagement.

Positioning games as systems of reasoning as well as representation (Champion, 2019), the students' work supports the potential of "playable arguments" – games that encourage critical reflection on the past through interactive means. The diversity of genres and styles – from solarpunk ecologies to dungeon crawlers – points to an expansive and creative understanding of heritage. Collaboration with cultural institutions further enriched the process, highlighting the value of co-curation and contextual storytelling.

These outcomes align with scholarship that views digital heritage not as static preservation but as an evolving, participatory practice shaped by audience interaction and speculative design (Salazar, 2018).

Students concluded the programme with strengthened technical capabilities and a heightened awareness of heritage as a living, negotiated construct. Their work potentially adds to growing evidence that making, particularly in interdisciplinary and collaborative contexts, can serve as a valuable mode of knowledge production.

ACKNOWLEDGEMENT

The authors would like to thank the external stakeholders – Museu da Oliveira e do Azeite (Portugal), Museu do Oriente (Portugal), Mirandela's Ecoteca (Portugal), Le Pavillon des Sciences (France), Musée de la Grande Guerre (France) – whose diverse contributions were essential in the co-creation of heritage-informed prototypes. Finally, the authors wish to thank all participants from the Heritage in Videogames BIP, as well as the hosting institution and institutional partners, for their active engagement and support.

REFERENCES

Anderson, E. F., McLoughlin, L., Liarokapis, F., Peters, C. & de Freitas, S. (2010). Developing serious games for cultural heritage: A state-of-the-art review. *Virtual Reality*, 14(4), pp.255–275. doi:10.1007/s10055-010-0177-3.

Bogost, I. (2007). *Persuasive games: The expressive power of videogames*. Cambridge, MA: MIT Press.

Bonacchi, C. & Krzyzanska, M. (2021). Digital heritage research re-theorised: ontologies and epistemologies. *Heritage*, 4(2), pp.671–691.

Cagiltay, K., Bichelmeyer, B. & Kaplan Akilli, G. (2015). Working with multicultural virtual teams: Critical factors for facilitation, satisfaction and success. *Smart Learning Environments*, 2(1), pp.1–16. https://doi.org/10.1186/s40561015-0018-7

Cerezo-Pizarro, M., Revuelta-Domínguez, F.-I., Guerra-Antequera, J., & Melo-Sánchez, J. (2023). *The cultural impact of video games: A systematic review of the literature. Education Sciences, 13*(11), 1116. https://doi.org/10.3390/educsci13111116

Champion, E. M. (2017). Single white looter: Have whip, will travel. In: A. Mol, C. Ariese, K. Boom & A. Politopoulos, eds. *The Interactive Past: Archaeology, Heritage, and Video Games*. Leiden: Sidestone Press, pp.43–56. Available at: https://doi.org/10.11141/ia.6.2 [Accessed 26 May 2025].

Champion, E. M. (2019). Games people dig: Are they archaeological experiences, systems or arguments? In: S. Hageneuer, ed. *Communicating the Past in the Digital Age*. London: Ubiquity Press, pp.13–25. Available at: https://doi.org/10.5334/bch.b [Accessed 26 May 2025].

Chapman, A. (2016). *Digital games as history: How videogames represent the past and offer access to historical practice*. New York: Routledge.

Ferdani, D. & Pagano, A. (2022). Immersive virtual museums and digital heritage: Methods and applications. *Heritage*, 5(1), pp.334–351.

Healy, J. P. & Cullen, C. (2022). Towards a model of the design process for games. [online] Available at: https://dl.digra.org/index.php/dl/article/view/1413 [Accessed 26 May 2025].

Liarokapis, F., Voulodimos, A., Doulamis, N. & Doulamis, A. (2020). *Visual computing for cultural heritage*. Cham: Springer. Available at: https://link.springer.com/book/10.1007/978-3-030-37191-3 [Accessed 26 May 2025].

Majewski, J. (2015). *Playing with the past: Digital games and the simulation of history*. New York: Bloomsbury. Available at: https://www.bloomsbury.com/us/playing-with-the-past-9781623567286/ [Accessed 26 May 2025].

Øygardslia, K. & Aarsand, P. (2018). Move over, I will find Jerusalem: Artifacts in game design in classrooms. *Learning, Culture and Social Interaction*, 19, pp.61–73. Available at: https://doi.org/10.1016/j.lcsi.2018.04.013 [Accessed 26 May 2025].

Salazar, J. F. (2018). Digital futures and heritage. In: S. Choudry, ed. *Critical Heritage Studies and the Future of Europe*. London: UCL Press, pp. 111–126.

Salazar, J. F. (2018). Digital futures and heritage: The mediation of cultural heritage through digital technologies. In: S. Nakamura & A. Saldanha, eds. *Cultural Sustainability and the Nature-Culture Interface: Livelihoods, Policies, and Methodologies*. London: Routledge, pp.123–139.

Schrier, K. (2014). *Knowledge games: How digital games can make a difference in education*. Baltimore: Johns Hopkins University Press.

Tavinor, G. (2009). *The art of videogames*. Malden, MA: Wiley-Blackwell.

DETECTION OF DRIVER FATIGUE USING MOBILE DEVICE SENSORS AND ARTIFICIAL INTELLIGENCE ON-DEVICE

Gonçalo Almeida[1,2], António Monteiro[1] and Bruno Correia[2]
[1]*Faculty of Engineering of the University of Porto, Portugal*
[2]*Pink Room, Lda, Portugal*

ABSTRACT

This paper presents a driver fatigue detection prototype leveraging smartphone sensors and Artificial Intelligence techniques, with real-time performance demonstrated in a controlled environment. The system uses facial analysis metrics including Eye Aspect Ratio (EAR), Mouth Aspect Ratio (MAR), Percentage of Eye Closure (PERCLOS), and head nod detection, calculated using Mediapipe and ML Kit AI models. A rule-based system then integrates these metrics with logical thresholds to detect fatigue-related behaviors such as prolonged eye closure, frequent yawning, and repetitive head nodding. Two datasets, DMD and YawDD, were used to develop and validate this system. Preliminary results demonstrate reliable extraction of fatigue-related facial features, supporting inference via the proposed rule-based system, suitable for resource-constrained mobile platforms.

KEYWORDS

Driver Fatigue, Facial Analysis, On-Device AI, Mediapipe, PERCLOS, Rule-Based System

1. INTRODUCTION

Driver fatigue is a silent killer on roads worldwide, responsible for a staggering 30% of all fatal traffic accidents in middle- and high-income countries, alongside factors like alcohol and inattention (European Commission 2024). Fatigue impairs cognitive function, slows reaction times, and affects decision-making, especially in modern driving environments, such as long highway drives or when drivers rely on automated systems like cruise control. While advanced driver-assistance systems (ADAS) have been developed to address these issues, such as Volvo's Driver Alert Control (Cars 2025), their high cost and complexity limit their adoption, particularly in lower-income regions. As an alternative, smartphones offer a promising solution. Equipped with sensors such as cameras, gyroscopes, and accelerometers, and benefiting from growing computational capabilities, they provide an accessible and scalable platform for real-time driver monitoring.

This work proposes a real-time fatigue detection system designed for mobile devices, as a low-cost platform already integrated into daily life that does not require dedicated in-vehicle infrastructure. By combining AI with facial analysis, the system aims to enhance driver alertness monitoring and accident prevention.

2. LITERATURE REVIEW

Driver fatigue detection has been widely explored using three main approaches: biological systems, vehicle-based systems, and driver-based systems. Biological methods, such as Electrocardiogram (ECG) and heart rate monitoring, are highly accurate but impractical for everyday use due to cost and invasiveness (Murugan et al. 2020). Vehicle-based approaches monitor patterns like steering behavior or lane deviation, but depend heavily on external factors, such as road conditions and vehicle type, limiting their reliability and scalability (Li et al. 2019). In contrast, driver-based systems, particularly those using facial analysis, offer a non-intrusive and accessible solution suitable for diverse environments (Galarza et al. 2018).

Metrics such as EAR, MAR, and PERCLOS are widely used for detecting fatigue (Dong et al. 2021). However, few studies assess their integration into mobile environments or compare performance across different AI tools.

Frameworks like Mediapipe and ML Kit allow real-time facial analysis on smartphones, offering a lightweight alternative to deep learning. However, most existing systems still rely on desktop-based or cloud--dependent models, which are impractical for mobile deployment. Comparative evaluations of Mediapipe and ML Kit in fatigue detection, particularly using both landmark and probability data, remain limited.

In addition, as summarized in Table 1, many approaches either require external hardware, such as embedded boards or physiological sensors, or rely on post-processing of recorded video using desktop-based tools. By contrast, the present work implements a hybrid rule-based system combining facial landmarks and probabilities, running fully on-device with real-time performance on smartphones. It evaluates the performance of Mediapipe and ML Kit using both landmark-based and probability-based data, offering a potentially lightweight alternative for fatigue detection in resource-constrained environments.

Table 1. Comparison of Related Fatigue Detection Approaches

Work	Input Type	Platform	Method	Execution
Murugan et al. (2020)	ECG Data	Jetson + Arduino	CNN (+ Heart Rate Data)	Embedded
Li et al. (2019)	Steering Angle Data	Vehicle Sensors	Fuzzy Recurrent NN	Real-world test
Dong & Lin (2021)	Video (Face)	PC + Jetson	Random Forest + CNN	Post-processing
Galarza et al. (2018)	Video (Face)	Android Smartphone	Rule-based (on-device)	Real-time
This Work	Face Landmarks & Probabilities Data	Android Smartphone	Rule-based (on-device)	Real-time

3. METHODOLOGY

This work proposes a prototype for real-time driver fatigue-related feature detection system that extracts facial metrics from video using lightweight AI tools. Metrics such as EAR, MAR, PERCLOS, head pitch, and eye openness probabilities are then processed through a rule-based decision system optimized for mobile devices.

3.1 Tools and Technologies

Mediapipe, developed by Google, is a cross-platform framework that has a solution for real-time detection of facial landmarks (478 3D points) using a single camera. It is optimized for mobile devices and provides high accuracy with low computational cost. For this project, Mediapipe's Face Landmarker task was used to extract facial landmarks and probabilities.

ML Kit, also by Google, is a mobile SDK that provides on-device face detection and landmark tracking solutions. Unlike MediaPipe, ML Kit is optimized for seamless integration into mobile apps and performs reliably under varying lighting conditions. In this work, two different modules were used: Face Mesh Detection (468 points) and Face Detection (133 points). The former provided full facial landmarks; the latter offered eye openness probabilities and a reduced set of mouth landmarks, which were still sufficient to analyze mouth openness.

To validate the system under realistic conditions, all inference was executed directly on an Android smartphone (Realme GT6) using a clean secondary environment with no background applications. Rather than capturing live video, frames extracted from dataset videos were processed locally at a consistent rate of 24 FPS, simulating real-time detection. Each frame was then fed into the fatigue detection pipeline on-device, with no cloud interaction or external processing. Results were logged in CSV format and retrieved via direct file transfer. Both Mediapipe and ML Kit variants were executed fully on-device, each confirming the feasibility of real-time fatigue detection on consumer-grade smartphones.

3.2 Facial Metrics Computation

This section outlines the facial metrics used to detect driver fatigue: eye closure, PERCLOS, blink count, yawns, and head nods (pitch). These features are extracted from facial landmarks around the eyes, mouth, and head. Figure 1 displays all 468 ML Kit face mesh points, which exclude the 10 iris landmark points present in Mediapipe's 478-point model but preserve the same structure for fatigue-related metrics and include the 133 landmarks used by the ML Kit face model. The following subsections detail how each of these metrics is computed using these facial landmarks or probabilities.

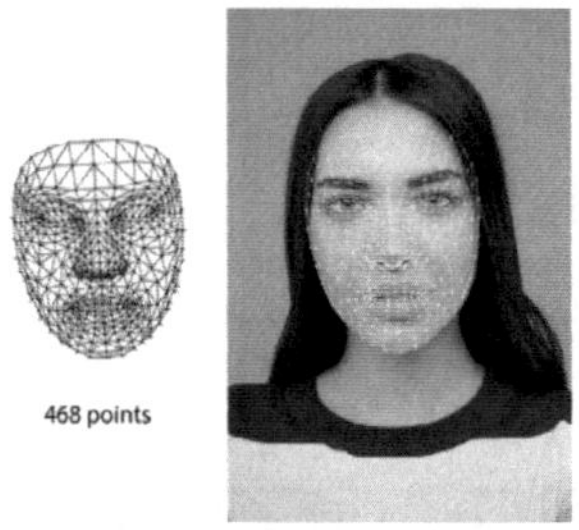

Figure 1. Facial landmarks detected by the ML Kit Face Mesh Detection AI model (Google, 2024)

3.2.1 Eye Closure

Eye closure detection was performed using both the Eye Aspect Ratio (EAR) and eye openness probabilities provided by Mediapipe and ML Kit.

The EAR is calculated based on specific eye landmarks as follows:

$$EAR = \frac{\|p_2 - p_8\| + \|p_3 - p_7\| + \|p_4 - p_6\|}{2 \times \|p_1 - p_5\|} \quad (1)$$

where p_i are specific eye landmarks. A decrease in EAR below a threshold of 0.25 over consecutive frames indicates eye closure. Additionally, eye openness probabilities were inverted to estimate blink probability, and the eye was considered closed when the blink value exceeded 0.45.

3.2.2 Yawning Detection

Yawning detection was performed using both the Mouth Aspect Ratio (MAR) and probability-based estimation. The MAR is calculated from specific mouth landmarks as follows:

The MAR is calculated from specific mouth landmarks as follows:

$$MAR = \frac{\|p_2 - p_8\| + \|p_3 - p_7\| + \|p_4 - p_6\|}{2 \times \|p_1 - p_5\|} \quad (2)$$

where p_i corresponds to mouth landmarks. Sustained high MAR values indicate yawning episodes, particularly when maintained above 2 for at least 1.5 seconds. In addition, yawning is detected when, for at least 1.5 seconds, the mouth openness probability exceeded 0.375, using Mediapipe.

3.2.3 Percentage of Eye Closure (PERCLOS)

PERCLOS represents the percentage of time the eyes are closed within a time window □ and is computed as:

$$PERCLOS = \frac{T_{closed}}{T} \times 100\% \quad (3)$$

Values above 70–80% over one minute suggest drowsiness.

3.2.4 Head Pitch (Nod Detection)

The head pitch angle is estimated using facial landmarks and the Perspective-n-Point (PnP) method. A nod is detected when the pitch exceeds 15° for at least 2 seconds.

3.3 Rule-Based Fatigue Detection System

The rule-based system integrates extracted facial metrics with threshold values defined in prior literature and was subsequently validated in this study using both the training and testing subsets of the DMD and YawDD datasets. These thresholds, summarized in Table 2, were kept fixed throughout the evaluation to prevent post hoc adjustments, ensuring consistent behavior across different subject profiles.

Table 2. Fatigue Detection Thresholds from Literature

Metric	Threshold / Condition	Reference
Eye closure	< 0.25 for ≥ 10 consecutive frames (calculated as 0.4 * FPS with FPS = 24)	Prasitsupparote et al. 2023
PERCLOS	> 70% over 1 minute	Arefnezhad et al. 2022
Blink Rate	< 8 or > 20 per minute	Karar et al. 2023
Yawns	≥ 2 in 10 sec or ≥ 4 in 1 minute	Kashevnik et al. 2019, Walizad et al. 2022
Head Nods (Pitch)	≥ 4 nods (>15°) in 2 minutes	Kashevnik et al. 2019

4. RESULTS AND DISCUSSION

Although the full system was not directly tested on real fatigue data, the consistent detection of eye closure and yawning features suggests potential for real-time fatigue monitoring on mobile platforms. The rule-based logic has been maintained, with the idea that although real-time fatigue detection has not yet been tested, the implemented feature detection logic enables efficient monitoring of the user's state.

Two datasets were used: DMD and YawDD. DMD, with annotations for both eye closure and yawning, allowed full evaluation of fatigue indicators. YawDD, annotated only for yawning, limited analysis to mouth features. Therefore, eye closure was tested only on DMD, while yawning was evaluated on both datasets. Performance metrics (True Positive/Negative, False Positive/Negative, etc.) are detailed in Tables 3 and 4.

False positives were mainly caused by abrupt movements or expressive gestures, while false negatives occurred under low-light or partial occlusion. Notably, use of probability-based signals improved robustness, especially with Mediapipe in the DMD dataset, where landmark mouth detection was more variable.

Table 3. Confusion Matrix and Performance Metrics Summary in DMD

Tool	Dataset	Approach	Feature	TP	FP	FN	Accuracy (%)	F-Score (%)	Recall (%)
Mediapipe	**DMD**	Landmarks	Eye	1416	78	273	95	99	85
Mediapipe	**DMD**	Landmarks	Mouth	27	4	11	87	78	71
Mediapipe	**DMD**	Probabilities	Eye	1445	29	340	98	81	89
Mediapipe	**DMD**	Probabilities	Mouth	30	3	10	91	75	82
MLKit	**DMD**	Landmarks	Eye	1498	129	211	92	90	88
MLKit	**DMD**	Landmarks	Mouth	27	2	11	93	81	71
MLKit	**DMD**	Probabilities	Eye	1603	257	198	86	88	89
MLKit	**DMD**	Landmarks	Mouth	26	4	14	87	74	65

Table 4. Confusion Matrix and Performance Metrics Summary in YawDD

Tool	Dataset	Approach	TP	TN	FP	FN	Accuracy (%)	F-Score (%)	Recall (%)
Mediapipe	**YawDD**	Landmarks	99	102	1	17	92	91	985
Mediapipe	**YawDD**	Probabilities	106	102	3	8	95	95	95
MLKit	**YawDD**	Landmarks	101	102	1	15	93	87	93
MLKit	**YawDD**	Landmarks	103	103	1	12	94	94	90

MediaPipe with probabilities reached the highest accuracy on DMD, while ML Kit offered more consistent performance and better efficiency for mobile use. Both tools reached around 90% accuracy, indicating the system's feasibility for real-time fatigue monitoring on mobile platforms.

The system also demonstrated low computational overhead during testing, consistently achieving 24 FPS with average latency below 40ms per frame and moderate CPU usage (12-18%) on the tested device. These metrics confirm the feasibility of on-device execution without additional hardware. Although the rule-based system was employed to process facial features, it was not used to infer fatigue. Instead, it served to assess the computational load of the pipeline, as the datasets used lacked ground-truth fatigue labels, which limited the evaluation to feature extraction and system performance.

5. CONCLUSION

This work presented a real-time driver fatigue detection system based on facial analysis, evaluated using Mediapipe and ML Kit on two datasets. Mediapipe showed slightly superior performance, while ML Kit proved more efficient for mobile deployment. The rule-based approach ensures low computational cost, making the system suitable for smartphone integration.

While the system benefits from on-device execution and broad hardware availability, mobile deployment also presents challenges, such as heterogeneous device capabilities, variable lighting conditions, and the absence of infrared or multi-sensor setups commonly used in embedded vehicle systems. Addressing these limitations requires more adaptive and robust models that can generalize better across usage scenarios. Future work will focus on validating the system in real-world scenarios through a proof-of-concept app. This system represents a preliminary step toward accessible driver monitoring using mobile devices, with further validation required in real-world conditions.

REFERENCES

Arefnezhad, S., Hamet, J., Eichberger, A., Frühwirth, M., Ischebeck, A., Koglbauer, I. V., et al. (2022). Driver drowsiness estimation using EEG signals with a dynamical encoder-decoder modeling framework. *Scientific Reports*, 12(1), 2650.

Cars, V. (2025). Driver Alert Control, 2023. Available: https://www.volvocars.com/pt/support/car/v40-cross-country/article/4da80d480d385962c0a801e80146fc4e/. Accessed, 2025-05-23.

Dong, B. T., & Lin, H. Y. (2021). An on-board monitoring system for driving fatigue and distraction detection. In *2021 22nd IEEE ICIT* (Vol. 1, pp. 850-855). IEEE.

European Commission (2024). *Road safety thematic report - Main factors causing fatal crashes*.

Galarza, E. E., Egas, F. D., Silva, F. M., Velasco, P. M., & Galarza, E. D. (2018). Real time driver drowsiness detection based on driver's face image behavior using a system of human computer interaction implemented in a smartphone. In *Proceedings of the ICITS 2018* (pp. 563-572). Springer International Publishing.

Google. (2025). ML Kit Face Mesh Detection. Available: https://developers.google.com/ml-kit/vision/face-detection. Accessed, 2025-05-23. Licensed under CC BY 4.0.

Karar, S., & Kanumuri, T. (2023). Assessment of driver fatigue and drowsiness based on eye blink rate. In *ICDAM 2023* (pp. 311-324). Springer Nature Singapore.

Kashevnik, A., Lashkov, I., & Gurtov, A. (2019). Methodology and mobile application for driver behavior analysis and accident prevention. *IEEE T-ITS*, 21(6), 2427-2436.

Li, Z., Yang, Q., Chen, S., Zhou, W., Chen, L., & Song, L. (2019). A fuzzy recurrent neural network for driver fatigue detection based on steering-wheel angle sensor data. *IJDSN 2019*, 15(9).

Murugan, S., Selvaraj, J., & Sahayadhas, A. (2020). Detection and analysis: Driver state with electrocardiogram (ECG). *Physical and engineering sciences in medicine*, 43(2), 525-537.

Prasitsupparote, A., Pasitsuparoad, P., & Itsarapongpukdee, S. (2023). Real-time driver drowsiness alert system for product distribution businesses in Phuket using Android devices. In *International JCSSE 2023* (pp. 351-355). IEEE.

Walizad, M. E., Hurroo, M., & Sethia, D. (2022). Driver drowsiness detection system using convolutional neural network. In *ICOEI 2022* (pp. 1073-1080). IEEE.

GENERATIVE ADVERSARIAL NETWORK: TOWARDS A ROBUST NEAR INFRARED IMAGE COLORIZATION

Patricia L. Suárez[1] and Angel D. Sappa[1,2]
[1]*ESPOL Polytechnic University*
Campus Gustavo Galindo, Guayaquil, Km. 30.5 Vía Perimetra, Ecuador
[2]*Computer Vision Center*
Campus UAB, 08193 Bellaterra, Barcelona, Spain

ABSTRACT

This paper proposes a novel method for generating RGB representations from near-infrared (NIR) images based on a stacked generative adversarial network (SC-GAN). The architecture incorporates a triplet-level learning strategy within a conditional framework to enhance generalization capability during training. A multi-term loss function is introduced to further improve colorization performance, combining adversarial, intensity-based, and structural similarity components. Extensive experiments conducted on real-world datasets demonstrate that the proposed method achieves robust colorization results across various object categories. Quantitative and qualitative comparisons against existing architectures confirm the effectiveness and advantages of the proposed approach in accurately translating NIR information into realistic visible spectrum representations.

KEYWORDS

Image Colorization, Convolutional Neural Networks, GAN, NIR Imaging

1. INTRODUCTION

In the field of computer vision, near-infrared (NIR) spectral information has become increasingly valuable, as it enables the detection of material properties that are less discernible in the visible spectrum. Applications leveraging NIR imaging include action interpretation in video sequences, driver assistance systems, remote sensing, and cultural heritage preservation. For instance, in remote sensing, NIR images facilitate the distinction between water bodies, built-up areas, and vegetation by enhancing spectral contrast, allowing for the assessment of plant health when combined with visible spectrum data (Wang and Gordon, 2018). In addition, NIR imaging is employed in reflectography to reveal underdrawings in paintings, and in pharmacology to detect the presence of active compounds through infrared transmission measurements.

The increasing integration of NIR-sensitive sensors into modern imaging devices has expanded the scope of these applications. Unlike visible-spectrum imaging, which is highly dependent on lighting conditions and surface color, NIR imaging captures reflected radiation independently of brightness or color, often revealing clearer structural details. This advantage has been exploited in areas such as image restoration under low-light conditions, as demonstrated by (Honda et al.,2015).

Despite these benefits, when images must be interpreted by human observers for decision-making or monitoring, the preferred format remains the RGB (visible spectrum) representation, which aligns with human visual perception. Therefore, transforming NIR images into realistic RGB outputs—known as colorization— *has become an essential task* to bridge the perceptual gap between human vision and NIR data.

Image colorization has been explored through various approaches, including predefined pattern-based methods (Larsson et al., 2016) and statistical color transfer methods (Wang et al., 2015; Oliveira et al., 2015). Early efforts in image colorization relied heavily on traditional image processing techniques, differing in both the strategies used and the way features were modeled to establish the correspondence between grayscale and color information. (Chen et al., 2018), introduces an adaptive quadtree-based clustering strategy for efficient editing propagation, minimizing detail loss in both grayscale colorization and color image recoloring.

With the rise of deep learning, convolutional neural network (CNN)-based models have significantly advanced colorization tasks, predicting chrominance components from grayscale input images (Guadarrama et al., 2017). However, while grayscale-to-RGB colorization infers only the chrominance, NIR-to-RGB colorization must also reinterpret luminance-related information, presenting additional challenges.

In (Dong et al., 2018) the authors propose an encoder-decoder architecture augmented with an auxiliary network for improved contextual understanding and fine-grain localization, requiring no external user input to NIR colorization. (Su et al., 2018) introduces a deep colorization model in the YUV color space, applying progressive edge vectorization refinements to boost quality. Among the various learning-based methods, GAN-based architectures have gained prominence due to their ability to generate highly realistic data representations. The original GAN framework introduced by (Goodfellow et al., 2014) established the adversarial training paradigm, where a generator and discriminator are jointly optimized. This approach was further extended to conditional GANs (Mirza and Osindero, 2014), allowing conditioning on auxiliary information such as labels or multimodal data. In the context of NIR image colorization. Furthermore, (Salimans et al., 2016) introduced virtual batch normalization to enhance GAN training stability and reduce convergence time, an approach incorporated into subsequent colorization models, including those proposed by (Suárez et al., 2017).

Some approaches based on adversarial architectures for NIR colorization, have achieved progressive improvements by independently modeling the R, G, and B channels (Suárez et al., 2017). Moreover, incorporating the NIR channel into the learning process for the red channel has been shown to enhance fine details by exploiting spectral overlaps (Soria et al., 2017).

Building upon this foundation, the present work proposes a hierarchical learning framework based on a stacked generative adversarial network (StackGAN). The main contributions of this paper are as follows:

1. Introduce a stacked GAN framework that reduces the training process, prevents overfitting, and minimizes model complexity.
2. Introducing a multi-term loss function that combines adversarial, intensity-based, and structural similarity terms to enhance training robustness.

The remainder of this paper is organized as follows. Section II presents the proposed methodology. Section III describes the experimental results. Section IV discusses the analysis, and Section V concludes the paper.

2. PROPOSED APPROACH

This work proposes an enhanced architecture for near-infrared image colorization, building upon the stacked model introduced by (Huang et al., 2016). The proposed system is based on a multi-level stacked conditional GAN (SC-GAN), where each level generates representations conditioned on the outputs of the preceding higher-level representations. This design enables the optimization of high-level features through hierarchical multi-level learning, as depicted in Figure 1 (*right*), while conditioning the training process on NIR images combined with Gaussian noise to enhance color diversity and improve generalization.

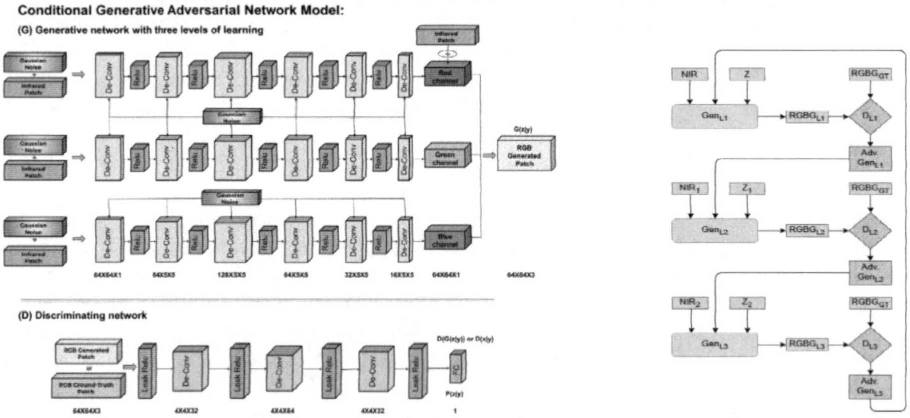

Figure 1. Illustration of the proposed: (*left*) Triplet GAN architecture; (*right*) stacked GAN

The core architecture is illustrated in Figure 1. It consists of a generator and a discriminator network where the NIR input is concatenated with Gaussian noise, and this noise is also introduced at each stage of the triplet learning architecture. This design choice encourages greater diversity in the colorized outputs and supports more rapid learning. To prevent overfitting and reduce model saturation, an L1 regularization term is applied at each generator layer, effectively contributing to shortening the training time.

The training process is guided by a composite loss function that integrates three complementary components: adversarial, intensity and structural similarity loss. Adversarial loss encourages the generator to produce outputs that are indistinguishable from real, and it is defined as:

$$L_{Adversarial} = -\sum_i log\, D\left(G_w(I_{z|y}), (I_{x|y})\right), \tag{1}$$

where G_w represents the function generating synthetic color images $(I_{z|y})$ for each channel, which are evaluated by the discriminator function D against the real images $(I_{x|y})$.

Another loss that measures the pixel-wise intensity differences, penalizing large errors but tolerating small deviations is known as Intensity loss, which is defined as:

$$L_{Intensity} = \frac{1}{NM} + \sum_{i=1}^{N} \sum_{j=1}^{M} \left(\mathrm{RGB}_{NIR_{(i,j)}} - \mathrm{RGB}_{GT_{(i,j)}}\right)^2, \tag{2}$$

where $\mathrm{RGB}_{\mathrm{NIR}(i,j)}$ denotes the estimated RGB representation and $\mathrm{RGB}_{\mathrm{GT}(i,j)}$ the corresponding ground-truth RGB image. Furthermore, to address the limitations of simple intensity-based loss, SSIM loss (Wang et al., 2004) is incorporated. This loss is defined as:

$$L_{SSIM} = \frac{1}{NM} + \sum_{p=1}^{P} \left(1 - SSIM(p)\right), \tag{3}$$

where SSIM(p) denotes the Structural Similarity Index centered at pixel p within patch P. The final loss function (L_{final}) used in this work is a weighted sum of the individual loss components:

$$L_{final} = 0.65\, L_{Adversarial} + 0.20\, L_{Intensity} + 0.15\, L_{SSIM}. \tag{4}$$

The weights assigned to each loss component are empirically determined based on the variability of the corresponding values during training. Loss components exhibiting greater variability are assigned higher weights in the model's regularization process.

3. EXPERIMENTAL RESULTS

The proposed stacked conditional GAN (SC-GAN) has been evaluated using near-infrared (NIR) images and their corresponding RGB ground-truth images obtained from the RGB-NIR Scene Dataset by (Brown and Susstrunk, 2011). Two categories, *Urban* and *Oldbuilding*, were selected for the evaluation due to their challenging characteristics, which include high variability in tones, contours, textures, and the frequent presence of blue shades that do not necessarily correspond to sky regions. The *Urban* category comprises 58 image pairs (1024×680 pixels), while the *Oldbuilding* category contains 51 image pairs (1024×680 pixels). From each category, 280,000 pairs of patches (64×64 pixels) were extracted for training, with an additional 5,600 patch pairs per category reserved for testing. It is important to note that the dataset is perfectly registered, ensuring pixel-to-pixel correspondence between the NIR and RGB images.

Table 1. Mean Squared Error from the proposed approach using multiple loss functions

Architectures	MSE	
	Urban	Oldbuilding
Conditional GAN from (Suárez et al., 2017)	18.91	18.25
SC-GAN with $L_{Adversarial} + L_{Intensity}$	18.74	18.11
SC-GAN with $L_{Adversarial} + L_{SSIM}$	18.53	18.02
SC-GAN with proposed L_{final}	17.63	17.34

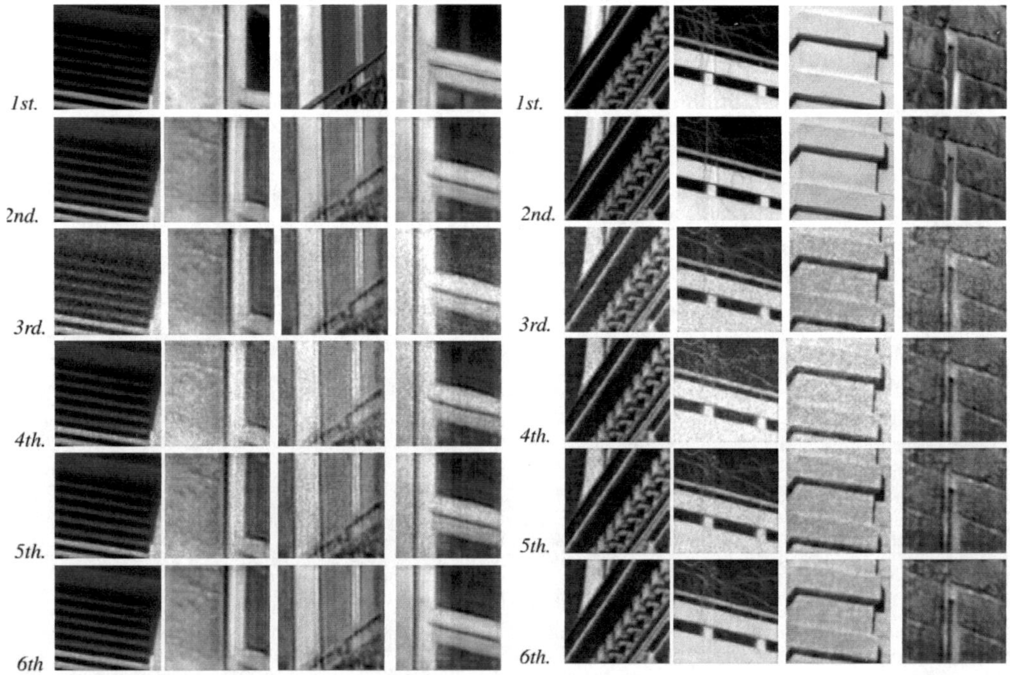

Figure 2. Urban category (*left*) and Oldbuilding (*right*): (1st row) NIR images. (2nd row) Ground-truth images; (3rd row) Results from (Suárez et al., 2017) (DCGAN); (4th row) colored images from (Loss Function: $L_{Adversarial} + L_{Intensity}$). (5th row) colored images from (Loss Function: $L_{Adversarial} + L_{SSIM}$). (6th row) colored images from (Loss Function: L_{final})

Table 2. Average SSIM obtained from the proposed Approach

Architectures	SSIM	
	Urban	Oldbuilding
Conditional GAN from (Suárez et al., 2017)	0.84	0.84
SC-GAN with $L_{Adversarial} + L_{Intensity}$	0.86	0.87
SC-GAN with $L_{Adversarial} + L_{SSIM}$	0.90	0.91
SC-GAN with proposed L_{final}	0.90	0.92

Table 3. Average Angular Error (AE) obtained from the proposed approach

Architectures	AE	
	Urban	Oldbuilding
Conditional GAN from (Suárez et al., 2017)	5.77	5.96
SC-GAN with $L_{Adversarial} + L_{Intensity}$	5.43	5.21
SC-GAN with $L_{Adversarial} + L_{SSIM}$	5.32	4.97
SC-GAN with proposed L_{final}	5.04	4.78

Quantitative evaluation was conducted using the metrics Angular Error (AE), Mean Squared Error (MSE), and Structural Similarity Index Metric (SSIM). The AE metric is particularly relevant as it closely aligns with human visual perception (Gijsenij et al., 2008) and is widely recognized as a reliable performance indicator in color constancy research. The results for the *Urban* and *Oldbuilding* categories are summarized in Tables 1, 2, and 3, demonstrating that the SC-GAN with the proposed multi-term loss function (see Equation 4) outperforms the earlier approach presented in (Suárez et al., 2017).

Qualitative results further illustrate the improvements achieved by the proposed model. Figure 2 presents sample outputs from the *Urban* (*left*) and *Oldbuilding* (*right*) categories, respectively. The figure displays, from top to bottom: the original NIR images, the corresponding ground-truth RGB images, the results from (Suárez et al., 2017) (DCGAN), and the results generated by the proposed method using different loss functions—namely, the adversarial loss combined with intensity loss, the adversarial loss combined with SSIM loss, and the final multi-term loss L_{final}. As observed, the colorized images produced by the proposed SC-GAN closely match the ground-truth references, exhibiting enhanced structural consistency and more accurate color rendering compared to the baseline method.

In addition to these comparisons, the proposed approach was evaluated against the method developed by (Dong et al.,2018). Table 4 reports the quantitative comparison, showing that the SC-GAN achieves a consistently lower angular error across both categories. Complementary qualitative results are presented in Figure 3, which highlights the superior visual quality achieved by the proposed model compared to Dong et al.'s technique, further validating the effectiveness of the proposed approach.

Table 4. Average Angular Error (AE) obtained from the proposed approach

Architectures	AE	
	Urban	Oldbuilding
S-SHAPE Encoder-Decoder from (Dong et al., 2018)	5.11	5.96
SC-GAN with L_{final}	5.04	4.78

The Angular Error (AE) between the resulting images *(RGB_{NIR})* and their corresponding ground-truth RGB images *(RGB_{GT})* is defined as: $AE = \cos^{-1}\left(\frac{dot(RGB_{NIR}, RGB_{GT})}{norm(RGB_{NIR}) \cdot norm(RGB_{GT})}\right)$.

Figure 3. Results from Oldbuilding: (1st row) and Urban (2nd row) categories: (1st column) NIR images; (2nd column) results from (Dong et al., 2018); (3rd column) results from SC-GAN with proposed L_{final} loss function; (4th column) ground-truth RGB images

4. CONCLUSION

This work proposes a new stacked conditional generative adversarial network (SC-GAN) model for the colorization of NIR images. The proposed architecture achieves convergence during training due to the hierarchical learning structure introduced. Moreover, conditioning the learning process on NIR images combined with Gaussian noise allows for an increased diversity of colors during training. Additionally, the incorporation of a multiple-term loss function further facilitates the optimization of the learning process. The experimental results demonstrate that the proposed approach generates high-quality color images across different scenes. As future work, the evaluation of alternative network architectures, both for the generator and the discriminator, is planned, along with the exploration of new loss functions to further accelerate the training process.

ACKNOWLEDGEMENT

This material is based upon work supported by the Air Force Office of Scientific Research under award number FA9550-24-1-0206; and partially supported by the Grant PID2021-128945NB-I00 funded by MCIN/AEI/10.13039/501100011033 and by "ERDF A way of making Europe"; and by the ESPOL project CIDIS-003-2024-T. The second author acknowledges the support of the Generalitat de Catalunya CERCA Program to CVC's general activities, and the Departament de Recerca I Universitats from Generalitat de Catalunya with reference 2021SGR01499.

REFERENCES

Brown, M. and Susstrunk, S. (2011). Multi- spectral SIFT for scene category recognition. *In Computer Vision and Pattern Recognition (CVPR), pages 177–184. IEEE.*

Chen, Y., Zong, G., Cao, G., and Dong, J. (2018). Efficient manifold-preserving edit propagation using quad-tree data structures. *Multimedia Tools and Applications, 77(6):6699–6712.*

Dong, Z., Kamata, S.-i., and Breckon, T. P. (2018). Infrared image colorization using a s-shape network. *In 25th IEEE International Conference on Image Processing (ICIP), pages 2242–2246. IEEE.*

Gijsenij, A., Gevers, T., and Lucassen, M. P. (2008). A perceptual comparison of distance measures for color constancy algorithms. *In European Conference on Computer Vision, pages 208–221. Springer.*

Goodfellow, I., Pouget-Abadie, J., Mirza, M., Xu, B., Warde-Farley, D., Ozair, S., Courville, A., and Bengio, Y. (2014). Generative adversarial nets. *In Advances in neural information processing systems, pages 2672–2680.*

Guadarrama, S., Dahl, R., Bieber, D., Norouzi, M., Shlens, J., and Murphy, K. (2017). Pixcolor: Pixel recursive colorization. *arXiv preprint arXiv:1705.07208.*

Honda, H., Timofte, R., and Van Gool, L. (2015). Make my day-high-fidelity color denoising with near-infrared. *In Proceedings of the IEEE Conference on Computer Vision and Pattern Recognition Workshops, pages 82–90.*

Huang, X., Li, Y., Poursaeed, O., Hopcroft, J., and Belongie, S. (2016). Stacked generative adversarial networks. *arXiv preprint arXiv:1612.04357.*

Larsson, G., Maire, M., and Shakhnarovich, G. (2016). Learning representations for automatic colorization. *In European Conference on Computer Vision, pages 577–593. Springer.*

Mirza, M. and Osindero, S. (2014). Conditional generative adversarial nets. ArXiv, abs-1411-1784.

Oliveira, M., Sappa, A. D., and Santos, V. (2015). A probabilistic approach for color correction in image mosaicking applications. *IEEE Transactions on Image Processing, 24(2):508–523.*

Salimans, T., Goodfellow, I., Zaremba, W., Cheung, V., Radford, A., and Chen, X. (2016). Improved techniques for training GANs. *In Advances in Neural Information Processing Systems, pages 2226–2234.*

Soria, X., Sappa, A. D., and Akbarinia, A. (2017). Multispectral single-sensor rgb-nir imaging: New challenges and opportunities. *In Seventh International Conference on Image Processing Theory, Tools and Applications (IPTA), pages 1–6. IEEE.*

Su, Z., Liang, X., Guo, J., Gao, C., and Luo, X. (2018). An edge-refined vectorized deep colorization model for grayscale-to-color images. *Neurocomputing.*

Suárez, P. L., Sappa, A. D., and Vintimilla, B. X. (2017). Colorizing infrared images through a triplet conditional dcgan architecture. *In 19th International Conference on Image Analysis and processing.*

Wang, Z., Bovik, A. C., Sheikh, H. R., and Simoncelli, E. P. (2004). Image quality assessment: from error visibility to structural similarity. IEEE transactions on image processing, 13(4):600–612.

Wang, L., Xiao, L., and Wei, Z. Color equalization and retinex. (2015). *In Color Image and Video Enhancement, pages 253–289. Springer.*

Wang, M. and Gordon, H. R. (2018). Sensor performance requirements for atmospheric correction of satellite ocean color remote sensing. *Optics express, 26(6):7390–7403.*

VISUALIZATION OF THE PROPAGATION OF ELECTROMAGNETIC WAVES, ENHANCING EDUCATION AND SCIENCE COMMUNICATION

Mark Ferreira, Viktor Kretzschmar, Stefan Valentin, Benjamin Meyer and Elke Hergenröther
Department of Computer Science, Hochschule Darmstadt, Germany

ABSTRACT

Traditional methods make it difficult to visualize electromagnetic wave propagation, especially in modern wireless systems like 5G, 6G and Wi-Fi. This paper introduces a VR-based prototype that employs ray-based simulations and semi-realistic 3D environments to demonstrate wave behavior, including reflection and attenuation. Users can interactively explore signal propagation from a first-person perspective, adjusting emitter placement and observing the effects of different materials. Designed for clarity and conceptual understanding, the system runs in real time on standalone VR hardware and paves the way for future educational evaluations.

KEYWORDS

Virtual Reality, Raytracing, Radiation Propagation Visualization

1. INTRODUCTION

Understanding how electromagnetic waves propagate through space and materials is essential to education and engineering. However, phenomena such as reflection, diffraction, and interference are difficult to grasp using traditional diagrams or static simulations. This challenge is further compounded by modern communication technologies, such as Wi-Fi, 5G, and 6G, which operate at higher frequencies and are more sensitive to materials, geometry, and line of sight.

This paper introduces a prototype virtual reality (VR) application that visualizes the propagation of electromagnetic waves in realistic 3D environments. Users can place virtual antennas and observe how rays reflect and attenuate across surfaces from a first-person perspective. The system combines ray-based simulation with real-world city layouts and material modeling to demonstrate wave dynamics.

Instead of striving for physical accuracy, the tool prioritizes visual and interactive clarity to promote conceptual understanding in education and scenario-based planning. VR provides an embodied, spatial experience in which invisible wave phenomena become tangible and explorable.

2. RELATED WORK

Virtual and augmented reality technologies have been increasingly explored as tools for visualizing electromagnetic phenomena in educational and professional settings. Fu et al. developed a VR-based learning system that allows users to interact with virtual charges and observe the resulting electromagnetic fields. This demonstrates the pedagogical benefits of immersive 3D environments. This work is part of the broader initiatives of the Immersive Learning Lab at ECE Illinois [ECE, 2021], which uses constructivist principles to improve conceptual understanding through hands-on VR interaction.

Similarly, Wicaksono et al. proposed the use of VR-based media to teach electromagnetic wave radiation concepts, demonstrating increased student engagement and comprehension compared to traditional methods (Wicaksono et al., 2021). These efforts underscore the importance of interactivity and spatial immersion in helping learners grasp challenging wave-based concepts.

Some AR systems overlay field visualizations in real-time for lab-scale interaction (Smith et al., 2021).

While other projects focus on small-scale visualization or abstract principles, our work shifts the focus to wave propagation in complex environments, such as urban layouts. Using real-world 3D maps, dynamic ray-based simulations, and material-based reflection models, our system supports the experiential learning of wave interactions, such as multipath effects and shadowing. These phenomena are critical in modern wireless networks, yet they are often difficult to visualize. Unlike existing tools, our VR prototype aims to bridge the gap between spatial intuition and wave theory at architectural scales.

3. METHODS

The goal of the VR system is to provide an interactive, spatially intuitive representation of electromagnetic wave propagation. This is achieved through a combination of ray-based wave simulation, user-controlled emitters, and real-world-inspired 3D environments. The system does not aim for precise accuracy but rather for accessible and configurable visualization that aids conceptual understanding in educational contexts and supports scenario exploration in network planning.

3.1 Electromagnetic Wave Simulation

At the core of the system is a ray-casting engine that simulates the propagation of waves from configurable sources, such as 5G antennas. Each emitter (ray caster) uses the Fibonacci sphere algorithm (González, 2009) to uniformly distribute rays in all directions. There is also an optional cone mode that can be used to simulate directional antennas.

Unity's physics engine handles collision detection. During surface interactions, rays reflect, transmit, or are absorbed according to a bidirectional scattering distribution function (BSDF) model (Butler and Cosgrove, 1991), with energy reduced based on material throughput. Rays are color-coded based on intensity and eliminated below a minimum threshold or when unobstructed.

The number of rays per emitter is limited to 500 to preserve frame rates on standalone headsets. In multi-source scenarios, users can deploy additional ray casters to simulate complex interactions, such as overlapping coverage zones or interference.

Materials in the environment are tagged in Unity and mapped to BSDF behavior. This allows users to visually explore how structural features and material choices affect wave propagation.

3.2 Environment and Interaction Design

To provide spatial context for wave interactions, virtual city environments were created in Blender using the Blosm plugin (Kirsanov, 2024). This plugin imports real-world data from OpenStreetMap (OpenStreetMap, 2024) and ArcGIS (Esri, 2025). These scenes were then optimized and imported into Unity. While not perfectly photorealistic, the scenes provide meaningful structural geometry for simulating wave interactions in urban settings.

Studies have shown that interactive VR experiences enhance learning by improving engagement, spatial understanding, and knowledge retention. Parong and Mayer found that VR environments promote deeper cognitive processing than passive learning does (Parong and Mayer, 2018), while Makransky et al. demonstrated that interactive VR simulations improve conceptual understanding and motivation regarding complex scientific topics (Makransky et al., 2019). Building on these findings, this VR application enables users to interact with wave sources using VR controllers. Users can move the wave source to explore wave behaviors in different settings firsthand.

To support this movement while maintaining user comfort, the application uses VR locomotion techniques such as teleportation-based movement and snap turning to minimize motion sickness when navigating the scene (Fernandes and Feiner, 2016).

Interactive UI elements further enhance control, allowing users to change values that can influence the environment and the positioning of the user. By enabling users to actively manipulate both the scene and simulation variables, the application concretely supports conceptual understanding in educational settings and scenario testing in professional applications—thereby fulfilling the research aim of bridging abstract electromagnetic theory with tangible, spatially-aware experiences.

4. RESULTS

The system was tested on a Meta Quest 3 standalone headset featuring 6DoF tracking and a high-resolution display. Due to the device's limited processing power compared to tethered VR systems, performance optimizations were necessary to enable real-time visualization. The application maintains an average frame rate of around 70 FPS by limiting the number of rays per source at 500, limiting ray length, and terminating low-energy rays early. Short performance dips occur when the ray count is dynamically adjusted or new emitters are added, but interaction remains smooth and usable for educational purposes. Figure 1 shows a recording of the Framerate on the Meta Quest 3.

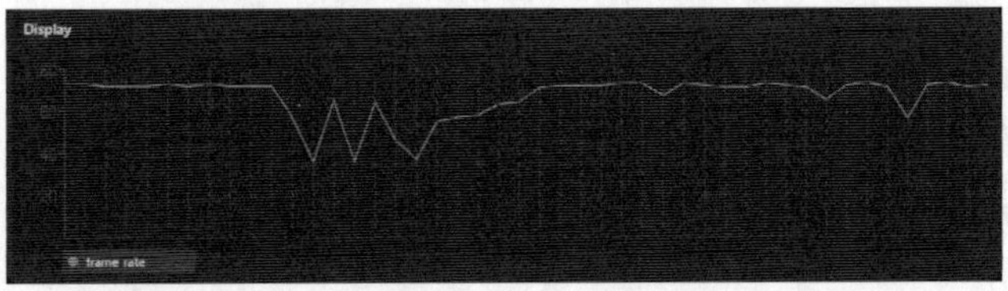

Figure 1. Frame rate recording

Figures 2 to 4 show a scene where two ray caster were placed and how increasing the ray count improves the visual resolution of wave interactions. In a test environment that simulates a narrow alleyway between buildings, low ray counts capture general propagation paths. Higher ray densities reveal multiple reflections and signal diffusion. While not physically exact, the simulation effectively conveys key wave behaviors, such as reflection off surfaces, shadowing behind obstacles, and intensity drop-off due to material absorption.

These results demonstrate the feasibility of real-time, user-driven exploration of electromagnetic propagation in VR. Although the system is not intended to be scientifically accurate, it allows users to observe signal behavior in complex spatial settings, which supports the development of intuition in educational contexts and provides conceptual insights for planning scenarios.

Figure 2. Showcase Scene

Figure 3. 50 Rays per Ray Caster

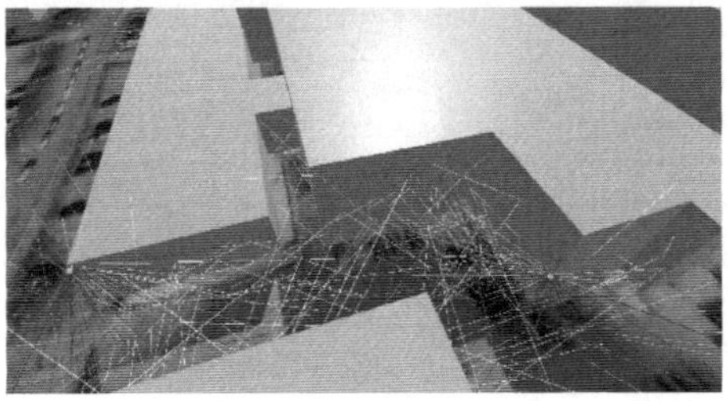

Figure 4. 100 Rays per Ray Caster

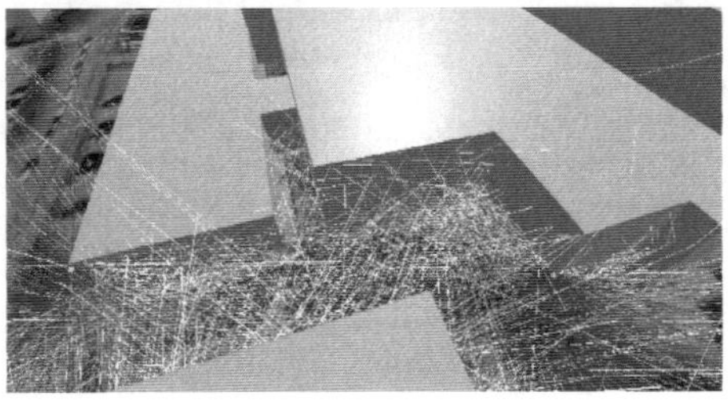

Figure 5. 500 Rays per Ray Caster

5. CONCLUSION AND FUTURE WORK

This paper introduces a VR-based electromagnetic wave visualization system for exploring signal propagation in 3D environments. The system combines real-time ray-based simulations, simplified material models, and 3D environments based on real-world data. This allows users to observe how waves reflect, attenuate, and interact with structures. Although the system is not physically precise, it prioritizes clarity and interactivity to support spatial reasoning and conceptual understanding of key wave behaviors.

Future development should focus on improving material modeling and scaling to larger environments. From an educational standpoint, a structured classroom evaluation is a key next step to assessing learning outcomes and usability. Further extensions may include augmented reality modes to visualize wave behavior in physical spaces. These enhancements will evolve the system into a versatile educational tool and an early-stage network design tool, bridging theory and real-world understanding.

REFERENCES

Butler, J.J. and Cosgrove, A.B., (1991). The Bidirectional Scattering Distribution Function (BSDF) and its role in optical metrology. *Journal of Research of the National Institute of Standards and Technology*, 96(2), pp.215–225.

Esri, (2025). *ArcGIS - Geographic Information System*. Online. Available at: https://www.arcgis.com

Fernandes, A.S. and Feiner, S.K., (2016). Combating VR sickness through subtle dynamic field-of-view modification. *Proceedings of the IEEE Symposium on 3D User Interfaces (3DUI)*. Greenville, SC, USA, pp.201–210.

Fu, H. et al., (2021). VR-based electromagnetic field education in immersive learning environments. *Immersive Learning Lab*. University of Illinois. Available at: https://www.ilie.ece.illinois.edu/immersive-learning-lab

González, Á., (2009). Measurement of areas on a sphere using Fibonacci and latitude–longitude lattices. *arXiv preprint*, arXiv:0912.4540. Available at: http://arxiv.org/pdf/0912.4540

ECE, (2021). *Immersive Learning Lab*. University of Illinois. Available at: https://www.ilie.ece.illinois.edu/immersive-learning-lab

Kirsanov, V., (2024). *Blosm: Blender OpenStreetMap Addon – Documentation*. GitHub. Available at: https://github.com/vvoovv/blosm/wiki/Documentation

Makransky, G., Terkildsen, T.S. and Mayer, R.E., (2019). Adding immersive virtual reality to a science lab simulation causes more presence but less learning. *Learning and Instruction*, 60, pp.225–236.

OpenStreetMap, (2024). *OpenStreetMap*. Online. Available at: https://www.openstreetmap.org

Parong, J. and Mayer, R.E., (2018). Learning science in immersive virtual reality. *Journal of Educational Psychology*, 110(6), pp.785–797.

Smith, J., Doe, R. and Johnson, M., (2021). Real-time electromagnetic visualization using augmented reality. *Proceedings of the IEEE Conference on Electromagnetic Applications*. Location not specified, pp. [n/a if not known]. Available at: https://ieeexplore.ieee.org/document/9645933

Unity, (2025). *Physics*. Unity Documentation. Available at: https://docs.unity3d.com/Manual/PhysicsSection.html

Wicaksono, A., Rahmatullah, N. and Sukarno, T., (2021). Development of virtual reality-based learning media on electromagnetic wave radiation material. *ResearchGate*. Available at: https://www.researchgate.net/publication/351467906_Development_of_virtual_reality-based_learning_media_on_electromagnetic_wave_radiation_material

COLLABORATIVE AI-DRIVEN DESIGN AND REALISTIC 3D SIMULATION OF DYNAMIC FABRIC BEHAVIOR

João Santos[1], Nuno Dinis[2], Luís Romero[1] and Pedro Miguel Faria[1]
[1]Instituto Politécnico de Viana do Castelo, Viana do Castelo, Portugal
[2]Riopele, Vila Nova de Famalicão, Portugal

ABSTRACT

This paper incorporates the use of artificial intelligence and collaborative visualization tools to provide an alternative approach to fabric/simulating 3D environments. The main aim is to create a machine learning model that follows the approach by classifying textile parameter combinations (i.e. composition, weight, elasticity) as 'good' or 'bad' to simplify the validation process. Approved combinations are exported to 3D modeling software for virtual visualization and then integrated into Unity, enabling real-time, collaborative interaction with the simulated fabrics.

KEYWORDS

3D Modeling, Real-Time Collaboration, Textile Simulation, Machine Learning

1. INTRODUCTION

The development of three-dimensional simulation systems for analyzing textiles, clothing or footwear behavior plays an important role in evaluating how these materials behave in different fields of design. These applications, often equipped with machine learning technologies, are based on models of physical behavior to produce realistic simulations, and are used in the areas of fashion, product design, engineering and digital games, predicting results more efficiently and accurately. However, the definition and validation of fabrics in 3D environments often still depends on physical samples, and this process can be costly, time-consuming, and sometimes incompatible with more agile workflows. That said, this paper presents an innovative idea: initially, the use of a machine-learning AI model capable of classifying combinations of the parameters of a certain fabric as "good" or "bad". With this solution, you explicitly define the characteristics of a fabric (such as composition, weight, thickness, elasticity, etc.) and immediately receive an assessment of the viability of that combination. If the combination is successful, it will be exported to modeling software, allowing it to be visualized and validated in a three-dimensional environment. It will then be exported to Unity, creating a collaborative mode where different users can interact in real time with the simulated fabrics.

This paper initially presents the work related to the proposed solution, then describes the architecture of the solution exploring each part of it and finally the conclusion and future work.

This system offers significant advantages over traditional methods of testing physical fabric products, which are both expensive and time consuming, as it can test these products in virtual environments much faster, cheaper and allow for collaboration, reducing time to market, and enabling sustainable design workflows. The aim of this system is to enable virtual evaluation and collaborative visualization of fabrics, reducing the need for physical samples and accelerating the design-validation loop in textile innovation.

2. RELATED WORK

A few research studies have explored alternative approaches to the topic incorporating AI into textile simulation, virtual environments and collaborative environments. Different studies utilize deep learning models, such as convolutional neural networks (CNNs), gated recurrent units (GRUs) and extreme gradient boosting (XGBoost), for analyzing fabric, as well as analyzing wrinkle models (Yang, 2024), fabrics with defects (Sajitha & Priya, 2023) and fabric quality assessment (Shifani et al., 2024). Other studies looked into customizing the avatars within the virtual environment with traditional clothing (Jalori et al, 2024) as well as simulated tactile experiences with electro-vibration and AI (Chen et al, 2019).

There is a tremendous opportunity for AI in the 3D modeling and collaborative technical space to transform the textile and fashion industry through improved workflows and more engaging and productive design and training environments.

In summary, these studies demonstrate how AI can be effectively applied to textile analysis and simulation, both visually and interactively. These AI approaches not only optimize processes and reduce human error but also open up numerous possibilities for solving diverse problems. Integrating AI into the textile industry is not just promising, it is becoming open for staying competitive in a rapidly evolving world.

In terms of collaboration, several studies have explored different approaches. Luyao et al. (2019) proposed a virtual collaborative platform developed in Unity, using a client-server architecture to support real-time multi-user interaction. The Unity-based client handles scene visualization and user interactions, while the server manages and synchronizes data in real time.

Huang et al. (2024) developed a virtual simulation system with VR support, also using Unity. Their system was tested with university students and demonstrated improved content comprehension, reinforcing the potential of collaborative VR environments, which can be extended to fields like textiles.

Hall et al. (2022) introduced a system for co-creation and visualization of 3D environments, using XR technologies and accessible tools like Unity Mirror for networking. They combined traditional meshing algorithms with deep learning methods, offering an affordable pipeline.

However, they also highlighted limitations, such as challenges with the Point2Mesh model when reconstructing large-scale urban areas, and technical issues with HoloLens2, revealing the complexity of integrating various XR platforms. Despite these challenges, the study confirms the value of XR-based collaborative environments in domains such as urban planning and training, while pointing to areas requiring further research.

3. SYSTEM ARCHITECTURE

This section presents the workflow for fabric evaluation and visualization in a 3D collaborative environment. The proposed architecture is represented in the UML Activity Diagram (Figure 1).

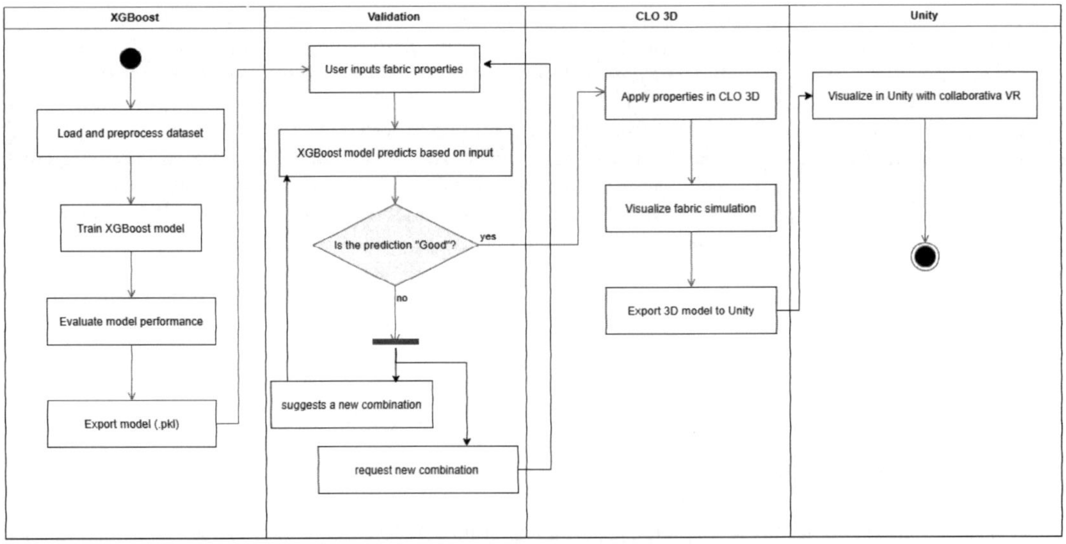

Figure 1. Proposed workflow for the automatic validation of fabric property combinations using XGBoost, realistic simulation in CLO3D, and collaborative visualization in Unity

3.1 XGBoost

The first block of the program will orient around the XGBoost algorithm. XGBoost (Extreme Gradient Boosting) is a machine learning algorithm that optimizes a loss function using a number of decision trees. New trees improve on previous ones by enabling learning from errors. XGBoost was selected for this application based on its speed, regularization methods, and strong performance in classification tasks.

Within the dataset there will be around 500 rows each representing different combinations of fabric physical and mechanical properties (i.e., weight, thickness, elastic properties, composition). Each row has a label of "Good" or "Bad", which will be designated by a human expert through pre-defined performance criteria for the textile simulation.

The first step before we say orients refusal will be to preprocess the dataset to remove poor quality data and verify the data is relatively consistent. The first step will include normalizing the numerical attributes of the underlined variables and using one-hot encoding for any categorical variables (e.g., type of fiber).

Whenever there are unequal classes, like in this project with "Good" and "Bad", if there is class imbalance, it will be possible to oversample the underrepresented class. One way to determine where class imbalance exists will be to consult with experts in textile simulation regarding performance ratios, in this case for each category of fabric simulation.

Prior to training the model, the dataset will be preprocessed for data quality and consistency. Normalization will be applied to numerical attributes while categorical variables (e.g., fiber type) will be converted via one-hot encoding. If there are any discrepancies in class distributions, oversampling will be used to balance the distribution between "Good" and "Bad" samples.

The model will entail a training, validation and testing split with 70% of the sample being train, 15% being validation and 15% being test samples. The performance of the model will be assessed based on accuracy, precision, recall, and F1 measure, though in future runs, cross-validation approaches will be used to improve the model's robustness and generalizability.

The goal of this initial phase of the workflow will develop a useful model that can automatically evaluate if a given combination of fabric parameters will work for realistic 3D simulation and collaborative visualization.

3.2 D Simulation

Once the combination has been approved by the XGBoost algorithm, it is then applied to software for a realistic simulation of the fabric. Initially, Maya was chosen as the main software, using the NCloth plugin. However, nCloth does not allow certain physical and mechanical parameters of the fabric to be simulated adequately, which forced us to resort to other more specific software for textile simulations. An analysis was then made of the best software to use in this study, as shown in Table 1.

Table 1. Comparison of textile simulations software's

Software	Realism	Ease of use	Export to Unity	Integration with AI	Academic License
Style3D	4/5	4/5	FBX/OBJ	Yes	Available
CLO 3D	5/5	4/5	FBX/GLTF	Limited	Free
Browzwear	5/5	3/5	OBJ	No	Commercial

Among the choices looked at, CLO 3D was picked because of its great level of realness (5/5), simple use, and fit with common export types like FBX and GLTF. Also, the partner company in this project already uses CLO 3D in their design workflow which helps back up the choice by keeping things standard with market habits and making future teamwork easier.

3.3 Unity

For the part of the system dedicated to collaborative visualization and real-time interaction, Unity stands out due to several technical and functional aspects that make Unity an advantageous option for three-dimensional collaborative environments, in a context of fabric simulation and intelligent systems integration.

Firstly, Unity provides native support for virtual reality (VR) and augmented reality (AR), which favor remote collaboration between users. The addition of avatars, interaction interfaces and virtual environments, as well as the possibility of real-time synchronization in interactions, facilitate communication and decision-making in design and engineering projects.

4. SYSTEM DEVELOPMENT

This section presents the development plan. The first step will be to develop the classification model using the XGBoost algorithm. A structured dataset will be drawn up which will include various combinations of physical and mechanical fabric properties. For example, physical properties based on bitmap textures include attributes such as base color (diffuse), normal maps, displacement maps, opacity, roughness, and metalness. Mechanical properties, extracted from.zfab or .json files, cover parameters such as mass, thickness, friction, bending, stretchiness, shear, linearity, and shrinkage behavior. Each dataset entry will be associated with a binary class, categorized as "Good" or "Bad", whether or not it is suitable for realistic 3D production/simulation.

Before training the model, the data will be pre-processed to ensure quality and uniformity, using techniques such as oversampling or under sampling to avoid an uneven distribution between the samples considered good or bad. Techniques such as One-Hot Encoding or Label Encoding will be applied to convert categorical variables, such as the type of fibers present in the composition of the fabric, into numerical formats that can be interpreted by the model. Next, the model will be trained using the XGBoost algorithm, and after training and validation, the final model will be exported so that it can be used in the next stage of integration.

Once the combination of properties has been validated, they will be applied in a 3D simulation environment. The CLO3D software allows direct modification of the physical and mechanical parameters of fabrics and also allows export to Unity-compatible formats (FBX/OBJ).

The last phase consists of creating a three-dimensional collaborative environment using Unity. The models simulated in CLO3D will be imported into Unity, allowing for real-time visualization. Remote collaboration functionality will be implemented using Virtual Reality (VR), allowing several users to interact with simulated fabrics.

5. CONCLUSION AND FUTURE WORK

This paper details an innovative use case that integrates machine learning and 3D simulation for textiles design and evaluation. Working with XGBoost for classification, CLO 3D for realistic simulated fabric, and Unity for collaborative VR environments, the solution supports product development and reduces the reliance on physical samples. The system is still in development, and the future work will be to build a viable prototype, and test usability and performance.

ACKNOWLEDGEMENT

This work received financial support from the integrated project Pacto Mobilizador TEXP@CT – Innovation Pact for the Digitization of Textiles and Apparel (TC-C12-i01, Sustainable Bioeconomy No. 02/C12-i01/202), promoted by the Recovery and Resilience Plan (PRR), Next Generation EU, for the period 2021-2026.

REFERENCES

Chen, T., & Guestrin, C. (2016). XGBoost: A scalable tree boosting system (Version 1.7) [Software]. https://xgboost.readthedocs.io/

Chen, Y., Qiu, W., Zhang, M., & Wang, X. (2019). 2019 IEEE the 2nd International Conference on Micro/Nano Sensors for AI, Healthcare, and Robotics (NSENS). IEEE.

CLO Virtual Fashion Inc. (2025). CLO 3D [Software]. https://www.clo3d.com/

Hall, B., Kessler, J., Edo-Ohanba, O., Collins, J., Zhang, H., Allegreti, N., Duan, Y., Wang, S., Palaniappan, K., & Calyam, P. (2022). Networked and multimodal 3D modeling of cities for collaborative virtual environments. In Proceedings - 2022 IEEE/ACM 9th International Conference on Big Data Computing, Applications and Technologies (BDCAT 2022) (pp. 204–212). Institute of Electrical and Electronics Engineers Inc. https://doi.org/10.1109/BDCAT56447.2022.00037

Huang, H., Wang, S., Tang, Z., Yue, S., Zheng, Y., & Tian, L. (2024). Immersive virtual simulation system for principles of communications based on Unity 3D. In Proceedings - 2024 39th Youth Academic Annual Conference of Chinese Association of Automation (YAC 2024) (pp. 2377–2380). Institute of Electrical and Electronics Engineers Inc. https://doi.org/10.1109/YAC63405.2024.10598462

Jalori, A., Prajod, A., Pandey, A., Pandey, A., & Kanwal, P. (2024). Enhancing 3D avatar realism with Indian clothing and motion capture data. In Proceedings of CONECCT 2024 - 10th IEEE International Conference on Electronics, Computing and Communication Technologies. Institute of Electrical and Electronics Engineers Inc. https://doi.org/10.1109/CONECCT62155.2024.10677335

Luyao, X., Honghai, D., Jianfeng, L., & Hao, Z. (2019). IICSPI: 2018 IEEE International Conference of Safety Produce Informatization: 10–12 December 2018, Chongqing, China (p. 475). Institute of Electrical and Electronics Engineers.

Sajitha, N., & Priya, S. P. (2023). Artificial intelligence based optimization with extreme gradient boosting for fabric defect detection and classification model. In 2nd International Conference on Sustainable Computing and Data Communication Systems (ICSCDS 2023) - Proceedings (pp. 509–515). Institute of Electrical and Electronics Engineers Inc. https://doi.org/10.1109/ICSCDS56580.2023.10104910

Shifani, S. A., Suresh, M. D., Paramaiyappan, M., Selvi, M. S. F. T., Giri, J., & Kanan, M. (2024). Intelligent deep learning model for real-time fabric quality evaluation using EfficientNet, GRU and XGBoost. In Proceedings of

Style3D. (2024). Style3D (Version 3.2) [Software]. Style3D Inc. https://www.style3d.com/

Unity Technologies. (2024). *Unity* (Version 2022.3.18f1) [Software]. Unity Technologies. https://unity.com/

Yang, H. (2024). 3D clothing wrinkle modeling method based on Gaussian curvature and deep learning. In Proceedings - 2024 Asia-Pacific Conference on Image Processing, Electronics and Computers (IPEC 2024) (pp. 136–140). Institute of Electrical and Electronics Engineers Inc. https://doi.org/10.1109/IPEC61310.2024.00033

Reflection Papers

PROPOSAL TO DESIGN A DIGITAL TWINS INTERFACE WITH VIRTUAL REALITY FOR TELECOMMUNICATION SITE, AN OVERVIEW

Miguel Ángel Gómez Garza, Leticia Amalia Neira Tovar and Juan Alberto Torres Lopez
Universidad Autónoma de Nuevo León, Mexico

ABSTRACT

Telecommunications are currently indispensable for humans, and maintaining and monitoring server sites is essential to keep the equipment in optimal operating condition. However, conventional tools for this purpose are limited and require the presence of an agent to conduct reviews, which leads to a waste of time and human resources and increases the risk of human error. Digital twins aim to monitor and diagnose server site to help prevent failures and expedite maintenance. Access to servers through a VR environment for control is also included, and their use for immersive server training is contemplated. This paper presents an overview of the current literature on digital twins, telecommunication site monitoring systems, and the application of VR and AR for training support to justify the development and proposal of a digital twin interface for monitoring telecom sites.

KEYWORDS

Training Support, Digital Twin, Telecommunication Server, Monitoring, Virtual Reality Interface

1. INTRODUCTION

The purpose of this review is to showcase various papers regarding the use of **Digital Twins (DT)** technology for monitoring and controlling applications across diverse fields, including **Telecommunications**, as well as the management of resources utilized for designing **Assisted Training** through **Virtual Reality (VR)** and **Augmented Reality (AR)**. It also aims to justify future projects that incorporate immersive technologies.

The concept of DT defines a virtual model interconnected with a physical system in real time for a functional purpose (Boyes 2022, Singh 2021). This is possible thanks to a set of new Industry 4.0 technologies focused on implementing intelligent systems, such as the Internet of Things (IoT), Big Data, simulation and artificial intelligence (AI). It can be utilized in fields like industrial processes, health, and smart cities (Fuller 2020). **Telecom Servers** is an area of interest due to the potential for remote monitoring and control, and the establishment of a secure environment for operations (RAJ 2023). VR technology is also planned for **Assisted Training**, creating an immersive scenario of DT Sites and training operators to manage the tools it provides access to.

2. RESEARCH METHODOLOGY

Certain guidelines were established. They must originate from reliable or sites scientific sector, in English and after 2015. Papers will be considered if they address the three main topics Figure 1. The collection includes case studies and reviews. It is classified into the following categories: **experimentation**, **prototypes**, **patents**, **literature review** and **discussion**. These categories are based on this work's classification (Liu 2022).

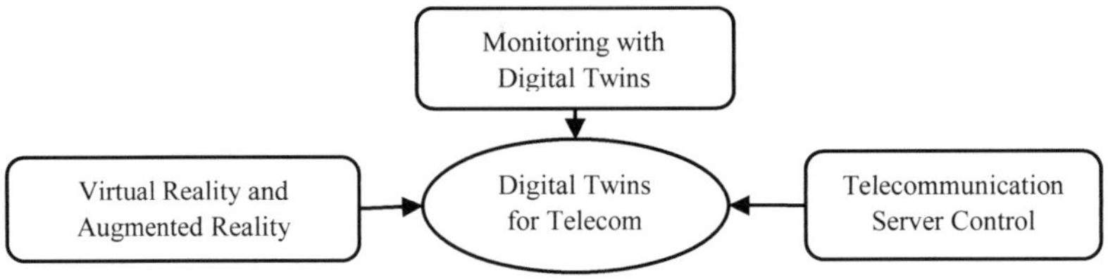

Figure 1. Conceptual Diagram about Topics correlation

The information sought in the papers concerns the main problems to be solved, the tools and technologies used in their development, the results, and future considerations improvements.

3. RESULT RESEARCH

The following is a summary of **32 articles** and proportions of topics can be visualized in Figure 2.

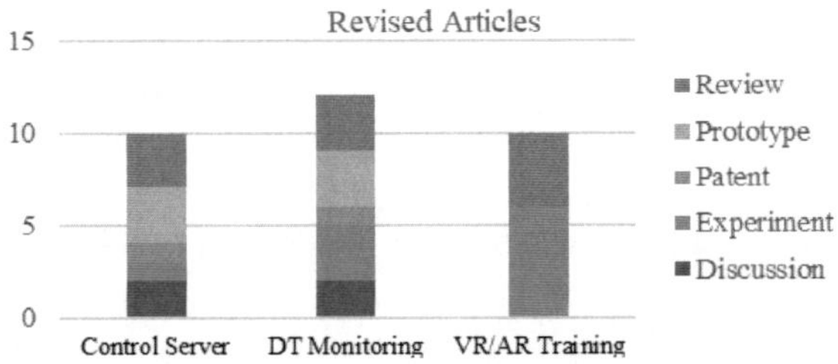

Figure 2. Graphic about the amount of revised works

3.1 Monitoring with Digital Twins

Table 1. Reviewed literature for Digital Twins

Ref	Year	Type	Field	Topic to resolve
Boyes	2022	Prototype	General	Concept
Brahmi	2024	Experiment	Healthcare	Predictive Monitoring
Feng	2023	Experiment	General	Predictive Monitoring
Fuller	2020	Review	General	Concept
Grieves	2016	Discussion	Manufacturing	Predictive Monitoring
Hosseinkhani	2024	Discussion	General	Predictive Monitoring
Kim	2019	Patent	Smart City	Predictive Monitoring
Liu	2022	Review	Industry	Predictive Monitoring
Liu	2024	Experiment	Manufacturing	Predictive Monitoring
Singh	2021	Review	Industry	Concept
Sosa-Méndez	2023	Prototype	Healthcare	Training
Tao	2017	Prototype	Manufacturing	Predictive Monitoring

Some papers focus on general (Boyes 2022, Feng 2023, Fuller 2020, Hosseinkhani 2024), but some works are also applied to healthcare (Brahmi 2024, Sosa-Méndez 2023), industry and manufacturing (Grieves 2016, Liu 2022, Liu 2024, Singh 2021, Tao 2017), and smart cities (Kim 2019). The list can be checked in Table 1.

A significant amount of literature highlights interest in developing predictive monitoring systems to prevent failures and detect violations of functionality (Grieves 2016, Hosseinkhani 2024, Liu 2022). Tools used for this purpose include predictive algorithms (Feng 2023), Artificial Intelligence (Brahmi 2024, Liu 2024). Other applications of DT include Big Data (Tao 2017) and simulation (Kim 2019, Sosa-Méndez **2023)**. Although it appears as a promising system with many future possibilities, commonly mentioned issues include the need to optimize the method of data collection due to the large volume of data to manage (Boyes 2022, Brahmi 2024, Fuller 2020, Grieves 2016, Liu 2022, Liu 2024, Singh 2021); the complexity and cost of infrastructure required to store it (Boyes 2022, Fuller 2020, Sosa-Méndez 2023); security and privacy concerns (Boyes 2022, Fuller 2020); and a lack of standardization in DT development (Boyes 2022).

3.2 Monitoring with Digital Twins

While these works focus on server management, some specialize in specific infrastructures such as telecommunications (Hilt 2016, Mehmood 2023, Poorzare 2025, Suzuki 2019) and mobile networks **(Moysen 2017, Sanz 2023)**. The list can be checked in Table 2.

Although there is interest in remote monitoring of server operations (Poorzare 2025, RAJ 2023, Sanz 2023, Verdecchia 2024), the majority is dedicated to optimization methods that enhance the **Quality of Service (QoS)** of servers, employing ML to manage server workloads (Almasan 2022, Haolin 2024, Mehmood 2023, Moysen 2017, Suzuki 2019). This optimization is added to a **Software Defined Networking (SDN)** for server control and management through software (Mehmood 2023, RAJ 2023).

Table 2. Reviewed literature for Telecommunication Control

Ref	Year	Type	Field	Topic to resolve
Almasan	2022	Discussion	General	Simulation
Haolin	2024	Patent	General	Control
Hilt	2016	Discussion	Telecom	Concept
Mehmood	2023	Experiment	Telecom	Proposal
Moysen	2017	Review	Mobile Net	Optimization
Poorzare	2025	Review	Telecom	Control
RAJ	2023	Prototype	General	Optimization
Sanz	2023	Prototype	Mobile Net	Concept
Suzuki	2019	Prototype	Telecom	Optimization
Verdecchia	2024	Review	General	Concept

An NDT project (Sanz 2023) presented the methodology for its proposed prototype, as well as several tools used, including server parameter collection software (ALTO, SNMP, Iperf3), multi-signal messaging protocols (MQTT), and cryptographic tools (TLS, OpenSSL). The current challenges to be solved are like those faced by Digital Twins in general, especially regarding optimization and data security issues (Moysen 2017, Poorzare 2025, RAJ 2023, Sanz 2023).

3.3 Virtual Reality and Augmented Reality

The collected literature is divided into the use of **Virtual Reality (VR)** technology (Bajuri 2021, Corelli 2020, Di Pasquale 2024, Freina 2015, Kubr 2024, Mirauda 2020), **Augmented Reality (AR)** (Gonzalez-Franco 2016, Lamberti 2014, Morales 2024), and both **(XR)** (Hoover 2021). The list can be checked **in Table 3.**

The main tool in a VR application is a headset and a compatible engine that supports the technology (Corelli 2020, Freina 2015, Mirauda 2020). In the case of AR is enough to have a camera and a processor to use it, like a smartphone (Lamberti 2014).

The advantages of using **Immersive Reality (XR)** for training include repeatability and low costs, creating a safe environment for skill development and even simulating hazardous scenarios (Corelli 2020, Di Pasquale 2024, Gonzalez-Franco 2016, Kubr 2024, Mirauda 2020), For AR can be used to assist in task execution by offering guidance (Lamberti 2014, Morales 2024).

The main goal of these studies is to demonstrate the effectiveness of XR for skill development. Some works focus on studying user retention (Bajuri 2021, Kubr 2024, Mirauda 2020), the effectiveness of immersion (Corelli 2020, Kubr 2024), and comparisons between XR and traditional training methods (Gonzalez-Franco 2016). Nevertheless, although satisfactory results are comparable to face-to-face training, a barrier remains since most people are not familiar with XR. Moreover, there is limited evidence showing practical improvement in real world situations due to XR training.

Table 3. Reviewed literature for VR and AR Support Training

Ref	Year	Type	Field	Technology
Bajuri	2021	Review	Healthcare	VR
Corelli	2020	Experiment	Public Security	VR
Di Pasquale	2024	Review	Manufacturing	VR
Freina	2015	Review	General	VR
Gonzalez-Franco	2016	Experiment	Industry	AR
Hoover	2021	Experiment	Manufacturing	XR
Kubr	2024	Experiment	Industry	VR
Lamberti	2014	Experiment	Others	AR
Mirauda	2020	Experiment	Others	VR
Morales	2024	Review	Industry	AR

4. CONCLUSION

The information gathered on DT and XR for Assisted Training indicates a wide range of technological applications. Implementing them in telecom servers could enhance performance with lower energy consumption. Furthermore, studies demonstrate methodologies that can serve as a foundation for future work. However, due to the lack of design standards and current technological limitations still presents a significant challenge. In any case, the development of a DT for Telecom Sites is feasible with the tools available, allowing for the establishment of a foundation to develop and implement more features.

REFERENCES

Almasan, P. et al. (2022). Network Digital Twin: Context, Enabling Technologies and Opportunities. *ArXiv*. doi: 10.48550/arXiv.2205.14206

Bajuri, M. Y. et al. (2021). Critical Success Factors for Virtual Reality Applications in Orthopaedic Surgical Training: A Systematic Literature Review. *IEEE Access*, Vol. 9, pp. 128574–128589. doi: 10.1109/access.2021.3112345

Boyes, H., & Watson, T. (2022). Digital twins: An analysis framework and open issues. *Computers in Industry*, Vol. 143, pp. 103763. doi: 10.1016/j.compind.2022.103763

Brahmi, R. et al. (2024). Elaboration of Innovative Digital Twin Models for Healthcare Monitoring With 6G Functionalities. *IEEE Access*, Vol. 12, pp. 109608–109624. doi: 10.1109/access.2024.3439269

Corelli, F. et al. (2020). Assessing the Usability of Different Virtual Reality Systems for Firefighter Training. *Proceedings of the 15th International Joint Conference on Computer Vision, Imaging and Computer Graphics Theory and Applications*, pp. 146–153. doi: 10.5220/0008962401460153

Di Pasquale, V. et al. (2024). Virtual Reality for Training in Assembly and Disassembly Tasks: A Systematic Literature Review. *Machines*, Vol. 12, No. 8, p. 528. doi: 10.3390/machines12080528

Feng, H. et al. (2023). Model-Based Monitoring and State Estimation for Digital Twins: The Kalman Filter. *ArXiv*. doi: 10.48550/ARXIV.2305.00252

Freina, L. et al. (2015). A LITERATURE REVIEW ON IMMERSIVE VIRTUAL REALITY IN EDUCATION: STATE OF THE ART AND PERSPECTIVES. *eLearning and Software for Education*. doi:10.12753/2066-026x-15-020

Fuller, A. et al. (2020). Digital Twin: Enabling Technologies, Challenges and Open Research. *IEEE Access*, Vol. 8, pp. 108952–108971. doi: 10.1109/access.2020.2998358

Gonzalez-Franco, M. et al. (2016). Immersive Augmented Reality Training for Complex Manufacturing Scenarios. *ArXiv*. doi: 10.48550/ARXIV.1602.01944

Grieves, M. et al. (2016). Digital Twin: Mitigating Unpredictable, Undesirable Emergent Behavior in Complex Systems. *Transdisciplinary Perspectives on Complex Systems*, pp.85–113. doi:10.1007/978-3-319-38756-7_4

Haolin, F. (2024). *Model transmission method and server*. (CH. Patent No. 118400069A). XFUSION DIGITAL TECHNOLOGIES CO LTD. https://worldwide.espacenet.com/patent/search?q=pn%3DCN118400069A

Hilt, A. et al. (2016). Availability Prediction of Telecommunication Application Servers Deployed on Cloud. *Periodica Polytechnica Electrical Engineering and Computer Science,* Vol. 60, No. 1, pp. 72–81. doi: 10.3311/PPee.9051

Hoover, M., & Winer, E. (2021). Designing Adaptive Extended Reality Training Systems Based on Expert Instructor Behaviors. *IEEE Access*, Vol. 9, pp. 138160–138173. doi: 10.1109/access.2021.3118105

Hosseinkhani, E. et al. (2024). A Model-Based Approach for Monitoring and Diagnosing Digital Twin Discrepancies. *Schloss Dagstuhl – Leibniz-Zentrum für Informatik*. doi: 10.4230/OASICS.DX.2024.2

Kim, T. G. (2019). *Computing system for virtual sensor implementation using digital twin and method for realtime data collection thereof.* (U.S. Patent No. 20220197231A1) Korea Digital Twin Lab Inc. https://patents.google.com/patent/US20220197231A1/en

Kubr, J. et al. (2024). Immersive Virtual Reality Training in Industrial Settings: Effects on Memory Retention and Learning Outcomes. *IEEE Access*, Vol. 12, pp. 168270–168282. doi: 10.1109/access.2024.3496760

Lamberti, F. et al. (2014). Challenges, Opportunities, and Future Trends of Emerging Techniques for Augmented Reality-Based Maintenance. *IEEE Transactions on Emerging Topics in Computing*, Vol. 2, No. 4, pp. 411–421. doi: 10.1109/tetc.2014.2368833

Liu, H. et al. (2022). Digital Twin-Driven Machine Condition Monitoring: A Literature Review. *Journal of Sensors*, Vol. 2022, pp. 1–13. doi: 10.1155/2022/6129995

Liu, Z. et al. (2024). Digital twin-based anomaly detection for real-time tool condition monitoring in machining. *Journal of Manufacturing Systems*, Vol. 75, pp. 163–173. doi: 10.1016/j.jmsy.2024.06.004

Mehmood, K. et al. (2023). Enhancing QoS of Telecom Networks through Server Load Management in Software-Defined Networking (SDN). *Sensors*, Vol. 23, No. 23, pp. 9324. doi: 10.3390/s23239324

Mirauda, D. et al. (2020). Sustainable Water Management: Virtual Reality Training for Open-Channel Flow Monitoring. *Sustainability*, Vol. 12, No.3, p. 757). doi: 10.3390/su12030757

Morales, G, et al. (2024). Impact of Augmented Reality on Assistance and Training in Industry 4.0: Qualitative Evaluation and Meta-Analysis. *Applied Sciences*, Vol. 14, No. 11, p. 4564. doi: 10.3390/app14114564

Moysen, J. et al. (2017). From 4G to 5G: Self-organized Network Management meets Machine Learning. *ArXiv*. doi: 10.48550/arXiv.1707.09300

Poorzare, R. et al. (2025). Network Digital Twin Toward Networking, Telecommunications, and Traffic Engineering: A Survey. *IEEE Access*, Vol. 13, pp. 16489–16538. doi: 10.1109/access.2025.3531947

RAJ, D. R. R. et al. (2023). Building a Digital Twin Network of SDN Using Knowledge Graphs. *IEEE Access*, Vol. 11, pp. 63092–63106. doi: 10.1109/ACCESS.2023.3288813

Sanz, M. et al. (2023). Digital Twins for 5G Networks: A Modeling and Deployment Methodology. *IEEE Access*, Vol. 11, pp. 38112-38126. doi: 10.1109/ACCESS.2023.3267548

Singh, M. et al. (2021). Digital Twin: Origin to Future. *Applied System Innovation*, Vol. 4, No. 2, pp. 36. doi: 10.3390/asi4020036

Sosa-Méndez, D., & García Cena, C. E. (2023). Robotic digital twin as a training platform for rehabilitation health personnel. *Enfoque UTE*, Vol. 14, No. 3, pp. 19–26. doi: 10.29019/enfoqueute.971

Suzuki, A. et al. (2019). Extendable NFV-Integrated Control Method Using Reinforcement Learning. *ArXiv*. doi: 10.48550/arXiv.1912.09022

Tao, F. et al. (2017). Digital twin-driven product design, manufacturing and service with big data. *The International Journal of Advanced Manufacturing Technology*, Vol. 94,No. 9–12, pp. 3563–3576. doi:10.1007/s00170-017-0233-1

Verdecchia, R. et al. (2024). Network Digital Twins: A Systematic Review. *IEEE Access*, Vol. 12, pp. 145400-145416. doi: 10.1109/ACCESS.2024.3453034

GAMIFICATION AS AN ENABLER FOR TRANSFORMATION: A SCIENTIFIC REFLECTION ON THE INTEGRATION OF PLAYFUL ELEMENTS IN SKILLS DEVELOPMENT AND INNOVATION

Manuela Sachse, Tim Neumann and Jessica Melzer
Westsächsische Hochschule Zwickau, Kornmarkt 1, 08056 Zwickau, Germany

ABSTRACT

The digital transformation is confronting companies, educational institutions and organizations with far-reaching change processes. Gamification, defined as the strategic incorporation of game-based elements into non-game contexts, has emerged as a successful approach to fostering motivation, learning and behavioral change. This review paper specifically investigates the potential of gamification as a catalyst for transformation in skilled labor development, innovation promotion, and sustainability. Rather than presenting original empirical research, it draws on recent studies and theoretical frameworks such as the Self-Determination Theory, the Fogg Behavior Model, and Flow Theory to analyze critical mechanisms of action. The analysis is supplemented by selected practical examples and a critical reflection on potential risks such as gamification fatigue, ethical manipulation and cultural context factors. The results demonstrate that gamification, when designed adaptively and with consideration for specific contexts, can be an effective tool in participatory and sustainable transformation processes.

KEYWORDS

Gamification, Transformation, Development of Skilled Workers, Innovation and Sustainable Behavioral Change

1. INTRODUCTION

Digital transformation exerts a profound influence on all facets of society and the economy, thereby presenting considerable challenges to businesses, educational institutions, and organizations. Gamification can be defined as the strategic integration of game mechanics into non-game environments with the aim of enhancing motivation, engagement, and behavioral change (Ruhi, 2015).

This paper contributes to the academic discourse on gamification by exploring its function as a facilitator in transformation processes. The focus lies on its potential applications and limitations in the development of skilled labor, innovation promotion, and sustainable behavioral change. As a review article, this study is based exclusively on recent empirical findings and established theoretical models and does not present new empirical data. The analysis centers on frameworks such as Self-Determination Theory (SDT), the Fogg Behavior Model (FBM), and Flow Theory, providing a conceptual foundation for understanding gamification's mechanisms of action.

2. GAMIFICATION AS A TRANSFORMATION TOOL

2.1 Theoretical Perspective of Gamification

Gamification can support transformation by lowering acceptance barriers, enhancing engagement, and stimulating innovation (Smiderle, Rigo & Marques, 2020). Its effectiveness is rooted in psychological and learning theories, notably Self-Determination Theory (SDT), the Fogg Behavior Model (FBM), and Flow Theory.

According to SDT (Deci & Ryan, 1985), intrinsic motivation arises from autonomy, competence, and relatedness. Gamified systems activate these needs through progress indicators, social challenges, and choice options. Sailer et al. (2017) show that adaptive feedback and difficulty levels enhance motivation when all three components are addressed.

FBM emphasizes that behavior requires motivation, ability, and triggers. Gamification contributes via rewards, accessible learning tasks, and cues for action. Takács and Balkányi (2023) confirmed this in digital learning contexts.

Flow Theory (Csikszentmihalyi, 1990) focuses on immersive engagement achieved by balancing challenge and skill. Yu et al. (2024) demonstrated that adaptive gamification can sustain flow and boost workplace productivity. Thus, theoretical grounding is crucial for sustainable gamified design..

2.2 Gamification in the Development of Skilled Labor

Digital transformation is reshaping skill demands. Gamified training offers an engaging alternative to traditional learning by creating interactive, adaptive scenarios that activate cognitive and emotional processes (Sailer et al., 2017). Core elements include point systems, ranking, and rewards to incentivize learning; immersive storytelling fosters exploratory and emotional engagement (Baah, Govender & Subramaniam, 2024).

Simulations and interactive challenges enhance experiential learning, while real-time feedback and personalized content increase effectiveness. Collaborative gamification strengthens social interaction (Baah et al., 2024). Pavlovic (2023) found significant learning motivation gains in adult vocational training. Grobbelaar & Alsemgeest (2024) showed that gamified financial education promotes engagement and long-term retention. Darden & Pesina (2025) highlighted increased self-efficacy and reduced tech-related anxiety among professionals in digital environments.

2.3 Gamification as a Catalyst for Innovation Processes

Gamification fosters creative problem-solving and participatory idea generation, especially in design thinking, innovation platforms, and prototyping (Leonhardt et al., 2025). It promotes divergent thinking and low-threshold participation.

Key mechanisms include group creativity games, decision-making simulations, feedback-based learning cycles, rapid prototyping, and team-based competitions. Studies show that these elements enhance self-directed learning and collaboration. Mitsea et al. (2025) emphasize gamification's role in developing meta-skills like critical thinking and adaptive learning.

A practical example is the Gamification meets Entrepreneurship program at European universities, where design thinking was combined with badges, storytelling, and challenge modules. Müller et al. (2024) found this approach increased motivation, team performance, and idea quality. Effective implementation requires balancing playfulness with pedagogical structure and combining gamification with established innovation methods.

2.4 The Application of Gamification as a tool to encourage sustainable behavioral change

Gamification is increasingly used to promote sustainable behaviors such as energy efficiency and eco-friendly consumption. Based on SDT and FBM, these systems enhance motivation, enable behavioral change, and support long-term engagement (Smiderle et al., 2020).

Effective features include real-time feedback on consumption, narrative elements to create emotional ties, social comparisons (e.g., low-emission rankings), and virtual sustainability goals to visualize progress. Studies show that combining feedback, scoring, and personalization can significantly reduce energy use. Personalized interaction, often missing in traditional campaigns, is key to sustained impact.

Nonetheless, symbolic gamification—so-called "greenwashing through play"—can erode trust and obscure actual sustainability performance. To ensure credibility and effectiveness, game elements must be applied transparently and meaningfully within broader ecological strategies.

2.5 Practical Examples: Gamification in Real Transformation Processes

Case studies confirm that well-implemented gamification can stimulate transformation in education, innovation, and sustainability.

Chávez-Reyes, García-Peñalvo & Ramírez-Montoya (2022) demonstrated that SDG-focused service learning enhances technical knowledge, self-efficacy, and social skills—especially in structurally weak regions. Buck, Abu-Hassan & AlDarwish (2024) showed that playful SDG challenges in English lessons increased participation, sustainability engagement, and civic motivation.

In business, Lamba et al. (2025) document how gamified stakeholder platforms—incorporating pitch contests, feedback cycles, and innovation sprints—improved solution quality, emotional commitment, and participation.

These examples underscore gamification's transformative potential—if participation, target group relevance, clear rules, feedback logic, and transparent reward structures are carefully designed.

3. REFLECTION: CHALLENGES AND LIMITS

Although the potential of gamification is promising, there are both scientific and practical challenges that need to be carefully considered when implementing it. Furthermore, several systematic limitations and critical side-effects have been identified that should not be overlooked in practice.

The phenomenon of gamification fatigue, defined as a decline in user engagement resulting from excessive exposure to gamification elements, has been a subject of considerable debate within the field. This risk increases when gamified systems rely too heavily on repetitive tasks, superficial rewards, or lack adaptive challenge levels. To counteract this effect, gamification should be designed with variability, personalization, and long-term value beyond mere entertainment. A recurrent critique pertains to gamification fatigue, which is defined as the progressive diminution of motivation that occurs with repeated utilization of playful components. A comprehensive meta-analysis by Schöbel et al. (2021) demonstrates that non-adaptive systems have the potential to lead to either excessive demands or indifference. Consequently, gamified processes must be customizable and scalable to circumvent the occurrence of overstimulation and demotivating effects.

A growing ethical problem that is currently coming to light concerns the boundary between motivation and manipulation. Gamification, whether intentionally or not, has the capacity to exert control over user behavior through design elements that exploit psychological triggers. This becomes especially critical when users are unaware of how their actions are being guided. The concept of "dark gamification" (Khanna, 2024) describes such practices, where emotional reward loops and addictive mechanics may lead to stress, digital dependency, or ethically questionable forms of engagement, particularly in commercial or educational settings.

A considerable number of gamification systems are designed to record usage data, behavioral patterns and personal preferences to generate rewards or recommendations. This practice gives rise to significant privacy concerns. Srivastava et al. (2023) have highlighted that the absence of stringent regulations regarding the use of gamification in online communities or learning environments can be a potential violation of privacy.

Gamified approaches demonstrate cultural variability in their acceptance. In a multicultural study, Fernandes et al. (2022) found that competitive elements are better accepted in individualistic societies, while cooperative forms of play are more effective in collectivist cultures. This finding underscores the necessity for a nuanced and culturally sensitive adaptation of game mechanics, with due consideration for the cultural context of the respective country.

4. CONCLUSION

Gamification has the potential to provide sustainable support for transformation processes in a variety of social and economic domains. The efficacy of gamification can be observed in its capacity to facilitate learning and behavioral processes, enhance motivation, and render complex challenges perceptible. The integration of reward, feedback, and emotional engagement has been demonstrated to be particularly effective in circumstances where traditional strategies reach their limits.

Empirical evidence indicates that gamification can contribute to the development of skilled labor, the promotion of innovation and sustainability. However, it is important to note that there are certain reservations regarding the effectiveness of this approach. The long-term implications of gamification depend crucially on the adaptability, target group-orientation and context sensitivity of the system. The utilization of gamification also requires an ethical framework that avoids manipulation, guarantees transparency and respects data protection.

This article is based on a review of recent theoretical and empirical studies and does not include original research.

Future research should concentrate on the long-term effects and sustainability of gamification approaches in different sectors, differentiated impact factors depending on user group, age, culture and application context, hybrid formats that combine gamification with artificial intelligence, augmented reality or social learning, social scalability, e.g. through use in smart cities or sustainable mobility. Theoretical frameworks such as Self-Determination Theory, the Fogg Behavior Model, and Flow Theory provided the conceptual basis for evaluating gamification's mechanisms and limitations.

In summary, the following assertion can be made: When conceived in an appropriate manner, gamification can be regarded as a tool that extends beyond the scope of a mere motivational device. Indeed, it has the potential to become a transformative principle in shaping sustainability.

REFERENCES

Baah, C., Govender, I., & Subramaniam, P. R. (2024). Enhancing Learning Engagement: A Study on Gamification's Influence on Motivation and Cognitive Load. Education Sciences, 14(10), 1115.Csikszentmihalyi, M. (1990). *Flow: The psychology of optimal experience.* New York: Harper & Row.

Buck, R. H., Abu-Hassan, J., Jimenez, M., & AlDarwish, S. (2024). Implementing SDGs in a pre-sessional English classroom. Open Scholarship of Teaching and Learning, 3(1), 96–106.

Chávez-Reyes, C., García-Peñalvo, F. J., & Ramírez-Montoya, M. S. (2022). Service learning and SDGs: A study of transformative competencies in higher education. Sustainability, 14(6), 3481. https://doi.org/10.3390/su14063481

Darden, D. L., & Pesina, R. (2025). *Integrating three-dimensional mentoring with workforce development training: A collaborative autoethnographic examination of skill transfer.* University of Texas at Tyler Repository.

Deci, E. L., & Ryan, R. M. (1985). *Intrinsic Motivation and Self-Determination in Human Behavior.* Berlin: Springer Science & Business Media.

Fernandes, A., Melo, M., & Machado, C. F. (2022). The Use of Gamification in Training and Socialization Processes in a Multicultural Context. In Technological Challenges: The Human Side of the Digital Age (pp. 93-108). Cham: Springer International Publishing.

Grobbelaar, C., & Alsemgeest, L. (2024). Gamification as an Educational Tool for Retirement Planning. Adult Learning, 10451595241286913.

Khanna, P. (2024). Dark gamification: A tale of consumer exploitation and unfair competition. In Demystifying the dark side of AI in business (pp. 138-147). IGI Global.

Lamba Sahdev, S., Hassan, A., Krishnan, C., Mariappan, J., & Salazar Chang, I. (2025). Metaverse and ESG governance: Addressing social and environmental challenges in the virtual world. In C. Krishnan, A. Behl, S. Dash, & P. D. Yadav (Eds.), The metaverse dilemma: Challenges and opportunities for business and society (pp. 149–161). Emerald Publishing. https://doi.org/10.1108/9781837975242.

Leonhardt, S., Neumann, T., Kretz, D., Teich, T., & Bodach, M. (2022). I*nnovation und Kooperation auf dem Weg zur All Electric Society.* Springer.

Leonhardt, S., Neumann, T., Kretz, D., Teich, T., & Bodach, M. (Eds.). (2022). Innovation und Kooperation auf dem Weg zur All Electric Society (1st ed.). Springer Vieweg. https://doi.org/10.1007/978-3-658-38706-8

Müller, J., Pippig, M., Fischer, H., Schmiedgen, P., Köhler, T., Letonja, M., Mertens, L., Slingerland, R., Urgacz, P., Farrand, Y., & Seré, D. (2024). Gamification meets entrepreneurship – Piloting a gamified European study program to foster the next generation of entrepreneurs. In ICERI2024 Proceedings (pp. 6169–6177). IATED.

Pavlović, G. (2023). Gamification: An innovative approach to employee training and skill development. In Proceedings of the 14th International Conference on e-Learning 2023 (pp. 108–117). Belgrade Metropolitan University. CEUR Workshop Proceedings. https://ceur-ws.org

Ruhi, U. (2015). Level Up Your Strategy: Towards a Descriptive Framework for Meaningful Enterprise Gamification. Technology Innovation Management Review, 5(8), 5–16. https://doi.org/10.22215/timreview/918.

Sailer, M., Hense, J. U., Mayr, S. K., & Mandl, H. (2017). How gamification motivates: An experimental study of the effects of specific game design elements on psychological need satisfaction. Computers in human behavior, 69, 371-380.

Sailer, M., Hense, J., Mandl, H., Klevers, M. (2017). Fostering Development of Work Competencies and Motivation via Gamification. In: Mulder, M. (eds) Competence-based Vocational and Professional Education. Technical and Vocational Education and Training: Issues, Concerns and Prospects, vol 23. Springer, Cham. https://doi.org/10.1007/978-3-319-41713-4_37

Schöbel, S., Schmidt-Kraepelin, M., Janson, A., & Sunyaev, A. (2021). Adaptive and personalized gamification designs: Call for action and future research. AIS Transactions on Human-Computer Interaction, 13(4), 479-494.

Smiderle, R., Rigo, S. J., Marques, L. B., Peçanha de Miranda Coelho, J. A., & Jaques, P. A. (2020). The impact of gamification on students' learning, engagement and behavior based on their personality traits. Smart Learning Environments, 7(1), 3.Srivastava,

Srivastava, G., Bag, S., Rahman, M.S., Pretorius, J.H.C. and Gani, M.O. (2023), "Examining the dark side of using gamification elements in online community engagement: an application of PLS-SEM and ANN modeling", Benchmarking: An International Journal, Vol. 30 No. 9, pp. 2921-2947. https://doi.org/10.1108/BIJ-03-2022-0160

Takács, P. (2023). *Achieving flow-state through gamification in education* [Master's thesis, Eötvös Loránd University]. ResearchGate. https://doi.org/10.13140/RG.2.2.16614.40004

Yu, D., Yue, A., & Rau, P. L. P. (2024). A gamified approach on inducing energy conservation behavior. In P. L. P. Rau (Ed.), Cross-cultural design (Lecture Notes in Computer Science, Vol. 14699, pp. 147 -160. Springer. https://doi.org/10.1007/978-3-031-60898-8_10

ACCEPTANCE OF GAMIFIED AND ESPORTS-BASED TRAINING FORMATS: A THEORETICAL APPROACH USING UTAUT AND DIFFUSION OF INNOVATIONS

Manuela Sachse and Lisa Strauch
Westsächsische Hochschule Zwickau, Germany

ABSTRACT

The acceptance of gamified and eSports-based training formats in the context of securing skilled workers in the district of Zwickau is analyzed using an extended theoretical framework. This is based on the Unified Theory of Acceptance and Use of Technology (UTAUT) and the Diffusion of Innovations model. While UTAUT captures central psychological and social determinants of individual technology acceptance, the diffusion model supplements the perspective with organizational and cultural dynamics. On this basis, a mixed-methods design is being developed that combines quantitative surveys on user expectations and qualitative analyses of individual and organizational influencing factors. The aim is to gain differentiated insights into the acceptance conditions of gamified training formats in small and medium-sized enterprises and to systematically take industry-specific and cultural differences into account.

KEYWORDS

Gamification, Esports, Securing Skilled Workers, Further Training, Technology Acceptance, UTAUT, Diffusion of Innovations, Mixed Methods, Digitalization, Employer Attractiveness

1. OPPORTUNITIES FOR GAMIFICATION IN COMPANIES - REFERENCE TO SKILLS SHORTAGE, DIGITAL TRANSFORMATION, YOUNG TARGET GROUPS

The research project “Change through gamification and eSports”, which is being carried out in collaboration with the Zwickau District Skilled Workers Alliance and the Saxony Development Bank, is investigating companies in Zwickau and analyzing regional challenges. Small and medium-sized companies in the Zwickau region have not yet fully exploited the potential of gamification and eSports in the areas of marketing and HR management. These strategies offer an opportunity to position themselves as attractive employers. The aim of the project is to design innovative training and awareness-raising offers for the recruitment and retention of skilled workers through the use of gamification and eSports.

Gamification elements can be used strategically to recruit and retain qualified personnel by creating a positive working environment and promoting employee motivation, commitment and professional development. In the context of skills shortages and digital transformation, younger generations, shaped by technological advances and societal changes, show a strong desire for meaningful employment, environmental responsibility and individual development. Research shows that companies need to adapt more to their employees in order to attract and retain them (Kochhan & Cichecki, 2024). Gamification and eSports are particularly attractive tools for Generation Z, born from 1997 onwards (Dimock, 2019). A study shows that 60-70% of Generation Z and younger millennials consider technology-supported, flexible and innovative working environments to be crucial when choosing an employer. (Deloitte, 2022). These figures underline the relevance of playful approaches in HR marketing and training for younger target groups.

Gamification and eSports have proven to be effective tools in the recruitment process to communicate company values to potential applicants or existing employees, as part of team building and employee retention initiatives, and in employer branding (Abuladze & Hasimi, 2023). Companies have the opportunity to use eSports and gamification to develop an innovative and interactive work environment that is in line with the younger workforce's increasing preference for digital technologies and ludic environments (Brademann & Piorr, 2019). At the same time, there are risks that need to be considered during implementation. Prioritizing playful elements in continuing education can lead to pedagogical quality standards being neglected and the offer being perceived as entertainment rather than a serious educational measure (Hamari et al., 2014).

2. THEORETICAL FRAMEWORK

The research aim is to analyze the acceptance of continuing education formats with gamification on the basis of the Unified Theory of Acceptance and Use of Technology (UTAUT). As part of this, an empirical survey design is being developed. The UTAUT theory integrates key elements from eight older models of technology acceptance research, including the theory of reasoned action, the technology acceptance model and the theory of innovation diffusion (Venkatesh et al., 2003).

While the UTAUT model approach enables a systematic description of central psychological and social determinants of the acceptance of new technologies, the implementation of gamification and eSports in the context of continuing education requires a more in-depth analysis. In order to adequately capture the entirety of organizational dynamics, the Diffusion of Innovations model is also used. This allows a systematic analysis of innovation decision processes and social influencing factors within organizations (Rogers, 2003).

A differentiated consideration of individual and cultural factors that influence the acceptance of gamification and eSports in continuing vocational training is only made possible by the combined application of UTAUT and Diffusion of Innovations.

3. PLANNED EMPIRICAL APPROACH AND USE OF THE RESULTS

According to statistical surveys conducted by the State Statistical Office of Saxony, the number of legal entities in the state of Saxony amounted to 154,877 units in 2023 (Statistics Saxony, 2024). Of these, 53 units were based in the district of Zwickau, employing a total of 15,315 people ("City of of Zwickau", 2024). The focus of the planned study is on analyzing the acceptance of continuing education formats that integrate gamification elements or references to eSports. The target group is young professionals, trainees and HR managers in companies. The survey design is based on the UTAUT model and captures the constructs of performance expectation, effort expectation, hedonic motivation and social influence.

In methodological terms, a mixed methods approach is being pursued: A quantitative online survey is used to determine the general patterns of acceptance. These are supplemented by qualitative interviews, which serve to deepen the acceptance patterns and analyze individual and organizational influencing factors. Building on the theoretical framework, the assumption that employer attractiveness automatically increases through the implementation of gamification and eSports is examined in particular. This examination takes into account cultural and industry-specific differences. Initial indications can be derived from the available literature that in traditional industries or in corporate cultures that are characterized by a hierarchical structure, there may be certain reservations about game-based learning (Rogers, 2003; Peek et al., 2014).

In the planned study, both individual acceptance factors according to UTAUT and organizational and cultural dynamics according to the model of diffusion of innovations are taken into account. The focus is on the balance between playful motivation and pedagogical effectiveness in order to ensure that gamified formats not only entertain, but also sustainably promote skills.

REFERENCES

Abuladze, L., & Hasimi, L. (2023). The Effectiveness and Attractiveness of Employer Branding: The Effects and Role of Gamification in Recruitment Activities. Conference Paper, Economics.

Brademann, I., & Piorr, R. (2019). Generation Z - Analysis of the needs of a generation on the move into working life. In B. Hermeier, & T. Heupel, Working worlds of the future - How digitalization is changing our jobs and ways of working.Wiesbaden: Springer Gabler.

Deloitte. (2022). Global 2022 Gen Z and Millennial Survey. https://www2.deloitte.com/global/en/pages/about-deloitte/articles/genzmillennialsurvey.html (last accessed: 28. April 2025)

Dimock, M. (2019). Defining generations: Where Millennials end and Generation Z begins. Pew research center, 17(1), 1-7.

Hamari, J., Koivisto, J., & Sarsa, H. (2014). Does Gamification Work? – A Literature Review of Empirical Studies on Gamification. 47th Hawaii International Conference on System Sciences, 3025–3034.

Kochhan, C., Cichecki, L. (2024). Generation Z und Arbeitsmarkt. In: Recruiting einer neuen Generation von Hochschulabsolventen. Springer Gabler, Wiesbaden.

Rogers, E. M. (2003). Diffusion of Innovations (5th ed.). New York: Free Press.

Sebastiaan T.M. Peek, Eveline J.M. Wouters, Joost van Hoof, Katrien G. Luijkx, Hennie R. Boeije, Hubertus J.M. Vrijhoef, Factors influencing acceptance of technology for aging in place: A systematic review, International Journal of Medical Informatics, Volume 83, Issue 4, 2014, Pages 235-248

Stadt Zwickau. (2024). Wirtschaftsdaten – Standortfaktoren der Stadt Zwickau. https://www.zwickau.de/de/wirtschaft/standort/faktoren/wirtschaftsdaten.php (last accessed: 23. April 2025)

Statistisches Landesamt des Freistaates Sachsen. (2024). Unternehmensregister. https://www.statistik.sachsen.de/html/unternehmensregister.html (last accessed: 23. April 2025)

Venkatesh, V., Morris, M. G., Davis, G. B., & Davis, F. D. (2003). User Acceptance of Information Technology: Toward a Unified View. MIS Quarterly, 27(3), 425–478.

Posters

CONTACT: AN INSTALLATION GAME

Andrew Hieronymi
Pennsylvania State University, University Park PA 16802, USA

ABSTRACT

In this paper I would like to describe my single-player installation game titled CONTACT. CONTACT invites players to engage in physical movement and digital play. It was conceived as an interactive art installation with an evolving iterative design approach, using custom hardware and software akin to a framework and test bed for game design explorations. The paper asks the following questions: can a digital interactive playful environment provide a contemplative experience for the player encouraging them to reflect and develop awareness of the interplay between their bodies, the digitally simulated world they interact with, and the underlying computational system that links them together? And through this contemplation, can players develop a consciousness of the collective realities surrounding them beyond the immersive isolation digital media so often reinforces?

KEYWORDS

Human-Computer Interaction, Interactive Art, Video Games, Embodiment, Artificial Life

1. INTRODUCTION

> "The epistemic potential of interactive art is based on an oscillation between flow and distancing and between action and reflection that originates in the processes of interaction." (Kwastek, 2013)

CONTACT was conceived in the context of the arts. It is designed to be experienced in various public settings such as art galleries, media festivals and symposiums for a wide variety of audiences. As an interactive art piece, it requires active participation and is encouraging participants to reflect on their interaction with the system triggering new ways of thinking about the language of the aesthetic encounter it generates. Learning the rules of the system, fine tuning the correct motions, developing non-verbal, gestural communication takes precedence over achieving a prescribed end-goal.

Most contemporary commercial video games favorize an experience centered around three main features: one-size-fits-all, friction free input devices, a digitally simulated photo-realistic three-dimensional audio-visual environment, and a competitive goal-oriented task-based game play. Many games don't have all three characteristics but most commonly share at least two out of three. CONTACT is circumventing all three features attempting instead to provide a more contemplative and self-reflective experience for the player. Ultimately, players could get in touch with a more critical consciousness of their day-to-day relationship with interactive technologies.

2. SETTING

> "How do we parse the shifting experiences, subtle and not so, across bodies, time and machines? This is in part a theoretical inquiry into the entanglement of bodies and machines, what these entanglements feel like, and how they register at the interface of computation, representation, and proprioception." (Anable, 2018)

In CONTACT, a participant stands in front of a screen projection and uses custom controllers, oversized dual joysticks anchored to a base. With these devices requiring upper-body physical movement to activate, the participant controls the orientation, rotation, and movement of an onscreen two-dimensional circular cell-like shape and guides it as it negotiates encounters within its two-dimensional virtual environment, a world made up of autonomous agents, other similar-looking cell-like shapes.

3. GAMEPLAY

A player engaging with CONTACT can go through three successive phases:

First, by manipulating the custom input devices, players attempt to make sense of how to use them to control the cell-like avatar. Eventually they discover that the use of a single stick rotates the avatar and changes its color, the angle rotation corresponding to a given color on a color wheel. The use of both sticks at the same time allows for the avatar to accelerate and move around its environment. A third behavior happens when the sticks are not used, the avatar stays still and a large circular "breathing" membrane around its body slowly expands and contracts. Gradually the player learns to alternate between these three behaviors, rotating, moving and breathing.

Secondly, the player starts to question the behavior of the other moving cell-like agents and their interaction with their avatar. The agents are all single-colored similar sized circles. They also alternate between moving and breathing like the player's avatar, but they don't rotate nor change colors. Color matching between the player's rotating body and the color of breathing agents or vice versa, the colors of the player's breathing membrane and of the moving agents is the core mechanic of the game. When colors match, the moving body can enter the membrane and get attracted to the breathing body. This action can be challenging because as the colors shift, the moving body gets repelled by the membrane. Moving agents can also make contact with breathing agents. The breathing membranes act as an obstacle to contact between bodies. They attract the moving cell to the breathing cell if the colors are matching, but otherwise they repel them.

Finally, the player develops an understanding of the consequence of their actions. Making contact with agents kills them. However, agents making contact with each other gives birth to a new agent. If the player does not attempt contact, the agents proliferate and ultimately overwhelm the world and immobilize the player. On the other hand, if the player kills too many agents, they stop birthing and the world depopulates completely. Maintaining a balanced number of agents keeps the game in virtual homeostasis.

4. DESIGN CONCEPT

The game is pared down to the essence of what game theorist Fruin defines as the spatial models and graphical logics key to most video games: *"collision detection, movement physics, and navigation." (Fruin, 2020)*

The 3D printed joysticks are reminiscent in their affordances of 1980s arcade dual sticks except for their enlarged size. Enlarging the dual sticks so that arms instead of just fingers get engaged emphasizes the role of the body during interaction with the digital interface.

Controlling the avatar with the sticks can be challenging, as instead of responsive controls traditionally found in digital games, the system's output involves a slightly delayed response due to the way the simulated physics are scripted. As players attempt to use the sticks to learn and master the game, they gradually accept this less responsive control and experience alternating moments of frustration and elation. The friction created by the system prevents players to immerse themselves fully in the game, and instead, when not quitting in frustration, they gradually surrender the desire for control and develop a level of acceptance, patience and curiosity that can lead to a calm, contemplative game experience.

The gameplay experience then, becomes reminiscent of David Toop description of ambient music:

> "Structure emerges slowly, minimally or apparently not at all, encouraging states of reverie and receptivity in the [participant] that suggest (on the good side of boredom) a very positive rootlessness." (Toop , 1995)

At that stage the player can feel a lack of clearly defined goals and closure, and experience aimless meandering. The limited vision the player has of the game environment due to the cropped framing of the game world, resembles what game theorist Anable relates to the act of spelunking.

> "To spelunk is to explore a potentially vast space that can be apprehended only a small section at a time. To spelunk is to risk disorientation in space and time". (Anable, 2018)

This disorientation prevents player to fully immerse themselves in the game, breaking with the design values of our contemporary digital experiences. Today's interaction with devices often integrates natural gestures such as real-time audio-visual response to finger taps and swipes so seamless that the interface becomes transparent, leading us to fall in a visual-centric, bodiless rabbit hole of impulsive, addictive activity.

CONTACT instead reminds us that as our bodies interact with computer systems, analog movements are transformed into digital signals. Those signals are then translated into information sent back to us. As game theorist Keogh writes,

> "Cyborgism puts back into play the corporeality of videogame engagement, the play of bodies, that is commonly displaced by calls to "gameplay" and "immersion" and "interactivity" as pregiven qualities. . [...] It renders legible [...] a more nuanced understanding of videogame experience as an embodied textuality that flickers across actual and virtual worlds as a play of bodies." (Keogh, 2018)

5. EVALUATION

Various iterations of CONTACT were exhibited since 2022. Reactions of players hovered between frustration and elation. Players able to move beyond phase one of the gameplay tended to communicate the most satisfaction with their experience. The learning curve required to master the color matching mechanic of phase two is what caused the most trouble to casual players. Reaching the third phase brings the game into a more goal-oriented game management mechanic, highlighting the need for human intervention in the lives of these virtual autonomous agents.

Is the game ultimately able to attain its goal of raising awareness about the addictive, immersive relationship we entertain with our digital devices? CONTACT remains an ongoing project with future iterations attempting to get closer and closer to answering this question.

ACKNOWLEDGEMENT

Special thanks to my Penn State colleagues Tom Lauerman for his expertise in designing the 3D-printed input devices and WooHun Joo for his atmospheric sound effects.

REFERENCES

Anable, A. (2018). Playing with Feelings: Video Games and Affect. University of Minnesota Press, Minneapolis, MN.
Keogh, B. (2018). A Play of Bodies: How We Perceive Videogames. MIT Press, Cambridge, MA.
Kwastek, K. (2013). Aesthetics of Interaction in Digital Art. MIT Press, Cambridge, MA.
Toop, D. (1995). Ocean of Sound: Aether Talk, Ambient Sound and Imaginary Worlds. Serpent's Tail, London, UK.
Wardrip-Fruin, N. (2020). How Pac-Man Eats: . MIT Press, Cambridge, MA (2020).

SIMULATION FRAMEWORK FOR EVALUATING DRIVER MONITORING SYSTEMS USING FACS-BASED VIRTUAL DRIVERS

Jonghwa Kim, Kyunglim Lee and Wonsang Lee
MORAI Inc.
Seoul, Republic of Korea

ABSTRACT

This work proposes a simulation-based framework that uses Facial Action Coding System (FACS)-driven virtual drivers to evaluate Driver Monitoring Systems (DMS). By leveraging MetaHuman Animator in Unreal Engine, facial behaviors such as fatigue and visual distraction are recreated using precise mappings between Action Units (AUs) and facial control curves. The simulation system allows repeatable, scalable testing under regulatory conditions (UNECE R157, Euro NCAP) without human data collection. Preliminary implementation demonstrates the capability to simulate key driver states and assess DMS accuracy in varied conditions.

KEYWORDS

Driver Monitoring System, FACS (Facial Action Coding System), Simulation, Automated Driving

1. INTRODUCTION

In Level 3 automated driving systems, it is essential that the driver remains available to take control when requested. This requirement has led to the widespread integration of Driver Monitoring Systems (DMS), designed to detect driver states such as visual distraction and fatigue. Conventional validation approaches are hindered by high costs, inconsistencies, and reliance on human participants. Regulatory standards such as UNECE R157 (2021) and the Euro NCAP Driver Monitoring Protocol (2023) outline precise requirements for DMS operation, highlighting the need for scalable, controllable, and reproducible validation methods. To address these limitations, this study presents a simulation framework employing virtual drivers modeled with the Facial Action Coding System (FACS) to validate DMS functionality. Using the MetaHuman system in Unreal Engine, facial animations representing typical driver states are programmatically generated. This approach aims to reduce validation cost and complexity, enhance reproducibility, and support evaluation across diverse driver characteristics.

2. SYSTEM DESIGN

The proposed system includes three main functional modules. The first module, SIM (Simulation Generator), is responsible for generating synthetic images of virtual drivers using the MetaHuman Animator. Specific FACS Action Units (e.g., AU41: Lid Droop, AU45: Blink) were mapped to MetaHuman control curves.

The second module, EVA (Evaluation Manager), receives image datasets from the SIM module and streams them to the DMS under test. The module manages scenario logic and evaluates the DMS output in terms of detection accuracy, response latency, and compliance with evaluation protocols.

The third module, DEV (DMS Software), represents the black-box implementation of the DMS being evaluated. The system processes input from the virtual camera and outputs driver state classifications based on internal detection models such as gaze tracking and eyelid closure monitoring.

This system is capable of adjusting various test parameters, including lighting conditions, driver demographics such as age and skin tone, and occlusion factors like sunglasses or facial accessories.

2.1 Scenario Implementation

Scenarios were implemented based on specific combinations of FACS Action Units. For example, fatigue was modeled using AU41 (lid droop) and AU45 (blink), which corresponds to lid droop, in combination with AU45, which represents blinking. Visual distraction was simulated using AU61 through AU64, which indicate lateral and vertical eye movements. Unresponsiveness was simulated by representing a lack of facial motion for a continuous duration of over 30 seconds.

The SIM module generated facial image sets corresponding to each scenario and demographic variation. These datasets were subsequently used by the EVA module to assess DMS detection performance.

2.2 Preliminary Evaluation

Initial experiments showed that the system successfully generated more than 50 distinct driver profiles based on configurable AU combinations. The evaluation process remained consistent and repeatable across lighting conditions ranging from 1 lux to 100,000 lux. Some DMS models demonstrated recognition failures, particularly in scenarios where eyelid features were underrepresented due to factors such as darker skin tones or partial occlusion.

3. CONCLUSION

The proposed simulation framework provides a robust, reproducible, and scalable method for evaluating Driver Monitoring Systems using FACS-based virtual drivers. The approach enables systematic validation without human subjects and aligns with current regulatory evaluation needs. Future work will include the development of simulation capabilities for non-transient cognitive distraction states and the incorporation of full-body behavior modeling using Body Action Coding Systems (BACS), which will be addressed in a separate study.

ACKNOWLEDGEMENT

This research was supported by a grant(code RS-2024-00403108) from R&D Program funded by Ministry of Trade, Industry and Energy of Korean government.

REFERENCES

Aloui, S., et al. (2022). Driver Monitoring Systems in Automated Interactions: A Real-Time, Thermographic-Based Algorithm. Proceedings of the Human-Computer Interaction Slovenia 2022, Ljubljana: CEUR Workshop Proceedings, Vol. 3300, pp. 392-401.

Ekman, P. and Friesen, W.V. (1978). *Facial Action Coding System: A Technique for the Measurement of Facial Movement*. Palo Alto, CA: Consulting Psychologists Press.

Ekman, P., et al. (2002). *Facial Action Coding System: Investigator's Guide*. Salt Lake City: Research Nexus.

Euro NCAP. (2023). *Protocol - Driver Monitoring Systems*. European New Car Assessment Programme.

Mersinger, M. C., et al. (2023). Driver Monitoring Systems: Design Considerations for Aging Drivers. Proceedings of the International Conference on Human-Computer Interaction, 2023. Open Access.

Nees, M. (2021). Driver Monitoring Systems: Perceived Fairness of Consequences when Distractions are Detected. Proceedings of the International Conference on Human-Computer Interaction, 2021.

UNECE. (2021). *UN Regulation No. 157 - Automated Lane Keeping Systems (ALKS)*. United Nations Economic Commission for Europe.

EEGVIS - A VISUALIZATION PROJECT TO SIMPLIFY PSYCHOPHYSICAL USER EXPERIENCE ANALYSIS

Melanie Steiner and Dieter Meiller
Ostbayerische Technische Hochschule (OTH) Amberg-Weiden,
Kaiser-Wilhelm-Ring 23, 92224, Amberg, Germany

ABSTRACT

This article deals with suitable methods for the user experience evaluation of experience worlds. It is on the use of encephalography as a measurement and presentation method for psychophysical questions in the User Experience context. An overview of the EEG method and the visualization of their results is given. Finally, the EEGVis project is described. It shows an optimized visualization of brain activity for the untrained computer scientist. This visualization cockpit should serve as the basis for an EEG atlas with specific UX use cases.

KEYWORDS

User Experience, Evaluation, Software Engineering, Electrical Activity

1. INTRODUCTION

In software engineering the user experience evaluation play an important role in quality of interactive products. The products are individual and entire worlds of digital experiences in which the user is immersed. The interactive product worlds are often a mix of the real world and digital solutions.

Various methods can be used to analyze these complex product worlds (e.g. usability tests, observations and surveys). Psychophysical methods such as eye tracking or using electroencephalography (EEG) are also used. They make body reactions and mental processes measurable, visualizable and interpretable. This offers the opportunity to optimize the quality of the entire product worlds.

User attention is a suitable parameter for assessing the user experience. Human attention is a basic biological and psychological function that includes both cognitive and non-cognitive aspects. It is an important parameter for user concepts as it can be recorded, interpreted and optimized before, during and after use.

Conducting analyses with EEG can be done with less effort to measure user attention (Cano, 2020). However, interpreting the results is more difficult. In medicine, graphical representation is typical, but not in the computer science. Resource constraints make it difficult to familiarize oneself with special analyses. This thesis deals with the visualization and simplified presentation of EEG results for less trained computer scientists. As part of a student project, EEG cockpits were created. It can simplify the interpretation of long term measurements. The results serve as basis of a computer science atlas for specific UX use cases.

2. ELECTROENCEPHALOGRAPHY IN USER EXPERIENCE ANALYSIS

If interactive products are to be evaluated users are the focus of consideration according to the user experience concept. It is more difficult to capture non-cognitive aspects. They offer a huge opportunity for a better understanding of users and unexpected new aspects for product optimization. The interpretation of attention as an index of a user journey helps to illustrate connections between product optimizations and user experience changes. Questionnaires, interviews or even observations are combined with bio- and neuro signal measurement methods for the holistic recording of the UX.

Recording the activity of the human brain it is useful to measure user attention. The brain is the human motor among the organs. It collects and processes all information. Analyses of brain activity reflect human behavior, bodily reactions as well as various psychological processes and functions (Steiner, 2023).

The EEG is suitable for measuring UX issues due to its valid results, low technical and financial outlay, high user acceptance. This method records the electrical potential with a high spatial and temporal resolution and displays the results. It is possible to record real time and over long time period. Participants can move around to a limited extent. The method can be used beyond static and medically stationary context.

The necessary technical systems for measurement are available specifically for UX context. Results should not be used as a basis for diagnostics. Such systems are small, usually self-explanatory, designed for easy handling and are also offered as mobile variants and usually with a graphical solution.

The expertise required to carry out the tests can be classified as low to medium due to the highly simplified technical systems. In order to obtain valid results, the exact placement of several electrodes along the scalp is necessary. Mostly the 10-20 electrode system is used but this manual electrode placement requires professional knowledge. Integrated systems simplify the effort and deliver valid results with less electrodes.

EEG is a method that is subject to the problem of artifacts. An excessively mobile context triggers muscle artifacts due to the excessive movement of the participant's muscles. Electrical charges in the immediate vicinity influence the derivation of the electrical signals and trigger electrical artifacts. Improperly placed electrodes trigger signal artifacts by superimposing them.

2.1 Visualization of an Electroencephalogram

The usual representation of the measurement results of an EEG is the electroencephalograph. This is a bipolar measurement of the signals. Depending on the number of measuring points used, the wave diagrams are usually displayed vertically separated. The descriptive unit of measurement for EEG waves is Hz and is in the range of milliseconds and microvolts of electrical signals. The recording of small electrical signals in short periods of time enables a good representation of the activity of human neurons in the brain.

The amplitude and wave width are decisive for analysis. EEG waves are assigned to frequency bands. These are known as alpha, beta, delta, teta and gamma rhythms, providing information on the activity level of individual brain regions. The basic rhythm of the participant, various artifacts and evoked potentials (EPs) can be of particular interest. These special patterns allow interpretations of specific questions.

A basic distinction is made between quantitative and qualitative EEG analysis. Quantitative analysis is suitable for measuring medium and long periods of time in order to analyze an overall picture. Aspects such as the rhythmicity of the EEG signal, for example by means of chaos analysis, or the entire frequency spectrum are considered here (Barry, 2003). As part of a qualitative analysis, for example, individual evoked potentials can be analyzed that are directly related to a specific reaction of the user. Both types of analysis are of interest for UX evaluation.

For easier interpretation of the results, EEG atlases are available for graphical representation by the measurement system. These are provided in both printed and digital form for training and analysis purposes.

The patterns are usually depicted as wave diagrams with description. Mostly they serve for medical diagnostics and describe the EEG patterns with this focus (Stern, 2005). For the untrained observer, it is necessary to familiarize themselves with the interpretation of the EEG wave diagrams. This requires more time and the necessity of application possibilities must be taken into account. Use cases that are suitable as standard for the interpretation of UX issues are rarely found in such atlases.

Many EEG systems offer further display variants that allow localization of the rhythms. This is also useful for precise diagnostics, but not necessary for many UX applications. Signals from an EEG are non-linear and largely random. It is therefore often difficult to make an interpretation based purely on observation. However, technical systems can help here by extracting signals using suitable signal processing techniques (Subha, 2010).

Results can be reproduced as individual key figures, such as the percentage of alpha waves. Categorization of the patient states in a holistic view are possible then. Many systems offer corresponding reports that are generated from a recording. These reports are differently structured and need training to be understood.

2.2 Display of Measurement Results in a Cockpit

An EEG cockpit was created as part of a study project to solve the existing basic problem of making EEG results difficult to understand for inexperienced UX professionals. This form of presentation is based on key figure cockpits. These are used in management to quickly provide decision-makers with the most important information on one page (Roth, 2015).

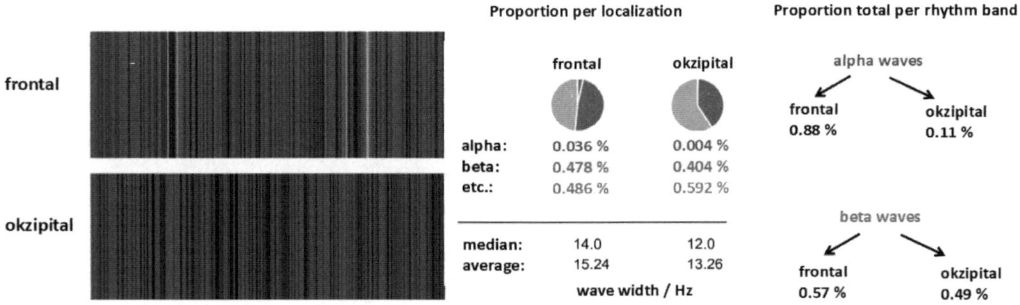

Figure 1. EEG measurement cockpit within key performance visualization

In the EEGVis project, media informatics students developed visualizations using a combination of histograms, pie charts and percentage key figures of EEG activity. The aim of the presentation was to display EEG measurements of medium-term duration (> 15 minutes), at least alpha and beta frequencies, at least 2 channels in a comprehensible manner in the aforementioned visualization forms on a single sheet. The measurement intensity used was 1000 Hz with recording at F1, F2 frontal and O1, O2 occipital. The data of the presentation base on a study from 2021 which was conducted to analyze attention during the use of augmentative media.

3. CONCLUSION

Due to the development of entire product worlds, user experience evaluation is more important than ever for the qualitative development of products with a focus on people. A suitable parameter for the evaluation of specific UX issues is the phenomenon of attention. This can be assessed by applying the EEG method and analyzing the human brain. The method can now be used for UX cases thanks to simplified technical systems. However, analyzing and interpreting the results is difficult due to the fact that UX professionals usually lack medical training. In the EEGVis project, EEG results were successfully presented in a simplified form as an EEG cockpit. The cockpit presentation is used in practice for optimized management decisions. It fulfills the goal of a simplified presentation of medium-term measurements, several frequencies and different display variants on one page. In a further step, the visualization will be is used to create an EEG atlas that is to be created specifically for user experience applications.

REFERENCES

Barry, R. J., Clarke, A. R., & Johnstone, S. J. (2003). A review of electrophysiology in attention-deficit/hyperactivity disorder: I. Qualitative and quantitative electroencephalography. *Clinical neurophysiology*, *114*(2), 171-183.

Cano, S., Araujo, N., Guzman, C., Rusu, C., & Albiol-Pérez, S. (2020). Low-cost assessment of user experience through EEG signals. *IEEE Access*, *8*, 158475-158487.

Roth, A. (2015). Management Cockpit as a layer of integration for a holistic performance management. Quarterly review of business disciplines, 2(2), 165-175.

Steiner M., Meiller D. (06/2023): Simple measurement of user response. In:17th Multi Conference on Computer Science and Information Systems 2023. IADIS Press.

Stern, J. M. (2005). *Atlas of EEG patterns*. Lippincott Williams & Wilkins.

Subha, D.P., Joseph, P.K., Acharya U, R. et al. EEG Signal Analysis: A Survey. J Med Syst 34, 195–212 (2010). https://doi.org/10.1007/s10916-008-9231-z

AUTHOR INDEX